D1327644

The Visitation of
Hereford Diocese
in 1397

EDITED AND TRANSLATED BY

IAN FORREST AND CHRISTOPHER WHITTICK

THE CANTERBURY AND YORK SOCIETY

The Boydell Press

2021

First published 2021

A Canterbury and York Society publication
published by The Boydell Press
an imprint of Boydell & Brewer Ltd
PO Box 9, Woodbridge, Suffolk IP12 3DF, UK
and of Boydell & Brewer Inc.
668 Mt Hope Avenue, Rochester, NY 14620–2731, USA
website: www.boydellandbrewer.com

ISBN 978-0-907239-84-0

A CIP catalogue record for this book is available
from the British Library

Details of previous volumes are available from Boydell & Brewer Ltd

The publisher has no responsibility for the continued existence or accuracy of URLs for
external or third-party internet websites referred to in this book, and does not guarantee
that any content on such websites is, or will remain, accurate or appropriate

This publication is printed on acid-free paper

Printed and bound in Great Britain by
TJ Books Limited, Padstow, Cornwall

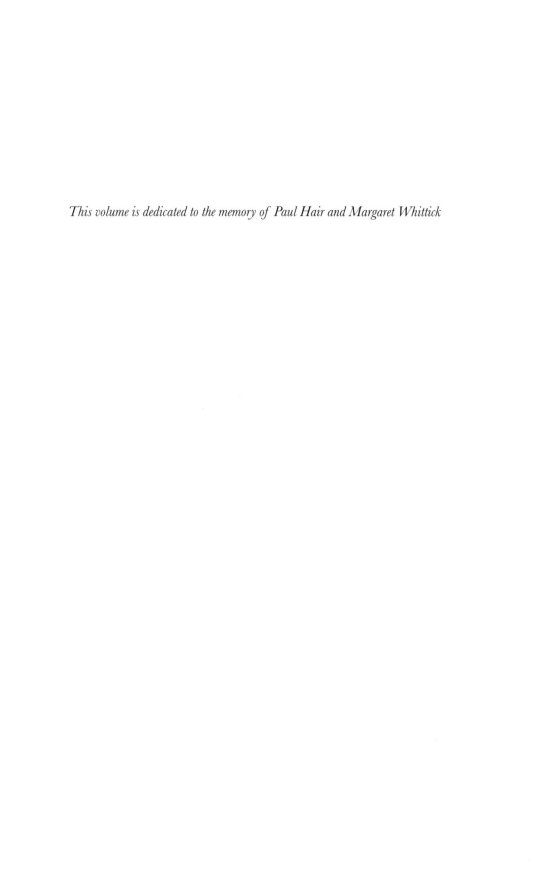

This volume is dedicated to the memory of Paul Hair and Margaret Whittick

CONTENTS

Acknowledgements   ix

Introduction   xi

    Description of the document   xi

    Custodial history of the document   xii

    History of scholarly work on the manuscript   xii

    Visitation in the late medieval church   xv

    Visitation in late medieval Hereford   xvii

    The geography and personnel of the visitation   xxiv

    Procedure and the composition of the record   xxvii

    The parishioners   xxxi

    Clerical faults in the visitation   xxxii

    Lay faults in the visitation   xxxvi

    The community of the faithful   xxxviii

    Conclusion   xli

Editorial method   xliii

TEXT AND TRANSLATION   1

Index of place-names   233

Index of personal names   241

Index of subjects   261

ACKNOWLEDGEMENTS

This editorial project has been long in the gestation and many thanks are due. The editors would like to acknowledge the assistance received from successive custodians of the visitation record – the late Miss Penelope Morgan, Rosalind Caird and Rosemary Firman of Hereford Cathedral Library and Archives, and Rhys Griffiths of the Herefordshire Archive and Records Centre; Josette Reeves of Liverpool University Archives provided help with our enquiries about Paul Hair's archive; we received advice on the text and translation from the late Lesley Boatwright, on the rendition of Welsh names from James January-McCann and Prys Morgan, and on place-names from Richard Coates of the University of the West of England; Michael Athanson prepared the map; academic colleagues have been generous with their advice on a number of points, and we would like to thank Judith Bennett, Chris Briggs, Andrew Honey, Paul Hyams, Ruth Karras, Lindsay McCormack of Lincoln College Archives, and Shannon McSheffrey. Essential funding for the preparation of the index was received from the Marc Fitch Fund, Oriel College, and the Oxford History Faculty. The index was compiled with great skill and patience by Ann Hudson. Barbara Bombi of the Canterbury and York Society made forensic and judicious suggestions for the improvement of the text, and Caroline Palmer and Nick Bingham at Boydell & Brewer were, as ever, exemplary in overseeing the production of the volume. Finally, Christopher Whittick would like to thank Ian Forrest, who has provided all that could be wished of a collaborator and given the impetus and encouragement that has ensured the final appearance of this edition after so many decades, while Ian Forrest wishes to express his gratefulness for the scholarship and friendship of Christopher Whittick.

Introduction

Since the thirteenth century, visitations have been the means by which bishops informed themselves of the condition of their dioceses. Surviving medieval visitation records are comparatively rare and of great value and interest to historians. The surviving text of Bishop John Trefnant's visitation of his diocese of Hereford, begun in the parish church of Burghill, four miles north-west of the city, on 30 April 1397, is contained in Hereford Cathedral Archives (HCA) 1779. This edition presents the Latin text with an English translation on facing pages. The text forms entries **1–1336**, and entries **1337–67** comprise the extensive contemporary notes written on the inside of the cover.

DESCRIPTION OF THE DOCUMENT

The text is written in a paper book of 26 leaves, foliated in Roman numerals and measuring 23.5 centimetres by 33 centimetres, all with a watermark resembling Briquet 3112–18, Italian paper attributable to 1349?–1421 but with dated examples of 1387 and 1397, albeit from continental manuscripts.[1] The folios are in two unequal but intact gatherings, the first comprising folios 1–14 and the second 15–26. The cover (now separated from it) that formerly contained the book is formed from a single piece of rough parchment measuring 33 by 66 centimetres overall, with a narrow gap on its outer margin where a clasp has been torn off. Despite its cover, the paper book has suffered considerable damage; indeed, the dirty appearance of its outer folios suggests that the cover may have been re-united with its former contents only relatively recently, and the vertical fold to which the book has evidently been subject is not visible in the cover. Apart from discolouration to the top-right corner of each folio, probably caused by the leaves being turned by licked fingers, the damage is confined to both bottom corners. Many of the folios have lost a triangular segment at the bottom-right corner, broken along fold-cracks; damage to the bottom-left corners seems to be the result of mould and general decay, encouraged by bookworm. A small amount of additional text was evidently visible in 1929 when elements of the text were first published, and it is possible that the ragged edges were tidied up during conservation in 1957. The document presents all the appearances of having been compiled or at least substantially augmented in the field, though it is clear from the extensive annotations to the text that it remained in active administrative use for many months or even years after the visitation itself had ended. Apart from its current reference on the cover, HCA 1779 bears no trace of any former archival arrangement.

At least two hands can be seen in the compilation of the document. Both the presentments themselves, and the procedural and other notes written inside the cover, are almost certainly the work of the same hand. The slightly more formal aspect of the latter is perhaps explicable from having been written on parchment.

---

[1]   Charles-Moïse Briquet, *Les filigranes: dictionnaire historique des marques du papier dès leur apparition vers 1282 jusqu'en 1600*, 4 vols (Amsterdam, 1968), vol. 1: 212, vol. 2: 3112–18.

The appearance of the cover entries in particular bears a striking similarity with the hand in which the register of Bishop Trefnant is written.[2] This may be the hand of the diocesan registrar, who was present during at least part of the visitation (**495**). The notes of process and judgements (*comperta*) – hastily written and far more heavily abbreviated – fall into two categories. The first, written in the more cursive form of the presentments themselves and largely in brown ink, we ascribe to the same author. The second, written with a broader nib and in greyer ink, mostly record the termination of cases, usually by the dismissal of the parties. These are written in a different hand, possibly belonging to the scribe of the commissary court (for which see below).

CUSTODIAL HISTORY OF THE DOCUMENT

The document was discovered in the archives of the dean and chapter of Hereford in 1907 or 1908 by William Wolfe Capes, formerly reader in ancient history at Oxford, who had been installed as a residentiary canon of the cathedral in 1904 and for whom the office of keeper of the archives was revived in the following year.[3] It is not unusual to find the record of an episcopal visitation in the archive of a dean and chapter. The survival among the same muniments of 13 texts of, or relating to, diocesan visitations undertaken between 1276 and 1300 suggests that there was little or no formal separation of episcopal and capitular archives.[4] In 1940 or 1941, the cathedral archives were removed to the crypt and in 1943 to the National Library of Wales, whose catalogue was completed a decade later. In 1955, the archives were returned to a new muniment room at Hereford, from which they were transferred to the new cathedral library in 1996.[5] In June 1957, two years after its return from Aberystwyth, HCA 1779 was repaired and bound at the Bodleian Library, probably by Leslie Frank Fifield, at a cost of two guineas.[6]

HISTORY OF SCHOLARLY WORK ON THE MANUSCRIPT

The sole evidence of attention being paid to the manuscript before the beginning of the twentieth century consists of gall stains, applied on the first folio to the part of the heading that contains the date and to the end of the first presentment and

[2]   Herefordshire Archive and Records Centre, Register of Bishop John Trefnant; *Registrum Johannis Trefnant, episcopi Herefordensis A.D. 1389–1404*, ed. William Wolfe Capes, Canterbury and York Society, 20 (London, 1916) [hereafter *Register of John Trefnant*].

[3]   For Capes, see J. R. Magrath, 'Capes, William Wolfe (1834–1914)', *Oxford Dictionary of National Biography* (Oxford, 2004), and Brian Smith 'The Archives', in Gerald Aylmer and John Tiller (eds), *Hereford Cathedral: A History* (London, 2000), 552–3; Paul Hair, in 'Mobility of Parochial Clergy in Hereford Diocese c.1400', *Transactions of the Woolhope Naturalists' Field Club*, 43 (1980), 164–80, n.1, attributes the discovery to 'around 1905', but its omission from Capes's *Charters and Records of Hereford Cathedral*, published in 1908, points to a later date.

[4]   For these texts, see Ian Forrest and Christopher Whittick, 'The Thirteenth-Century Visitation Records of the Diocese of Hereford', *English Historical Review*, 131 (2016), 737–62.

[5]   For the cathedral archives, see Smith 'The Archives', 544–56.

[6]   The repair, at the expense of Cathedral Library Funds, is recorded on a label pasted to the inside of the back cover. Fifield worked at the Bodleian from 1929 to 1969 and eventually became the supervisor of the bindery; we are most grateful to Andrew Honey, Book Conservator at the Bodleian, for his assistance and unsuccessful attempts to establish whether a photographic record of the work was made.

its additions. That the stains are so limited suggests that the application of the fluid, the purpose of which was to highlight faded writing, might have taken place during the preparation of a catalogue of the cathedral muniments, perhaps during the eighteenth century.[7] Capes announced his discovery in the *Hereford Diocesan Messenger* of January 1909, and in 1915 his text was reprinted in *Old Hereford and Other Papers* (Hereford, 1915).[8]

In the 1920s, another canon, Arthur Thomas Bannister, began work on the document, using it extensively in a 1927 article and publishing a partial text, serialised in four issues of the *English Historical Review*, in 1929 and 1930.[9] Bannister's foreword begins with the claim that 'I recently discovered … an unsightly and tattered manuscript …', the same words used by Capes in his announcement in the *Diocesan Messenger* two decades before. Bannister furthermore failed to make clear that his text was not a complete edition. Although the presentments – *detecta* – were transcribed with a fair degree of accuracy, the overwhelming majority of the judgements and notes of process – *comperta* – far more abbreviated and much harder to read – were silently omitted. As might be expected, until the text that forms the basis of the present edition began to be circulated in draft, and a copy placed in the County Record Office, citations of the visitation record by historians were most often based solely upon Bannister's edition, without reference to the original text.[10]

[7]   For correspondence of 1776 on the use of a solution of oak gall in madeira by Richard Gough, see Catherine Delano-Smith *et al.*, 'New Light on the Gough Map', *Imago Mundi*, 69:1 (2017), 5.

[8]   We owe this reference to Dr Rosemary Firman of Hereford Cathedral Library.

[9]   Arthur Thomas Bannister, 'Parish Life in the Fourteenth Century', *The Nineteenth Century*, 102 (1927), 394–404; 'Visitation Returns of the Diocese of Hereford in 1397', *English Historical Review*, 44 (1929), 279–89, 444–53; 45 (1930), 92–101, 444–63. Arthur Thomas Bannister (1861–1936), son of Joseph Bannister, a master baker of Chester, was educated at The King's School Chester and Lincoln College, Oxford; he was ordained in 1890, and after curacies in Cambridgeshire and Kent became vicar of Ewyas Harold in Herefordshire in 1898, rural dean of Abbeydore in 1905, and a canon of Hereford Cathedral in 1908; one of a succession of liberal scholars whose appointment to the chapter prompted dissention in the diocese, he became warden of St Katherine's Hospital at Ledbury in 1909, and precentor of Hereford in 1916; an appreciation on his retirement was published in the *Hereford Diocesan Messenger* of May 1936, and a frank and perceptive obituary in September 1936 by his fellow canon A. L. Lilley, who pointed out that Bannister 'paid the penalty of his nature which was one of singular simplicity and directness'; for a discussion of the appointments to the chapter by Bishop John Perceval, including a photograph of Bannister, see Aylmer and Tiller (eds), *Hereford Cathedral*, 167–71.

[10]   Historians reliant upon Bannister include Robert N. Swanson, *Church and Society in Late Medieval England* (Oxford, 1989); Richard Morris, *Churches in the Landscape* (London, 1989); Beat Kümin, *The Shaping of a Community: The Rise and Reformation of the English Parish c. 1400–1560* (Aldershot, 1996). Conversely, research by Katherine L. French, *The Good Women of the Parish: Gender and Religion after the Black Death* (Philadelphia, 2008), and Janelle Werner, 'Promiscuous Priests and Vicarage Children: Clerical Sexuality and Masculinity in Late Medieval England', in Jennifer D. Thibodeaux (ed.), *Negotiating Clerical Identities: Priests, Monks and Masculinity in the Middle Ages* (Basingstoke, 2010), 159–81, made use of a draft of the present edition. William J. Dohar, *The Black Death and Pastoral Leadership: The Diocese of Hereford in the Fourteenth Century* (Philadelphia, 1995), was unusual in consulting the original text besides Bannister's transcriptions.

The next substantive engagement with the manuscript, which ultimately brought about the present edition, was made by Paul Hair (1926–2001) of Liverpool University, to which he had been appointed as a lecturer in African history in 1965. His wide-ranging research interests included the study of sexual behaviour in early modern England, and his *Before the Bawdy Court* was published in 1972.[11] Possession of a caravan in Herefordshire drew Hair to the records of that county, and in 1970, already familiar with Bannister's articles, he visited the cathedral library, obtained a photocopy of HCA 1779, and soon established both that the published transcription was incomplete, and that he lacked the palaeographic and linguistic skills to produce a new edition to modern standards. His solution, adopted in 1975, was to walk down the corridor to the classroom of the trainee archivists in the School of History and ask for volunteers. The call was answered by Margaret Truran and Christopher Whittick, who initially worked independently on different sections of the text. After Liverpool, Margaret became assistant archivist at Bedford County Record Office for a year but entered Stanbrook Abbey in September 1976.[12] In 1975, Christopher married Margaret Rutherford (1947–95), herself a graduate of the Liverpool Archives Course, and they worked together on the text, conferring with Hair several times a year. In about 1980, a copy of their text was deposited at the County Record Office and made available to interested scholars. In 1980 and 1993, Hair published two articles based on his own research and that of his collaborators.[13] It was always Hair's intention to publish the visitation entries as pendants to an architectural and topographical description of each parish, an approach that led to some dissention with the editors. Margaret Whittick's death in 1995 and Hair's in 2001 injected a spirit of urgency into the project, and in 2005 Christopher Whittick was contacted about the manuscript by Ian Forrest, then of All Souls College, Oxford, which saw the beginning of their present collaboration.[14] In 2016, their article on the thirteenth-century antecedents to Trefnant's visitation was published.[15] Every aspect of this edition has been a collaborative endeavour, although the remainder of this introduction is largely the work of Forrest, and the text and translation largely that of Christopher and Margaret Whittick; the index is by Ann Hudson.

[11]   Paul Edward Hedley Hair, *Before the Bawdy Court: Selections from Church Court and Other Records Relating to the Correction of Moral Offences in England, Scotland and New England, 1300–1800* (London, 1972).
[12]   Christopher subsequently visited Stanbrook in the hope of discussing the text with Margaret Truran but was turned away by the novice mistress.
[13]   Hair, 'Mobility of Parochial Clergy'; Hair, 'Defaults and Offences of Clergy and Laity, 1397', *Transactions of the Woolhope Naturalists' Field Club*, 47 (1993), 318–50.
[14]   Appreciations of Paul Hair by David Henige, Adam Jones, Robin Law, Bruce Mouser, Konrad Tuchscherer, and Selena Winsnes, with a bibliography, were published in *History in Africa*, 29 (2002), 1–37; his archive, including papers on the visitation project, is held at the Special Collections and Archives, University of Liverpool, reference HAI, which includes a fuller biography than that published in *History in Africa*.
[15]   Forrest and Whittick, 'Thirteenth-Century Visitation Records of the Diocese of Hereford'.

VISITATION IN THE LATE MEDIEVAL CHURCH

The episcopal visitation of the laity, and of the secular clergy who served them, was an important feature of late medieval Latin Christianity. Visitations were occasions when lay ideas about the church and morality came into contact with those held by the parish clergy and the episcopal hierarchy. It is likely to have been a formative experience for all concerned. While it is doubtful whether visitation played any significant part in early medieval society, by the mid- to late-thirteenth century it was well established in several regions of Europe, and in the late-fourteenth century it was part of the common experience of most Latin Christians.[16] For many people, visitation would have been a regular occurrence. Some bishops visited every three years or thereabouts, in accordance with the presumption of canon law texts.[17] Others visited their dioceses less regularly. In some dioceses, archdeacons also made visitations, though these are not so well documented and their relationship to episcopal visitation remains poorly studied. Scattered across most dioceses there were also a number of detached or unitary jurisdictions – 'peculiars' – operated by the rectors of independent churches, monasteries with residual jurisdiction over parishes, or bishops with historic rights in other dioceses.[18] These may have been especially closely supervised, and perhaps quite difficult places in which to live.

As one might expect with such a ubiquitous institution, there was a great deal in common between visitations conducted by a bishop, an archdeacon, or another authority. Accordingly, much of the necessary background to understanding the visitation of Hereford diocese in 1397 is common to the western medieval church. However, visitation also involved much that was particular to certain times and places, deriving from local administrative habits or political exigency. An appreciation of these variable factors demands close attention to the form and content of each particular document and to the circumstances in which a visitation was undertaken.

Across Latin Christendom, visitation performed three functions: administrative, pastoral, and judicial. The administrative function consisted mainly in checking the clergy's written proofs of ordination and appointment, hearing reports about the physical condition of the rectory estate and chancel of the church (the responsibility of the rector) and of the nave (the responsibility of the parishioners), and collecting 'procurations', which were the fees or sustenance that churches were expected to provide to the visitor and his party.[19] The pastoral function included

---

[16] Noel Coulet, *Les visites pastorales* (Turnhout, 1977) provides an overview of visitation documents, though one sorely in need of updating. For more recent comment on visitation, see Swanson, *Church and Society in Late Medieval England*, 163–5; Daniel Bornstein, 'Priests and Villagers in the Diocese of Cortona', *Ricerche Storiche*, 27 (1997), 93–106; Katherine L. French, *The People of the Parish* (Philadelphia, 2001), 31–6; Ian Forrest, 'The Transformation of Visitation in Thirteenth-Century England', *Past and Present*, 221 (2013), 3–38; Michelle Armstrong-Partida, *Defiant Priests: Domestic Unions, Clerical Violence and Masculinity in Fourteenth-Century Catalunya* (Ithaca, 2018), 31–3.

[17] Gratian, *Decretum*, C. 10 q. 3 cc. 7, 9 in *Corpus iuris canonici*, ed. Emil Richter and Emil Friedberg, 2 vols (Leipzig, 1879–81), vol. 1: 624–6.

[18] Robert N. Swanson, 'Peculiar Practices: The Jurisdictional Jigsaw of the Pre-Reformation Church', *Midland History*, 26 (2001), 69–95.

[19] As the practice of visitation became more common, its associated costs frequently caused resentment, and by the fourteenth century a body of papal decretals and English

attention to the ministrations received by parishioners, covering the ability and willingness of the clergy and each church's possession of the correct liturgical equipment. Beyond this, in their desire to mould a Christian society, visitors were concerned with behaviour and, to a lesser extent, belief. The judicial function arose from the integration of visitation with the system of diocesan courts and the bishop's legal authority as a judge. Every duty that flowed from membership of the church was capable of being enforced by its courts, and visitation sat mid-way along a spectrum of coercion that ran from confession and fraternal correction to the bishop's consistory and excommunication.[20]

However, despite the depth at which legal thinking and procedure were embedded in visitation, there was no discrete body of canon law devoted to it. Procurations, as noted above, attracted a great deal of prescription, but the actual conduct and purposes of visitation were governed largely by the general principles of canon law and the expectations and assumptions of those participating in it. These might be derived from a number of sources. Some bishops made use of extensive written visitation articles, sending out what was, in effect, a questionnaire to every church they intended to visit.[21] However, it is not clear that this happened in all cases, and there was no requirement for it. A small body of procedural writing was in circulation, including a short section on *infamia* and parish visitation in the *Speculum iuris* of William Durandus, and a few treatises appended to lists of visitation articles, discussing issues such as procurations and the size of the visitor's party.[22] Such writings must have been influential in conveying legal ideas, but the actual practices of visitation and its attendant record-keeping, which are broadly similar across dioceses, were most probably transmitted between jurisdictions and over the generations by clerical administrators trained in reading and writing some

---

conciliar and synodal constitutions had combined to limit the size of a visitor's party and establish the principle of no payment without visitation. *Decretals*, X 2.26.16, X 3.39.23, X 3.39.25, VI 1.16.4, VI 3.20.2–3, and *Extrav. comm.* 3.10.1 in *Corpus iuris canonici*, ed. Richter and Friedberg, vol. 2: 388–9, 632–3, 987–8, 1057–8, 1280–4; *Decretales D. Gregorii papae IX una cum glossis* (Paris, 1612), ordinary gloss to X 2.26.16 v. *consuetudine*; *Constitutiones Concilii quarti Lateranensis una cum Commentariis glossatorum*, ed. Antonio García y García, Monumenta Iuris Canonici Series A: Corpus Glossatorum, 2 (Vatican, 1981), 436; Hostiensis, *Aurea Summa* (Venice, 1605), Book 3, *De censibus et exactionibus et procurationibus*, §19 (col.1174); *Councils and Synods with other Documents Relating to the English Church*, II: *A.D. 1205–1313*, ed. Frederick M. Powicke and Christopher R. Cheney (Oxford, 1964), 36, 93, 114, 263–4, 308, 457–9, 553, 613–14, 649, 718, 749, 907–8, 1011, 1034–6.

[20] For confession and the courts, see Joseph Goering, 'The Internal Forum and the Literature of Penance and Confession', in Wilfried Hartmann and Kenneth Pennington (eds), *The History of Medieval Canon Law in the Classical Period, 1140–1234: From Gratian to the Decretals of Pope Gregory IX* (Washington, D.C., 2008), 379–428. For fraternal correction, see Edwin Craun, *Ethics and Power in Medieval English Reformist Writing* (Cambridge, 2010), 10–34.

[21] For example, see John Shinners and William H. Dohar (eds), *Pastors and the Care of Souls in Medieval England* (Notre Dame, Ind., 1998), 288–91; *The Register of John Waltham Bishop of Salisbury 1388–1395*, ed. T. C. B. Timmins, Canterbury and York Society, 80 (Woodbridge, 1994), 210–11.

[22] Guilelmi Durandi Episcopi, *Speculum Iuris* (Basel, 1574), Book 3, part 1, §2, section 6; Oxford, Balliol College MS 158, ff. 171r–175v; Cambridge, Peterhouse MS 84, ff. 179v–183v; Cambridge University Library MS Ii.3.14, ff. 213v–218r. These would all repay further study.

generic forms of legal record.[23] Visitation of the laity also drew extensively upon the practices involved in the visitation of religious houses, although there were important differences: typically the visitor had more control over the agenda and outcome of a monastic visitation, and the religious were questioned individually rather than transmitting their grievances through representatives.[24] A great deal of visitation procedure was also shared with other forms of inquiry. At Hereford, the early decades of visitation may have been influenced by the Herefordshire and Shropshire eyres of 1292, and by the papal inquiry into the miracles of Thomas Cantilupe in 1307.[25]

VISITATION IN LATE MEDIEVAL HEREFORD

Hereford was one of several dioceses in England where the visitation of parishes and other small churches is known to have been practised and, crucially, recorded from the fourth quarter of the thirteenth century onwards. Mandates, citations, and memoranda relating to visitation were copied into the registers of every bishop between Thomas Cantilupe (1275–82) and Trefnant's predecessor John Gilbert (1375–89).[26] In addition to these notices in the bishops' registers, a handful of documents survive among the records of the dean and chapter of Hereford. HCA 1050a is a copy, datable to c.1335, of a visitation made of parishes in the Leominster area in 1284. The original does not survive, but the copy was probably commissioned by Bishop Thomas Charlton (1327–44) as evidence to support a jurisdictional claim against Leominster Priory. HCA 1076 is a list of places visited by Bishop Richard Swinfield (1283–1317) in 1293, with notes on paid and unpaid procurations. A further roll recording a visitation made by Swinfield in 1286 was

[23] See comments of Paul Harvey, *A Medieval Oxfordshire Village: Cuxham 1240 to 1400* (Oxford, 1965), 20–5; H. G. Richardson, 'Business Training in Medieval Oxford', *American Historical Review*, 46 (1941), 259–80.
[24] Christopher R. Cheney, *Episcopal Visitation of Monasteries in the Thirteenth Century* (Manchester, 1931).
[25] David Crook, *Records of the General Eyre* (London, 1982), 175; Patrick H. Daly, 'The Process of Canonization in the Thirteenth and Early Fourteenth Centuries', in Meryl Jancey (ed.), *St Thomas Cantilupe Bishop of Hereford: Essays in his Honour* (Hereford, 1982), 129–33. For the connections between visitation and the eyre, see Forrest, 'Transformation of Visitation', 11–13.
[26] *The Register of Thomas de Cantilupe, Bishop of Hereford (A.D. 1275–1282)*, ed. R. G. Griffiths and W. W. Capes, Canterbury and York Society, 2 (London, 1906–7), 46–9, 79–80, 87–9, 95, 116–17, 144–50, 219, 237–40, 256–8; *Registrum Ricardi de Swinfield Episcopi Herefordensis, 1283–1317*, ed. W. W. Capes, Canterbury and York Society, 6 (London, 1909), 131–2, 149–50, 161–2, 288–9, 388–9; *Registrum Ade de Orleton, Episcopi Herefordensis, A.D. MCCCXVII–MCCCXXVII*, ed. A. T. Bannister, Canterbury and York Society, 5 (London, 1908) [hereafter *Register of Adam Orleton*], 68, 81–3, 172–4, 180, 285–8, 316–18; *Registrum Thome de Charlton, Episcopi Herefordensis, A.D. MCCCXXVII–MCCCXLIV*, ed. W. W. Capes, Canterbury and York Society, 9 (London, 1908), 24, 29–30; *Registrum Ludowici de Charltone episcopi Herefordensis A. D. MCCCLXI–MCCCLXX*, ed. J. H. Parry, Canterbury and York Society, 14 (London, 1914) [hereafter *Register of Lewis Charlton*], 7–8 (see also HCA 1449); *Registrum Johannis de Trillek, Episcopi Herefordensis, A.D. MCCCXLIV–MCCCLXI*, ed. J. H. Parry, Canterbury and York Society, 8 (London, 1907), 30–1, 62, 73, 90, 96, 108, 177–8, 183, 215, 221–2, 236–8, 246–7, 252–3; *Registrum Johannis Gilbert episcopi Herefordensis, A.D. MCCCLXXV–MCCCLXXXIX*, ed. J. H. Parry, Canterbury and York Society, 18 (London, 1915) [hereafter *Register of John Gilbert*], 16–17, 77–9, 109 (see also HCA 1453 and 1548).

deposited in the County Record Office but has been misplaced. This has been published, along with HCA 1050a and 1076, by the present editors.[27] In addition to these registered, copied, and original documents, two medieval lists of records shed light on the practice of visitation. In 1353 and 1354, Bishop John Trillek (1344–60) was contesting the claims of Bromfield and Monmouth priories to be able to visit their appropriated parish churches. In order to produce evidence of episcopal rights, Trillek ordered two canons of the cathedral to search its archives for any records of visitation. Their efforts located numerous visitation rolls from the episcopates of Cantilupe and Swinfield, numbered 'first circuit', 'second circuit', and so on. Together with the documents described above, these lists suggest that triennial visitation was more or less adhered to in the late-thirteenth century. The fourteenth-century evidence suggests a similar pattern, and there is even one explicit mention of 'triennial' visitation in 1385.[28]

Trefnant's episcopal register, however, provides much less evidence that he conducted regular visitations of the parishes in his diocese. It is certain that he sometimes visited religious houses.[29] A few details in HCA 1779 point to the fact that he had also visited the parishes of his diocese on at least one previous occasion: in 1397, the rector of Ullingswick was said to have failed to return a breviary purchased by the parishioners, which he had sworn to do at 'the last visitation' (**593**), and a parishioner of Clunbury was reminded that he was bound to provide his church with a candle weighing two pounds, repeating an injunction from the 'last visitation' (**1186**). We do not know exactly when this previous visitation took place, but we can be fairly sure it was during Trefnant's episcopate, since a key member of Trefnant's household, Reynold of Woolaston, had dealt with its pastoral and judicial aftermath (**593**, **612**).[30] The latest time this could have taken place may be inferred from a comment made about several male offenders in 1397 that they were absent 'in Ireland' (**957**, **992**, **1038**, **1201**, **1250**, **1282**). These men were likely part of Roger Mortimer's contingent within Richard II's expeditionary force to Ireland, which departed on 1 October 1394 and would have been mustered some weeks before that. While the king's household troops returned to England in May 1395, the Mortimer soldiers were still away in 1397.[31] If we assume, as seems likely, that visitation worked along similar lines to the eyre, dealing with offences that had occurred since the last tribunal, then the previous visitation must have taken place under Trefnant, but no later than late summer or early autumn of 1394.

---

[27]   Forrest and Whittick, 'Thirteenth-Century Visitation Records of the Diocese of Hereford'.
[28]   *Register of John Gilbert*, 77–8.
[29]   *Register of John Trefnant*, 22–4.
[30]   Woolaston was a canon who became vicar general in 1389, acting as witness to episcopal *acta* or as a judge on numerous occasions; on Trefnant's death in 1401, he was appointed guardian of the see: *Register of John Trefnant*, 5, 28, 39, 155.
[31]   They came mostly from lands within or adjacent to Mortimer estates in north-west Herefordshire and south-west Shropshire (Wigmore, Burrington, Churchstoke, Wistanstow): Nigel Saul, *Richard II* (New Haven, 1997), 277, 287; Anthony Tuck, *Richard II and the English Nobility* (Ann Arbor, 1973), 175, 205; Melville Richards, *Welsh Administrative and Territorial Units Medieval and Modern* (Cardiff, 1969), 240; Adrian R. Bell, *War and the Soldier in the Fourteenth Century* (Woodbridge, 2004), 189; Adam Chapman, *Welsh Soldiers in the Late Middle Ages 1282–1422* (Woodbridge, 2015), 100–1.

This is as much as we know about Trefnant's visitations beyond the evidence provided by HCA 1779.[32] But does this mean that Trefnant was a negligent visitor, or a negligent record keeper? Idiosyncrasy, rather than negligence, is the overriding impression gained from an examination of his main register. Many aspects of a bishop's usual work are scantily recorded, and a great deal of space is instead taken up by documents relating to legal disputes. In particular, the trials of the prominent heresy suspects William Swinderby and Walter Brut are recorded with what Anne Hudson has called 'unparalleled amplitude'. While it was common for summary notices of heresy trials to be recorded in bishops' registers, Trefnant went much further by including long letters accusing and defending the two men, as well as protracted trial proceedings.[33] Trefnant was a lawyer by training and long experience who brought a large personal library of canon law texts with him to Hereford. He has been called 'litigious but hard-working' by May McKisack, and Richard Davies wrote of his 'ability and fierce determination'.[34] The papers on heresy trials sit alongside other detailed legal arguments relating to the election of John Prophet as dean of Hereford, the contested union of Bullinghope prebend with the decanal estates (for further details of which, see below), testamentary jurisdiction, and a dispute with the papal camera over first fruits.[35] It is an unusually learned episcopal register, but also – we note – rather lax in recording quotidian business. This peculiarity makes it possible that Trefnant was indeed a regular visitor of his diocese, merely failing to record his acts in the surviving general episcopal register.

However, there is evidence that the visitation of 1397 took place in exceptional circumstances, and that the preservation of HCA 1779 was driven by the bishop's relationship with authorities beyond the diocese. For much of Trefnant's episcopate, the archbishop of Canterbury was William Courtenay (1381–96), a zealous ecclesiast who energetically prosecuted the claim of Canterbury to 'metropolitan' status: that is, the archbishop's putative right to supersede the jurisdiction of his diocesan bishops from time to time. None of the English or Welsh bishops within the province of Canterbury were very happy about this, and Courtenay's register – to say nothing of those of the bishops – contains numerous documents relating

---

[32]   A visitation of the city parishes carried out in March 1400 took place under the authority of the dean, whose jurisdiction was quite separate to that of the bishop, and jealously guarded: HCA 1155. The end, in 1677, of the cathedral's and deanery's independence from episcopal visitation is discussed in Alan Bray, *The Friend* (Chicago, 2003), 234–9.

[33]   *Register of John Trefnant*, 231–411; the quotation is from Anne Hudson's preface to Fiona Somerset, Jill C. Havens, and Derrick G. Pitard (eds), *Lollards and their Influence in Late Medieval England* (Woodbridge, 2003), 3; see also Anne Hudson, 'The Problem of Scribes: The Trial Records of William Swinderby and Walter Brut', *Nottingham Medieval Studies*, 94 (2005), 80–9.

[34]   A. B. Emden, *A Biographical Register of the University of Oxford to A.D. 1500* (Oxford, 1957–9), vol. 3: 1900–2; May McKisack, *The Fourteenth Century 1307–1399* (Oxford, 1959), 301; Richard G. Davies, 'The Episcopate in England and Wales, 1375–1443' (Unpublished doctoral thesis, University of Manchester, 1974), 134. It cannot really be countenanced, as Peter McNiven has argued, that Trefnant was 'insufficiently dynamic' to catch up with Swinderby: *Heresy and Politics in the Reign of Henry IV: The Burning of John Badby* (Woodbridge, 1987), 54. Trefnant's books are listed in his will: *Testamentary Records of the English and Welsh Episcopate 1200–1413*, ed. Christopher M. Woolgar, Canterbury and York Society, 102 (Woodbridge, 2011), 258–62.

[35]   *Register of John Trefnant*, 53–6, 73–90, 103–14, 131–5.

to their struggles.[36] Diocesan bishops were justifiably worried that the usurpation of their jurisdiction would lead to the confiscation of their revenues and questions about their suitability, though it was not always easy to resist a determined archbishop.

Most late-fourteenth-century bishops therefore pursued a policy of vigorous objection and controlled capitulation to their archbishop's demands and Trefnant was no exception. In 1388, he agreed to Courtenay's proposed visitation of his diocese, but no action seems to have followed.[37] When Courtenay resumed his plans, writing on 15 April 1396 to express his purpose to visit the cathedral, city, and diocese of Hereford beginning on 5 June that year, Trefnant was more belligerent. He replied angrily to the archbishop's order that he prepare for metropolitan visitation, saying that these were 'sinister and pointed' machinations against him and his church. He protested against Courtenay's presumption to issue citations, suspensions, interdicts, and excommunications, all of which were – he wrote – his prerogative as the diocesan bishop. Trefnant appealed to the pope on 30 April, thundering against Courtenay's condescension in requiring him – the bishop! – to act as the archbishop's servant. He was no summoner, he wrote, a functionary whose office was 'vile and counted among the sordid things ... unworthy to be assigned to a bishop as it may be done by any clerk or layman'.[38]

Between the dates of those two attempted metropolitan visitations, Trefnant had clashed with Courtenay over testamentary jurisdiction, a struggle the archbishop had abandoned as a lost cause.[39] However, Trefnant's protest against the second proposed visitation ultimately proved unnecessary, as Courtenay was prevented by ill-health and then death from carrying it out.[40] Courtenay's successor as archbishop was Thomas Arundel (1396–7, 1399–1414), the politically astute younger son of Richard Fitzalan the earl of Arundel. Thomas had served Richard II as chancellor (1386–9, 1391–6) as well as having been bishop of Ely (1374–88) and archbishop of York (1388–96). Upon his promotion to Canterbury, Arundel did not pursue his predecessor's plan for a metropolitan visitation of Hereford. But this was not for want of interest in such activity. Arundel carried out visitations of the cathedrals, religious houses, and deaneries of Canterbury diocese in March 1397, Chichester between April and July 1400, Coventry and Lichfield between October 1400 and February 1401, and Ely in September and October 1401.[41] It may be that the primary visitation of his own diocese had diverted Arundel's attention from any plans for Hereford, but new political alignments may also have

---

[36]   *The Metropolitan Visitations of William Courtenay Archbishop of Canterbury 1381–1396: Documents Transcribed from the Original Manuscripts of Courtenay's Register, with an Introduction Describing the Archbishop's Investigations*, ed. Joseph H. Dahmus (Urbana, Ill., 1950), 7–8.

[37]   HCA 1548, 1857.

[38]   *Register of John Trefnant*, 120–2, 123–5.

[39]   *Register of John Trefnant*, 100–15.

[40]   *Metropolitan Visitations of William Courtenay*, 61–3.

[41]   Lambeth Palace Library, Register of Thomas Arundel, vol. 1, ff. 469r–496r; selections have been printed in S. J. A. Evans, 'Metropolitan Visitation of Archbishop Thomas Arundel', *Camden Miscellany*, Camden Society, third series, 64 (1940), 44–56. Arundel also attempted a metropolitan visitation of London diocese: London Guildhall, MS 9531/3, ff. 485v–494v.

worked in Trefnant's favour.[42] Trefnant had been a beneficiary of Fitzalan family patronage while he was a clerk in London; he was named as a debtor of Earl Richard on his death in 1376. He was then associated with them – but no more than this – during the appellant crisis of the late 1380s, and would be one of the bishops chosen to put the case against Richard II in 1399.[43] This relationship may have disposed the new archbishop to drop his claim (which the two men had had opportunity to discuss at the February 1397 convocation in London), although he did try to renew it during the vacancy that followed Trefnant's death in 1404.[44]

While Arundel was visiting his own diocese, Trefnant pressed ahead with the visitation of Hereford in late April 1397. It is likely that Courtenay's threats had stimulated the Hereford administration to be more than usually careful in preserving documentation of this visitation (though not in the general register), and that after Arundel was exiled by the king in September that same year uncertainty about the future prompted the retention of this record when so many of a similar nature were destroyed.[45] Although the 1397 visitation was not a completely exceptional 'performance' of the bishop's rights over his diocese, we can nevertheless be fairly sure that political uncertainty in both church and realm created incentives for the unusual preservation of the visitation book. It is clear, however, that HCA 1779 was not specially prepared to support litigation over jurisdiction. As we discuss below, it is very much a working document, full of the interlineations, additions, and corrections that were commonly ironed out of clean 'presentation' copies.[46]

---

[42]   The bull *Romana ecclesia* (VI 3.20.1 in *Corpus iuris canonici*, ed. Richter and Friedberg, vol. 2: 1056–7), initially drafted in 1246, had stipulated that archbishops should not conduct metropolitan visitations until they had completed a tour of their own diocese, and this was a well-known requirement.

[43]   Margaret Aston, *Thomas Arundel: A Study of Church Life in the Reign of Richard II* (Oxford, 1967), 17; *Register of John Trefnant*, 6–7; R. G. Davies, 'Trefnant, John (d. 1404)', *Oxford Dictionary of National Biography* (Oxford, 2004). The Fitzalans were also Marcher lords with lands in the diocese (**1026**).

[44]   Lambeth Palace Library, Register of Thomas Arundel, vol. 1, ff. 431r–v, 442r–v; *Records of Convocation* IV: *1377–1414*, ed. Gerald Bray (Woodbridge, 2005), 170.

[45]   Ian Forrest, 'The Survival of Medieval Visitation Records', *Archives*, 37 (2013), 1–10.

[46]   The following are examples of clean copies of visitation records: HCA 1050a (Hereford 1284, diocesan); York, Borthwick Institute, Register 8A (York 1311, metropolitan); Canterbury Cathedral Archives DCc/VR/4 (Canterbury 1328, diocesan); Durham Cathedral Archives 1.9.Pont.9 (Durham mid-fifteenth century, diocesan).

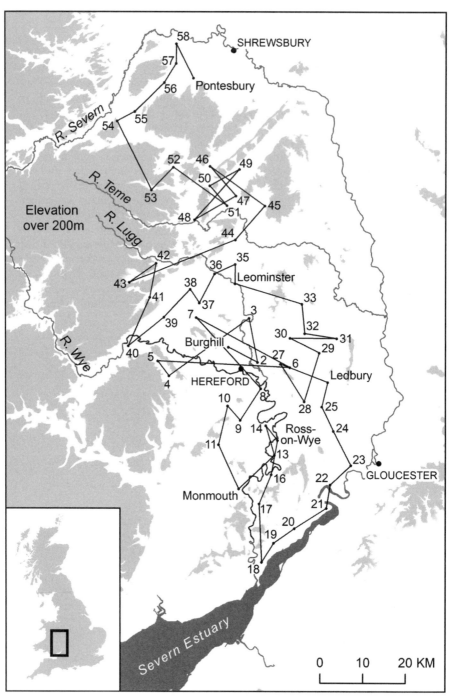

Route of Bishop Trefnant's visitation in 1397

Key:

1	Burghill	30 April
2	Lugwardine	1 May
3	Bodenham	2 May
4	Peterchurch	3 May
5	Dorstone	4 May
6	Staunton-on-Wye	5 May
7	Weobley	7 May
8	Holme Lacy	8 May
9	Llanwarne	9 May
10	Much Dewchurch	10 May
11	Garway	11 May
12	Monmouth	12 May
13	Walford	13 May
14	Sellack	14 May
15	Ross-on-Wye	15 May
16	English Bicknor	16 May
17	Newland	17 May
18	Tidenham and Lancaut	18 May
19	Woolaston and Alvington	19 May
20	Lydney	20 May
21	Awre	21 May
22	Westbury-on-Severn	22 May
23	Churcham	23 May
24	Newent	24 May
25	Dymock	25 May
26	Ledbury	26 May
27	Stoke Edith	27 May
28	Much Marcle	28 May
29	Bosbury	29 May
30	Much Cowarne	30 May
31	Cradley	31 May
32	Bishops Frome	1 June
33	Bromyard	3 June
34	Leominster	5 June
35	Eye	6 June
36	Kingsland	7 June
37	Dilwyn	8 June
38	Pembridge	9 June
39	Almeley	11 June
40	Clifford	12 June
41	Kington	13 June
42	Presteigne	14 June
43	Old Radnor	15 June
44	Richards Castle	18 June
45	Bitterley	19 June
46	Wistanstow	20 June
47	Stanton Lacy	21 June
48	Leintwardine	23 June
49	Diddlebury	24 June
50	Stokesay	25 June
51	Bromfield	26 June
52	Lydbury North	27 June
53	Clun	28 June
54	Montgomery	29 June
55	Chirbury	30 June
56	Worthen	2 July
57	Westbury	3 July
58	Alberbury	4 July
59	Pontesbury	5 July

THE GEOGRAPHY AND PERSONNEL OF THE VISITATION

Between 30 April and 5 July 1397, the bishop's visitation toured most of the diocese. The medieval diocese of Hereford comprised the whole of modern Herefordshire, the southern half of Shropshire, several parishes in Powys and Worcestershire, and the Forest of Dean in Gloucestershire. The visitation began in Burghill, just north of the city of Hereford (which itself lay outside the bishop's ordinary jurisdiction), and then spiralled rather eccentrically around the central and south-western parts of Herefordshire, before taking a more predictable course through the Forest of Dean and up the River Severn. The bishop's party then travelled in an arc taking in Ledbury, Bosbury, Bromyard, and Leominster, after which it progressed into the portions of the diocese that lay in Wales and Shropshire.⁴⁷ At this point, however, a question mark hangs over the relationship between Trefnant's itinerary and the evidence of the visitation book. There are no entries for Burford, Wenlock, or Stottesdon deaneries, which would have completed his tour of the diocese minus the exempt cathedral deanery. It looks as though there were plans to continue to Much Wenlock, given two instructions for offenders in Pontesbury deanery to appear there.⁴⁸ Although there are no further entries in the visitation book after 5 July (at Pontesbury), Trefnant was indeed at Wenlock on 9 July as planned, where we know he was dealing with a matrimonial case he had first heard at Chirbury on 30 June (**1359**).⁴⁹ In the meantime, he had been to Burford on 8 July with his key aide Reynold of Woolaston.⁵⁰

If the visitation had continued onwards from Pontesbury, we might assume that it would have followed the route taken by Bishop Swinfield in his visitation of 1293, for which we have a surviving itinerary. Swinfield visited Wenlock, Stottesdon, and Burford deaneries in the middle of his itinerary, travelling down the eastern edge of the diocese from Wenlock to Burford, stopping at 13 centres in 12 days, with incursions westward to take in Rushbury and Doddington.⁵¹ Afterwards, he continued on to Ludlow deanery. One of the centres in 1293, Tenbury, is mentioned in entries for Leominster (**709**) and Bishops Castle (**1110**) in the 1397 book, but only as a place where absent offenders were living. Trefnant's prorogation of the Westbury case to Much Wenlock would have involved a wait of six days, and in 1293 there were five days between the two places, which does suggest similar plans. However, something seems to have disrupted the progress of the 1397 visitation, with several pieces of evidence suggesting that the visitation party was being disbanded. First, from Westbury onwards (**1294**) the scribe of the commissary court – who had hitherto made additions only to occasional entries – records every

---

⁴⁷ For the extent of the medieval diocese, see David M. Smith, *Guide to Bishops' Registers of England and Wales* (London, 1981), 95; H. W. Phillott, *Diocesan Histories: Hereford* (London, 1888), 28–36 and frontispiece map.

⁴⁸ On 3 July, the chaplain of Westbury (Pont. deanery) was told to cite two offenders to appear at Much Wenlock on 9 July (**1294**), and in an undated note on the cover (**1342**) a portioner of Pontesbury was ordered to appear at Much Wenlock. There is one mention of Stottesdon, at Caynham in Ludlow deanery on 19 June (**1005**) where the vicar of Kinlet in Stottesdon deanery was cited for fornication.

⁴⁹ See also *Register of John Trefnant*, 144.

⁵⁰ *Register of John Trefnant*, 151.

⁵¹ Forrest and Whittick, 'Thirteenth-Century Visitation Records of the Diocese of Hereford', 751.

stage following the initial presentments. This strongly suggests the book was physically handed over to the commissary general, whose staff completed the visitation. Moreover, if a similar route to Swinfield's was planned by Trefnant it would seem odd to head 40 kilometres south from Pontesbury (5 July) to hear a case in Burford (8 July) only to travel 35 kilometres back north to Much Wenlock (9 July), had he anticipated being in Burford on his visitation itinerary perhaps a week to ten days later. It is therefore possible that the business of visitation was hastened somewhat in its latter stages, with the date of the hearing at Worthen being brought forward from 3 July (planned in a prorogation noted on the cover: **1360**) to 2 July (items **1281–93**), though this could equally be a mistake, or of no consequence. Lastly, the final page of the visitation book is very grubby, indicating that it functioned as the back cover for a long time; the book consists of two intact gatherings, arguing against leaves having fallen off.[52]

The surviving document records that the lord bishop 'made a visitation' at 60 central places, to each of which the representatives of several communities were summoned to present their reports. In all, 253 parishes, chapelries, and vills were 'visited' in this way. Compared to some other bishops of late medieval England, Trefnant devoted a relatively generous amount of time to the business of each reporting unit. The way visitations were organised spatially varied greatly. For example, whereas Bishop Giffard of Worcester (1268–1302) spent just one day in each deanery in his late-thirteenth-century visitations, three decades later his successor Bishop Montacute (1334–7) devoted three to five days to each deanery.[53] In 1395, the *sede vacante* visitation of the massive deanery of Cumbria was dispatched by the vicar general of York at Penrith parish church in a single day, whereas the usual practice for the diocese of York was to do as Trefnant did and spend several days in each deanery, spreading the work between a number of central places.[54] The basic principle of frequent stops in many centres seems to have been established at Hereford since at least the days of Bishop Swinfield, whose 1293 visitation stopped at 74 centres.[55]

The route of the visitation, as described above, does not adequately capture all the travelling that it occasioned. Thinking about the personnel involved tells a much more complex and interesting story. The bishop is named at the head of the document, and we tend to assume that he was present at each centre, but this

[52] An alternative explanation would be that the visitation did indeed continue, and that a whole gathering of leaves covering the three missing deaneries became detached from the rest of the book at an early date. Had the visitation continued, it would have covered perhaps 13 more centres and heard presentments from around 50 further parishes, chapels, and vills, depending on what units reported. This could have added about 20% to the business of the visitation, so it is a plausible surmise, but needs to be weighed against the evidence for abandonment at Pontesbury. On balance, the evidence for Pontesbury being the final centre, with continuations planned but not carried out (except for some tidying up at Wenlock), seems strongest.

[53] *Episcopal Registers, Diocese of Worcester: Register of Bishop Godfrey Giffard*, ed. J. W. Willis Bund (Oxford, 1902), 232, 313, 530–1; Richard M. Haines, *The Administration of the Diocese of Worcester in the First Half of the Fourteenth Century* (London, 1965), 163.

[54] York, Borthwick Institute, Register 14, f. 79v; for the usual practice, see Borthwick Institute, Register 11, f. 93v.

[55] Forrest and Whittick, 'Thirteenth-Century Visitation Records of the Diocese of Hereford', 751.

may not have been the case. Trefnant may have been represented by some other officer if business called him away. For example, on 6 June he dictated a letter from Leominster while the visitation tribunal took place in Eye (**745–8**). Eye is only three miles from Leominster, so it is possible that he travelled between the two places, but equally likely that he delegated the business of visitation that day.[56] We know that the official and registrar were present from time to time (**495, 612**), while the commissary general was frequently instructed to follow up cases in his own itinerant court (**1359–60**), which may have been following in the wake of the visitor's party, necessitating much coming and going and posing a great many logistical challenges.[57] At least one royal officer, the escheator of Herefordshire, John Maunce, was also involved (**114**).[58]

Procurations in kind and the resources of episcopal manors may have provisioned the party in places, but payments in money would have meant someone had to purchase food, drink, and other necessities from local producers and dealers. The daily bustle would also have included messengers coming and going to make sure the clergy and parish representatives appeared where and when they were supposed to. Because the visitation was organised around centres, most parish delegations and individual offenders had to travel to deliver their reports and receive their correction. In some places, notably near the Welsh border and around Leominster, the visitor also required the presence of local clergy and rural deans to carry out the correction of offenders (**761–8, 773, 785, 882, 890, 1221**). This may have been because these places were off the commissary general's usual itinerary, or because local knowledge and linguistic ability were deemed particularly important. However, frequent marginal annotation with the names of deaneries indicates that the attendance and involvement of rural deans was more generally expected. Offenders could indeed be recalcitrant, failing to appear on many occasions. This fact, and our reconstruction of the many journeys occasioned by visitation, lends the whole undertaking a fissiparous shapelessness that complicates the linear progression suggested by the documented itinerary.

For the most part, the visitation received reports from the representatives of the parishes of the diocese, but other units made reports too. At Bromfield in the deanery of Ludlow, representatives of the dependent chapel of Ludford and Syde, for example, gave the visitor the message that all was well with their church (**1088**). They saw themselves as a community and organised their dealings with the visitor to reflect this; the parishioners of Bromfield itself complained that their neighbours in Ludford and Syde did not contribute to necessary repairs to the bells of the parish church (**1090**), understandably so if they had their own church to attend to. Perhaps more surprisingly, several reports were received from 'vills' or settlements that were not defined by any parochial or chapel identity. Eaton, Adforton, Clun, Bicton, and Spoad were all described in this way (**719, 1032, 1193, 1213–14**). This was not, in fact, unusual in England. Most visitations of the northern province of York took the secular vill as the basic unit of ecclesiasti-

[56]   *Register of John Trefnant*, 144–5.
[57]   Charles Donahue (ed.), *The Records of the Medieval Ecclesiastical Courts*, II: *England* (Berlin, 1994), 169.
[58]   Maunce received the sequestered fruits of Mansell Gamage; he is named as escheator in The National Archives, SC/8/339/15988, and (in 1402) as a donor to the cathedral: HCA 1921.

cal discipline.[59] This was probably born of necessity. In many areas of upland England, the secular vill or township, and not the parish, was the administrative unit possessing geographical coherence and a sense of community. Vills were also used in some lowland areas, such as Ely and Wisbech where in 1401 Thomas Arundel confirmed the bishop of Ely's jurisdiction over 'vills, hamlets and parishes'.[60] Also, in some towns, the street and not the parish was the unit of visitation.[61] Since visitation relied upon communal identity, local elites, and self-policing, it was sensible to receive reports from whatever unit was locally meaningful, and where administrative structures already existed.

PROCEDURE AND THE COMPOSITION OF THE RECORD

Local meaning is omnipresent in the visitation book, but it is not straightforwardly accessible to the historian. To access it, we must first understand how the document was produced. As discussed above, the entry for each reporting unit was compiled in several distinct episodes. There are three main episodes in evidence in HCA 1779: presentments submitted in advance, corrections and augmentations made 'on the day' of the visitation, and notes of pastoral or judicial outcomes that occurred up to a year or more later. We argued above that the diocesan registrar was responsible for recording the first and second episodes, while the third was typically entered by the scribe of the commissary court. Not all episodes appear in every entry.

The presentments are the reports of representatives from each reporting unit. Where they are described in this record, the representatives are called 'the parishioners', though this should be read as a technical term denoting a limited and largely self-selecting group rather than the whole parish. In many visitation mandates, they were called the 'trustworthy men' of the parish.[62] This group was not synonymous with those who would – in later centuries – be called churchwardens; these are separately identified as 'procuratores' or 'custodes' (**213**, **261**, **367**, **574**, **613**). The presentments themselves are written out neatly with minimal spacing, and gaps are sometimes left at the foot of each entry. We do not know for certain how reports were submitted, but blank spaces left for names to be filled in and the insertion of additional information during the hearings are suggestive of written presentments, sometimes augmented with further and better particulars at the hearing.[63] A list of visitation articles may have been pre-circulated or proclaimed,

[59]   See for example York, Borthwick Institute, Register 10, ff. 67r, 69v, 156v, 212v; *The Register of William Greenfield Lord Archbishop of York 1306–1315*, volume 2, ed. William Brown and Alexander Hamilton Thompson, Surtees Society, 149 (1934), 27; *The Register of Thomas Langley Bishop of Durham 1406–1437*, volume 3, ed. Robin L. Storey, Surtees Society, 169 (1967), 181–2.

[60]   *Vetus Liber Archidiaconatus Eliensis*, ed. C. L. Feltoe and Ellis H. Minns (Cambridge, 1917), 182.

[61]   For example: *Register of Bishop Waltham*, 129–36 (Wilton in 1394); Lichfield Record Office, D30/9/3/1 (Lichfield in 1461–71); Taunton, Somerset Heritage Centre, D/D/Ca/9 (Wells in 1533).

[62]   Forrest, 'Transformation of Visitation', 15–21; Forrest, *Trustworthy Men: How Inequality and Faith Made the Medieval Church* (Princeton, N.J., 2018).

[63]   The unusual survival of ephemeral parchment slips listing the presentments of parishes in a 1299 visitation of Lincoln diocese shows that this stage could rely on written rather than oral reports: Lincolnshire Archives, D&C A/1/14.

but equally the representatives may have passed on their knowledge and expectations regarding the 'things in need of correction' from one generation to the next.
Some presentments are incomplete stubs, while elsewhere the initial presentments
are all that is recorded, for example at Weston (**35–8**).

After the presentments had been written into the book, hearings took place in
the visitation centres in the presence of the visitor or his representative. Presentments were reports of *fama* or fame, that is, legally sanctioned rumour or common
knowledge. In formal terms, fame, or 'common fame' (**216**, **616**, **981**, **1035**), was
widespread opinion reported by at least two people. It was not in itself proof of an
allegation, and its truth had to be tested.[64] The visitor would cite the alleged offenders or a responsible person or group (such as the clergy, 'parishioners', or proctors),
and put the fame to them in a question. The scribe made abbreviated notes on
whether the offence was admitted or denied, whether any party failed to appear,
and what outcome was ordered by the visitor. Sometimes missing names are filled
in or corrected. The arrangement of certain entries can be used to demonstrate
that the presentments and 'on-the-day' hearings were written up in batches, centre
by centre, as the visitor's party made its way around the diocese. For example,
the initial presentments for Monmouth (**257–75**) took up about a quarter of the
space on folio 6r. Before writing the next set of presentments, those for Dixton, the
scribe left a large gap, clearly expecting that there would be more presentments
made for Monmouth on the day of the hearing. He was right to do so, but the
additional entries for Monmouth were so numerous that he had to begin another
section, headed 'Item Monemuth' (**276–86**), which in the manuscript follows the
Dixton presentments and continues for a few lines on folio 6v. There was space to
do so because Dixton was the last place scheduled for visitation at the Monmouth
centre, and the scribe had not yet placed the heading for the next centre. The book
was gradually filled with presentments and on the day hearings, centre by centre.

Some offenders who failed to appear at their own centre, or who could not give
a satisfactory account of themselves, might be told that they 'have a day' a little
later in the itinerary on which to appear to explain themselves or provide proofs.
For example, the parish representatives of Welsh Bicknor were due to appear at
Monmouth on 12 May but did not (**249**) and so the stub for the primary entry was
revised from 'The parishioners say' to 'The parishioners have a day at English Bicknor.' The scribe seems to have been interrupted in writing 'dicunt' ('they say') to
be told that they were not present, so he crossed this out and indicated where they
would be told to appear instead. The hand that continues this sentence 'where
they said that ...' is the same one, but the ink is the much darker one that he was
using at English Bicknor (folio 7v), showing that the compilation of the primary
entries and many of the 'on-the-day' notes was here undertaken by the same man,
as suggested above. Similarly, at Burghill the parish representatives did not appear
(**7**), and their appearance was postponed until the visitation reached Wormsley, at
which time the day of their appearance (Sunday) was added into a blank space,
and nine presentments were entered. Both postponements were also noted on the
book's cover (**1343**, **1348**).[65] However, at Burghill, a presentment about the need

---

[64]   Forrest, 'Transformation of Visitation', 23–7; Thelma Fenster and Daniel Lord Smail
(eds), *Fama: The Politics of Talk and Reputation in Medieval Europe* (Ithaca, 2003).
[65]   A note on the cover, however (**1343**), inexplicably contradicts this, saying that the
parishioners of Burghill did *not* appear at Wormsley.

for the rector and vicar to repair the chancel roof was known about and recorded on the first appointed day in a completely different ink from the Sunday entries. Despite the 'batching' of initial entries, it is clear that the reports of each parish were not necessarily all delivered at the same time.

The third episode that often goes to make up a single entry is a note of follow-up proceedings, often written in a distinctive hand, perhaps that of the scribe of the commissary court. Most of this is undated and undatable, but one entry (**9**) stipulates a date for an offender to appear the following February, almost ten months after the initial presentment. This must indicate future judicial proceedings in the itinerant commissary court, which followed up particular cases in the visitor's wake. Indeed, sometimes the parishioners were explicitly told to initiate litigation themselves if they thought the issue was serious enough, for example over the multiple faults of the vicar of Weobley (**140**, **141**, **144**), a missing book at Llanwarne (**171**), a missing chalice at Llangarron (**326**), the failure to properly execute a will at Staunton-on-Arrow (**792**), or defamation at Bitterley (**998**). From this, it is clear that Trefnant made a procedural distinction between matters that could be dealt with pastorally and corrected on the spot, and things that required judicial settlement in another forum. The most serious or delicate cases were referred to the bishop's consistory that sat in Hereford (**2**, **128**, **131**, **137**, **172**, **420**, **1000**, **1046**, **1280**). Some disputes might result in a private lawsuit without the visitor's explicit instruction, such as the report of bigamy at Richards Castle (**978**), which was then pursued as matrimonial litigation (**1358**). Indeed, the bishop's register mentions a number of cases arising from presentments to the visitation. Leominster Priory complained formally to the bishop about the behaviour of some of its parishioners, in response to the parishioners' own complaints about the monks (**688–97**, **713–14**).[66] At Chirbury, the bishop heard the case of Margery Deheubarth, who claimed she was married to Roger ap Ieuan ap Llewelyn, whereas he denied their union, saying he was married to Sybil Herdemon (**1359**); the main register records that the bishop annulled the marriage between Margery and Roger.[67]

Most presentments were, however, dealt with on the day by the visitor, issuing penances, requiring people to make good their faults, and orchestrating informal solutions to disputes. Some offenders had already been corrected at an earlier visitation, in the courts, or perhaps in confession. The presentment might note that they had returned to their offence 'since the time of correction', while subjects might also deny their alleged recidivism in the same terms (**895**, **1277**, **1297**). The 'correction' that the visitor dealt out was intended to reform behaviour, and there was not an absolute distinction between pastoral and judicial outcomes. Penances were meant to persuade the sinner to reform, and to set an example to his or her neighbours. Sometimes the nature of penance was not specified (**94**, **323**), but most often offenders were ordered to be beaten a number of times around their local church or marketplace (e.g. **521**, **892**, **963**), occasionally carrying a candle while being beaten (**252**, **254**, **297**, **1233**). Sometimes they were merely required to provide a candle for the church (**612**, **1186**). An occasion on which a pregnant woman had her penance for fornication postponed until she had given birth (**786**) indicates beating was intended to be a painful physical ordeal and not just a sham-

---

[66]   *Register of John Trefnant*, 140–2.
[67]   *Register of John Trefnant*, 143–4; Margery's father, David Deheubarth of Montgomery, was reported for adultery at the visitation (**1221**).

ing ritual. If penances were not carried out, an offender could find themselves excommunicated (**829**, **831**, **1011**). Besides penance, offenders might be ordered to right a wrong or change their behaviour: unmarried couples reported for having sex might be given a chance to marry by a certain date (**705**, **706**, **943**, **1199**, **1255**), debtors to pay their debts (**1219**), cadgers to return borrowed goods (**592**), and cruel or violent husbands to treat their wives better (**42**, **913**). If the person reported for an offence denied it, they might be given the chance to undergo purgation, which meant finding a number of people willing to swear to one's innocence and good name; for example, purgation 'with six hands' (**95**, **361**, **424**) involved finding six people who would raise their hand in an oath. One option mid-way between dealing with offences on the day and sending them up to the diocesan courts was to impose an arbitrated settlement, as happened at Eardisley, where the deeply unpopular vicar and his parishioners were told to reach an amicable agreement through four 'good men', two chosen by each side (**1340**).

The complexity of the record – as a series of distinct episodes, produced over quite a long period, incorporating a variety of interests and voices, and drawing on external documents and memories going back at least three years – is reflected in its arrangement. The three main episodes sometimes create an impression of chaos and confusion, but this is a working record and clearly functioned quite efficiently. There are many interlineations, but very few cases in which the records of hearings completely burst out of the space left by the positioning of the presentments.[68] The overall arrangement is defined by date and place headings for each visitation centre, where the name of the centre is wrapped in a rectangular box. The deanery name also occasionally appears at the head of the folio or beside a parish, probably because the rural deans were responsible for citing the clergy and lay representatives, and for carrying out corrections.[69] The names of each unit visited were also written in the left-hand margin. These features may have functioned as finding aids, imposing documentary order on a dynamic process, and were perhaps useful to officers in the diocesan courts, searching for the origins of a case. Marginal procedural notes also highlighted particular cases and outcomes. For example, when an offender was recorded as excommunicated in the main entry, a marginal note often adds that a signification of excommunication had also been sought from the crown (**51**, **74**, **119**, **413**, **460**, **462**, **743**, **783**, **877**–**9**, **940**, **1041**, **1132**, **1223**, **1257**, **1310**).[70] The conclusion of particularly tricky cases is sometimes noted with 'expeditum' (**166**) or, more commonly, 'dimissus est' (**284**, **1191**–**2**).

---

[68]   Items that exceed their available space occur at f. 10v (**495**); f. 22v where it is the sheer number of additional items, made in the annotating hand (**1094**–**7**), rather than extensive follow-up hearings that drive the text into the margin; f. 24r, where case notes relating to the chaplain of Clunbury flow into the margin (**1171**). Sometimes the scribe found it easiest to insert an additional item above the first he had written, in which cases he would draw a line to indicate where that place's reports began, for example at Orcop on f. 4r (**174**).

[69]   For rural deans issuing citations to visitations, see *Register of Lewis Charlton*, 7–8, and *Register of John Gilbert*, 78–9.

[70]   For significations of excommunication, see F. Donald Logan, *Excommunication and the Secular Arm in England: A Study in Legal Procedure from the Thirteenth to the Sixteenth Century* (Toronto, 1968).

THE PARISHIONERS

The dominant voices in the initial presentments are those of the parish representatives, who are mostly anonymous in this record, but elsewhere can be shown to have been the male heads of wealthier peasant households.[71] The extent to which these men were truly able to represent the concerns of their fellow parishioners is a question of great interest. It seems likely that they reported some issues of general concern and filtered other matters, using visitation as an organ of local social control. Moreover, they knew how to make visitation serve their own interests, often referring to previous decisions of the bishop's consistory or to legal obligations that had not been met (**323**, **612**, **776**, **838**).

Only at Newland (**351**) were a group of parishioners named. Why here? Their inclusion is anomalous. It was usual for parishes or other reporting units to be represented by between four and eight 'trustworthy men' at the visitor's command, but here we have 15 names. Newland was a visitation hub for Burford deanery, and so this may be an ecclesiastical version of the secular grand jury, sifting and weighing the reports from outlying places. In Bishop Orleton's time (1317–27), the visitation of Burford deanery had been undertaken with juries of 12 men from the visitation centres and just four or six representatives of the neighbouring churches. In the Yorkshire deaneries in 1301 and 1304, the archbishop of York required certain parish representatives to 'respond to things [already] discovered in the visitation', suggesting a filtering and response role for such juries.[72] If this was general in 1397, it might suggest that the reports of the parishioners were subjected to an additional layer of lay scrutiny and selection.

Moreover, neither 'the parishioners' nor any putative grand jury were the only voice of a parish, as indicated by another peculiar feature of the record, the appearance of separate 'accusers' on the day of a hearing (**52**, **122**, **297**, **332**, **352**, **405**, **410**, **545**) making reports in addition to those of the parish representatives. In canon law, *accusatio* describes a very different process from visitation reporting: the report of a single named person rather than an anonymous collective.[73] Most likely it was simply an expedient way to describe a group of people who were not the delegated representatives of a parish or other unit. At Kenchester, for example, 'the parishioners' said that all was well, but on the day of the hearing 'accusers' turned up to say that a will had been executed without licence (**122**). At other times (see comment below on the phrase *omnia bene*), such additions are incorporated silently. It would be extremely odd if there had not been disagreement within parishes about what should be reported to the visitor, but the 1397 visitation makes this more than usually explicit.

Aside from 'accusers', parishioners outside the narrow social circle of the official representatives generally appear only as named offenders, subject to correction by the combined agency of their neighbours and the visitor. They may have felt an affinity with some of the customs and old practices alluded to by their representatives, but we should not assume so. Occasionally, the record provides echoes of other voices. We might suppose, for example, that the 'friends' of Annot Howel

---

[71] Forrest, *Trustworthy Men*, 129–57.
[72] *Register of Adam Orleton*, 287; *The Register of Thomas of Corbridge, Lord Archbishop of York, 1300–1304*, volume 1, ed. William Brown, Surtees Society, 138 (1925), 55, 126–7, 146–7.
[73] James A. Brundage, *Medieval Canon Law* (London, 1995), 142–3.

who remonstrated with the chaplain of Woolaston about her readmission to the church after childbirth (**386**) were distinct from the parish representatives who reported the incident. But for the most part lay parishioners are a silent majority, and only careful contextual study can reveal the relationships and motivations behind the record.

Interpretative challenges only serve to make the business of the visitation more intriguing. The book is an unrivalled source for the investigation of social and religious life on the borders of late medieval England. What did the bishop, clergy, parishioners, and accusers think were the 'things in need of correction'?[74] In 59 of the 253 places visited, the answer was nothing – all is well, *omnia bene* – a message that could be read as a reflection of parochial harmony or as an attempt to keep the bishop out of local affairs. On a few occasions (**123**, **126**, **330**, **417**, **458**, **585**, **662**, **851**, **1002**) *omnia bene* was followed by an 'except ...' that may indicate disagreement within the parish and an un-signalled intervention by *accusatores*, or at the least caution in dealing with the bishop. Once, at Mitcheldean (**411**), where the parishioners had sent the message that all was well, a proctor acting for the bishop said that he dared not cite them to appear, providing a salutary reminder that medieval churchmen were not all-powerful.

More often, they had plenty to say.[75] The parish representatives in this visitation do not seem to have been responding to every item on a list of visitation articles; indeed, it is possible that no such list was used on this occasion. While there are themes – such as church fabric and sexual morality – that recur from place to place, the transition from the presentments of one parish to those of another can be notably sharp, with different subjects dominating the reports of neighbouring places.

CLERICAL FAULTS IN THE VISITATION

Before the late-thirteenth century, visitations mainly involved an inspection of the church fabric and possessions, and this was still an important task in 1397. The visitor heard reports about church walls, windows, and roofs in disrepair, things that were the fault of the clergy if it were the chancel (e.g. **486**) and of the parishioners if in the nave (e.g. **1148**). The proper enclosure of churchyards was also sometimes mentioned (e.g. **964**, **973**) because consecrated ground could be 'polluted' if stray animals wandered in. The condition of the wider rectory estate (e.g. **118**, **492**) was also of great concern to patrons of churches and clerics involved in the market for benefices, who saw their rights to rectories and vicarages as items of real property. The representatives of many parishes reported on the provision of liturgical books and objects, and they may have been as keen as the bishop that things were done properly in their church, whether out of a sense of piety, respectability, or pride. At Peterchurch and Wigmore, for example, they reported their rectors for failing to provide psalters, antiphonals, and breviaries (**60–1**, **954**), books that were seen as the property of the parish, and at Llanwarne, Welsh Bicknor, and Ullingswick

---

[74]   This was a common phrase used in mandates to summon parishioners and clergy to a visitation; for example in *Registrum Roberti Winchelsey Cantuariensis Archiepiscopi*, ed. Rose Graham, Canterbury and York Society, 51–2 (London, 1952–6), 225.

[75]   A descriptive account of the lay and clerical faults reported in the visitation is given in Hair, 'Defaults and Offences of Clergy and Laity, 1397'.

the parishioners complained that various clerics had taken books and refused to return them, or had lent them privately (**171**, **249**, **592**). Parishioners sometimes demanded that their rectors provide deacons who would take care of the parish's books and ornaments (**137**, **232**, **626**). At Leominster, there was only one old and worn book for the office of burial, while it was said that not even two sufficed in times of plague when there could be 16 or 18 bodies to bury in one day (**689**). The absence of liturgical objects such as chalices (**326**, **594**, **839**, **1219**) was noted and, if the font could not be locked to prevent misuse of holy water (**37**, **649**), the visitor was interested. Likewise, if the clergy did not have proper vestments, as at Dilwyn (**787**), the basic material provision for divine services was deficient. If the church was dark and it was difficult for the clergy to read from their service books, the lack of lights would also be noted (e.g. **144**, **192**, **340**). Such complaints might combine the interests of lay people and the visitor, but sometimes it was the parishioners who were at fault, as at Wentnor (**1145**), where they were said to have failed to provide a surplice for the chaplain, a lock for the font, and a light for the chaplain to use when visiting the sick at night.

Besides the physical fabric of the church and its contents, the main concern of the bishop was the management of the parish clergy, whose behaviour had the potential to cause scandal, hinder the provision of pastoral care, upset both patrons and parishioners, divert tithe receipts, and devalue the real property of their livings.[76] Visitation enabled bishops and archdeacons to achieve this management in concert with the parish representatives, whose desire for respectable clergy is one of the overriding themes of the visitation. This confluence of interests had the potential to make the clergy feel as though they were being criticised both from above and from below. At Coddington, for example, the rector was said to be a liability in almost all areas: he was 'extremely lukewarm' and negligent in celebrating divine services, he had enclosed parts of the churchyard, stored hay in the tower, was absent from the parish, kept a concubine, had failed to provide bell-ropes, and was working lands that were not part of the glebe (**534**–**40**). While the ability of clerics to show written titles to the benefices they held was probably more a matter for the bishop than the laity, in all these other areas the concerns of bishops and parishioners were potentially aligned. The first requirement of the clergy was that they should be present in their parishes, and their absence was often noted (**330**, **503**, **526**, **668**). Where a rector was absent legally, or the rectory was in the hands of an institution, the absence of the vicar (literally a deputy) might otherwise be reported (**230**, **1203**), and where a priest had died and not been replaced, this was also noted (**255**).

Most lay Christians felt strongly that they should be served by competent clergy. At Wentnor, for example, the parishioners complained that the rector did not conduct services 'in a praiseworthy manner' and that their chaplain was 'unworthy ... and one inadequate to serve God and the parishioners' (**1134**, **1138**). Vague though such judgements were, they are an indication of the depth of local feeling, and they chimed with the bishop's responsibility as pastor to his flock. A more specific complaint was failure to conduct services in church (**115**, **503**, **715**, **1047**, **1173**), and at Cusop the parishioners told the visitor that they had resorted to paying a priest to come and perform services for them (**868**), although this was part of a wider dispute about the status of their church (**91**, **860**). Where there was a

---

[76] Dohar, *The Black Death and Pastoral Leadership*, 121–48.

priest to celebrate mass and carry out other pastoral duties, the parishioners might still be unhappy. There is a palpable sense of anger in reports about baptisms not performed or done incorrectly (**536, 821, 1172**), or dying relatives who did not receive the last rites (**262, 820, 1171**). Such cases reveal values and beliefs that were fundamental to late medieval Christianity. For example, at Woolaston (**380**) the former vicar was said to have carried 'an empty pyx, without the Body of Christ' when visiting a dying woman, causing a great scandal in 'making the people adore the sacrament that was not present'. This was a scandal in the sense of hindering the salvation of the people. It was duplicitous, made lay persons into unwitting idolaters, and may have made people worry about their priest's own beliefs. Worship was clearly not merely psychological balm but a meaningful attempt to approach the divine. Although Christians were exhorted to have faith in an unseen God, it was through the physical presence of Christ in consecrated bread that they achieved this, and they were reliant upon the clergy as mediators of this holy matter. It is interesting that the presentments never mention preaching, either the lack of it or its quality, suggesting that lay people did not see this as an essential part of the parish priest's role. Unusual complaints such as a priest who demanded payment to hear confession (**844**) or an unruly and drunken priest who revealed the content of confession (**219**), indicate that lay reports about their clergy were much more than mechanical responses to the visitor's concerns.

This was perhaps especially so when clerical sexual morality was reported. It would be easy to imagine that such presentments – which are very common – are evidence that parish representatives shared the church's official views on clerical celibacy, but it is possible to look at them in a different way. Some clerics were simply seen as promiscuous, such as Richard Sterr of Cradley (**614**), but where reports suggest a long-term sexual or domestic partnership there may have been years of tolerance, ended only by some change in the politics of the parish. As Janelle Werner's work on this visitation book has shown, the label 'clerical concubinage' threatens to divert our attention from the stability and customary nature of such relationships.[77] The lives of priests could also clash with canonical expectations in more complex ways. For example, clerics were not necessarily confirmed in their vocation from an early age: Richard Stokke of Dymock had been ordained after his betrothal to Isabel Waren, with whom he was suspected of continuing a relationship (**483**). In such cases, it is hard to tell what moral attitudes and local politics lay behind visitation presentments, and further contextual study will undoubtedly reveal more. What is clear, however, is that clerical failings are not evidence of decline or terminal inadequacy in the pre-Reformation church. Instead, visitation reporting of clerical offences should be seen either as a translation of the values of reform into a local ethic of lived religion, or as the creative use of a powerful institution in pursuit of local goals.

Lay priorities were not always determinative, however. In several items recorded only on the cover of the visitation book, the bishop dealt with clerics not mentioned in the general parish entries. This may indicate a two-tier system of correction, one in which the visitor was happy to be seen as the public ally of the parishioners, and another more private tier (**1338–9, 1341–2, 1352–4, 1356–7**) that allowed him to protect the reputations of certain clerics. Other tensions in the

---

[77] Werner, 'Promiscuous Priests and Vicarage Children'; her analysis is based on the fifteenth-century consistory court books of Hereford as well as the 1397 visitation.

diocese are not apparent unless one compares the contents of the visitation book with the main register. For example, the parishioners of Leominster, whose parish church was a shared part of the priory church, brought a long list of complaints to Trefnant's attention: the monks – as rector of Leominster – were alleged to withhold a key from the bell-ringers so that the bells could not be rung; to prevent the parishioners from decorating the church as they wished; not to provide a clerk to carry a bell and lamp in front of the vicar when he visited the sick; not to have provided the right liturgical books; and to have prevented lay people from receiving communion unless they paid for it (**688–91, 713–14**). The monks did not get a chance to respond in the recorded visitation hearing, but Trefnant's main register shows that they made a series of counter-allegations against the parishioners: that they had enclosed an area of the church around an altar dedicated to Saints Mary Magdalen, Katherine, and Margaret, and that their services were disturbing the monks' singing of the holy office. These seem to be the other side of the parishioners' comments about access and control of space in the shared church and the creation of a new structure, perhaps comprising wooden screens. Although visitation gave an outlet to lay complaints, in this instance the bishop sided with the priory and ordered the parishioners to demolish their construction.[78]

Leominster was also the location for one of the more puzzling presentments in the visitation book, concerning the chaplain William Crompe (**693**). This cleric was clearly unpopular with his parishioners: they complained that he bought and sold livestock at a profit, perhaps implying that he was evading market rules, but also that he shared in the profits arising from 'baggerts crafte'. This appears to be a reference to fraudulent religious begging, of the kind lambasted in William Langland's poem *The Vision of Piers Plowman*, in which 'baggards' are people who pretend to be mendicant friars or hermits in order to collect alms from the gullible. 'Baggard' comes from the Middle Dutch word 'beghard', the masculine form of beguine and often an insult paired with another loan word: lollard. Beghard also appears to be the etymological root of the English 'beggar'.[79] If this interpretation is correct, the Leominster 'baggert' was resented as a pious fraud.

Certain powerful clergy required more careful handling, and one notable instance indicates the limits of the usual business of visitation. Bishop Trefnant had objected to the election of John Prophet as dean of Hereford in 1395, and in 1397 was criticising him for pluralism and questioning his right to the prebend of Overhall. Prophet's case was recorded only on the cover of the visitation book (**1354, 1357**) before being written up in the main register, suggesting it was too complicated or sensitive to be dealt with among parochial business.[80]

---

[78]   *Register of John Trefnant*, 140–3.
[79]   The Latin–Middle English glossary known as *Medulla Grammatice* (c.1425) has 'baggard' as the translation of 'lustrator', a wanderer and frequenter of suspect places: *Middle English Dictionary* (Online edition, 2014); see also the *Dictionary of Medieval Latin from British Sources*. William Langland, *Piers Plowman: The C-Text*, ed. Derek Pearsall (Exeter, 1994), Passus IX, lines 98–105, at p. 165. For the Dutch background, see Robert Lerner, *The Heresy of the Free Spirit in the Later Middle Ages* (Notre Dame, 1972), 168–74; Margaret Deanesly, *The Lollard Bible and Other Medieval Biblical Versions* (Cambridge, 1920), 69.
[80]   *Register of John Trefnant*, 52–6, 138–40; Richard G. Davies, 'Prophete, John (c.1350–1416)', *Oxford Dictionary of National Biography* (Oxford, 2004).

LAY FAULTS IN THE VISITATION

The parish representatives spent at least as much time thinking about the behaviour of their lay neighbours as they did about the clergy. The largest category of offences reported to the visitor concerned lay sexual morality, with additional attention paid to domestic violence and cruelty. As with clerical faults, the things in need of correction were determined by general moral principles and local circumstances rather than by the systematic application of canon law. It is safe to assume that the parish representatives chose to report the faults that offended their sense of propriety, and that they thought could be addressed by the publicity, deterrence, and coercion that visitation offered. While spousal litigation in the church courts has received a great deal of historiographical attention, the distinctive character of visitation evidence has not hitherto been appreciated: cases at the visitation emerged from the collective judgement of a male peasant elite, not by individual legal action. There is therefore scope for quantitative and contextual analysis.

For example, visitations provide a fuller picture than that gained from church court records of the range of long-term sexual and domestic relationships entered into by lay people at this time, as demonstrated in Michelle Armstrong-Partida's work on Catalunya.[81] The far-from-simple story of the Peterchurch quartet of John ap Tommi, Agnes Robynes, Richard Hamonde, and Agnes Pye (**67**, **68**) is a case in point. Robynes and Hamonde had been married in the past but had divorced because of Hamonde's impotence.[82] But when Ap Tommi entered into a relationship with Robynes, he was reported to the visitor for illicit sexual activity, she being canonically still married to Hamonde. It was not Hamonde who brought this complaint, for he had by this time married Pye, overcome his impotence, and had children with her. The presentment must have been made because these arrangements offended sections of parish opinion, or because there was confusion over the legal standing of their separation. To complicate matters further, the new partners of Robynes and Hamonde (that is, John ap Tommi and Agnes Pye) were themselves also having an affair with each other. The status of these four relationships is impossible to determine fully on the basis of the visitation record alone, but it does seem that there were more ways of being in a long-term sexual partnership than canon law permitted, and that there was also local disagreement about what amounted to a breach of propriety.

Illicit lay sexual relationships threatened to disturb the order of households, either through a breach of patriarchal authority – by a wife, daughter, son, or servant – or a failure of self-control on the part of the male head. As Werner has shown, the women involved in proscribed sexual acts in Hereford diocese were punished more harshly than the men.[83] Nevertheless, masculine weakness was addressed in other spheres, notably husbands' cruelty towards their wives, which

[81]   Armstrong-Partida, *Defiant Priests*. See also, Ruth Mazo Karras, *Unmarriages: Women, Men, and Sexual Unions in the Middle Ages* (Philadelphia, 2012).
[82]   Here and in other instances in the book (**9**, **638**, **859**, **1016**, **1162**, **1245**), 'divorce' could mean either lawful separation or annulment. The former could be granted only because of male impotence or cruelty, leaving the parties still married and unable to re-marry; the latter relied upon the discovery of an impediment, following which the parties could re-marry. For the canon law on divorce, see Richard H. Helmholz, *Marriage Litigation in Medieval England* (Cambridge, 1974), 74–111.
[83]   Werner, 'Promiscuous Priests and Vicarage Children', 171–2.

could take many forms, though the presentments tell only the most truncated stories. 'Mistreatment' often went hand in hand with a husband's adultery (**220**, **246**, **1221**, **1225**), and could involve depriving the woman of food, clothing, and other necessaries (**250**, **913**); at Westbury-on-Severn, there were two cases of refusing to support children as well as wives (**420**, **421**). Actual physical violence was rarely alleged since husbands were expected to beat their wives, so community disapproval was triggered only when men went beyond what was called 'reasonable chastisement', for example permanent maiming or putting a woman in fear of her life (**225**).[84] A man mistreated by his wife was a sign of disorder and patriarchal failure in a different way: male weakness and an inversion of the proper hierarchy of power (**375**). Interpersonal violence between men was a social problem that did not fall squarely within the remit of visitation or indeed the church, but it was nevertheless occasionally raised by the parish representatives when it involved the pollution of churches and churchyards by bloodshed (**381**, **399**), or when the victim was a cleric (**1222**).

In addition to their role in policing sexual morality and married life, the parish representatives were the arbiters of neighbourliness and status within their communities. Although reports of unruly behaviour or harmful speech were usually framed in general terms as damaging to 'neighbours' or as a hindrance to peace in church, in practice offences such as defamation (**28**, **133**, **473**, **735**, **743**, **772**, **849**) and talking in church (**29**) were heavily gendered female: most reported offenders were women. The exceptions, for example of a man reported for defaming a married woman, proves the rule (**771**): he had been boasting about having had sex with her, and this talk was harmful to her husband's – rather than simply to her – reputation. So in public as well as in private morality, the behaviour and speech of women seems to have been more closely scrutinised and judged than that of men, and disorder was understood as female. This gendered social order was even policed in spatial terms. For example, at Brilley we see two reports about social position and seating in church: one stated that laymen were sitting in the chancel, which was presumably a complaint of the clergy, but the second noted that women were sitting too far forward in the nave, contravening an old custom (**899**, **900**). In this juxtaposition, usurping another's proper place was associated with femininity and used as a means of controlling both men and women.[85]

Fellow-feeling with one's neighbours was shot through with habitual ideas and actions that maintained inequalities: between the sexes, between employers and employees, and between wealthier and poorer villagers. The precise ways in which the visitation was used as a forum for the maintenance of status and hierarchy, and how this intersected with the search for communal peace and order, would certainly repay detailed study.

[84] For a discussion, see Sara Butler, *The Language of Abuse: Marital Violence in Later Medieval England* (Leiden, 2007).
[85] For a discussion of women and parish churches, see Katherine L. French, 'Women in the Late Medieval English Parish', in Mary C. Erler and Maryanne Kowaleski (eds), *Gendering the Master Narrative: Women and Power in the Middle Ages* (Ithaca, 2003), 163–4.

THE COMMUNITY OF THE FAITHFUL

Some of the most important assumptions about order and disorder in the presentments and their treatment by the visitor have to do with the boundaries of belonging in late medieval England. These include the distinction between the English
and the Welsh, between healthy and unhealthy bodies, between resident members
of parishes and people who had left, and between right and wrong belief.

In many parts of the diocese, and not only in the west, there were substantial
numbers of Welsh speakers. This is amply attested by the personal names in the
visitation book. Some were members of long-settled families while others may
have been more recent economic migrants, as suggested by locative surnames
referring to Elfael, Rhayader, Arwystli, and Deheubarth. In some areas, Welsh was
the dominant language. For example, the parishioners of Garway in Archenfield
deanery, which lay in the ancient Welsh kingdom of Ergyng, complained that a
parish chaplain was incapable of undertaking the cure of souls 'because he does
not know the Welsh language, and most parishioners there ... do not know the
English language' (**222**). The inhabitants of Aston and Churchstoke – both places
that were disputed between the bishops of Hereford and St Asaph – had made
a similar claim in 1307, and also recalled that when Thomas Cantilupe came to
preach in that area, he had needed a translator to make himself understood.[86]
These particular experiences may, however, have been exceptional, as there were
many clergy with Welsh names. Bishop Trefnant himself came from a Welsh area,
had a Welsh name, and employed Welsh-speaking scribes in his household.[87] This
multilingualism was crucial to the success of institutions such as visitation and the
itinerant consistory court, which regularly had to hear presentments in Welsh and
translate them into administrative Latin. Against this background of ostensible co-
existence, the extent of disharmony between Welsh and English speakers is hard to
assess. A fuller picture would undoubtedly emerge from more detailed quantitative
work on the inter-ethnic interactions attested in the visitation book. Although it
would, in many instances, be unwise to pronounce on the identity of people with
mixed English and Welsh names, sometimes the clear identification of an offender
as Welsh suggests that significant, though perhaps unconscious, feelings of differ-
ence and inequality played a part in the micro-politics of the parish. For example,
at Culmington the parishioners reported that 'Isabel of Wales fornicates with a
Welshman whose name they do not know' (**1065**). At Stokesay, John Hir's long-
term yet extra-marital sexual partner was identified as 'Dyddgu the Welsh woman'
(**1084**), tacitly associating moral laxity with ethnic identity.

The visitation also provides evidence for a great deal of mobility. Besides the
soldiers away in Ireland (mentioned above), many other offenders are noted as
absent in the record. The rather opaque formula used by the scribe is 'extra' (out-

[86]   Llinos Beverley Smith, 'The Welsh Language before 1536', in Geraint H. Jenkins (ed.),
The Welsh Language before the Industrial Revolution (Cardiff, 1997), 15–44, at 17–18.
[87]   Richard G. Davies, 'Trefnant, John (d. 1404)', in *Oxford Dictionary of National Biography*
(Oxford, 2004); Merja Black, 'Lollardy, Language Contact and the Great Vowel Shift:
Spelling in the Defence Papers of William Swinderby', *Neuphilologische Mitteilungen*, 94 (1998),
53–69; Llinos Beverley Smith, 'A View from an Ecclesiastical Court: Mobility and Marriage
in a Border Society at the End of the Middle Ages', in R. Rees Davies and Geraint H.
Jenkins (eds), *From Medieval to Modern Wales: Historical Essays in Honour of Kenneth O. Morgan and
Ralph A. Griffiths* (Cardiff, 2004), 64–80, at 72–3.

side), leaving the reason unspecified: they may have fled so as not to have to appear before the bishop, been forced to leave as a communal sanction for the reported offence, migrated, or simply been away from home. It is, moreover, unclear where is meant by 'outside': it may signify an offender beyond either the bishop's or the rural dean's jurisdiction, or simply someone whom the parishioners could not locate. Occasionally, the sparse contextual detail permits a little more clarity. For example, at Churchstoke a couple reported for fornication appeared before the bishop and were assigned the penance of being beaten three times around the church at Chirbury (**1263**), but the scribe then added that they were now in the village of Harry Stoke, which is near Bristol. It would seem that they had eloped rather than do penance and remain in Churchstoke. Of course, much else about this case remains unknowable, chiefly why their relationship met with disapproval. Wherever the truth lies in this instance, the cumulative effect of such cases is to establish a structural rhetorical distinction between the settled (and present) parish representatives and the offenders who had gone 'outside' their community. The single instance of a man at Norton 'smitten by leprosy' (**937**) whom the parishioners requested be 'separated from the company of people' lest he infect them, reminds us that visitation could disturb the course of some people's lives so much that they could not remain at home.

Other boundaries of Christian belonging were more cognitive and emotional than geographical. In general, there was little reason for the parishioners to make presentments concerning religious belief and practice, except when norms had been transgressed. Of course, this was a subjective judgement, and we should assume that much behaviour that verged on the unorthodox was accepted because it was deeply embedded in local practice. When, therefore, the parishioners did report some unusual belief or practice, it must be because it had disturbed local consensus or shocked the leaders of parish society in some way. At Kilpeck, the parishioners said that a chaplain seemed to them infirm in his faith 'because he has often made boast that he goes about at night-time with fantastic spirits' (**187**), while at Ruardean Nicholas Cuthler was reported for keeping vigil at his father's grave, expecting to meet his ghost 'to the great scandal of the catholic faith, as they believe' (**300**). The circumspection of these presentments – 'as it seems to them', 'as they believe' – hints both at strongly held local convictions about Christian propriety and an awareness that only the bishop was in a position to *judge* whether a belief was contrary to the faith.[88]

For all the attention he gave to heresy in the diocese, it is interesting that Trefnant did not have any overt reports of heretical ideas or behaviour recorded in the visitation book. Heresy is nowhere addressed head on, but the visitor and his party must have been conscious of it as they moved around the parishes where William Swinderby and Walter Brut were known to have preached. What are we to make, for example, of the report that all was well at Croft, despite an active heresy case against the esquire of Croft Castle?[89] However, looking for echoes of heresy is a risky business for historians, given that Wyclif's followers touched many of the raw nerves of late medieval Christianity. Much of the behaviour that bishops sought to correct sat on a spectrum that ran towards heresy. For example, it is

---

[88] For a discussion of this circumspection about matters of belief, see Forrest, *Trustworthy Men*, 261–3.
[89] *Register of John Trefnant*, 147–50.

impossible to establish any causal link between Swinderby's preaching at Whitney on Wye in 1389 and Hywel Says' failure to receive the Eucharist, reported to the visitation there in 1397 (**811**), but equally it is impossible to categorically rule out such a connection.[90]

On the other hand, there is evidence that lollards or Wycliffites did influence the places where they preached. At Eardisley in the west, where Swinderby and Brut were both active, a remarkable report that Agnes and Isabel, who were servants of the vicar, 'ring the bells and help the vicar to celebrate' (**816**), stands out from the more commonplace concerns about the clergy not doing their duty. Margaret Aston wondered whether 'conditions in these western regions [were] perhaps peculiarly favourable' to Brut's support for female ministry, although there is little else to support this. The vicar of Eardisley was also reported (**822**) for scandalising his parishioners with his command to the dead-and-buried body of John Boley: 'Lie there, you excommunicate!'[91] At first glance, there might not seem much to link these two reports, but employing female celebrants and making an implicit claim to possess power of excommunication were both challenges to ecclesiastical authority. At Bromyard farther to the east, the two issues again came together: Alison Broun allegedly maintained that 'when she curses any man ... by her imprecation God without delay will take vengeance on him'. She was said to have 'often boasted about this, which is against the catholic faith and tempts God' (**658**). Broun's words may be understood as magical cursing, but it is also possible they were influenced by Brut's conviction that women could excommunicate ('curse' in Middle English) just as well as clerical men. Although Brut had no known association with Bromyard, it was the place where, in 1397, John Pollyrbache, who would become an associate of the more famous Wycliffite William Thorpe, was ordained a subdeacon.[92] However, excommunication was a complicated issue, and both the Eardisley and Bromyard reports could be read in a different way. Swinderby, for one, believed that it was impossible for ecclesiastical authorities to remove someone from the church because this implied unverifiable knowledge of that person's state of grace. In this light, we may understand the parish representatives of Eardisley themselves to have been influenced by Wycliffite ideas, objecting to what they saw as unreasonable claims by any clergy to know and command God.[93]

Apart from these possible connections and echoes, heresy seems to have been purposely excluded from the business of the visitation. It was, after all, a 'reserved case' dealt with exclusively by bishops and delegated inquisitors, and it is possible Trefnant was worried about fanning the flames of notoriety if heresy was dealt with in public. This looks to have happened in the case of Isabel Prustes from Whitbourne, which was the site of an episcopal manor on the Herefordshire–Worcestershire border. At the Bromyard hearing on 3 June (**652–61**), the

[90] *Register of John Trefnant*, 245; Kenneth Bruce McFarlane, *Wycliffe and English Non-Conformity* (Harmondsworth, 1972), 115.

[91] Margaret Aston, 'Lollard Women Priests?', in her *Lollards and Reformers: Images and Literacy in Late Medieval Religion* (London, 1984), 70; McFarlane, *Wycliffe and English Non-Conformity*, 115; Hudson, 'Problem of Scribes', 83–6, 94. The vicar of Eardisley was very unpopular with his parishioners (**815–17, 822–7, 832, 835, 838, 840, 844–5, 1340**).

[92] Aston, 'Lollard Women Priests', 52; Maureen Jurkowski, 'The Arrest of William Thorpe and the Anti-Lollard Statute of 1406', *Historical Research*, 75 (2002), 279.

[93] Ian Forrest, 'William Swinderby and the Wycliffite Attitude to Excommunication', *Journal of Ecclesiastical History*, 60 (2009), 246–69.

parishioners of Whitbourne had merely reported two sexual offences, but just two days later the bishop issued an order to absolve Prustes of heresy, strongly suggesting that he had heard of her case while dealing with visitation reports from her parish and yet decided not to have it recorded in the visitation book. Prustes had been accused of 'wrongfully despising the keys of the church', meaning that, in common with William Swinderby and other Wycliffites, she did not believe in the bishop's power of excommunication.[94] Her view was explicitly stated and relatively simple, unlike the implied reservations and abuses contained in the reports from Bromyard and Eardisley, and this may have caused Trefnant to remove it immediately from such a public forum.

CONCLUSION

HCA 1779 is arguably the most detailed and interesting record of visitation proceedings to survive from late medieval England. Properly contextualised and critically read, it provides abundant source material for further investigations of social and religious history. It is not an objective record of what was happening in medieval parishes, being in fact much more fascinating than that. The document is a detailed record of how hundreds of lay persons and clergy sought to use a powerful institution for a multitude of purposes. Their claims and counter-claims, strategies and goals, successes and failures lie behind every single entry. Moreover, in addition to such active use of visitation, we can read against its institutional grain to uncover something of the experiences of those who found themselves the targets or victims of people more powerful than themselves. Some such experiences were highly personal, born of unusual circumstances, whereas others were shared by people defined by sex, status, or ethnicity.

[94]   *Register of John Trefnant*, 144–5; Prustes swore an oath of repudiation on 21 July 1397.

Editorial method

The edition has been produced in accordance with the principles set out by R. F. Hunnisett in 1977.[1] The text of the visitation arises from three distinct 'episodes' of writing (for discussion of the hands, see above), each of which comprehended entries made on different occasions during the working life of the document. These consist of presentments of faults and offences; corrections and augmentations made at the hearing; and finally notes of the completion of the sentences and penalties imposed, some of which can be shown to have been made up to a year or more later. Episodes two and three, together with completions of stub presentments made at a later stage, have been represented within angle brackets as recommended by Hunnisett, in both the Latin text and the translation. The Latin text is presented in Roman type throughout; the translation employs Roman for the presentments, but for the sake of clarity presents the judicial/pastoral process and later additions to stub presentments in italic. Aspects of such entries that we judge to have been written on a single occasion have been separated by commas and terminated with a full stop. Entries relating to different individuals (almost exclusively parties in cases of sexual misconduct), or to different episodes of judicial/pastoral process, have been separated by semi-colons. The determination of such episodes of writing is not easy, and often relies on a combination of the appearance of the text – colour of ink, interlineations – with an analysis of the several phases through which such cases passed. In many instances, the sequence and grouping of the entries relies on our joint editorial judgement; it goes without saying that readers doubting a particular interpretation are well advised to consult the original.

The editorial commentary on the text is limited to the Latin side, and the English translation renders the document in its final form, without reference to deletions and with conjectural material in square brackets silently included.

The many Welsh names that occur in the document have required special treatment. The Welsh patronymic indicators *ap* (son of) and *verch* (daughter of) have been retained and not translated; where individuals with Welsh names are called *filius* (son of) and *filia* (daughter of) in the Latin text these have been translated into English to reflect the contemporary distinction, whatever that might have implied. Welsh nouns indicating occupational names, such as *y Famaeth* (the wet-nurse) and *y Ceisiad* (the serjeant of the peace or bailiff) (**721**, **1214**), and epithets such as *Moel* (bald) and *Cwta* (short) (**1034**, **1202**) have been rendered in the translation in the Welsh forms used in the text, and their modern forms and meanings supplied in footnotes. In the translation, Welsh names have been rendered in the forms given by Morgan and Morgan;[2] those not included there are given in the forms recommended by Dr James January-McCann of the University of Aberystwyth who has also offered advice on the meaning of non-patronymic epithets.

---

[1] R. F. Hunnisett, *Editing Records for Publication* (London, 1977).
[2] Thomas John Morgan and Prys Morgan, *Welsh Surnames* (Cardiff, 1985). We are grateful to Prys Morgan for his personal guidance and advice.

Text and Translation

[f. 1]

Visitatio facta per reverendum in Christo patrem dominum Johannem Trefnant Dei gracia episcopum Hereforden' incepta in ecclesia parochiali de Burghull in decanatu de Weston die lune videlicet ultimo mensis Aprilis anno Domini millesimo trecentesimo nonagesimo septimo et consecrationis dicti reverendi patris octavo

Decanatus de Weston

Brunshop <West'>

1   Parochiani[1] dicunt quod cancellus est defectius in tectura in defectu prioris Lanthon' prime rectoris ibidem. <sequestrentur fructus et committitur custodia vicario et Johanni Sholdewyk>

2   Item dicunt quod Margareta Baylyf de Brunshop subtrahit j toftum valoris viij d per annum deputatum quondam per quendam Radulphum Torel dominum ibidem ad sustentationem servicii Beate Marie in eadem ecclesia et subtraxit xv annis elapsis. <ad proximum consistorium Heref'>

3   Item dicunt quod Thomas Baylyf fecit sepem infra cimiterium longitudinis duorum pedum et ultra et occupat illam terram sacram frangendo limites cimiterii. <in tractando>

4   Item dicunt quod baptisterium non est seratum in defectu parochianorum. <citra Pascham reparetur sub pena de iij s iiij d>

5   Item dicunt quod quidam Thomas Symondes <absens> et Matilda quam tenet pro uxore sunt illegitime copulati eo quod quidam dominus Willelmus Peny consanguineus dicti Thome infra quartum gradum precognovit eandem Matildam ante contractum inter dictos Thomam et Matildam initum. <mulier comparet, fatetur precognitionem set negat consanguinitatem>

Welynton <West'>

6   Parochiani[2] nichil dicunt quia omnia ut asserunt stant bene ibidem.

Burghull <eadem>

7   Parochiani respiciuntur usque ad diem dominicam[3] proximam futuram apud Wormesley ubi dicunt quod cancellus est defectivus in tectura in defectu rectoris et vicarii unde injunctum fuit eisdem huiusmodi cancellum reparari citra festum nativitatis Sancti Johannis Baptiste proximum futurum sub pena xx s. <sequestrentur fructus rectorie et vicarie quorum custodia committitur Rogero Burchull, Johanni Bolt et Philippo Fourches>

---

[1]   The word *parochiani*, appearing very many times in the document, is always written with the abbreviation for *par*, a letter p with a bar through the descender. But in places the clerk follows it with the letter r, implying the form *parrochiani*. It occurs too frequently to be merely a slip, but perhaps it was a standard abbreviation for a common word, although strictly inaccurate. We have retained *parochiani* throughout.

[2]   Followed by *dicunt*, struck through.

[3]   In same ink as entries **8–16**.

[f. 1]

Visitation made by the Reverend father in Christ John Trefnant, by the grace of God lord bishop of Hereford, begun in the parish church of Burghill in the deanery of Weston on Monday the last day of April, in the year of our Lord 1397 and in the eighth year of the consecration of the said reverend father [30 April 1397]

Deanery of Weston

BRINSOP <*Weston*>

1   The parishioners say that the chancel is defective in its roof by the fault of the prior of Llanthony Prima, the rector there. <*the revenues to be sequestrated and custody committed to the vicar and John Sholdewyk*>

2   Next, they say that Margaret Baylyf of Brinsop withholds a toft [of land] worth 8 pence a year formerly assigned by a certain Ralph Torel, the lord there, to the upkeep of the service of the Blessed Mary in the same church, and she has withheld it for 15 years past. <*to the next consistory at Hereford*>

3   Next, they say that Thomas Baylyf has made a fence within the churchyard two foot and more in length and occupies that holy ground, breaking the bounds of the churchyard. <*under discussion*>

4   Next, they say that the font is not locked, by the fault of the parishioners. <*to be put right before Easter, under penalty of 3 shillings and 4 pence*>

5   Next, they say that a certain Thomas Symondes <*absent*> and Maud whom he keeps as a wife are unlawfully joined because a certain Sir William Peny, a blood-relative of the same Thomas within the fourth degree, previously knew the same Maud [sexually] before the contract between the said Thomas and Maud was entered into. <*the woman appears, she admits the previous knowledge but denies the blood-relationship*>

WELLINGTON <*Weston*>

6   The parishioners say nothing because, as they assert, all remains well there.

BURGHILL <*same*>

7   The parishioners are given a postponement until <*Sunday*> following [6 May 1397] at Wormsley, where they say that the chancel is defective in its roof by the fault of the rector and the vicar, who are ordered to repair the chancel before the feast of the Birth of St John the Baptist next [24 June 1397] under a penalty of 20 shillings. <*the revenues of the rectory and vicarage to be sequestrated, their custody to be committed to Roger Burchull, John Bolt, and Philip Fourches*>

8   Item quod Johannes Watys carpentarius solutus fornicatur cum Sibilla Wyston.[1] <non citati ideo citentur ad proximam>

9   Item quod Harry Daundevyl tylarius recusat cohabitare cum uxore sua legitima nec tractat eam affectione maritali et adulteratur cum Matilda quam tenet in domo sua apud Pyoniam. <vir apud Webb'; allegat divorcium, ad exhibendum apud Staundoun octavo die Februarii>

10   Item quod Davy Elvel fornicatur cum Matilda de Wallia attingente eundem infra quartum gradum affinitatis. <vir fatetur, abjurat, fustigetur ter per mercatum et ecclesiam; mulier comparet, abjurat, fustigetur eodem modo>

11   Item quod Walterus Heryng <absens> fornicatur cum Agnete nuper concubina Willelmi Leper. <mulier suspensa>

12   Item quod Davy Matys fornicatur cum Issabella Preston conjugata ut creditur. <comparent, abjurant, fustigentur vj per mercatum et ecclesiam>

13   Item quod eadem Issabella recusat invenire panem benedictum in cursu suo. <emendabit ut dicit>

14   Item quod Jankyn Wadyns, Harry Twychere, Robyn Strange, Ieuan Kyfflyhode, Jankyn Godych <et> Hugyn Hulle de Hulle sunt communes operarii diebus festivis et dominicis. <promittunt emendare>

15   Item quod Johanna Twycher, Joh<anna> Bolte, Margareta Been, Agnes Coppe, Agnes Scote <jurant de emendando> non veniunt diebus dominicis et festivis ad ecclesiam. <emendabunt ut dicunt>

16   Item quod Cecilia Glovere et Elena Strange et Alicia Wadyns, Johanna uxor Willelmi Wadyns et Clemens Wolfe et Rosa Tryge non veniunt ad ecclesiam. <juraverunt emendare sub pena j libre cere>

17[2]   Dicunt quod cancellus est[3] male coopertus in defectu rectoris. <reparetur sub pena xx s citra Pascham>

18   Dicunt quod Ricardus Pluntyng conjugatus adulteratur cum Alicia Frensh. <mulier[4] purget se; vir suspensus>

19   [Item] dicunt quod Johannes serviens Ricardi Smyth contraxit cum eadem carnali copula subsecuta n[ec vu]lt eam ducere ... in ecclesiam. <vir excommunicatus quia non vult abjurare peccatum; mulier abjurat quousque; vir postea comparuit ..>

20   [Item] quod Agnes Holder fornicatur cum [Johanne][5] Blake. <comparent, abjurant, fustigentur ter per mercatum et [ecclesiam] ..>

---

[1]   Followed by *suspensi*, struck through.

[2]   An irregular portion, varying in length between three-quarters of an inch and three inches, has been lost from the foot of this page, including the margin at the point where any heading for entries **17–24** would have been written. Although entry **16** is followed by a gap of an inch, the lack of *parochiani* suggests that they form a continuation of the return for Burghill, perhaps a presentment by *accusatores*, rather than the return for another parish.

[3]   Followed by *d[efectivus]*, struck through.

[4]   Followed by *ad purgandum coram*, struck through.

[5]   Supplied from Bannister.

8   Next, [the parishioners say] that John Watys, carpenter, a single man, fornicates with Sybil Wyston. <*not cited, so let them be cited to the next*>

9   Next, that Harry Daundevyl, tiler, refuses to live with his lawful wife nor does he treat her with marital affection, and he commits adultery with Maud whom he keeps in his house at Pyon. <*the man at Weobley; he alleges a divorce, to show proof at Staunton-on-Wye on 8 February*>

10   Next, that Davy Elvel fornicates with Maud of Wales, who is related to him within the fourth degree of affinity. <*the man admits, abjures, to be beaten three times through the marketplace and the church; the woman appears, abjures, to be beaten in the same way*>

11   Next, that Walter Heryng <*absent*> fornicates with Agnes, lately the concubine of William Leper. <*the woman suspended*>

12   Next, that Davy Matys fornicates with Isabel Preston, a married woman, as is believed. <*they appear, abjure, both to be beaten six times through the marketplace and the church*>

13   Next, that the same Isabel refuses to provide the holy bread in her turn. <*she will amend, she says*>

14   Next, that Jankin Wadyns, Harry Twychere, Robin Strange, Ieuan Kyfflyhode, Jankin Godych, and Hugyn Hulle of Hill are habitual workers on feast days and Sundays. <*they promise to amend*>

15   Next, that Joan Twycher, Joan Bolte, Margaret Been, Agnes Coppe, and Agnes Scote <*they swear to amend*> do not come to church on Sundays and feast days. <*they will amend, they say*>

16   Next, that Cecily Glovere, Helen Strange, Alice Wadyns, Joan, wife of William Wadyns, Clemence Wolfe, and Rose Tryge do not come to church. <*they have sworn to amend, under the penalty of one pound of wax*>

17   They say that the chancel is badly roofed, by the fault of the rector. <*to be repaired by Easter, under penalty of 20 shillings*>

18   They say that Richard Pluntyng, a married man, commits adultery with Alice Frensh. <*the woman to purge herself; the man suspended*>

19   Next, they say that John, servant of Richard Smyth, contracted with the same woman and that bodily union followed, but he will not marry her ... in church. <*the man excommunicated because he will not abjure the sin; the woman abjures until [marriage]; the man later appeared ...*>

20   Next, that Agnes Holder fornicates with John Blake. <*they appear, abjure, to be beaten three times through the marketplace and [the church]*>

21   [Item quod] ... ..ong fornicatur cum ... ...kes. <vir suspensus; mulier fatetur, mulier ... penitenciam ..>

22   [Item quod] ... ...alker. <mulier comparet, purgavit se, ..>

23   [Item quod] ... ...Walker. <vir fatetur, ..>

24   [Item quod] ... ... serviente Willelmi D... <... sub ... ambo usque ..> ...

[f. 1v]

Visitatio facta in ecclesia parochiali de Lugwardyn die martis primo mensis Maii
videlicet in festo apostolorum Philippi et Jacobi anno Domini supradicto

>Sutton Sancti Michelis

25   Parochiani dicunt quod <omnia stant bene ibidem>.

>Dormyton

26   Parochiani dicunt quod Ricardus Huggys tenet injuste et contra voluntatem parochianorum diversa ornamenta altaris et alia in custodia et recusat ea
liberare ad usum parochianorum.

27   Item dicunt quod idem Ricardus detinet j summam frumenti et xj bussellos
avenarum collectos in partibus pro reconsiliatione cimiterii et recusat huiusmodi
blada vel valorem restituere.

28   Item dicunt quod Agnes uxor eiusdem Ricardi est communis diffamatrix
inter vicinorum[1] et communis suscitatrix discordiarum in magnum dampnum et
periculum inhabitantium ibidem.

29   Item dicunt quod Margareta Northyn est garulatrix in ecclesia et impedit
divinum servicium.

30   Item[2]

>Sutton Sancti Nicholai

31   Parochiani dicunt quod Johannes Gorde[3] adulteratur [cum][4] Cecilia oth'
Home conjugata.

32   <Dominus Ricardus Prykes capellanus suspensus>

>Lugwardyn

33   Parochiani dicunt quod Walterus Aldeford tenet Aliciam Wych consanguineam suam infra quartum gradum in concubinam. <mulier comparet, negat a
tempore correctionis et purgat se legitime et dimissa est>

[1]   Recte *vicinos.*
[2]   Unfinished.
[3]   Followed by *fornicatur*, struck through.
[4]   Omitted.

21   Next, that ... ...ong fornicates with ... ...kes. <*the man suspended; the woman admits, the woman ... ... penance ...*>

22   Next, that ... ...alker. <*the woman appears; she has purged herself, ...*>

23   Next, that ... ...Walker. <*the man admits, ...*>

24   Next, that ... ... a servant of William D... <*... under ...; both to ...*> ...

[f. 1v]

Visitation made in the parish church of Lugwardine on Tuesday, 1 May, the feast of the Apostles Philip and James, in the year of Our Lord as above

SUTTON ST MICHAEL

25   The parishioners say that <*all remains well there*>.

DORMINGTON

26   The parishioners say that Richard Huggys keeps in his custody, wrongfully and against the will of the parishioners, various altar ornaments and other things, and refuses to release them for the benefit of the parishioners.

27   Next, they say that the same Richard withholds one measure of wheat and 11 bushels of oats collected in the neighbourhood for the reconsecration of the churchyard, and he refuses to restore this corn or its value.

28   Next, they say that Agnes, wife of the same Richard, is a habitual defamer of her neighbours and a habitual provoker of arguments, to the great damage and danger of the people living there.

29   Next, they say that Margaret Northyn is a chatterer in church and disturbs divine service.

30   Next, [*not completed*]

SUTTON ST NICHOLAS

31   The parishioners say that John Gorde commits adultery [with] Cecily oth' Home, a married woman.

32   <*Sir Richard Prykes, chaplain, suspended*>

LUGWARDINE

33   The parishioners say that Walter Aldeford keeps Alice Wych, his blood-relative within the fourth degree, as a concubine. <*the woman appears, denies since the time of correction and lawfully purges herself, and is dismissed*>

34   Item quod Willelmus Neubry conjugatus adulteratur cum Agnete Taelour soluta. <vir negat, ad purgandum se[1] et dimissus est ab instancia officii; mulier infirma>

Weston

35   Parochiani dicunt quod dominus Johannes Pole qui obtinet cantariam in ecclesia de Weston et tenetur celebrare singulis diebus ibidem nec facit set absentat se ab huiusmodi ecclesia, aliquando per mensem continue, aliquando per iij septimanas, onus sibi incumbens negligenter omittendo.

36   Item dicunt quod idem dominus Johannes asportavit diversos lapides ecclesie usque ad quantitatem duorum vel trium plaustratorum sine licencia parochianorum de cimiterio quos restituere recusat.

37   Item dicunt quod idem dominus Johannes portavit seram baptisterii de ecclesia et quod huiusmodi baptisterium non est seratum in defectu eiusdem domini Johannis.

38   Item dicunt quod idem dominus Johannes non est obediens vicario eiusdem ecclesie nec eius mandatis licitis et honestis nec vult interesse divinis serviciis una cum dicto vicario in ecclesia set in quantum potest impedit commodum ecclesie oblationes et alia emolumenta.

Visitatio facta in ecclesia parochiali de Bodenham die mercurii videlicet secunda mensis Maii anno Domini supradicto.

Bodenham

39   Parochiani dicunt quod baptisterium non est seratum tamen est competenter custoditum alio modo.

40   Item dicunt quod aliter omnia stant bene ibidem.

[f. 2]
Peterchurche <Webbley>. Visitatio facta ibidem die jovis tertia dicti mensis Maii etcetera.

Thornaston

41   +Parochiani dicunt quod Ricardus Gogh conjugatus adulteratur cum Lleuku Kedy, Margareta Hunte <absens est>, Elena filia Trahaearn <absens> et Lleuku filia Eynon. <vir excommunicatus; vir negat quo ad omnes, ad purgandum; vir purgavit se a tempore correctionis quo ad omnes>

42   <Ricardus Goch <suspensus> comparuit eisdem die et loco et injunctum est sibi quod compareat cras apud Dorston ad recipiendum penitenciam sibi injungendam pro commissis et quod tractet uxorem debite sub pena excommunicationis in futuro>[2]

---

[1]   Followed by *mulier infirma*, struck through.

[2]   This entry inserted later above **41**, presumably in the course of one of the hearings recorded in that entry.

34   Next, that William Neubry, a married man, commits adultery with Agnes Taelour, a single woman. *<the man denies, to purge himself, and is dismissed at the instance of the official; the woman is sick>*

WESTON BEGGARD

35   The parishioners say that Sir John Pole who acquired a chantry in the church of Weston and is bound to celebrate every day there does not do so, but absents himself from this church, sometimes for a month at a time, sometimes for three weeks, negligently failing to carry out the duty incumbent on him.

36   Next, they say that the same Sir John has carried off from the churchyard various stones belonging to the church, as much as two or three waggon-loads, without the permission of the parishioners, which stones he refuses to restore.

37   Next, they say that the same Sir John has carried away the lock of the church font, and that this font is not locked, by the fault of the same Sir John.

38   Next, they say that the same Sir John is not obedient to the vicar of the same church nor to his lawful and proper commands, and that he will not be present at divine services with the said vicar in the church, but as much as he can he obstructs the welfare of the church, the offerings, and other income.

Visitation made in the parish church of Bodenham on Wednesday, 2 May, in the year of Our Lord abovesaid

BODENHAM

39   The parishioners say that the font is not locked, but it is adequately guarded another way.

40   Next, they say that otherwise all remains well there.

[f. 2]

Peterchurch *<Weobley>*. Visitation made there on Thursday, 3 May, etc.

TURNASTONE

41   +The parishioners say that Richard Gogh, a married man, commits adultery with Lleucu Kedy, Margaret Hunte *<she is absent>*, Helen, daughter [of] Trahaearn *<absent>*, and Lleucu, daughter of Einion. *<the man excommunicated; the man denies as to them all, to purge; the man has purged himself since the time of correction as to them all>*

42   *<Richard Goch <suspended> appeared at the same day and place and is ordered to appear tomorrow at Dorstone [73] to receive the penance to be imposed on him for the things he has done, and that he should treat his wife properly, under penalty of being excommunicated in future>*

43   Gwladus[1] alias Alson filia Ricardi <suspensa> soluta fornicatur cum Harry filio Ricardi de diocese Men'.

Bacton

44   [*in margin*] + <vicarius suspensus; vicarius excommunicatus>

45   Parochiani dicunt quod Philippus Vardd solutus fornicatur cum Dydgu Wasmair <et continuarunt peccatum suum xij annis etcetera; suspensi>

46   Item quod David Turnour solutus fornicatur cum Issabella Scote. <conjuges sunt; suspensi>

47   Item dicunt quod vicarius celebrat bis diebus dominicis et festivis.

48   Item dicunt quod cancellus patitur defectum in tectura et in muris eiusdem et quod una fenestra in fronte cancelli est ruinosa in defectu rectoris.

49   Item quod dominus Walterus Bunte vicarius incontinens est cum Alicia Torr. <negat a tempore correctionis, ad purgandum in proximam>

Vowechurch

50   Parochiani dicunt quod ecclesia est aliqualiter discooperta in defectu parochianorum, tamen dicunt quod fecerunt pactum cum carpentario pro reparationibus et habent pecuniam in promptu.

51   [*in margin*] <+ significatum>

Item dicunt quod Willelmus Turnour <suspensus; excommunicatus> conjugatus[2] adulteratur cum Johanna 3yfker <suspensa; excommunicata> et tenet eam in domo sua continue nec habitat cum uxore sua ymmo eam omnino affectione maritali tractare recusat. <denunciati sunt ut dicitur>

52   Item Vowechurch accusatores[3] dicunt quod Walterus Mulward laycus habet ecclesiam ad firmam sine dispensatione domini episcopi et habuit <per[4] tres annos et ultra; citetur ad proximam; dimissus>

53   Item quod non habetur portiforium in ecclesia pro matutinis horis et vesperis dicendis in defectu parochianorum et rectoris. <prosequantur etcetera>

54   Item non habetur processionale pro processionibus fiendis in ecclesia in defectu parochianorum.

55   Item non habentur ornamenta pro processionibus videlicet nec capa nec tunicule etcetera.

56   Item campanile patitur defectum in tectura et muris in defectu parochianorum.

57   Item cancellus est male coopertus in defectu rectoris.

---

[1]   Followed by *f,* struck through.
[2]   Followed by *f,* struck through.
[3]   In margin; **52–8** follow **59–71** at the foot of the page.
[4]   Interlined.

43   Gwladus otherwise Alison, daughter of Richard *<suspended>*, a single woman, fornicates with Harry son of Richard of St David's diocese.

BACTON

44   [*in margin*]: +*<the vicar suspended; the vicar excommunicated>*

45   The parishioners say that Philip Vardd,[1] a single man, fornicates with Dyddgu Wasmair *<and they have continued their sin for 12 years and more; both suspended>*

46   Next, that David Turnour, a single man, fornicates with Isabel Scote. *<they are married; both suspended>*

47   Next, they say that the vicar celebrates twice on Sundays and feast days.

48   Next, they say that the chancel is defective in its roof and walls, and that a window at the end of the chancel is in a state of ruin, by the fault of the rector.

49   Next, that Sir Walter Bunte, the vicar, is incontinent with Alice Torr. *<he denies since the time of correction, to purge at the next>*

VOWCHURCH

50   The parishioners say that the church is partially unroofed, by the fault of the parishioners, but they say that they have made an agreement with a carpenter for the repairs and they have the money ready.

51   [*in margin*]: < + *signified*>

Next, they say that William Turnour *<suspended; excommunicated>*, a married man, commits adultery with Joan Yyfker *<suspended; excommunicated>* and keeps her in his house continually, and does not live with his wife, indeed he wholly refuses to treat her with marital affection. *<they are denounced, it is said>*

52   Next, the Vowchurch accusers say that Walter Mulward, a layman, has the church to farm without a dispensation from the lord bishop and has had it for three years and more. *<cite to the next; dismissed>*

53   Next, that there is no breviary in the church for saying matins, hours, and vespers, by the fault of the parishioners and the rector. *<let them prosecute etc.>*

54   Next, there is no processional for performing processions in the church, by the fault of the parishioners.

55   Next, there are no ornaments for processions, that is, neither cope nor tunicle etc.

56   Next, the bell-tower is defective in its roof and walls, by the fault of the parishioners.

57   Next, the chancel is badly roofed, by the fault of the rector.

---

[1]   Recte *Fardd*, the poet.

58   I[tem]¹ quod David Gyffe de Monyton decessit intestatus cuius bona ministravit [*blank*] filius eiusdem [sine] licencia ordinarii seu ministrorum suorum. <dimissus>

Peterchurch

59   [*in margin*] <vicarius suspensus est>

60   Parochiani dicunt quod non habent portiforium in ecclesia pro matutinis horis et vesperis dicendis in ecclesia in defectu rectoris.

61   Item dicunt quod idem rector tenetur de antiqua consuetudine invenire parochianis duo portiforia <et> duo gradalia pro servicio divino faciendo ibidem nec facit.

62   Item dicunt [quod non habent]² missas nec servicia divina pro infirmis visitandis pro pueris baptizandis et aliis serviciis fiendis in defectu vicarii eo quod idem vicarius est infirmus et impotens ad deserviendum parochianis nec invenit alium capellanum.

63   + Item dicunt quod Hugo Cockes decessit intestatus set³ nesciunt an Ibel uxor sua ministravit⁴ de licencia commissarii vel non, ideo inquiratur. <suspensa; dimissus>

64   Item dicunt quod quedam pars clausure cimiterii cuius sustentatio spectat ad rectorem est defectiva in defectu eiusdem rectoris.

65   Item dicunt quod rector tenetur invenire unum capellanum diebus dominicis et festivis, feria iiijᵗᵃ et vj ad celebrandum in capella de Urysay nec facit.

66   Item dicunt quod tenetur ad idem in capella de Snowdell nec facit.

67   [*in margin*] + Heref'

Item dicunt quod Johannes ap Tommi <suspensus; excommunicatus> et⁵ Agnes Robynes <ad producendum litteram divorcii habent diem Heref'> sunt illegitime copulati eo quod dicta Agnes precontraxit cum Ricardo Hamonde adhuc vivente inter quos matrimonium fuit in facie ecclesie solempnizatum. Demum tamen⁶ ut pretenditur divorciati abinvicem propter frigiditatem et impotenciam dicti Ricardi Hamond. Quiquidem Ricardus postea duxit Agnetem <suspensa> <Pye> quam tenet de qua procreavit filios et filias.

68   +Item quod idem Johannes ap Tommy pretensus conjugatus adulteratur cum Agnete ap⁷ Pye <suspensi; excommunicati; vir abjurat, fustigetur in forma>

---

¹   A portion of the left-hand margin is perished, but this appears to be the only entry affected.
²   Omitted.
³   Altered from *et*.
⁴   Followed by *l* struck through.
⁵   Struck through, apparently in error.
⁶   Followed by *d*, struck through.
⁷   Followed by *Huypys*, struck through.

58   Next, that David Gyffe of Monnington died intestate, his son administered his goods without the licence of the ordinary or his officers. <*dismissed*>

PETERCHURCH

59   [*in margin*]: <*the vicar is suspended*>

60   The parishioners say that there is no breviary in church for saying matins, hours, and vespers in the church, by the fault of the rector.

61   Next, they say that, by ancient custom, the same rector is bound to provide for the parishioners two breviaries and two graduals for performing divine services there and does not do so.

62   Next, they say that they do not have masses, nor the divine services for visiting the sick and baptising children, and for performing other services, by the fault of the vicar because he is sick and incapable of serving the parishioners, nor does he provide another chaplain.

63   +Next, they say that Hugh Cockes died intestate, but they do not know whether Isabel, his wife, administered his estate by the licence of the commissary or not, so let it be looked into. <*suspended; dismissed*>

64   Next, they say that a certain part of the fence of the churchyard whose upkeep is the responsibility of the rector is defective, by the fault of the same rector.

65   Next, they say that the rector ought to provide a chaplain on Sundays and feast days, Wednesdays and Fridays, to celebrate in the chapel of Urishay, and does not do so.

66   Next, they say that he is bound to do the same in the chapel of Snodhill, and does not do so.

67   [*in margin*]: Hereford

Next, they say that John ap Tommi <*suspended; excommunicated*> and Agnes Robynes <*they have a day at Hereford to produce a letter of divorce*> are unlawfully joined because the said Agnes made a previous contract with Richard Hamonde, who is still alive, and a marriage between them was solemnised in the sight of the church. But later, as she claims, they were divorced from each other because of the frigidity and impotence of the said Richard Hamond. This Richard later married Agnes Pye <*suspended*>, whom he keeps, and by whom he has fathered sons and daughters.

68   + Next, that the same John ap Tommy, who claims to be a married man, commits adultery with Agnes ap Pye. <*both suspended; both excommunicated; the man abjures, to be beaten in due form*>

69   +Item quod Willelmus Weste conjugatus adulteratur cum[1] Issabella <ap Wylim soluta>[2] <abjurat, fustigetur in forma> et Johanna Dellok conjugata. <vicarius non audet citare; citentur per edictum, habent diem in proximam apud Staundon; vir comparet, abjurat peccatum et locum suspectum in forma, fustigetur quo ad utrasque>

70   Item dicunt quod cancellus patitur defectum in tectura et vitro fenestrarum ac muris.

71   Item quod frater Somon monachus ibidem celebrat bis in die et continuavit per annum et ultra.

[f. 2v]

Dorston.[3] Visitatio facta ibidem die veneris quarto mensis Maii predicti

          [Dorston]

72   [*in margin*] <vicarius suspensus>

73   <Ricardus Gogh comparuit et negat opposita sibi et indicta est sibi purgatio eidem>

74   [*in margin*] <significatum>

Parochiani ibidem dicunt quod Eva filia Ieuan ap Gwyn <suspensa; excommunicata; denunciata est; purget se> soluta fornicatur cum Jankyn ap Ieuan ap Llewelyn de diocese Men'.

75   Item quod Alicia filia Jak ap Roger <suspensa; excommunicata> soluta fornicatur cum eodem Jankyn.

76   Item quod Gwenllian verch Hoesgyn <suspensa; excommunicata> soluta fornicatur cum Gruffuth ap Madoc. <suspensus; vir extra>

77   Item quod Thomas ap Iorwerth <suspensus; excommunicatus> solutus fornicatur cum Gwenllian filia Ieuan ap Gwyn <suspensa; excommunicata; vir abjurat, fustigetur in forma>

78   Item idem Thomas fornicatur cum Beton<ia> filia Llewelyn Dewe de Talgarth. <suspensa; extra>

79   Item Jankyn Cravel <suspensus; excommunicatus> alienavit et subtraxit unum calicem de bonis capelle de capella Sancti Jacobi quem recusat restitutere.

80   Item idem Jankyn subtraxit j towellam dicte capelle nec vult restituere.

81   Item dicunt quod Johannes Cravel <suspensus> solutus fornicatur cum Margeria filia Gruffuth <suspensa; excommunicata>

82   Item David Werkemon <suspensus> solutus fornicatur cum Issabella <suspensa> quam tenet.[4] <extra>

---

[1]   Followed by *Juliana*, struck through.
[2]   *ap Wylim, soluta* interlined over *Blusy*, struck through.
[3]   Written over *Mokkas*, struck through.
[4]   Followed by *excommunicati*, struck through.

69   + Next, that William Weste, a married man, commits adultery with Isabel ap Wylim, a single woman <*abjures, to be beaten in due form*>, and Joan Dellok, a married woman. <*the vicar does not dare to cite; let them be cited by edict, they have a day at the next at Staunton-on-Wye; the man appears, abjures the sin and the suspicious circumstances in due form, let him be beaten in respect of both women*>

70   Next, they say that the chancel is defective in its roof, glass of the windows and walls.

71   Next, that Brother Somon, a monk there, celebrates twice a day, and has been doing it for a year and more.

[f. 2v]

Dorstone. Visitation made there on Friday, 4 May

[DORSTONE]

72   [*in margin*]: <*the vicar suspended*>

73   <*Richard Gogh appeared and denies the charges against him, and is ordered to purge himself for it*>

74   [*in margin*]: <*signified*>

The parishioners there say that Eve, daughter of Ieuan ap Gwyn <*suspended; excommunicated; denounced; to purge herself*>, a single woman, fornicates with Jankin ap Ieuan ap Llewelyn of St David's diocese.

75   Next, that Alice, daughter of Jack ap Roger <*suspended; excommunicated*>, a single woman, fornicates with the same Jankin.

76   Next, that Gwenllian verch Hoesgyn <*suspended; excommunicated*>, a single woman, fornicates with Gruffudd ap Madog. <*suspended; the man outside*>

77   Next, that Thomas ap Iorwerth <*suspended; excommunicated*>, a single man, fornicates with Gwenllian, daughter of Ieuan ap Gwyn <*suspended; excommunicated; the man abjures, let him be beaten in due form*>

78   Next, the same Thomas fornicates with Beton <*suspended; outside*>, daughter of Llewelyn Dewe of Talgarth.

79   Next, Jankin Cravel <*suspended; excommunicated*> has taken and removed a chalice from the chapel goods of the chapel of St James, which he refuses to restore.

80   Next, the same Jankin has removed one towel from the same chapel and will not restore it.

81   Next, they say that John Cravel <*suspended*>, a single man, fornicates with Margery, daughter of Gruffudd. <*suspended; excommunicated*>

82   Next, David Werkemon <*suspended*>, a single man, fornicates with Isabel <*suspended*> whom he keeps. <*outside*>

83   [*in margin*] <Snowdehull>

Item quod Willelmus West conjugatus adulteratur cum Johanna Dellok conjugata. <morantur apud Snowdhull>

84   Item idem Willelmus adulteratur cum Maiota Watys. <mulier suspensa, vir abjurat peccatum et locum suspectum; excommunicata mulier; mulier abjurat, fustigetur in forma>

85   Item quod Marcus Flesher solutus fornicatur cum Johanna Mulward. <suspensa; vir abjurat peccatum et locum suspectum, fustigetur in forma; mulier excommunicata>

86   Item Philippus Parnell fornicatur cum Duen quam tenet. <extra>

87   [*in margin*] <Norton>

Item quod Sibilla Ʒyfker fornicatur cum domino Johanne <Mathewe>[1] ut credunt, tamen ignorant an sic vocatur vel non; moratur tamen apud Norton.

88   Item Thomas Prat <absens> fornicatur cum Margareta Chepestere <suspensa> soluti ambo.

89   Item quod Johanna Dellok peperit unum filium cuius pater ignoratur. <apud[2] Snowdhull>

90   Item Johannes Hir fornicatur cum Agnete serviente Thome Partriche. <suspensi ambo>

91   Item quod Johannes Smyth et Maiota Yong sunt illegitime copulati eo quod dictus Johannes[3] habet aliam uxorem superstitem apud Hereford' nomine Tibota quam tenuit[4] xvj annis et ultra ante contractum inter se et dictam Maiotam. Item[5] ut dicunt quod habet tertiam apud Hereford' cum qua contraxit cuius nomen ignorant et dicunt quod matrimonium inter dictum Johannem et Maiotam fuit clamdestine celebratum apud Curshop per dominum Johannem Davys. <habet diem coram domino>

Bradewardyn

92   [*in margin*] <vicarius excommunicatus>

93   Parochiani dicunt quod fenestre cancelli patiuntur defectum in vitro in defectu rectoris et injunctum est rectori quod reparentur citra festum Sancti Michelis proximum futurum.

94   Item quod Robert Scote solutus fornicatur [cum] Johanna Nichols. <vir comparet, fatetur, abjurat, dimisit sibi penitentiam; mulier suspensa>

95   Item quod dominus Johannes Peer vicarius ibidem diffamatus est vehementer de incontinencia cum Dydgu Says. <citata de novo; vir comparet, fatetur, abjurat peccatum et locum suspectum, habet diem sabbati iiij[or] temporum apud BromƷord; iterum impetitur a tempore correctionis et negat, habet diem ad purgandum se xij[a] manu>

---

[1]   Interlined over *Smyth*, struck through.
[2]   Followed by *de*, struck through.
[3]   Followed by *pre[contraxit]*, struck through.
[4]   Followed by *v*, struck through.
[5]   Continues on same line.

83   [*in margin*]: <*Snodhill*>

Next, that William West, a married man, commits adultery with Joan Dellok, a married woman. <*they live at Snodhill*>

84   Next, the same William commits adultery with Maiota Watys. <*the woman suspended, the man abjures the sin and the suspicious circumstances; the woman excommunicated; the woman abjures, let her be beaten in due form*>

85   Next, that Mark Flesher, a single man, fornicates with Joan Mulward. <*she is suspended; the man abjures the sin and the suspicious circumstances, let him be beaten in due form; the woman excommunicated*>

86   Next, Philip Parnell fornicates with Duen, whom he keeps. <*outside*>

87   [*in margin*]: <*Norton*>

<Next, that Sybil Yyfker fornicates with Sir John Mathewe, as they believe, but they do not know whether she is called this or not; but she lives at Norton>

88   Next, Thomas Prat <*absent*> fornicates with Margaret Chepestere <*suspended*>, both of them single.

89   Next, that Joan Dellok has given birth to a son whose father is not known. <*at Snodhill*>

90   Next, John Hir fornicates with Agnes, servant of Thomas Partriche. <*both suspended*>

91   Next, that John Smyth and Maiota Yong are unlawfully joined, because the said John has another wife alive at Hereford, by name Tibota, whom he kept for 16 years and more before the contract between him and the said Maiota. Next, as they say, he has a third wife at Hereford with whom he contracted, whose name they do not know, and they say that the marriage between the said John and Maiota was clandestinely celebrated at Cusop by Sir John Davys. <*he has a day before his lordship*>

BREDWARDINE

92   [*in margin*]: <*the vicar excommunicated*>

93   The parishioners say that the glass of the chancel windows is defective, by the fault of the rector, and the rector is ordered to have them repaired by Michaelmas next.

94   Next, that Robert Scote, a single man, fornicates with Joan Nichols. <*the man appears, admits, abjures, a penance is given to him; the woman suspended*>

95   Next, that Sir John Peer, the vicar there, is vehemently defamed of incontinence with Dyddgu Says. <*she is cited anew; the man appears, admits, abjures the sin and the suspicious circumstances, he has a day on Ember Saturday [16 June 1397] at Bromyard; he is further accused since the time of correction and denies, he has a day to purge himself with 12 hands*>

96   Item dicunt quod Willelmus ap Roger et Walterus Walishe habent diversa tigna in cimiterio unde impediuntur processiones fieri in forma debita et consueta.[1] <emendatum est>

97   Item quod baptisterium non est seratum in defectu parochianorum. <suspensa ecclesia quousque fiat, habent diem citra festum Natalis Domini>

98   Item quod Robyn Brykkon <suspensus> parochianus ibidem alienavit unam vaccam debitam vicario ibidem pro mortuario uxoris sue in fraudem ecclesie etcetera.

99   Item Johannes Nichols[2] pari forma alienavit unum porcum. <concordati sunt vicarius et idem Johannes>

100   Item quod cimiterium non est clausum in defectu parochianorum. <claudatur debite citra Pentecostem sub pena x s>

101   Item dicunt quod non habent clericum ad deserviendum in ecclesia in defectu vicarii; ultra dicunt [quod][3] abbas et conventus de Wyggemor rectores ibidem tenentur solvere vicario pro inventione clerici ibidem annuatim xx s nec facere volunt.[4]

102   Item dicunt <quod> quidem Alanus quondam vicarius ibidem primo exoneravit rectores de dictis pecuniis.

103   Item dicunt quod Rogerus Vachan non dat decimas rerum suarum existentium in dicta parochia videlicet de lana et aliis minutis decimis nuncupatis alteragia.[5] <citetur ad proximam>

104   [*added in margin*] [Item dicunt quod] Thomas Smyth fornicatur cum Margareta quam tenet. <vir fatetur, abjurat, fustigetur ter; mulier citetur ad proximam>

105   [Accusatores dic]unt quod Cecilia Held conjugata adulteratur cum Roberto Huntelowe. <mulier comparet in ... [apud Here]ford>[6]

[Moccas]

106   [Parochiani dicunt quod omnia] sunt bene ibidem.

---

[1]   Followed by *suspensi*, struck through.
[2]   Interlined <*suspensus*>, struck through.
[3]   Omitted.
[4]   The bottom right-hand and left-hand corners of this page have perished; some letters are visible under the repair.
[5]   Followed by *v*, struck through.
[6]   The damage to the foot of the page has resulted in the loss of the beginning of this entry and the name of the next parish. Entry **105** seems to have been written with the preceding Bredwardine entries, but its place at the end, along with the positioning of *dicunt*, suggests that *Accusatores* rather than *Item* is lost.

96   Next, they say that William ap Roger and Walter Walishe have several timbers in the churchyard, which obstruct processions being made in the due and customary form. <*it has been put right*>

97   Next, that the font is not locked, by the fault of the parishioners. <*the church is suspended until it is done, they have a day before Christmas*>

98   Next, that Robin Brykkon <*suspended*>, a parishioner there, has taken a cow owed to the vicar there as the mortuary of his wife, to the fraud of the church, etc.

99   Next, John Nichols has taken a pig in the same way. <*the vicar and John are agreed*>

100   Next, that the churchyard is not fenced, by the fault of the parishioners. <*let it be properly fenced by Whitsun, under penalty of 10 shillings*>

101   Next, they say that they do not have a clerk to serve in the church, by the fault of the vicar; they further say that the abbot and convent of Wigmore, the rectors there, are bound to pay the vicar 20 shillings a year to provide a clerk there, and they are not willing to do so.

102   Next, they say that a certain Alan, formerly the vicar there, first discharged the rectors from the said sums.

103   Next, they say that Roger Vachan does not give tithes of his property in the said parish, that is to say of wool, and the other small tithes called altarage. <*let him be cited to the next*>

104   Next, they say that Thomas Smyth fornicates with Margaret whom he keeps. <*the man admits, abjures, let him be beaten three times; let the woman be cited to the next*>

105   The accusers say that Cecily Held, a married woman, commits adultery with Robert Huntelowe. <*the woman appears in ... at Hereford*>

[MOCCAS][1]

106   The parishioners say that all things are well there.

---

[1]   The name of this parish is deleted after Dorstone, the visitation centre, at the head of folio 2v.

[f. 3]

Standon. Visitatio facta ibidem die sabbati quinto mensis Maii anno domini supradicto

Monyton

107   [*in margin*] <Heref'>

Parochiani ibidem dicunt quod Ricardus Fox conjugatus adulteratur cum Emota uxore Adam Baker. <mulier moratur Hereford; vir comparet, fatetur, abjurat, fustigetur vj circa ecclesiam et vj ante processionem Heref' et vj per forum Heref'>

108   Item quod dicta Emota adulteratur cum Willelmo Walissh de qua procreavit unum filium. <vir moratur apud Welynton>

109   Item

Credenhull

110   Parochiani dicunt quod omnia sunt bene ibidem.

Streton

111   Parochiani dicunt quod omnia bene ibidem.

Malmeshull Gamage

112   Parochiani dicunt quod fenestre cancelli sunt fracte in defectu rectoris.

113   Item dicunt quod selura est defectiva in defectu eiusdem.

114   Item quod murus cancelli non est dealbatus nec honestus in defectu eiusdem rectoris. <sequestrantur fructus eo quod dantur ad firmam et commissa est custodia decano et Johanni Maunce ac vicario ibidem>[1]

115   Item dicunt quod dominus Reginaldus capellanus cantarie ibidem absentat se penitus ab huiusmodi ecclesia nec celebrat divina ibidem. <sequestrantur fructus cantarie>

Byford

116   Parochiani dicunt quod ecclesia patitur defectum in tectura et fenestrarum vitro in defectu parochianorum. <suspensa ecclesia, habent diem usque>[2]

117   Item quod cancellus est defectivus in tectura in defectu rectoris. <injunctum est quod reparetur>

118   Item quod mansum rectoris patitur defectum in tectura muris et clausuris. <injunctum est ut supra>

119   [*in margin*] <significatum>

Item quod Johannes Rydemarley conjugatus adulteratur cum <Tybota Fythler conjugata. Mulier excommunicata, vir absens est; mulier denunciata est>

---

[1]   This sentence is bracketed against **113–15**.

[2]   Unfinished.

[f. 3]

Staunton-on-Wye. Visitation made there on Saturday, 5 May, in the year of our Lord abovesaid

MONNINGTON

107 [*in margin*]: <*Hereford*>

The parishioners there say that Richard Fox, a married man, commits adultery with Emota, wife of Adam Baker. <*the woman lives at Hereford; the man appears, admits, abjures, let him be beaten six times around the church and six times before the procession at Hereford and six times through the marketplace at Hereford*>

108 Next, that the said Emota commits adultery with William Walissh of whom she has borne a son. <*the man lives at Wellington*>

109 Next, [*not completed*]

CREDENHILL

110 The parishioners say that all things are well there.

STRETTON SUGWAS

111 The parishioners say that all is well there.

MANSELL GAMAGE

112 The parishioners say that the windows of the chancel are broken, by the fault of the rector.

113 Next, they say that the ceiling is defective, by the fault of the same.

114 Next, that the wall of the chancel is not whitewashed nor in proper condition, by the fault of the same rector. <*let the revenues be sequestrated because they are farmed, and the custody committed to the dean, to John Maunce, and to the vicar there*>

115 Next, they say that Sir Reynold, chaplain of the chantry there, totally absents himself from this church and does not celebrate divine services there. <*let the revenues of the chantry be sequestrated*>

BYFORD

116 The parishioners say that the church is defective in its roof and the glass of the windows, by the fault of the parishioners. <*the church suspended, they have a day to [not completed]*>

117 Next, that the chancel is defective in its roof, by the fault of the rector. <*ordered that it be repaired*>

118 Next, that the house of the rector is defective in its roof, walls, and fences. <*ordered as above*>

119 [*in margin*]: <*signified*>

Next, that John Rydemarley, a married man, commits adultery with <*Tybota Fythler, a married woman; the woman excommunicated; the man is absent; the woman is denounced*>

120   Item quod Rys Ieuan son þe Walissh fornicatur cum¹ quadam quam tenet <nomine Wenllian. Vir comparet, abjurat, fustigetur ter circa ecclesiam parochialem; mulier comparet, abjurat, fustigetur ter circa ecclesiam; egerunt penitentiam>

Kenchestr'

121   Parochiani dicunt quod omnia sunt bene ibidem.

122   Accusatores² dicunt quod Thomas Pryll ministravit bona Johannis Alrete ab intestato decedentis absque licencia ordinarii seu ministrorum eiusdem et habet penes se xij marcas de bonis eiusdem Johannis. <negat, habet ad purgandum se Hereford>

Standon

123   Parochiani dicunt quod omnia sunt bene ibidem <excepto quod Johannes Gomond conjugatus adulteratur cum Johanna Smyth et Lucia quas tenet in domo sua uxore legitima repulsa>.

Probury

124   Parochiani dicunt quod omnia bene ibidem.

Malmeshull Lacy

125   Parochiani dicunt quod omnia bene ibidem.

[Bridge Sollers?]³

126   [Parochiani dicunt] quod omnia sunt bene ibidem <excepto quod Jankyn Berde adulteratur cum Issabella quam tenet conjugaliter> ... <... [citentur ad] proximam; mulier comparet, abjurat, fustigetur in forma; vir absens>

[unidentified place]

127   [Parochiani dicunt quod Will]elmus Tynker capellanus incontinens est cum⁴

128   <[Item dicunt quod] ... ... ibidem citatus per decanum quod compareat ... in proximo consistorio cum sua concubina>

[f. 3v]

ʒasor

129   Parochiani ibidem dicunt quod cantaria ibidem vacat ibidem et vacavit a diu eo quod <capellanus qui ultime obtinuit eandem> recessit hospite non soluta-to.⁵ [*margin*] <vacatio>

---

¹   Followed by *C*, struck through.
²   *Accusatores* written in the margin.
³   The damage to the foot of the page has resulted in the loss of the names of this and the next parish.
⁴   Unfinished.
⁵   Recte *soluto*.

120   Next, that Rhys Ieuan, son of the Welshman, fornicates with a woman whom he keeps <*named Gwenllian; the man appears, abjures, to be beaten three times around the parish church; the woman appears, abjures, to be beaten three times around the church; they have done their penance*>

KENCHESTER

121   The parishioners say that all things are well there.

122   The accusers say that Thomas Pryll administered the goods of John Alrete, who died intestate, without the licence of the ordinary or his officers, and has in his possession 12 marks [worth] of the same John's goods. <*he denies, has [a day] to purge himself at Hereford*>

STAUNTON-ON-WYE

123   The parishioners say that all things are well there <*except that John Gomond, a married man, commits adultery with Joan Smyth and Lucy, both of whom he keeps in his house, having driven out his lawful wife*>.

BROBURY

124   The parishioners say that all is well there.

MANSELL LACY

125   The parishioners say that all is well there.

[BRIDGE SOLLERS?]

126   The parishioners say that all things are well there <*except that Jankin Berde commits adultery with Isabel whom he keeps as though they were married ... ; ... [to be cited to] the next; the woman appears, abjures, to be beaten in due form; the man absent*>

[unidentified place]

127   The parishioners say that William Tynker, chaplain, is incontinent with [*not completed*]

128   <*Next, they say that ... there; cited by the dean that he appear ... at the next consistory with his concubine*>

[f. 3v]

YAZOR

129   The parishioners there say that the chantry there is vacant and has been vacant for a long time because <*the chaplain who last held it*> went away without paying his host

[*in margin*]: <*Vacancy*>

130	<Item dominus Willelmus Tynker capellanus incontinens est cum>[1]

131	Item quod Walterus Graunte fornicatur cum Agnete Pyschard quam tenet non obstante abjuratione alias facta etcetera. <vir comparet, negat, purget se cum vj^{ta} manu in proximo consistorio Heref', mulier citetur; vir deficit in purgatione, fatetur, abjurat, fustigetur ter ante processionem; difer usque post Epiphaniam>

132	Item dicunt quod dominus Thomas vicarius ibidem mutuavit cuidam Gylym de Erdeshop xl d et recepit nomine usure xij pulletos. Idem mutuavit eidem xx d et recepit <de> usura ij bussellos avene. <negat; purgavit se>

Bysshopeston

133	Parochiani dicunt quod Sibilla uxor Johannis de Norys est communis diffamatrix vicinorum unde oritur[2] scandalum in parochia, et presertim quod eadem Sibilla falso et maliciose diffamavit Rosam Daniel aviam Alicie uxoris Edwardi Smyth asserendo eam esse adulteram, ad effectum quod dicta Alicia heres dicte Rose amitteret hereditatem suam sibi jure hereditario debitam.

134	Item petunt respectum quo ad polutionem cimiterii apud Almaly.

Webley. Visitatio facta ibidem die lune vij^a mensis Maii anno Domini supradicto

[Weobley]

135	Parochiani dicunt quod portiforium in choro existens non est ligatum in defectu rectoris. <dicit procurator quod emendabitur>

136	Item dicunt [quod] blada rectoris ventilantur in cimiterio in magnam dehonestationem etcetera. <inhibitum est ne de cetero fiat>

137	Item dicunt quod idem rector debet invenire unum diaconum ad deserviendum in ecclesia et ad custodiendum libros et ornamenta ecclesie. <habent diem ambe partes in proximo consistorio Herefordie xix die Decembris>[3]

138	Item dicunt quod vicarius ponit equos vaccas et aucas ad pascua in cimiterio in magnam dehonestationem etcetera. <negat expresse>

139	Item dicunt quod campane non pulsantur in aurora <nec> ad vesperas diebus ferialibus nec campana dormitationis in defectu vicarii.[4] <emendabitur>

140	Item dicunt [quod][5] corde campanarum et earum sustentatio pertinent ad vicarium quod facere recusat. <dicit quod non tenetur, ideo prosequantur parochiani si velint>

141	Item quod vicarius recusavit ministrare sacralia sacramentalia cuidam Ieuan Slefmaker parochiano suo eo quod noluit reddere sibi decimas ad libitum suum. <negat, ideo prosequatur cuius intersit>

---

[1]	Unfinished.
[2]	Corrected from *moritur*.
[3]	Following *Novembris*, struck through.
[4]	Following *rectoris*, struck through.
[5]	Omitted.

130   *<Next, Sir William Tynker, chaplain, is incontinent with>* [*not completed*]

131   Next, that Walter Graunte fornicates with Agnes Pyschard whom he keeps, despite an abjuration previously made, etc. *<the man appears, denies, to purge himself with six hands at the next consistory at Hereford; the woman to be cited; the man fails in purgation, admits, abjures, to be beaten three times before the procession; defer until after Epiphany>*

132   Next, they say that Sir Thomas, the vicar there, made a loan of 40 pence to a certain Gylym of Yarsop and received, in usury, 12 pullets. He lent the same man 20 pence and received in usury two bushels of oats. *<he denies; he has purged himself>*

BISHOPSTONE

133   The parishioners say that Sybil, wife of John de Norys, is a habitual defamer of her neighbours, by which scandal is raised in the parish, and specifically that the same Sybil falsely and maliciously defamed Rose Daniel, grandmother of Alice, wife of Edward Smyth, asserting that she is an adulterer, in order that the said Alice, Rose's heir, might lose the inheritance due to her by hereditary right.

134   Next, they seek a postponement as regards the pollution of the churchyard at Almeley.

Weobley. Visitation made there on Monday, 7 May, in the year of Our Lord abovesaid

[WEOBLEY]

135   The parishioners say that the breviary in the choir is not bound, by the fault of the rector. *<the proctor says that it shall be put right>*

136   Next, they say [that] the rector's corn is winnowed in the churchyard, with great impropriety, etc. *<prohibited from doing this in future>*

137   Next, they say that the rector ought to provide a deacon to serve in church and keep the church's books and ornaments. *<both parties have a day at the next consistory at Hereford on 19 December>*

138   Next, they say that the vicar puts horses, cows, and geese out to pasture in the churchyard, with great impropriety, etc. *<he denies expressly>*

139   Next, they say that the bells are not rung at dawn *<nor>* at vespers on weekdays, nor the passing-bell, by the fault of the vicar. *<it shall be put right>*

140   Next, they say that the bell-ropes and their upkeep are the responsibility of the vicar, which he refuses to perform. *<he says that he is not bound, so let the parishioners prosecute if they want to>*

141   Next, that the vicar would not administer the holy sacraments to a certain Ieuan Slefmaker, his parishioner, because he would not pay him tithes at his will. *<he denies, so let whoever is concerned prosecute>*

142   Item quod idem vicarius alienavit diversa tigna et lapides de solo ecclesie. <dimissus est>

143   Item dicunt quod aliquando idem vicarius aliquando absentat se per quindenam nec invenit alium capellanum ad deserviendum in divinis pro se nisi prout alii capellani ibidem commorantes faciunt sua bona voluntate. <negat vicarius, inhibitum est quod non faciat de cetero>

144   Item dicunt quod idem vicarius tenetur invenire omnibus et singulis capellanis celebrantibus in ecclesia panem, vinum et luminaria ad celebrandum nec facit. <dicit vicarius quod non tenetur, ideo prosequantur si velint>

145   Item dicunt quod idem vicarius tenetur invenire duos cereos ardentes coram summo altari diebus dominicis et festivis dum alta missa celebratur loco quorum cereorum ponit candelas parvas. <dicit quod inveniet>

146   Item dicunt quod Ricardus Lunteley subtrahit ij s vj d ordinatos quondam annuatim pro quadam parcella terre Walteri Dewall[1] ad sustentationem unius lampadis ardentis coram summo altari et subtraxit tribus annis elapsis. <negat, prosequantur parochiani>

147   Item Radulphus Barton subtrahit pari forma iij d ad sustentationem eiusdem lampadis. <absens est, citatus>

148   Item Harry Daunderfeld subtrahit xiiij d[2] ad sustentationem eiusdem lampadis. <absens est, citatus ad proximam; prosequantur quorum etcetera>

149   Item[3] Hugo Lunteley <prosequantur quorum interest> subtrahit xij d ad idem opus deputatos pro tenemento <ubi> Johannes Spilspekes moratur.

150   +Item quod Johannes Taelour conjugatus adulteratur cum Johanna <suspensa> quam tenet. <vir comparet,[4] negat post correctionem, purget se cum vj^{ta} manu coram vicario etcetera; mulier excommunicata>

151   +Item quod Johannes Dounwode solutus fornicatur cum Maiota Burton <suspensa>. Abjuraverunt alias coram commissario archidiaconi ideo perjuri. <vir comparet, fatetur, abjurat peccatum et locum suspectum, fustigetur ter circa ecclesiam de Dilwe; mulier abjurat; fustigetur in forma>

152   Item quod Willelmus Dounwode solutus fornicatur cum Agnete Burton. Abjuraverunt alias peccatum coram commissario archidiaconi. <vir absens, citatus, habet diem apud Leom' die jovis; mulier comparet, fatetur, abjurat, fustigetur ter circa ecclesiam parochialem; comparuit ibidem, fatetur, abjurat, fustigetur semel>

153   Item quod dominus Philippus Heilin capellanus perjurus est publice in curia laycali prout fama laborat. <absens est apud Payon> [*in margin*] Payon

154   Item dicunt quod Katerina Ondys <suspensa> pregnans est nescitur cum quo set ut creditur cum rectore de Sarnesfeld. <purget se> [*in margin*] ...n

---

[1]   Perhaps *de Wallia* was intended.
[2]   Altered from *xij d* by the interlineation of *ij d*.
[3]   Preceded by *Item Harry Teylor subtrahit*, struck through.
[4]   Followed by *fatetur*, struck through.

142 Next, that the vicar has taken several timbers and stones from the church land. *<it is dismissed>*

143 Next, they say that the vicar sometimes absents himself for a fortnight and does not provide another chaplain to serve in divine office for him, except when the other chaplains living there do it by their good will. *<the vicar denies, forbidden to do so in future>*

144 Next, they say that the vicar is bound to provide bread, wine, and lights to celebrate for each and every chaplain celebrating in the church, and does not do so. *<the vicar says he is not bound, so let them prosecute if they want to>*

145 Next, they say that the vicar ought to provide two wax candles burning before the high altar on Sundays and feast days while high mass is being celebrated, in the place of which he places small candles. *<he says that he will provide>*

146 Next, they say that Richard Lunteley withholds 2 shillings and 6 pence formerly established annually in respect of a piece of land owned by Walter Dewall, for the upkeep of a lamp burning before the high altar, and he has withheld it three years past. *<he denies, let the parishioners prosecute>*

147 Next, Ralph Barton in the same way withholds 3 pence for the upkeep of the same lamp. *<he is absent, cited>*

148 Next, Harry Daunderfeld withholds 14 pence for the upkeep of the same lamp. *<he is absent, cited to the next; let those concerned prosecute, etc.>*

149 Next, Hugh Lunteley *<let those concerned prosecute>* withholds 12 pence for the same purpose, assigned for the tenement where John Spilspekes lives.

150 Next, that John Taelour, a married man, commits adultery with Joan *<suspended>*, whom he keeps. *<the man appears, denies since correction, to purge himself with six hands before the vicar, etc.; the woman excommunicated>*

151 Next, that John Dounwode, a single man, fornicates with Maiota Burton *<suspended>*. They previously abjured before the archdeacon's commissary, so are perjured. *<the man appears, admits, abjures the sin and the suspicious circumstances, to be beaten three times around the church of Dilwyn; the woman abjures, to be beaten in due form>*

152 Next, that William Dounwode, a single man, fornicates with Agnes Burton. They previously abjured the sin before the archdeacon's commissary. *<the man absent, cited, has a day at Leominster on Thursday; the woman appears, admits, abjures, to be beaten three times around the parish church; he appeared there, admits, abjures, let him be beaten once>*

153 Next, that Sir Philip Heilin, chaplain, is publicly perjured in a lay court, as fame has it.[1] *<he is absent; at Pyon>* [*in margin*]: Pyon.

154 Next, they say that Katherine Ondys *<suspended>* is pregnant and it is not known by whom but, it is believed, by the rector of Sarnesfield. *<she is to purge herself>* [*in margin*]: ...n

---

[1]   The meaning of *fama* is discussed in the introduction, page xxviii.

155   Item dicunt quod Willelmus Saundrys absentat se ab ecclesia et officio divino diebus dominicis et festi[vis][1] <negat … exerceat de cetero>

156   Item quod [idem] Willelmus perjurus est eo quod alias juravit coram clerico Marchichie quod nunquam … exerceret … artem et postea non obstante huiusmodi juramento exercuit et adhuc exercet. <dimissus est>

157   Johannes Gall <excommunicatus> fornicatur cum Margeria Pyper conjugata. <vir comparet,[2] negat post correctionem, postea fatetur … ; mulier excommunicata; dimissi sunt>

[f. 4]

Wormesley <Irchenfeld>

158   Parochiani dicunt quod cimiterium patitur defectum in clausura in defectu parochianorum.

Homme Lacy. Visitatio facta ibidem die martis viij Maii anno Domini supradicto

Bolyngham

159   Parochiani dicunt quod omnia sunt bene ibidem.

Deuchurch Cholle

160   Parochiani dicunt quod omnia bene ibidem.

Boleston

161   Parochiani dicunt quod omnia bene sunt ibidem.

Homme Lacy

162   Parochiani dicunt quod decime garbarum non reponuntur in solo ecclesie ymmo alibi in domo Ricardi Caldecote.

163   Item mansum rectoris est ruinosum et in parte prostratum. <suspensus a celebratione divinorum et sequestrati sunt fructus>

164   Item dicunt quod rector prosecutus est vicarium[3] maliciose per brevia regia coram judicibus secularibus.

165   Item dicunt quod Walterus Berwalle <suspensus; excommunicatus> tenet unum calicem ecclesie quem recusat restituere in prejudiciam parochianorum.

166   Item dicunt quod Johannes Tymberlak <suspensus; excommunicatus> subtrahit unam lampadem ardentem coram ymagine crucifixi ad cuius sustentationem tenetur ratione terrarum que fuerunt quondam Stephani Colyer. [*in margin*] <expeditum>

---

[1]   The bottom left-hand and right-hand corners of this page have perished.
[2]   Followed by *fatetur*, struck through.
[3]   Followed by *p*, struck through.

155   Next, they say that William Saundrys absents himself from church and the divine office on Sundays and feast days. *<he denies ... [promises] to do so in future>*

156   Next, that the same William is perjured because he previously swore before the Clerk of the Marches that he would never practise ... [his] craft ... and later, despite this oath he practised it and still does. *<he is dismissed>*

157   John Gall *<excommunicated>* fornicates with Margery Pyper, a married woman. *<the man appears, denies since correction, later admits ... ; the woman excommunicated; they are dismissed>*

[f. 4]

WORMSLEY *<Archenfield>*

158   The parishioners say that the churchyard is defective in its fence, by the fault of the parishioners.

Holme Lacy. Visitation made there on Tuesday, 8 May, in the year of Our Lord abovesaid

BALLINGHAM

159   The parishioners say that all things are well there.

LITTLE DEWCHURCH

160   The parishioners say that all is well there.

BOLSTONE

161   The parishioners say that all things are well there.

HOLME LACY

162   The parishioners say that the tithes of sheaves are not stored on church land, but rather elsewhere in the house of Richard Caldecote.

163   Next, the house of the rector is ruinous and partly collapsed. *<suspended from the celebration of divine services and the revenues are sequestrated>*

164   Next, they say that the rector is prosecuting the vicar maliciously by royal writs before secular judges.

165   Next, they say that Walter Berwalle *<suspended; excommunicated>* is holding a chalice belonging to the church that he refuses to restore, to the prejudice of the parishioners.

166   Next, they say that John Tymberlak *<suspended; excommunicated>* withholds a lamp burning before the image of the crucifixion, to the upkeep of which he is bound by reason of the lands that formerly belonged to Stephen Colyer. [*in margin*]: *<settled>*

167   Item quod Ricardus Caldekot <suspensus; excommunicatus; Heref';
denunciatus est> prout fama laborat adulteratur cum Ibel Tyler <suspensa>
uxore Johannis Tyler.

168   Item quod Hugyn Glasbury <suspensus; excommunicatus> fornicatur
cum Maiota Wilson ambo soluti. <mulier comparet, fatetur, abjurat, fustigetur
circa ecclesiam parochialem>

Lanwaran. Visitatio facta ibidem die mercurii ix mensis Maii anno Domini
supradicto

Landynabo

169   Parochiani dicunt quod omnia sunt bene ibidem.

Lanwaran

170   Parochiani ibidem dicunt quod campanile patitur defectum in tectura in
defectu parochianorum. <reparetur sub pena xl s citra festum nativitatis Sancti
Johannis>

171   Item dicunt quod quidam Jak Coke quondam parochianus ibidem accomodavit unum portiforium domino Waltero Crokenek tunc sellerario de Lanthon'
quod portiforium fuit parochianorum ibidem et prior et conventus ibidem habent
huiusmodi librum in custodia sua et recusant restitutionem eiusdem. <prosequan-
tur parochiani si velint>

172   Item dicunt quod dominus Johannes ap Adam capellanus parochialis
ibidem incontinens est cum Cecilia Veyr <citata per edictum per Mauricium
rectorem ad comparendum Heref' in consistorio> quam tenet in domo sua die
noctuque ut <si essent>[1] vir et uxor. <vir comparet, fatetur, abjurat, jejunet omni
feria vj^ta per septemanam, tenet panem et aquam et dicat j psalterium>

173   Item dicunt quod Johannes Robyns <citatus ad proximam> serviens Jak
Daykys non recepit sacralia sacramentalia in ecclesia parochiali in die Pasche nec
alibi prout scitur. +

Orcobe

174[2]   Primo parochiani dicunt quod rector dat fructus ad firmam licencia ordinarii non petita nec obtenta. <sequestramus fructus>

175   Parochiani dicunt quod dominus Rys <excommunicatus>[3] rector de
Landynabo tenet quandam Sussannam <suspensa; excommunicata> quondam
concubinam suam secum in domo sua an peccant invicem vel non nesciunt. <in
proximo Heref'>

176   Item dicunt quod fons baptismalis non est seratus. <reparetur citra festum
Natalis sub pena vij s>

---

[1]   Replacing *ut*, struck through.
[2]   The whole entry interlined above **175**.
[3]   Preceded by <*suspensus*>, struck through.

167 Next, that Richard Caldekot <*suspended; excommunicated; at Hereford; he is denounced*>, as fame has it, commits adultery with Isabel Tyler <*suspended*>, the wife of John Tyler.

168 Next, that Hugyn Glasbury <*suspended; excommunicated*> fornicates with Maiota Wilson, both single. <*the woman appears, admits, abjures, let her be beaten around the parish church*>

Llanwarne. Visitation made there on Wednesday, 9 May, in the year of Our Lord abovesaid

LLANDINABO

169 The parishioners say that all things are well there.

LLANWARNE

170 The parishioners there say that the bell-tower is defective in its roof, by the fault of the parishioners. <*let it be repaired by the feast of the birth of St John [the Baptist, 24 June], under penalty of 40 shillings*>

171 Next, they say that a certain Jack Coke, formerly a parishioner there, lent a breviary to Sir Walter Crokenek, then cellarer of Llanthony [Priory], which breviary belonged to the parishioners there; and the prior and convent there have this book in their keeping and refuse to restore it. <*let the parishioners prosecute if they wish*>

172 Next, they say that Sir John ap Adam, parish chaplain there, is incontinent with Cecily Veyr <*cited by edict by Maurice, the rector, to appear at Hereford in the consistory*> whom he keeps in his house day and night as <*if they were*> man and wife. <*the man appears, admits, abjures, let him fast every Friday weekly, keeping to bread and water and saying one psalter*>

173 Next, they say that John Robyns <*cited to the next*>, servant of Jack Daykys, did not receive the holy sacraments on Easter Sunday in the parish church nor elsewhere, as far as is known.

ORCOP

174 First, the parishioners say that the rector farms out the revenues without the licence of the ordinary having been sought or obtained. <*we sequestrate the revenues*>

175 The parishioners say that Sir Rhys <*excommunicated*>, the rector of Llandinabo, keeps a certain Susan <*suspended; excommunicated*>, his former concubine, with him in his house, but whether they sin together or not they do not know. <*at the next [consistory] at Hereford*>

176 Next, they say that the baptismal font is not locked. <*let it be repaired by Christmas, under penalty of 7 shillings*>

177 Item quod Morys ap Ivor conjugatus adulteratur cum Wenllian filia Morgan. <suspensa;[1] vir comparet, negat, purget se coram commissario in pro[ximam]>[2]

178 Item quod Philippus ap Llewelyn <non est citatus; suspensus> et Margret filia Ieuan ap Philip <non est citata; suspensa> contraxerunt adinvicem carnali copula subsecuta set nolunt matrimonium inter eos facere solempnizari.

179 [Item dicunt] quod dominus Johannes Bugeyl capellanus[3] parochialis de Byrche Sancti Thome usurpat sepultur[am parochian]orum[4] de Lanwaran et spoliavit rectorem ibidem de tribus corporibus non obstante eiusdem rectoris recla[matione] ... Willelmus Byrche, Meuric ap Gwilim, Gruffuth Waty et Johannes Fryer ac Mychel Jak ... [noct]urno sepelierunt huiusmodi corpora. <concitentur sub spe concordie de consensu partium>

[f. 4v]

Rythir

180 Dicunt parochiani quod mansum rectoris est prostratum ad terram et tigna eiusdem vendita in defectu domini Rogeri Gorpa nuper rectoris ibidem defuncti. <quia mortuus est moritur et actio>

Deuchurch. Visitatio facta ibidem die jovis decimo mensis Maii anno Domini ut supra

Kenderchurch

181 Dicunt quod rectores non inveniunt aliquem capellanum ad deserviendum Deo et parochianis ibidem nec habetur ibidem procurator ad respondendum ordinariis etcetera. <sequestrantur fructus>

Kilpek

182 Parochiani dicunt quod Maiota Leduart <suspensa; excommunicata> soluta fornicatur cum domino Johanne ap Gwilim ap Rys <extra> capellano nuper ibidem. <mulier comparet, fatetur, abjurat, fustigetur in forma>

183 Item quod Margareta filia Robyn oth' Noke <extra> fornicatur cum eodem domino Johanne.

184 Item quod <Johannes> Hull pyper <infirmus; suspensus> fornicatur cum Alson <suspensa;[5] excommunicata> quam tenet consanguineam quondam uxoris in secundo gradu. <vir abjurat, fustigetur in forma; mulier>[6]

---

[1] Followed by <*absens*>, struck through.
[2] The bottom left-hand and right-hand corners of this page have perished.
[3] Replacing *parochianus*, struck through.
[4] *sepulturam parochianorum* seen or conjectured by Bannister, whose transcript ends at *corporibus*.
[5] *suspensa* repeated in error and expunged.
[6] Unfinished.

177 Next, that Morys ap Ifor, a married man, commits adultery with Gwenllian, daughter of Morgan. *<suspended; the man appears, denies, to purge himself before the commissary at the next>*

178 Next, that Philip ap Llewelyn *<he is not cited; suspended>* and Margaret, daughter of Ieuan ap Philip *<she is not cited; suspended>*, contracted together, followed by bodily union, but they will not have the marriage between them solemnised.

179 Next, they say that Sir John Bugeyl, parish chaplain of Much Birch, usurps the burial of the parishioners of Llanwarne, and has robbed the rector there of three corpses, despite the challenge of the same rector ... William Byrche, Meurig ap Gwilym, Gruffudd Waty, John Fryer, and Michael Jak ... by night have buried these bodies. *<let them be jointly cited in the hope of an agreement with the consent of the parties>*

[f. 4v]

TRETIRE

180 The parishioners say that the house of the rector has collapsed to the ground and its timbers have been sold, by the fault of Sir Roger Gorpa, lately the rector there, deceased. *<because he is dead the action is dead too>*

Much Dewchurch. Visitation made there on Thursday, 10 May, in the year of our Lord as above

KENDERCHURCH

181 They say that the rectors do not provide any chaplain to serve God and the parishioners there, nor do they have a proctor there to answer to the ordinaries etc. *<the revenues to be sequestrated>*

KILPECK

182 The parishioners say that Maiota Leduart *<suspended; excommunicated>*, a single woman, fornicates with Sir John ap Gwilym ap Rhys *<outside>*, the chaplain lately there. *<the woman appears, admits, abjures, to be beaten in due form>*

183 Next, that Margaret, daughter of Robin oth' Noke *<outside>*, fornicates with the same Sir John.

184 Next, that *<John>* Hull, piper *<sick; suspended>* fornicates with Alison *<suspended; excommunicated>*, whom he keeps, a blood-relative of his former wife in the second degree. *<the man abjures, to be beaten in due form; the woman [not completed]>*

185   Item quod David Webbe <extra> fornicatur cum Eva Elvell <extra>

186   Item quod Howel Gwtta <suspensus; absens> non venit ad ecclesiam pro servicio divino audiendo ultra ter in anno nec uxor sua. <dimissus>

187   Item dicunt quod prefatus dominus Johannes capellanus ut eis videtur non est firmus in fide eo quod pluries fecit pompam suam quod de vadit tempore nocturno cum spiritibus fantasticis.

Deuchurch <non citati>

188   Parochiani dicunt quod non habent portiforium ad dicendum matutinas et horas in defectu rectoris.

189   Item quod vicarius tenetur invenire unum diaconum ad deserviendum in ecclesia nec facit.

190   Item dicunt quod Ibel Thomkyns impedit executionem testamenti Elizabethe Deveros.

191   Item quod Johannes Carpenter et uxor sua, Henricus Gurney et uxor sua et Wenllian Clenston absentant se diebus dominicis et festivis ab ecclesia.

192   Item dicunt quod cancellus est obscurus et tenebrosus ita quod clerici non possunt legere propter defectum luminis in defectu rectoris.

193   Item idem[1] cancellus in fronte est ruinosus in defectu rectoris.

194   Item dicunt quod Ricardus Cherwynd fornicatur cum Margareta Lloyt.

195   <Item quod Jankyn Taelour junior solutus adulteratur cum Jonet uxore Lewys Taelour>

Sayn Dyvrykes

196   Parochiani dicunt quod <omnia sunt bene ibidem>.

Byrch Sancti Thome

197   Parochiani dicunt quod[2] ornamenta ecclesie male custodiuntur in defectu capellani et clerici ibidem.

198   Item quod unum coopertorium ordinatum in ecclesia est dilaceratum et consumptum in usu capellani.

199   Item quod fenestra ecclesie est fracta in defectu eorundem.

200   Item quod capellanus parochialis fregit ramos arborum crescentium in cimiterio et fecit asportari ad domum suam et ibidem cremari.

201   Item quod non habuerunt neque missam neque vesperas in die dedicationis ecclesie ultimo preterito in defectu capellani.

---

[1]   Repeated in error.
[2]   Followed by *q*, struck through.

185 Next, that David Webbe <*outside*> fornicates with Eve Elvell <*outside*>.

186 Next, that Hywel Gwtta <*suspended; absent*> does not come to church to hear divine service more than three times in the year, nor does his wife. <*dismissed*>

187 Next, they say that the aforesaid Sir John, chaplain, as it seems to them, is not firm in his faith, because he has often made boast that he goes about at night-time with fantastic spirits.

MUCH DEWCHURCH <*not cited*>

188 The parishioners say that they do not have a breviary for saying matins and the hours, by the fault of the rector.

189 Next, that the vicar is bound to provide a deacon to serve in church and does not do so.

190 Next, they say that Isabel Thomkyns obstructs the execution of the will of Elizabeth Deveros.

191 Next, that John Carpenter and his wife, Henry Gurney and his wife, and Gwenllian Clenston absent themselves from church on Sundays and feast days.

192 Next, they say that the chancel is dark and gloomy so that the clerks cannot read because of the lack of light, by the fault of the rector.

193 Next, the same chancel is in a ruinous state at the end, by the fault of the rector.

194 Next, they say that Richard Cherwynd fornicates with Margaret Lloyt.

195 <*Next, that Jankin Taelour the younger, a single man, commits adultery with Jonet, the wife of Lewis Taelour*>

ST DEVEREUX

196 The parishioners say that <*all things are well there*>.

MUCH BIRCH

197 The parishioners say that the ornaments of the church are badly looked after, by the fault of the chaplain and the clerk there.

198 Next, that an altar-cover in the church is torn and worn by the chaplain's use.

199 Next, that a window of the church is broken, by the fault of the same [chaplain and clerk].

200 Next, that the parish chaplain has broken the branches of the trees growing in the churchyard and has had them carried to his house and there burned.

201 Next, that they had neither mass nor vespers on the day of the dedication of the church last past, by the fault of the chaplain.

Garwy. Visitatio facta ibidem die veneris xj mensis Maii anno Domini ut supra

Keynchurch

202 Parochiani ibidem dicunt quod Howel ap John fornicatur cum Wladus quam tenet. <ambo suspensi; excommunicati>

203 Item quod Cadwgon Webbe <extra> fornicatur cum Jonet <extra> quam tenet.

204 Item quod Ieuan Webbe <extra> cum Eva Elvael <extra> fornicatur.

205 Item quod Roger ap Watkyn fornicatur cum Wenllian quam tenet. <ambo suspensi; excommunicati>

[f. 5]

Llanrutholl

206 Parochiani dicunt quod cancellus est discoopertus in defectu rectoris et vicarii.

207 Item dicunt quod fenestre huius cancelli sunt fracte in defectu eorundem.

208 Item quod rector tenetur invenire unum portiforium pro servicio divino fiendo nec facit.

209 Item quod rector dat fructus ecclesie ad firmam licencia non petita nec obtenta. <sequestrati sunt fructus>

210 Item dicunt quod prior de Monemuth violavit sequestrum alias interpositum in fructibus eiusdem ecclesie per reverendum patrem episcopum Hereford' qui nunc est.

211 Item quod Perwar <suspensa> uxor Thome Jerwerth adulteratur cum Nicholao Gamme. <suspensus; mulier purget>

212 <Item quod dominus David vicarius ministravit sacralia sacramentalia in die Pasche quibusdam Meuric Bengrych et Rys Duy excommunicatis eo quod injecerunt manus violentas in dominum Willelmum Watkyn capellanum, ipso domino David hoc sciente>

Saynwaynard

213 Parochiani dicunt quod vicarius de Lugwardyn tenetur invenire duos capellanos ad deserviendum videlicet unum apud Sayn Waynard et unum pro capellis de Tref Vranen et de[1] Penros nec facit. <sequestrati sunt fructus, commissa est custodia sequestrationis domino Thome capellano et domino Johanni capellano ad supervisionem procuratorum ecclesie> [*in margin*] <Nota, Ieuan Thomas et Ieuan Cogh de Penros et Trefvranen>

214 Item quod dominus Johannes capellanus ibidem exercet tabernas et ibidem inhoneste garulat[2] <in magnum scandalum etcetera>.

---

[1]   Followed by *Trefros*, struck through.
[2]   Followed by *ibidem*, struck through.

Garway. Visitation made there on Friday, 11 May, in the year of our Lord as above

KENTCHURCH

202 The parishioners there say that Hywel ap John fornicates with Gwladus whom he keeps. <*both suspended; both excommunicated*>

203 Next, that Cadwgan Webbe <*outside*> fornicates with Jonet <*outside*> whom he keeps.

204 Next, that Ieuan Webbe <*outside*> fornicates with Eve Elvael <*outside*>.

205 Next, that Roger ap Gwatkyn fornicates with Gwenllian whom he keeps. <*both suspended; both excommunicated*>

[f. 5]

LLANROTHAL

206 The parishioners say that the chancel is unroofed, by the fault of the rector and the vicar.

207 Next, they say that the windows of the chancel are broken, by the fault of the same.

208 Next, that the rector is bound to provide a breviary for carrying out divine service and does not do so.

209 Next, that the rector farms out the revenues of the church without a licence being sought or obtained. <*the revenues are sequestrated*>

210 Next, they say that prior of Monmouth has violated the sequestration previously imposed on the revenues of the same church by the reverend father, the present bishop of Hereford.

211 Next, that Perwar, wife of Thomas Jerwerth <*suspended*>, commits adultery with Nicholas Gamme. <*suspended; let the woman purge*>

212 <*Next, that Sir David, the vicar, administered the holy sacraments on Easter Sunday to Meurig Bengrych and Rhys Duy, both excommunicates because they laid violent hands on Sir William Watkyn, chaplain, the same Sir David being aware of this*>

ST WEONARDS

213 The parishioners say that the vicar of Lugwardine is bound to provide two chaplains to serve, namely one at St Weonards and one for the chapels of Treferanon and Penrose, and does not do so. <*the revenues are sequestrated, custody of the sequestration committed to Sir Thomas, chaplain, and Sir John, chaplain, under the supervision of the proctors of the church*> [in margin] <*Note, Ieuan Thomas and Ieuan Cogh of Penrose and Treferanon*>

214 Next, that Sir John, a chaplain there, frequents taverns and there gossips improperly <*to the great scandal etc.*>.

215 Item quod idem dominus Johannes incontinens est cum quadam Margareta cuius cognomen ignorant. <purgavit se, tamen inquirat commissarius>

216 Item dicunt quod prout communis fama laborat idem dominus Johannes inhabilis et ignarus ad gerendum curam animarum etcetera.

Garwy <expeditum>

217 <Dominus Johannes capellanus parochialis ibidem suspensus>

218 Parochiani dicunt quod Meuric Bengrych et Rys Duy injecerunt manus temere violentas in quendam dominum Willelmum Watkyn et Thomas Pengrych pater dicti Meuric dedit eis ad hoc consilium et auxilium.

219 <Item quod dominus Thomas Folyot exercet tabernas inordinate et exces­sive in magnum scandalum clericorum etcetera et quod detexit confessionem Roberti Scheppert parochiani sui in publico>

220 Item quod Johannes Smyth conjugatus adulteratur cum Alicia Wilkok concubina sua et male tractat uxorem suam <videlicet Agnetem Hunte de Whyteney; interrogata illa de conditione sua libera vel etcetera; vir excommunicatus quia etcetera; Alicia Wylkok suspensa>

221 Item dicunt quod dominus Ricardus capellanus parochialis ibidem celebrat bis in die videlicet hic apud Garwy et alibi apud Wormbrugg et recipit duplex salarium.

222 Item quod idem dominus est inhabilis ad gerendum curam animarum ibidem quia nescit linguam Wallicanam et quamplures parochiani ibidem nesciunt linguam Anglicanam.

223 Item quod Llewelyn ap Ieuan ap Madoc et Wladus Bach[1] juraverunt de matrimonio solempnizando inter eos nec faciunt. <diferuntur sub spe nubendi; solempnizatum est matrimonium>

224 Item quod Jankyn serviens Petri Smyth fornicatur cum Johanna Scheppert. <vir abjurat, fustigetur in forma; mulier extra>

225 Item quod Hugyn oth' Walle male tractat uxorem suam minando eam pluries interficere et eam atrociter verberando.

Neweton

226 Parochiani [dicunt][2] quod cancellus patitur defectum in tectura et in vitro in defectu rectoris.

227 Item quod idem rector tenetur invenire unum portiforium pro divino servicio fiendo ibidem nec facit.

228 Item quod Lleuky Bach tenetur solvere ad opus ecclesie parochialis xx d. legatos per David Paty maritum suum in suo testamento in quo constituit eandem Lleuky huiusmodi testamenti sui executricem et recusat huiusmodi denarios solvere. <concordes sunt et satisfecit>

---

[1] Followed by *conjugata*, struck through.
[2] Omitted.

215   Next, that the same Sir John is incontinent with a certain Margaret, whose surname they do not know. *<he has purged himself, but the commissary should inquire>*

216   Next, they say that, as common fame has it, the same Sir John is unsuitable and inexperienced at performing the cure of souls etc.

GARWAY *<settled>*

217   *<Sir John, parish chaplain there, suspended>*

218   The parishioners say that Meurig Bengrych and Rhys Duy laid violent hands without good reason on a certain Sir William Watkyn, and that Thomas Pengrych, the father of the said Meurig, gave them counsel and aid.

219   *<Next, that Sir Thomas Folyot frequents taverns in an unruly and excessive manner, to the great scandal of the clergy etc., and that he revealed the confession of Robert Scheppert, his parishioner, in public>*

220   Next, that John Smyth, a married man, commits adultery with Alice Wilkok, his concubine, and mistreats his wife, *<namely Agnes Hunte of Whitney; this woman questioned about her condition, whether a free woman or etc.; the man excommunicated because etc.; Alice Wylkok suspended>*

221   Next, they say that Sir Richard, parish chaplain there, celebrates twice in a day, namely here at Garway and elsewhere at Wormbridge, and he receives a double salary.

222   Next, that the same Sir [Richard] is unsuitable to perform the cure of souls there, because he does not know the Welsh language, and most parishioners there do not know the English language.

223   Next, that Llewelyn ap Ieuan ap Madog and Gwladus Bach swore that they would have marriage solemnised between them and they have not done so. *<deferred in the hope of them marrying; the marriage has been solemnised>*

224   Next, that Jankin, servant of Peter Smyth, fornicates with Joan Scheppert. *<the man abjures, to be beaten in due form; the woman outside>*

225   Next, that Hugyn oth' Walle mistreats his wife, often threatening to kill her and beating her terribly.

WELSH NEWTON

226   The parishioners say that the chancel is defective in its roof and glass, by the fault of the rector.

227   Next, that the rector is bound to provide a breviary for performing divine service there and does not do so.

228   Next, that Lleucu Bach is bound to pay for the benefit of the parish church 20 pence bequeathed by David Paty, her husband, in his will, in which will he made Lleucu his executrix, and she refuses to pay this money. *<they have agreed and she has paid>*

[Llang]aran[1]

229 Parochiani dicunt[2]

[f. 5v]
[M]onemuth.[3] Visitatio facta ibidem die sabbati xij mensis Maii anno Domini ut supra

Godrichecastell

230 Parochiani ibidem dicunt quod vicaria vacat ut credunt quia nec vicarius nec aliquis alius capellanus deservit ibidem in divinis unde iminet grave periculum animarum parochianorum ibidem quia non habent curatum. <constat domino>

231[4] <Item dicunt quod fenestre cancelli patiuntur defectum in vitro in defectu rectoris>

232 Item dicunt quod vicarius qui pro tempore fuerit debet invenire unum diaconum ad deserviendum in ecclesia et ad custodiendum libros et ornamenta quod nullatenus factum est.

233 <Item quod dominus Thomas prior de Flankeford incontinens est cum Johanna uxore Johannis Taelour. Prior comparet, negat, habet diem ad purgandum se coram commissario; vir purgavit se>

234 Item dicunt quod oleum et crisma non renovatur aliquando de triennino[5] in triennium ibidem.

235 Item dicunt quod non habuerunt matutinas in die Pasche ultimo preterito.

236 Item quod dominus Johannes Byterlowe celebrat bis in die videlicet apud <Godrich Castell et apud capellam de Honsham>.[6]

237 Item quod dominus Johannes Smyth celebrat bis in die videlicet apud <Godrich Castell et apud Honsham>.

238 Item quod idem Johannes Smyth incontinens est cum Maiota <Watcok> <suspensa> quam tenet. <vir[7] habet diem ad purgandum apud Ross>

239 Item quod idem dominus Johannes est ebriosus. <negat, habet diem ad purgandum>

240 Item quod prefatus dominus Johannes Byterlowe <non est citatus> obtulit alias unum calicem ymmo verius dedit de bonis <suis> ad celebrandum in ecclesia de Grodrych Castell perpetuo, quem calicem postea asportavit de eadem ecclesia licencia parochianorum ibidem non petita nec obtenta et ad usum suum proprium convertit.

[1] Both corners of this page are perished.
[2] Unfinished.
[3] A small piece is missing from the top left-hand margin of the page.
[4] The whole entry interlined above **230**.
[5] Recte *triennio*.
[6] Followed by *excommunicatus*, struck through.
[7] Interlined over *mulier*, struck through.

LLANGARRON[1]

229   The parishioners say [*not completed*]

[f. 5v]
Monmouth. Visitation made there on Saturday, 12 May, in the year of our Lord
as above

GOODRICH

230   The parishioners there say that the vicarage is vacant, as they believe,
because neither a vicar nor any other chaplain serves the divine offices there, from
which threatens grave peril for the souls of the parishioners there, because they do
not have a parish priest. <*a matter for his lordship*>

231   <*Next, they say that the glass of the windows of the chancel is defective, by the fault of
the rector*>

232   Next, they say that the vicar for the time being ought to provide a deacon
to serve in church and look after the books and ornaments, which is by no means
done.

233   <*Next, that Sir Thomas, prior of Flanesford, is incontinent with Joan, the wife of John
Taelour; the prior appears, denies, has a day to purge himself before the commissary; the man has
purged himself*>

234   Next, they say that the oil and the chrism are sometimes not renewed every
three years.

235   Next, they say that did not have matins last Easter Sunday.

236   Next, that Sir John Byterlowe celebrates twice in a day, namely at Goodrich
Castle and at the chapel of Huntsham.

237   Next, that Sir John Smyth celebrates twice in a day, namely at <*Goodrich
Castle and at Huntsham*>.

238   Next, that the same John Smyth is incontinent with Maiota Watcok <*suspended*> whom he keeps. <*the man has a day to purge at Ross-on-Wye*>

239   Next, that the same Sir John is a drunkard. <*he denies, has a day to purge*>

240   Next, that the aforesaid Sir John Byterlowe <*he has not been cited*> previously offered a chalice, indeed in truth he donated it out of <*his own*> goods,
for celebrating in the church of Goodrich Castle for ever, which chalice later he
carried off from the same church, without seeking or obtaining permission from
the parishioners there, and he converted it to his own use.

[1]   Although Bannister hypothesised that this entry represented Glangarren Farm in St
Weonards, it is more likely to relate to the parish of Llangarron, whose appearance may
have been expected at Garway, but which presented at Sellack, also in Archenfield deanery,
on 14 May (**326–8**, see also **1347**).

241   Item quod fructus ecclesie non reponuntur in solo ecclesie.

242   Item quod Willelmus Thomkyns tenetur ad opus ecclesie in xviij d quod recusat solvere. \<excommunicatus\>

243   Item quod Thomas Robyns tenetur ad opus eiusdem ecclesie in iiij s ij d quos solvere recusat. \<excommunicatus\>

244   Item quod Philippus Hankokes tenetur in xv d ad idem opus et recusat eos solvere. \<satisfecit\>

245   Item quod Willelmus Gelyf solutus fornicatur cum Matilda[1] \<suspensa; excommunicata quia etcetera\> aperte quam tenet. \<vir comparet, fatetur, abjurat, fustigetur ter circa ecclesiam parochialem publice; mulier fustigetur in forma\>

246   Item quod Rogerus Beveney conjugatus adulteratur cum Dynys Jevanes \<suspensa; excommunicata\> et male tractat uxorem suam.[2] \<vir comparet, abjurat,[3] fustigetur ter circa ecclesiam\>

247   Item quod Willelmus Gardenere solutus adulteratur cum Felicia Kydes uxore Roberti Kydes. \<non reperiuntur, ideo commissarius etcetera; dimissus\>

248   Item quod Thomas Botemon conjugatus adulteratur cum Margareta Hely. \<mulier moratur apud Ruwardyn; vir suspensus; citatus per edictum; vir comparet, negat post correctionem; purgavit se\>

Walissh Bykenor

249   Parochiani[4] habent diem apud Bykenor Englissh \<ubi dicunt quod dominus Johannes Bytyrlowe habet penes se unum librum continens in se officium baptismi, psalterium et alia diversa quem[5] tenuit penes se x annis et ultra et recusat restitutionem\>.

Whytchurch

250   Parochiani dicunt quod Willelmus Fox \<extra\> conjugatus adulteratur cum Johanna Hardyng \<extra\> quam tenet in concubinam et male tractat uxorem suam subtrahendo sibi victualia et alia sibi debita de jure.

251[6]   Item idem confessus est publice coram vicinis suis ibidem quod ipse precognovit Luciam[7] Wasmair sororem uxoris sue et ideo pretendit matrimonium inter se et dictam uxorem suam ea occasione dirimendum.

252   Item quod David Smyth et Wenllian uxor sua fecerunt matrimonium solempnizari clamdestine inter se bannis non editis extra in alia parochia videlicet in ecclesia de Geneyrryw. \<vir comparet, fatetur, fustigetur ter circa ecclesiam parochialem cum cereo et ter per forum Monemuth; mulier non comparet, suspensa\>

---

[1]   Preceded by *Mal*, struck through.
[2]   Followed by \<*ambo suspensi*\>, struck through.
[3]   Followed by *retraxit*, struck through.
[4]   Followed by *dicunt*, struck through.
[5]   Followed by *d*, struck through.
[6]   Continues on the same line as **250**.
[7]   Followed by *uxorem*, struck through.

241 Next, that the revenues of the church are not stored on church land.

242 Next, that William Thomkyns owes 18 pence for the benefit of the church, which he refuses to pay. *<excommunicated>*

243 Next, that Thomas Robyns owes 4 shillings and 2 pence for the benefit of the same church, which he refuses to pay. *<excommunicated>*

244 Next, that Philip Hankokes owes 15 pence for the same benefit and refuses to pay it. *<he has paid>*

245 Next, that William Gelyf, a single man, fornicates openly with Maud *<suspended; excommunicated because etc.>* whom he keeps. *<the man appears, admits, abjures, let him be beaten three times around the parish church publicly; let the woman be beaten in due form>*

246 Next, that Roger Beveney, a married man, commits adultery with Dynys Jevanes *<suspended; excommunicated>* and mistreats his wife. *<the man appears, abjures, let him be beaten three times around the church>*

247 Next, that William Gardenere, a single man, commits adultery with Felise Kydes, wife of Robert Kydes. *<they are not found, so the commissary etc.; dismissed>*

248 Next, that Thomas Botemon, a married man, commits adultery with Margaret Hely. *<the woman lives at Ruardean; the man suspended; cited by edict; the man appears, denies since correction; he has purged himself>*

WELSH BICKNOR

249 The parishioners have a day at English Bicknor *<where they say that Sir John Bytyrlowe has in his possession a book containing in it the office of baptism, the psalter, and various other things, which he has retained for ten years and more and refuses to give back>*

WHITCHURCH

250 The parishioners say that William Fox *<outside>*, a married man, commits adultery with Joan Hardyng *<outside>* whom he keeps as a concubine, and mistreats his wife, depriving her of food and other things due to her of right.

251 Next, the same man has confessed publicly before his neighbours there that he previously knew [sexually] Lucy Wasmair, sister of his wife, and so claims that for that reason the marriage between him and his wife should be nullified.

252 Next, that David Smyth and his wife Gwenllian had the marriage between them solemnised clandestinely, the banns not being given out in the other parish, that is, in the church of Ganarew. *<the man appears, admits, to be beaten three times around the parish church, with a candle, and three times through the marketplace of Monmouth; the woman does not appear, suspended>*

253   Item quod dominus Mauricius ap Ieuan ap Jerwerth presbiter Landav'[1] diocesis celebravit huiusmodi matrimonium clamdestine pro xij d et moratur apud Pennederyn Men' diocesis.

254   Item quod David Goch <correxit etcetera> et Wenllian quam tenet pro uxore fecerunt matrimonium clamdestine solempnizari [inter eos][2] in ecclesia de Penne y Klawde Landaven' diocesis bannis non editis per quendam dominum ... <vir comparet, fatetur, fustigetur tribus diebus dominicis circa ecclesiam parochialem cum j cereo et similiter per forum de Mone[muth]>

[f. 6]

Geneyryw

255   Parochiani dicunt quod ecclesia vacat per mortem domini Mauricii ultimi rectoris ibidem et vacavit per medium annum et ultra quare parochiani non habent divinum servicium etcetera.

256   Item quod Willelmus Staunton fecit tabernam communem in domo rectoris ibidem. <suspensus>

Monemuth

257   Parochiani dicunt quod matutine et vespere non fiunt cum[3] nota prout consuetum est in defectu rectoris et vicarii.

258   Item dicunt quod Walterus Catell parochianus ibidem recusat invenire panem benedictum in cursuo[4] suo prout alii parochiani faciunt. <dimissus>

259   Item quod Davy Vadyr et Lucia filia Johannis Robyn quam tenet abjurarunt peccatum[5] adinvicem et adhuc non obstante huiusmodi abjuratione cohabitant simul in una domo continuando[6] in peccato. <uterque abjurat, fustigentur in forma>[7]

260   Item quod Ieuan ap Philip <citetur> conjugatus adulteratur cum Gwladus <absens> quam tenet et non tractat uxorem suam affectione maritali.

261   Item dicunt quod vicarius est absens in curia Romana nec[8] invenit pro se aliquem capellanum ad deserviendum in ecclesia quia ut dicunt consuetum est ab antiquo quod vicarius in propria persona <deserviret> vel per alium capellanum in eius absencia faceret deserviri et alius capellanus parochialis deserviret in eadem ecclesia et modo non habent nisi unum solum capellanum parochialem. <sequestrati sunt fructus ad satisfaciendum pro vicario ad inveniendum unum capellanum ad celebrandum et commissa est custodia procuratoribus>

1   Interlined over *Men'*, struck through.
2   Both bottom corners of the page have perished.
3   Altered from *in*.
4   Recte *cursu*.
5   Followed by *al[ias]*, struck through.
6   Followed by *p[eccatum]*, struck through.
7   Followed by *mulier excommunicata quia etcetera*, struck through.
8   Preceded by *nec*, struck through.

253   Next, that Sir Maurice ap Ieuan ap Iorwerth, a priest of Llandaff diocese, celebrated this marriage clandestinely for 12 pence, and he lives at Penderyn in St David's diocese.

254   Next, that David Goch <*he has amended etc.*> and Gwenllian, whom he keeps as a wife, had the marriage between them solemnised clandestinely, the banns not having been given out, in the church of Penn-y-Clawdd in Llandaff diocese by a certain Sir ... <*the man appears, admits, to be beaten three Sundays around the parish church, with one candle, and three times through the marketplace of Monmouth*>

[f. 6]

GANAREW

255   The parishioners say that the church is vacant by the death of Sir Maurice, the last rector there, and has been vacant for half a year and more, as a result of which the parishioners do not have divine service etc.

256   Next, that William Staunton has made a common tavern in the rectory there. <*suspended*>

MONMOUTH

257   The parishioners say that matins and vespers do not take place with music, as is customary, by the fault of the rector and the vicar.

258   Next, they say that Walter Catell, a parishioner there, refuses to provide the holy bread in his turn, as the other parishioners do. <*dismissed*>

259   Next, that Davy Vadyr and Lucy, daughter of John Robyn, whom he keeps, abjured sinning together and despite such abjuration, they still live together in one house, continuing in sinning. <*each abjures, both to be beaten in due form*>

260   Next, that Ieuan ap Philip <*to be cited*>, a married man, commits adultery with Gwladus <*absent*> whom he keeps, and does not treat his wife with marital affection.

261   Next, they say that the vicar is absent, being at the papal court at Rome, and does not provide in his place any chaplain to serve in church, because, as they say, it has been the custom of old that the vicar <*should serve*> in person or else he should have it served in his absence by another chaplain, and another parish chaplain should serve in this church; and now they have only one parish chaplain. <*the revenues are sequestered to pay on the vicar's behalf for the provision of a chaplain to celebrate, and custody is committed to the proctors*>

262   Item dicunt quod mansum vicarie est usque ad terram prostratum in defectu rectoris in magnum dampnum parochianorum et periculum animarum quia de nocte in necessitatis articulo cum contigerit imminere parochochiani[1] non possunt intrare scepta prioratus pro vicario ad ministrandum viaticum infirmis sive extremam unctionem. <satisfactum est in articulo proximo superius>

263[2]   Item dicunt quod Ricardus Skynner et Emot quam tenet contraxerunt adinvicem nec faciunt matrimonium solempnizari inter se. <conjugati sunt>

264   Item dicunt quod Jankyn John conjugatus adulteratur cum Johanna quam tenet. <vir abjurat, fustigetur in forma, mulier suspensa>

265   Item quod Ricardus Scote[3] mercandizat diebus dominicis et festivis exercendo artem suam tempore indebito. <dimissus[4] est>

266   Item quod Gryge Corvyser <dimissus est> facit idem.

267[5]   Item Morys Corvyger <infirmus, citetur> facit idem.

268[6]   Item Johannes[7] Tresor idem. <dimissus>

269   Item quod Thomas Justyn solutus fornicatur cum serviente sua quam tenet in domo.

270   Item quod Johannes Went fornicatur cum <Sibilla>[8] serviente Tybote[9] Tannere. <vir abjurat, fustigetur, mulier;[10] fustigetur in forma bis; dimissi sunt> [*in margin*] <dimissi sunt>

271   Item quod Jankyn Ornel fornicatur cum Alicia Hawys. <vir absens, mulier suspensa>

272   Item quod Jankyn Cookes fornicatur cum Johanna Gergeamide. <mulier suspensa>

273   Item Jankyn Wade fornicatur cum Editha serviente sua <suspensa> qui contraxerunt adinvicem per verba de presenti.

274   Item Jankyn ap Gwilim fornicatur cum Alicia Prior. <suspensa>

275   Item Thomas Taelour fornicatur cum Johanna serviente Johannis Wade. <in puerperio; citentur>

276   [*in margin*] Item Monemuth.[11]

Jak Cookes conjugatus adulteratur cum quadam. <suspensus, Isabella>[12]

---

[1]   Recte *parochiani*.
[2]   Entries **263–9**, **271**, and **273–5** are each marginated *a*.
[3]   Corrected from *Scotey*.
[4]   Preceded by *suspensus*, struck through.
[5]   Follows **266** on the same line.
[6]   Follows **267** on the same line.
[7]   Preceded by *Ricardus*, struck through.
[8]   Replacing *Felicia*, struck through.
[9]   Preceded by *J*, struck through.
[10]   Followed by *suspensa*, struck through.
[11]   Continued in a gap left after the three Duxton entries, for which see **293–5**.
[12]   The name has been added in a later hand, so <*susp'*> must refer to the man.

262 Next, they say that the vicarage house has collapsed to the ground by the fault of the rector, to the great damage of the parishioners and the danger of their souls, because at night when the need is pressing, the parishioners cannot enter the precinct of the priory for the vicar to administer the viaticum to the sick or extreme unction. <*satisfied in the previous article above*>

263 Next, they say that Richard Skynner and Emot, whom he keeps, contracted together and have not had the marriage between them solemnised. <*they are married*>

264 Next, they say that Jankin John, a married man, commits adultery with Joan, whom he keeps. <*the man abjures, to be beaten in due form; the woman suspended*>

265 Next, that Richard Scote trades on Sundays and feast days, exercising his craft at a time when he ought not to. <*dismissed*>

266 Next, that Grug[1] Corvyser <*he is dismissed*> does the same.

267 Next, Morys Corvyger <*sick, to be cited*> does the same.

268 Next, John Tresor the same. <*dismissed*>

269 Next, that Thomas Justyn, a single man, fornicates with his servant, whom he keeps at home.

270 Next, that John Went fornicates with <*Sybil*>, servant of Tybota Tannere. <*the man abjures, to be beaten; the woman to be beaten in due form twice; they are dismissed*> [*in margin*]: <*they are dismissed*>

271 Next, that Jankin Ornel fornicates with Alice Hawys. <*the man absent; the woman suspended*>

272 Next, that Jankin Cookes fornicates with Joan Gergeamide. <*the woman suspended*>

273 Next, Jankin Wade fornicates with Edith, his servant <*suspended*>, the two having contracted together in the present tense.

274 Next, Jankin ap Gwilym fornicates with Alice Prior <*suspended*>.

275 Next, Thomas Taelour fornicates with Joan, servant of John Wade. <*in labour; to be cited*>

276 [*in margin*]: Next, Monmouth.

Jack Cookes <*suspended*>, a married man, commits adultery with a certain woman <*Isabel*>.

---

[1] Recte *Cryg*, defective of speech, stammering.

277   Item quod Matilda Thomas¹ tenet commune burdellum in domo sua receptando adulteros et fornicatores in domo sua. <purget² se coram curato>

278   Item quod Thomas Prophete fornicatur cum <Magiota> serviente sua quam tenet in domo sua. <purget se coram curato>

279   Item quod Johannes Hecey vadit diebus dominicis et festivis ad forum extra villam omittendo servicium divinum. <dimissus>

280   Johannes Knyght facit idem. <dimissus³ senior>

281   [Ite]m⁴ Jankyn filius eiusdem fornicatur cum <Johanna> serviente eiusdem patris sui. <suspensus>

282   [Ite]m quod Willelmus Sweynshull exercet forum diebus dominicis et festivis. <emendabit, dimissus>

283   [Item quod] Phylipott oth' Moore fornicatur cum serviente Parnell Bryde.

284   [Item Wilko]c⁵ Bounde exercet forum diebus dominicis etcetera. <dimissus est>

285   [Item quod Thomas Ever]⁶ de Monwystrete et Elizabeth uxor sua fecerunt matrimonium clamdestine solempnizari [inter se licencia] non [petita nec obtenta] etcetera.

286⁷   Item quod idem Thomas subtrahit ... ...les⁸ et ...

[f. 6v]

287   Item quod Walterus Tyler et Agnes Frunde quam tenet pro uxore fecerunt matrimonium clamdestine solempnizari inter se in diocesi Landav' non obstante reclamatione Marione pretendentis et asserentis precontractum cum eodem.

288   Item Johannes Lybykes <citetur> et Jak Laurens serviens eiusdem exercent forum extra diebus dominicis et festivis.

289   Item quod Jankyn Mason junior facit idem. <dimissus est>

290   Item quod David Dyer conjugatus adulteratur cum Agnete Norys conjugata. <extra>

291   Item dicunt quod cancellus ecclesie Sancti Thome ultra Wayan patitur defectum in tectura in defectu prioris.

---

¹   Followed by *ri*, struck through.
²   Preceded by <*suspensa*>, struck through.
³   Following *suspensus*, deleted; apparently includes the previous item.
⁴   Up to an inch from the left-hand margin and half an inch from the bottom of this page have perished; more was visible to Bannister in the 1920s.
⁵   Full name supplied from Bannister.
⁶   Supplied from Bannister.
⁷   Follows **285** on the same line.
⁸   Perhaps *decimas suas rationales*. Cf. **1129**.

277   Next, that Maud Thomas keeps a common brothel in her house, receiving adulterers and fornicators in her house. *<to purge herself before the parish priest>*

278   Next, that Thomas Prophete fornicates with *<Maiota>*, his servant, whom he keeps in his house. *<to purge himself before the parish priest>*

279   Next, that John Hetey goes to market on Sundays and feast days outside the town, missing divine service. *<dismissed>*

280   John Knyght does the same. *<dismissed>*

281   Next, Jankin, son of the same man, fornicates with *<Joan>*, servant of his father. *<suspended>*

282   Next, that William Sweynshull uses the market on Sundays and feast days. *<he will amend, dismissed>*

283   Next, Philipot oth' Moor fornicates with the servant of Parnell Bryde.

284   Next, Wilkoc Bounde uses the market on Sundays etc. *<he is dismissed>*

285   Next, that Thomas Ever of Monnow Street and his wife Elizabeth had a clandestine marriage solemnised between them, without seeking or obtaining a licence etc.

286   Next, that this Thomas withholds [?his reasonable tithes] and ...

[f. 6v]

287   Next, that Walter Tyler and Agnes Frunde, whom he keeps as a wife, had a clandestine marriage solemnised between them in Llandaff diocese, despite Marion's challenge, alleging and asserting a previous contract with the same man.

288   Next, John Lybykes *<to be cited>* and Jack Laurens, his servant, use the market outside [the town] on Sundays and feast days.

289   Next, that Jankin Mason the younger does the same. *<he is dismissed>*

290   Next, that David Dyer, a married man, commits adultery with Agnes Norys, a married woman. *<outside>*

291   Next, they say that the chancel of the church of St Thomas, Overwye, is defective in its roof, by the fault of the prior.

292 Item quod dominus Rogerus Monkes capellanus parochialis mercandizat videlicet emit et vendit diversa bona[1] pro lucro inde captando. <habet[2] diem ad respondendum Hereford' xix[3] die Decembris>

Duxton[4]

293 Parochiani dicunt quod cancellus est obscurus et tenebrosus ita <quod> in meridie servicium divinum non potest fieri ibidem sine candela in defectu rectoris et vicarii.

294 Item dicunt quod ostium cancelli est fractum in defectu eorundem rectoris et vicarii.

295 Item dicunt[5]

Walleford <Ross>. Visitatio facta ibidem die dominica xiij mensis Maii anno Domini supradicto

[Walleford]

296 Parochiani ibidem dicunt quod omnia sunt bene ibidem.

297 Accusatores[6] dicunt quod Wilkok Agyns <dimissus est>[7] fornicatur cum Ibel Smyth <suspensa> ambo soluti. <vir comparet, fatetur, abjurat, fustigetur semel circa ecclesiam cum j candela>

298 Item quod Thomas Underwode <extra> fornicatur cum Margareta Capestere <extra> ambo soluti.

Ruwardyn <Ross>

299 <Capellanus parochialis ibidem non comparet; suspensus>

300 Parochiani dicunt quod quidam Nicholaus Cuthler de Ruwardyn defuncto patre suo publice dixit quod spiritus eiusdem patris sui transivit de nocte in parochia predicta et fecit vigilias super tumulum dicti patris sui una nocte in magnum scandalum fidei catholice ut credunt.

301 Item quod Nicholaus Boweton solutus adulteratur cum Margareta Hobys conjugata. <ambo comparent, abjurant, fustigentur[8] circa ecclesiam vj et vj per forum>

302 Item quod Gwrwaret de Wallia fornicatur cum Johanna Ballard.

303 Item quod Hik Hwkesmon <adulteratur>[9] cum Lucia Baker conjugata.

---

[1] Followed by *lucrando etc*, struck through.
[2] Preceded by <*Webley Irch'*, struck through.
[3] *xix* entered in a gap in the text.
[4] The Duxton entries are on folio **6**, between **275** and **276**.
[5] Unfinished.
[6] *Acc[usatores]* in margin.
[7] Preceded by <*suspensus*>, interlined and struck through.
[8] Followed by *ter* corrected from *j*, and finally struck through.
[9] Replacing *fornicatur*, struck through.

292 Next, that Sir Roger Monkes, parish chaplain, trades, that is, he buys and sells various goods to take profit from it. <*he has a day to answer at Hereford on 19 December*>

DIXTON

293 The parishioners say that the chancel is so dark and gloomy that, at mid-day, divine service cannot be held there without a candle, by the fault of the rector and the vicar.

294 Next, they say that the chancel door is broken, by the fault of the same rector and vicar.

295 Next, they say [*not completed*]

Walford <*Ross*>. Visitation made there on Sunday, 13 May, in the year of Our Lord abovesaid

[WALFORD]

296 The parishioners there say that all things are well there.

297 [*in margin*]: Accusers

They say that Wilkok Agyns <*he is dismissed*> fornicates with Isabel Smyth <*suspended*> both single. <*the man appears, admits, abjures, to be beaten once around the church, with one candle*>

298 Next, that Thomas Underwode <*outside*> fornicates with Margaret Capestere <*outside*>, both single.

RUARDEAN <*Ross*>

299 <*the parish chaplain there does not appear, suspended*>

300 The parishioners say that a certain Nicholas Cuthler of Ruardean, on the death of his father, publicly said that the spirit of his father goes about at night in this parish, and he kept watch over the tomb of his father one night, to the great scandal of the catholic faith, as they believe.

301 Next, that Nicholas Boweton, a single man, commits adultery with Margaret Hobys, a married woman. <*both appear, both abjure, both to be beaten around the church six times and six times through the marketplace*>

302 Next, that Gwrwared of Wales fornicates with Joan Ballard.

303 Next, that Hik Hwkesmon commits adultery with Lucy Baker, a married woman.

304   Item quod cancellus est ruinosus in defectu rectoris <et vicarii>.

305   Item dicunt quod fructus illius ecclesie datur ad firmam. <sequestrati sunt fructus et commissa est custodia decano ibidem, Johanni Bayly et Thome Heyde>

Sellak <Irch'>. Visitatio ibidem die lune xiiij die mensis Maii anno Domini supradicto

Brydestowe

306   Parochiani dicunt quod quidam Gruffuth Sawyer <manet apud Madley> et Margareta Taelour de Madley fecerunt matrimonium clamdestine inter se in ecclesia de Madley per vicarium ibidem sine litteris curati dicti Gruffuth ac bannis non editis in ecclesia de Brydestowe, superstite ut creditur Maiota filia Willelmi Taelour uxore legitima dicti Gruffuth.

Sellak

307   Parochiani dicunt quod parochiani de Sellak commorantes apud Lytel Deuchurch et apud Combe tenentur visitare matricem ecclesiam de Sellak semel in anno videlicet in festo Sancti Thesiliaw patroni eiusdem ecclesie et ibidem illo die offerre et non[1] faciunt. <moniti sunt quod faciant sub pena excommunicationis>[2]

308[3]   Item quod iidem recusant contribuere ad sustentationem clausure cimiterii de Sellak pro rata etcetera.

309   Item parochiani de Sellak commorantes apud Hendre tenentur con- tribuere ad reformationem clausure cimiterii nec faciunt. <suspensi; et citati de novo>

310   Item parochiani de Sellak apud Bydelston tenentur ad idem et non faciunt.

311   Item quod Wilkok Owein de Rytir subtrahit jura parochialia ecclesie de Sellak et tenetur ad reformationem [clausure][4] cimiterii et non facit. <suspensus et citatus>

312   Item quod baptisterium non est seratum.

313   Item quod cimiterium non est clausum in defectu parochianorum. Injunc- tum est eisdem quod faciant ref[ormari] citra festum Sancti Michelis proximum futurum <sub pena xl s>.

---

[1]   Repeated in error and cancelled.
[2]   The judgement marginated and bracketed against **307–10**.
[3]   Runs on from **307** without a break.
[4]   The bottom right-hand corner of this page has perished.

304   Next, that the chancel is in a ruinous state, by the fault of the rector <*and of the vicar*>.

305   Next, they say that the revenues of this church are farmed. <*the revenues are sequestrated and custody committed to the dean there, to John Bayly and to Thomas Heyde*>

Sellack <*Archenfield*>. Visitation there on Monday, 14 May, in the year of Our Lord abovesaid

BRIDSTOW

306   The parishioners say that a certain Gruffudd Sawyer <*he lives at Madley*> and Margaret Taelour of Madley have had a clandestine marriage between them in the church of Madley conducted by the vicar there, without letters from Gruffudd's parish priest and without the banns being given out in Bridstow church, Maiota, daughter of William Taelour, Gruffudd's lawful wife, being alive, as is believed.

SELLACK

307   The parishioners say that the parishioners of Sellack living at Little Dewchurch and at Coombe ought to visit the mother church of Sellack once in the year, that is, on the feast of St Tysilio, patron of the same church, and to make an offering there on that day, and they do not. <*warned that they must do under penalty of excommunication*>[1]

308   Next, that they refuse to contribute their share to the upkeep of the fence of the churchyard of Sellack etc.

309   Next, the parishioners of Sellack living at Hendre ought to contribute to the reconstruction of the fence of the churchyard, but they do not do so. <*suspended and cited again*>

310   Next, the parishioners of Sellack at Biddlestone ought to do the same and do not.

311   Next, that Wilkok Owein of Tretire withholds the parish rights of the church of Sellack and ought to [contribute to] the reconstruction of the fence of the churchyard, and does not do so. <*suspended and cited*>

312   Next, that the font is not locked.

313   Next, that the churchyard is not fenced, by the fault of the parishioners. They are ordered to have it put right by Michaelmas next, <*under penalty of 40 shillings*>.

---

[1]   Applies to entries **307–10**.

[f. 7]

Capyll Regis

314 Parochiani dicunt quod cimiterium non est clausum in defectu parochi-anorum. <injunctum est parochianis reformari facere defectus clausure huius-modi citra festum Sancti Michelis proximum futurum; sub pena xl s>

Henllan

315 Parochiani dicunt quod cancellus patitur defectum in tectura muris et vitro fenestrarum in defectu rectoris.

316 Item quod Jankyn ap Ieuan alias Wlan <non noscuntur tales> solutus adulteratur cum Juliana uxore Ricardi Blakney et continuarunt peccatum vij annis.

317 Item dicunt quod dominus Matheus capellanus parochialis ibidem rec-usavit[1] ministrare sepulturam Johanne filie Davy Godemon defuncte sine causa justa et corpus eiusdem dimisit inhumatum per diem et noctem. <dimissus est>

318 Item[2]

Pennkoet

319 Parochiani dicunt [quod] David Wille <infirmus est> subtrahit iiij d debi-tos singulis annis pro quodam prato quod ipse tenet ad sustentationem luminis ante ymaginem crucifixi et subtraxit ix annis elapsis.

320 Item quod idem David executor Hugonis filii sui tenetur pro eodem defuncto ad opus ecclesie in xvj d quos solvere recusat.

Martynstowe

321 Parochiani dicunt quod omnia sunt bene ibidem.

Pyterstowe

322 Parochiani dicunt quod omnia sunt bene ibidem.

Foy

323 Parochiani dicunt quod Ieuan Schyryton <apud Mordeford> et Cecilia Taelour alias correcti sunt per commissarium generalem et abjuraverunt et hiis non obstantibus continuant peccatum et quod non fecerunt penitenciam alias per eundum commissarium eis injunctam.

324 Item quod cimiterium non est clausum in defectu vicarii. <negat, dimissus est>

325 Item[3]

---

[1]   Followed by *sepulturam*, struck through.
[2]   Unfinished.
[3]   Unfinished.

[f. 7]

KING'S CAPLE

314 The parishioners say that the churchyard is not fenced, by the fault of the parishioners. <*the parishioners are ordered to have this defect in the fence put right by Michaelmas next, under penalty of 40 shillings*>.

HENTLAND

315 The parishioners say that the chancel is defective in its roof, walls, and the glass of the windows, by the fault of the rector.

316 Next, that Jankin ap Ieuan otherwise Wlan[1] <*they do not know any such person*>, a single man, commits adultery with Julian, wife of Richard Blakney, and they have continued the sin for seven years.

317 Next, they say that Sir Matthew, parish chaplain there, refused without just cause to conduct the burial of Joan, the deceased daughter of Davy Godemon, and left her body unburied for a day and a night. <*he is dismissed*>

318 Next, [*not completed*]

PENCOYD

319 The parishioners say David Wille <*he is sick*> withholds 4 pence, due every year for a certain meadow that he holds towards the upkeep of the light before the image of the crucifixion, and has withheld it for nine years past.

320 Next, that the same David, the executor of Hugh, his son, owes on behalf of the same deceased 16 pence for the benefit of the church, which he refuses to pay.

MARSTOW

321 The parishioners say that all things are well there.

PETERSTOW

322 The parishioners say that all things are well there.

FOY

323 The parishioners say that Ieuan Schyryton <*at Mordiford*> and Cecily Taelour were previously corrected by the commissary general and they abjured, but nevertheless they have continued the sin and have not done the penance previously imposed on them by the same commissary.

324 Next, that the churchyard is not fenced, by the fault of the vicar. <*he denies, he is dismissed*>

325 Next, [*not completed*]

---

[1] Possibly for *Wlân*, wool.

Llangaran <Irch'>[1]

326   Parochiani dicunt quod duo calices de ecclesia sunt perditi in defectu domini Eynon capellani parochialis ibidem. <prosequantur parochiani>

327   Item quod idem dominus Eynon est vicarius de Neweton habens curam animarum ibidem et deservit in utraque ecclesia celebrando bis in die. <consulatur dominus super hoc>

328   Item quod Johanna uxor David Lloyt adulteratur cum Ieuan Martyn conjugato et cum Nicholao Langeston <purget se> conjugato. <Ieuan comparet, negat; purgavit se>

Ross. Visitatio facta ibidem die martis xv die mensis Maii anno Domini ut supra

329   Eisdem die et loco inhibitum est domino <auctoritate>[2] curie Cantuar' ne aliquid attemptaret contra Johannem Fyssher alias excommunicatum et[3] pro sic excommunicato publice denunciatum.

Aston

330   Parochiani dicunt quod rector non residet et quod nescitur ubi moratur; aliter omnia bene ibidem.

Ross

331   Parochiani dicunt quod omnia bene ibidem.

332   Accusatores[4] dicunt quod Thomas Berwe fornicatur cum Alicia Bryngwyn. <ambo comparent, fatentur, abjurant, fustigentur ter circa ecclesiam parochialem in forma penitencie>

333   Item quod Willelmus Chiltenham fornicatur cum Elena Wade. <citentur ad proximam quia vir absens, mulier infirma>

334   Item quod[5] Margareta[6] <Rys> quam tenet Tryhayarn ap Ieuan Whith. <suspensus; comparet; mulier fatetur, dimissa est>

335   Item quod Willelmus Schorn fornicatur cum Agnete filia Hugonis Taelour. <suspensa; vir comparet, fatetur, abjurat, jejunet in pane et aqua omni feria vj per annum>

336   Item quod Thomas Smyth fornicatur cum eadem Agnete. <vir purgavit se>

337   Item quod Agnes Tryg <suspensa> nuper fornicata est cum Willelmo Grange nuper defuncto.

---

[1]   Possibly added on account of its status as a chapel of Lugwardine.
[2]   Replacing *pro parte*, struck through.
[3]   *et* repeated in error.
[4]   Continues on the same line as **331**.
[5]   Followed by *Ieuan Goch Sawyer* <suspensus> *fornicatur cum*, struck through. Cf. **339**.
[6]   <*suspensa*> interlined and struck through.

LLANGARRON <*Archenfield*>

326 The parishioners say that two chalices belonging to the church are lost, by the fault of Sir Einion, the parish chaplain there. <*let the parishioners prosecute*>

327 Next, that the same Sir Einion is vicar of Welsh Newton, having the cure of souls there, and he serves in each church, celebrating twice in a day. <*his lordship is consulted about this*>

328 Next, that Joan, wife of David Lloyt, commits adultery with Ieuan Martyn, a married man, and with Nicholas Langeston <*to purge himself*>, a married man. <*Ieuan appears, denies; he has purged himself*>

Ross-on-Wye. Visitation made there on Tuesday, 15 May, in the year of Our Lord as above

329 On this day and at this place his lordship was inhibited, on the authority of the court of Canterbury, from taking any action against John Fyssher, previously excommunicated and as an excommunicate publicly denounced.

ASTON INGHAM

330 The parishioners say that the rector does not reside, and it is not known where he lives; otherwise all is well there.

ROSS-ON-WYE

331 The parishioners say that all is well there.

332 The accusers say that Thomas Berwe fornicates with Alice Bryngwyn. <*both appear, admit, abjure, to be beaten three times around the parish church in penitential form*>

333 Next, that William Chiltenham fornicates with Helen Wade. <*to be cited to the next because the man absent; the woman sick*>

334 Next, that Margaret <*Rhys*> whom Trahaearn ap Ieuan Whith[1] keeps. <*suspended; appears; the woman admits, she is dismissed*>

335 Next, that William Schorn fornicates with Agnes, daughter of Hugh Tae-lour. <*suspended; the man appears, admits, abjures, to fast on bread and water every Friday throughout the year*>

336 Next, that Thomas Smyth fornicates with the same Agnes. <*the man has purged himself*>

337 Next, that Agnes Tryg <*suspended*> lately fornicated with William Grange, recently dead.

---

[1] Possibly for *chwith*, left-handed.

338   Item quod Johannes Dawe <suspensus> fornicatur cum Margareta Smyth. <suspensa; conjuges sunt et vir purgavit usque ad solempnizationem et dimissi[1] sunt ab instancia officii etcetera> [*in margin*] <dimissi>

339   <Ieuan Gogh sawyer fornicatur cum Margareta <quam tenet>.[2] Ambo suspensi; non sunt citati>

[Lint]on[3]

340   Parochiani dicunt quod cancellus est defectius in tectura et est ita obscurus et tenebrosus quod presbiter celebrare non potest in eodem sine lumine candele <in defectu rectoris; sequestrati sunt fructus>

341   [Item] dicunt quod Johannes Huges <suspensus> tenetur solvere ij d annuatim ad sustentationem torcisiorum ad elevationem [corporis] Christi illuminandorum quos subtrahit et subtraxit viij annis et ultra. <prosequantur parochiani; postea habitis probationibus ... [condem]natus est et injunctum est eidem ad satisfaciendum citra festum Natalis Domini sub pena xx s vel etcetera>

342   [Item quod] campanile est defectius in tectura.

[f. 7v]

Brompton

343   <Parochiani dicunt quod omnia bene ibidem>[4]

Weston

344   Parochiani dicunt quod omnia bene sunt.

Bykenore English. Visitatio facta ibidem die mercurii xvj mensis Maii anno Domini supradicto

[Bykenore English]

345   Parochiani ibidem dicunt quod dominus Johannes Schorn nunc rector de Walish Bykenor quando fuit capellanus parochialis de Bykenor English asportavit de ecclesia de Bykenor English duas casulas <de serico> videlicet unam rubeam et aliam albam cum uno superpellicio novo in magnum dampnum parochianorum.

346   <Dominus capellanus parochialis ibidem non comparet; suspensus a celebratione divinorum>

347   Item dicunt quod Alexander Pullesdon injuste detinet de bonis ecclesie iiij s quod recusat restituere. <comparet, negat, prosequantur parochiani si velint>

[1]   Followed, at the beginning of a line, by *Item*, struck through.
[2]   Replacing *Rys*, struck through; the whole entry inserted. Cf. **334**.
[3]   The bottom left-hand corner of this page has perished.
[4]   The entry inserted at the head of the page.

338 Next, that John Dawe <*suspended*> fornicates with Margaret Smyth. <*suspended; they are married, and the man has purged himself up to the solemnisation and they are dismissed at the instance of the official etc.*> [*in margin*]: <*dismissed*>

339 <*Ieuan Gogh, sawyer, fornicates with Margaret whom he keeps; both suspended, they are not cited*>

LINTON[1]

340 The parishioners say that the chancel is defective in its roof and is so dark and gloomy that the priest cannot celebrate in it without the light of a candle <*by the fault of the rector; the revenues are sequestrated*>.

341 Next, they say that John Huges <*suspended*> ought to pay 2 pence annually to the upkeep of the torches that light the elevation of the Body of Christ, which he witholds and has withheld eight years and more. <*let the parishioners prosecute; later, having proofs ... he is sentenced and ordered to pay before Christmas, under penalty of 20 shillings or etc.*>

342 Next, that the bell-tower is defective in its roof.

[f. 7v]

BRAMPTON ABBOTTS

343 <*The parishioners say that all is well there*>

WESTON-UNDER-PENYARD

344 The parishioners say that all things are well.

English Bicknor. Visitation made there on Wednesday, 16 May, in the year of Our Lord abovesaid

[ENGLISH BICKNOR]

345 The parishioners there say that Sir John Schorn, now the rector of Welsh Bicknor, when he was parish chaplain of English Bicknor carried off from the church of English Bicknor two <*silk*> chasubles, one red and one white, with a new surplice, to the great loss of the parishioners.

346 <*the parish chaplain there does not appear; suspended from celebrating divine services*>

347 Next, they say that Alexander Pullesdon wrongfully detains 4 shillings from the goods of the church, which he refuses to restore. <*appears, denies, the parishioners to prosecute if they wish*>

---

[1] The identification based partly on the presence of a tower of the late fourteenth century: Alan Brooks and Nikolaus Pevsner, *Herefordshire* (London, 2012), 470.

348 Item dicunt quod Jak Nychol absentat se ab ecclesia et servicio divino die-bus dominicis et festivis per annum et quod recusat contribuere ad reparationem ecclesie, campanilis et cimiterii et etiam subtrahit jura parochialia etcetera.

349 Item Thomas Mychel est communis operarius diebus dominicis et festivis et absentat se ab ecclesia. <suspensus>

Newelond. Visitatio facta ibidem die jovis xvij mensis Maii anno Domini supradicto

[Newelond]

350 Episcopus Landaven' rector ibidem.

Dominus Ricardus Peer vicarius ibidem. <exhibet>

Dominus Nicholaus Mede capellanus. <exhibet>

Dominus Johannes Fowyer <non habet litteras ordinum, ymmo refert se ad registrum domini Johannis Trillek>

<Dominus Willelmus Davy exhibet>

351 [*in margin*] Parochiani[1]

Willelmus Courte, Jankyn Ely, Thomas Ely, Willelmus Robert, Willelmus Teer, Jak Burych, Willelmus Rolffe, Jak Watkyns, Harry Norton, Jankyn Nor-ton, Wate of Okel, Willelmus Brute, <Philippus Mychel, Rogerus Bollynghop', Thomas Druwe>.

[*in margin*] Accusatores

352 Parochiani dicunt quod dominus Walterus Hadyrley de Newelond capel-lanus incontinens est cum Johanna Sarney de Newelond conjugata. <ambo pur-garunt se apud Monemuth>

Staunton

353 Parochiani dicunt quod Ricardus Morys fecit matrimoniam solempnizari inter se et Matildam Flessher quam tenet pro uxore, superstite quadam Agnete Morys uxore sua legitima, per quendam capellanum de Wallia[2] in ecclesia de Saunton[3] sine licencia curati ibidem. <dimissi sunt quia non est verum quod sibi imponitur prout probationibus constat>

354 Item quod Thomas Smyth <suspensus> ammovit uxorem suam legiti-mam a sua cohabitatione injuste denegando eidem victum et vestitum ac alia jura conjugalia et devastat bona communia[4] etcetera.

355 Item[5]

---

[1] The names are in a single column but bracketed together.
[2] Followed by *sine*, struck through.
[3] Recte *Staunton*.
[4] Followed by *C*, struck through.
[5] Unfinished.

348 Next, they say that Jack Nychol absents himself from church and divine service on Sundays and feast days throughout the year, and that he refuses to contribute to the repair of the church, the bell-tower, and the churchyard, and also withholds the parochial rights etc.

349 Next, Thomas Mychel is a habitual worker on Sundays and feast days and absents himself from church. *<suspended>*

Newland. Visitation made there on Thursday, 17 May, in the year of Our Lord abovesaid

[NEWLAND]

350 The bishop of Llandaff, the rector there.

Sir Richard Peer, vicar there. *<exhibits>*

Sir Nicholas Mede, chaplain. *<exhibits>*

Sir John Fowyer *<does not have letters of ordination but rather refers himself to the register of his lordship, John Trillek>*

<Sir William Davy; exhibits>

351 [*in margin*]: The parishioners

William Courte, Jankin Ely, Thomas Ely, William Robert, William Teer, Jack Burych, William Rolffe, Jack Watkyns, Harry Norton, Jankin Norton, Wate of Okel, William Brute, *<Philip Mychel, Roger Bollynghop, Thomas Druwe>*.

[*in margin*]: The accusers

352 The parishioners say that Sir Walter Hadyrley of Newland, chaplain, is incontinent with Joan Sarney of Newland, a married woman. *<they have both purged themselves at Monmouth>*

STAUNTON

353 The parishioners say that Richard Morys had a marriage solemnised between himself and Maud Flessher, whom he keeps as a wife, by a certain chaplain from Wales in Staunton church without the leave of the parish priest there, a certain Agnes Morys, his lawful wife, being still alive. *<they are dismissed because the charge against them is not true, as is clear from the proofs>*

354 Next, that Thomas Smyth *<suspended>* wrongfully removed his lawful wife from their home, denying her food and clothing and other conjugal rights, and wasted their common possessions etc.

355 Next, [*not completed*]

Newelond

356   Parochiani dicunt quod cancellus est defectius in selura in defectu rectoris et vicarii.

357   Item quod fenestra cancelli patitur defectum in vitro in defectu eorundem.

358   Item quod rector tenetur invenire unum capellanum ad celebrandum pro domino rege et ... ... [1] in ecclesia de Newelond imperpetuum nec facit et subtraxit huiusmodi capellanum a festo Sancti M[ichelis] ... ...

[f. 8]

359   Item quod rector tenetur invenire unum portiforium in ecclesia ad deserviendum Deo et ecclesie quod non facit.

360   Item quod quidam Johannes Duglace <suspensus> et Jak Danger[2] absentant se ab ecclesia diebus dominicis et festivis. <Jak comparet; correctus est>

361   Item quod Johannes Haydon <suspensus> conjugatus adulteratur cum Maiota Dolle.[3] <mulier comparet, negat, purget se coram vicario cum v^{ta} manu; vir comparet Hereford', fatetur, abjurat, fustigetur ter, difertur super gesturam>

362   Item quod Philippus Denys fornicatur cum Maiota Blakemon <suspensa> quam alias abjuravit. <vir comparet, negat, purget se; purgavit se>

363   Item quod Marcus of Ely <suspensus> fornicatur cum Alicia Duy. <suspensa>

364   [*in margin*] <Ross> Item quod[4]

Tudenham et Langaute <Foresta>. Visitatio facta ibidem die veneris xviij mensis Maii anno Domini supradicto

[Tudenham]

365   Parochiani dicunt quod cancellus est ruinosus et defectius in tectura selura muris et fenestris in defectu rectoris et vicarii.

366   Item quod domus rectoris sunt prostrate ad terram in defectu rectoris.

367   Item quod Thomas Amney <suspensus; excommunicatus> nuper custos bonorum ecclesie injuste detinet de huiusmodi bonis vj s viij d quos dominus Galfridus Longhop legavit ad sustentationem torticiorum accendendorum ad elevationem corporis Christi et etiam detinet incrementum huius pecunie etcetera.

---

[1]   The bottom right-hand corner of this page is torn away.
[2]   Followed by *c[omparet]*, struck through.
[3]   Followed by *suspensa* deleted.
[4]   Unfinished.

NEWLAND

356   The parishioners say that the chancel is defective in its ceiling, by the fault of the rector and of the vicar.

357   Next, that a window of the chancel is defective in its glass, by the fault of the same people.

358   Next, that the rector ought to provide a chaplain to celebrate for the lord king and ... ... in the church of Newland in perpetuity and does not do so, and he has withheld this chaplain since Michaelmas ... ...

[f. 8]

359   Next, that the rector ought to provide a breviary in the church, to serve God and the church, which he does not do.

360   Next, that a certain John Duglace <*suspended*> and a certain Jack Danger absent themselves from church on Sundays and feast days. <*Jack appears, he is corrected*>

361   Next, that John Haydon <*suspended*>, a married man, commits adultery with Maiota Dolle. <*the woman appears, denies, to purge herself before the vicar with five hands; the man appears at Hereford, admits, abjures, to be beaten three times; deferred on [good] behaviour*>

362   Next, that Philip Denys fornicates with Maiota Blakemon <*suspended*> whom previously he abjured. <*the man appears, denies, to purge himself; he has purged himself*>

363   Next, that Mark of Ely <*suspended*> fornicates with Alice Duy <*suspended*>.

364   [*in margin*]: <*Ross*> Next, that [*not completed*]

Tidenham and Lancaut <*Forest*>. Visitation made there on Friday, 18 May, in the year of Our Lord abovesaid

[TIDENHAM AND LANCAUT]

365   The parishioners say that the chancel is in a ruinous state and defective in its roof, ceiling, walls, and windows, by the fault of the rector and the vicar.

366   Next, that the rector's buildings have collapsed to the ground, by the fault of the rector.

367   Next, that Thomas Amney <*suspended; excommunicated*>, lately warden of the goods of the church, wrongfully detains from the church's goods 6 shillings and 8 pence that Sir Geoffrey Longhop bequeathed for the upkeep of the torches that are lit at the elevation of the Body of Christ etc., and he also retains the interest on this money etc.

368 Item quod Johannes Longe <suspensus; excommunicatus> subtrahit et detinet de bonis ecclesie viij s.

369 Item quod Hik Aelward <suspensus; excommunicatus> detinet v s.

370 Item quod Willelmus Hayn <suspensus; extra> detinet ij s viij d.

371 Item quod Rogerus Rype <suspensus; excommunicatus> detinet xviij d.

372 Item quod quidam Stephanus Scheppert parochianus de Tudenham decessit intestatus et quod quidam dominus Willelmus[1] Broun capellanus nuper defunctus fabricavit unum testamentum in quo testamento ordinavit Johannem Croke de Bedesley executorem dicti defuncti et seipsum supervisorem; cuius falsi testamenti pretextu dictus Johannes Croke ministravit bona dicti defuncti. <inquirat commissarius generalis>

373 Dominus Johannes capellanus ibidem est apostaticus ordinis predicatorum <et vocatur frater Johannes Brugg'>. [*in margin*] <Nota>

374 Item quod Willelmus Croke <extra> tenetur invenire unam lampadem ardentem die noctuque coram ymagine crucifixi in ecclesia pro quibusdam terris quas tenet in parochia ibidem quod non facit <et subtractum est xx annis elapsis; prosequantur parochiani>

375 Item dicunt quod Isabella Montayn <suspensa; excommunicata> denegat opera conigalia[2] Willelmo Montayn marito suo et male tractat eundem.

376 Item quod Jak Wodeman <suspensus; excommunicatus> de parochia de Wolaston subtrahit ij s viij d ad opus ecclesie de Langaot ordinatos.

Wolaston et Alvynton <[Fore]sta>.[3] Visitatio facta ibidem die sabbati xix mensis Maii supradicti

[Wolaston]

377 Parochiani dicunt quod non habuerunt servicium divinum nec missas nec alia per quinque <vel sex> septimanas continuas in defectu domini Philippi tunc vicarii.

378 Item quod Johannes Raker solutus[4] fornicatur cum Johanna Walker. <ambo suspensi et citati; excommunicati>

379 Item quod fenestra cancelli capelle de Alvynton est fracta et cancellus est defectius in tectura et selura in defectu rectoris.

---

[1] Followed by *Cr*, struck through.
[2] Recte *conjugalia*.
[3] The bottom left-hand corner of this page is torn away.
[4] Preceded by *conjugatus*, struck through.

368   Next, that John Longe <*suspended; excommunicated*> withholds and detains 8 shillings from the goods of the church.

369   Next, that Hik Aelward <*suspended; excommunicated*> withholds 5 shillings.

370   Next, that William Hayn <*suspended; outside*> withholds 2 shillings and 8 pence.

371   Next, that Roger Rype <*suspended; excommunicated*> withholds 18 pence.

372   Next, that a certain Stephen Scheppert, a parishioner of Tidenham, died intestate and that a certain Sir William Broun, chaplain, lately deceased, forged a will in which he made John Croke of Beachley executor of the dead man and himself overseer, on the pretext of which false will John Croke has administered the effects of the deceased. <*the commissary general to inquire*>

373   Sir John, the chaplain there, is an apostate from the Order of Preachers <*and is called Brother John Brugg*>. [*In margin*]: <*note*>

374   Next, that William Croke <*outside*> ought to provide a lamp to burn night and day before the image of the crucifixion in the church, in respect of certain lands that he holds in the parish there, which he does not do <*and it has been withheld for the past 20 years; let the parishioners prosecute*>

375   Next, they say that Isabel Montayn <*suspended; excommunicated*> denies sexual intercourse to William Montayn, her husband, and mistreats him.

376   Next, that Jack Wodeman <*suspended; excommunicated*> of the parish of Woolaston withholds 2 shillings and 8 pence provided for the benefit of the church of Lancaut.

Woolaston and Alvington <*Forest*>. Visitation made there on Saturday, 19 May, abovesaid

[WOOLASTON]

377   The parishioners say that they did not have divine service or masses or other [ministries] for five <*or six*> weeks together, by the fault of Sir Philip, then the vicar.

378   Next, that John Raker, a single man, fornicates with Joan Walker. <*both suspended and cited; both excommunicated*>

379   Next, that a window of the chancel of the chapel of Alvington is broken and the chancel is defective in its roof and ceiling, by the fault of the rector.

380 Item dicunt quod dominus Philippus nuper vicarius venit cum[1] lumine et campana, superpellicio revestitus ut est moris, [ad visi]tandum[2] quandam Aliciam Clerk in mortis articulo constitutam cum[3] pixide vacuo sine corpore [Christi in] magnum scandalum faciendo populum adorare sacramentum ubi non erat etcetera. <dimissus est>

[f. 8v]

381 Item quod Robyn[4] Raglyn <suspensus; excommunicatus> percussit violenter cum pugno quendam Johannem Stywart in ecclesia ante maius altare.

382 Item quod Rogerus Saweterer <non citatus> fornicatur cum Johanna Baker. <suspensa; matrimonium est solempnizatum et dimissi sunt> [*in margin*] <dimissi>

383 Item quod Annot Lotmon suscitat dissensiones[5] inter curatum, <videlicet [*blank*]> et parochianos de Wolaston. <citetur ad proximam>

384 Item dicunt quod aliquando erat post nonam antequam finiatur missa diebus dominicis et festivis.

385 Item dicunt quod dominus Philippus nuper vicarius, nunc capellanus parochialis, non stat in pulpito set in cancello diebus dominicis[6] ad publicandum festa et vigilias ac alia ficienda ut est moris. <promisit facere de cetero>

386 Item dicunt quod prefatus dominus Philippus maliciose sine auctoritate alicuius superioris recusavit ministrare officium purificationis cuidam Annot Howel post partum, asserendo eam suspensam per commissarium generalem quod non fuit verum, et quod amici dicte mulieris petierunt ab eo an habuit ad hoc mandatum, nec aliquod voluit ostendere. <dicit quod habuit mandatum commissarii etcetera>

387 Item quod Nicholaus Wysbage <extra> fornicatur cum Ibel Conyng. <suspensa,[7] citata>

388 Item dicunt quod dominus Willelmus Clyffe vicarius ibidem absentat se a vicaria sua non obstante juramento suo etcetera. <permutavit>

389 Item[8]

---

[1]   Followed by *c*, struck through.
[2]   The bottom left-hand corner of this page is torn away, though the passage was apparently all seen or conjectured by Bannister.
[3]   Followed by *prox'*, struck through.
[4]   Preceded by *Johannes*, struck through.
[5]   Followed by *disc*, struck through.
[6]   Followed by *et festivis*, struck through.
[7]   Followed by *excommunicata*, deleted.
[8]   Unfinished.

380   Next, they say that Sir Philip, the late vicar, came with a light and a bell, dressed in a surplice, as is the practice, when visiting a certain Alice Clerk who was on the point of death, with an empty pyx, without the Body of Christ, to the great scandal, making the people adore the sacrament that was not present etc. <*he is dismissed*>

[f. 8v]

381   Next, that Robin Raglyn <*suspended; excommunicated*> struck a certain John Stywart violently with his fist in church before the high altar.

382   Next, that Roger Saweterer <*not cited*> fornicates with Joan Baker. <*suspended; the marriage is solemnised and they are dismissed*> [*In margin*]: <*dismissed*>

383   Next, that Annot Lotmon provokes disagreements between the parish priest, <*that is to say [blank]*>, and the parishioners of Woolaston. <*cite to the next*>

384   Next, they say that sometimes it has been after midday before mass was concluded on Sundays and feast days.

385   Next, they say that Sir Philip, the late vicar, now the parish chaplain, does not stand in the pulpit but in the chancel on Sundays to announce forthcoming feasts and vigils and other matters, as is customary. <*he promises to do so in future*>

386   Next, they say that the same Sir Philip maliciously and without the authority of any superior has refused to administer the office of purification to a certain Annot Howel after childbirth, alleging that she has been suspended by the commissary general, which was not true; and that the friends of this woman asked him whether he had a mandate for this, but he would not show anything. <*he says that he had a mandate of the commissary etc.*>

387   Next, that Nicholas Wysbage <*outside*> fornicates with Isabel Conyng <*suspended, cited*>.

388   Next, they say that Sir William Clyffe, the vicar there, absents himself from his vicarage despite his oath etc. <*he has exchanged*>

389   Next, [*not completed*]

Lydeney. Visitatio facta ibidem die dominica videlicet xx mensis Maii anno ut supra

[Lydeney]

390   Parochiani dicunt quod dominus David capellanus de Alvynton incontinens est cum Johanna Baker. <vir comparet, negat, purget se cum vj^{ta} manu>

391   Item quod Jankyn Rude <extra> solutus adulteratur cum Johanna Duffyll conjugata. <mulier comparet, fatetur, abjurat, fustigetur ter per forum et ter circa ecclesiam et jejunet omni feria vj per vij annos>

392   Item quod Harry Frunde conjugatus et Ibel Barne sunt graviter diffamati super adulterio. <vir non audet accedere quia indictatus, mulier comparet, negat, purget se coram curato cum v^{ta} manu>

393   Item quod Willelmus Scheppert adulteratur cum Ela Talbote ambo conjugati. <purgaverunt se coram commissario generali a tempore correctionis>

Sayn Brevoll

394[1]   Parochiani dicunt quod cancellus est defectius in tectura selura et vitro fenestrarum et quod ostium est fractum in defectu rectorum.

395   Item quod rectores tenentur invenire unam lampadem ardentem coram ymagine Beate Virginis diebus dominicis et festivis ac ferialibus dum missa celebratur ibidem nec faciunt et subtractum est xxx annis. <prosequantur parochiani>

396   Item quod rectores tenentur invenire unum bussellum frumenti pro pane fiendo ad celebrandum annuatim quod non faciunt nec fecerunt iij^{bus} annis elapsis. <prosequantur ut supra>

397   Item quod vestimenta et linthiamina altaris sunt immunda et inhonesta in defectu parochianorum eo quod non habent custodes deputatos etcetera.

398   Item dicunt quod non habent portiforium ad deserviendum Deo et ecclesie in defectu rectorum.

399   Item quod Rogerus Johenes <suspensus> percussit violenter Thomam Folyot cum baculo sine culpa <in cimiterio>.

400   <Item quod Phylipot Ryve fornicatur cum Alson Clyfdon> <suspensa; citati>

401[2]   Dicunt quod Willelmus Wethy adulteratur cum Agnete Jones ambo conjugati.

Huwelsfeld

402   Parochiani dicunt quod dominus Thomas Orchard est ebriosus et exercet tabernas continue contra honestatem clericorum nec facit servicium divinum debite; aliter omnia bene. <comparet, negat, purget se>

---

[1]   Entry **401** is inserted above this entry for lack of room at the end.
[2]   Inserted above **394** for lack of room here.

Lydney. Visitation made there on Sunday, 20 May, in the year as above

[LYDNEY]

390 The parishioners say that Sir David, chaplain of Alvington, is incontinent with Joan Baker. *<the man appears, denies, to purge himself with six hands>*

391 Next, that Jankin Rude *<outside>*, a single man, commits adultery with Joan Duffyll, a married woman. *<the woman appears, admits, abjures, to be beaten three times through the marketplace and three times around the church and to fast every Friday for seven years>*

392 Next, that Harry Frunde, a married man, and Isabel Barne are gravely defamed over adultery. *<the man does not dare to come near because he is indicted; the woman appears, denies, to purge herself before the parish priest with five hands>*

393 Next, that William Scheppert commits adultery with Ela Talbote, both married. *<they have purged themselves before the commissary general since the time of correction>*

ST BRIAVELS

394 The parishioners say that the chancel is defective in its roof, ceiling, and the glass of the windows and that the chancel door is broken, by the fault of the rectors.

395 Next, that the rectors ought to provide a lamp to burn before the image of the Blessed Virgin on Sundays, feast days, and on weekdays while the mass is celebrated there, but they do not do so, and it has been withheld for 30 years. *<let the parishioners prosecute>*

396 Next, that the rectors ought to provide a bushel of corn for making the bread for the celebration [of communion] annually, which they do not do nor have done for the past three years. *<let them prosecute as above>*

397 Next, that the vestments and the altar cloths are dirty and unsightly, by the fault of the parishioners because they do not have appointed custodians etc.

398 Next, they say that they do not have a breviary to serve God and the church, by the fault of the rectors.

399 Next, that Roger Johenes *<suspended>* violently struck Thomas Folyot with a staff, without cause, *<in the churchyard>*.

400 *<Next, that Philipot Ryve fornicates with Alison Clyfdon; suspended; they are cited>*

401 They say that William Wethy commits adultery with Agnes Jones, both married.

HEWELSFIELD

402 The parishioners say that Sir Thomas Orchard is a drunkard and he frequents taverns incessantly, contrary to the dignity of the clergy, and he does not take divine service properly; otherwise all is well. *<he appears, denies, to purge himself>*

Aur. Visita facta ibidem die lune xxj mensis Maii anno Domini ut supra

[Aur]

403   Parochiani dicunt quod cancellus est defectius in tectura selura et vitro in defectu rectoris. Injunctum est procuratori rectoris tunc ibidem presenti quod reformentur omnes defectus sub pena xl s citra festum Sancti Michelis archangeli. <est in reparando>

404   Item dicunt quod rector tenetur invenire unam lampadem ardentem coram summo altari die noctuque quod non facit. <pro[sequantur parochiani]>[1]

[*in margin*] Accusatores

405   Item quod Thomas Mason conjugatus adulteratur cum Johanna Mason quam tenet conjugata. <ambo suspensi et citentur; conjuges sunt et dimissi>

406   Item dicunt quod dominus Rogerus Mury capellanus de Lydeney incontinens est cum Juliana Webbe. <comparet, negat, purgavit se> [*in margin*] <Lydeney>

[f. 9]
Wesbury. Visitatio facta ibidem die martis xxij die mensis Maii etcetera

Blechedon

407   Parochiani dicunt quod omnia sunt bene.

Abenhale

408   Parochiani dicunt quod omnia bene ibidem.

Hunteley

409   Parochiani dicunt quod omnia sunt bene ibidem.

410[2]   <Accusatores dicunt quod dominus Willelmus Herte rector ibidem incontinens est cum Issabella quam tenet in domo sua. Vir comparet, negat, abjurat peccatum et locum suspectum, purget se vj^{ta} manu coram commissario, mulier citata ad proximam; purgavit se et dimissus est>

Magna Deen

411   Parochiani dicunt quod omnia sunt bene ibidem. <procurator juravit[3] quod non auderet citare parochianos etcetera>

412   Johannes Barne conjugatus adulteratur cum <Agnete>[4] Fyssher conjugata. <vir ad purgandum coram commissario[5] generali ibidem; purgavit se legitime>

---

[1]   The bottom right-hand corner of this page is torn away.
[2]   Follows **409** on the same line.
[3]   Followed by *de*, struck through.
[4]   Replacing *Maiota*, struck through.
[5]   Followed by *in prox'*, struck through.

Awre. Visitation made there on Monday, 21 May, in the year of Our Lord as above

[AWRE]

403   The parishioners say that the chancel is defective in its roof, ceiling, and glass, by the fault of the rector. The rector's proctor, then present there, is ordered that all the defects should be put right before Michaelmas, under penalty of 40 shillings. <*it is under repair*>

404   Next, they say that the rector ought to provide a lamp burning before the high altar day and night, which he does not do. <*let the parishioners prosecute*>

[*in margin*]: Accusers

405   Next, that Thomas Mason, a married man, commits adultery with Joan Mason whom he keeps, a married woman. <*both suspended and to be cited; they are married and are dismissed*>

406   Next, they say that Sir Roger Mury, chaplain of Lydney, is incontinent with Julian Webbe. <*he appears, denies, he has purged himself*> [*in margin*]: <*Lydney*>

[f. 9]
Westbury-on-Severn. Visitation made there on Tuesday, 22 May, etc.

BLAISDON

407   The parishioners say that all things are well.

ABENHALL

408   The parishioners say that all is well there.

HUNTLEY

409   The parishioners say that all things are well there.

410   <*The accusers say that Sir William Herte, the rector there, is incontinent with Isabel, whom he keeps in his house; the man appears, denies, abjures the sin and the suspicious circumstances, to purge himself with six hands before the commissary; the woman cited to the next; he has purged himself and is dismissed*>

MITCHELDEAN

411   The parishioners say that all things are well there. <*the proctor has sworn that he dare not cite the parishioners etc.*>

412   John Barne, a married man, commits adultery with Agnes Fyssher, a married woman. <*the man to purge before the commissary general there; he has purged himself lawfully*>

413 [*in margin*] <significatur>

Item quod Johannes Carles fuit et est excommunicatus per j quarterium anni ultimo preteriti et non dum est absolutus. <significatur>

414 Item quod dominus Johannes Harald capellanus incontinens est cum Margareta Conyng.

Longhop

415 Parochiani dicunt quod omnia sunt bene ibidem.

416 Harriot Flesher fornicatur cum Alicia Fox. <suspensa; vir comparet, fatetur,[1] abjurat, fustigetur ter>

Newenham et Lytell Deen

417 Parochiani dicunt quod omnia bene ibidem <excepto quod Ricardus Malot fornicatur cum Margareta Clerkes; suspensa; vir comparet, fatetur,[2] excommunicatus propter manifestam contumaciam>

418 <Johannes Hawekyn suspensus alias, nunc quia non comparet excommunicatus est ad instanciam Johanne Wyggemor suam contumaciam accusantis; in causa matrimoniali>

Wesbury

419 Parochiani dicunt quod Johannes Alayn non recepit corpus Christi in festo Pasche tribus annis elapsis prout quilibet christianus tenetur etcetera. <correctus est et juratus de emendando se etcetera>

420 Item quod Walterus Kadyle male tractat <Ibel> uxorem suam legitimam expellendo eandem a comitancia sua et denegando eidem victum et vestitum et alia debita conigalia de[3] qua procreavit unum filium quem recusat sustentare. <difertur sub spe concordie usque ad consistorium Heref'>

421 Item quod Symond oth' Hull pari forma male tractat uxorem suam ut supra. <vir comparet, asserit se paratum ad acceptandum uxorem suam debite etcetera; ideo citetur mulier ad proximam>

422 Item quod Johannes Brasyer <suspensus> et Ibella Vyell <suspensa> uxor Willelmi Vyell publice diffamati sunt adinvicem de adulterio commisso inter eos. <vir comparet, negat, purget se cum iij^a manu, mulier purget se pari forma>

423 Item quod Walterus Wodemon fornicatur cum Juliana Arthur <suspensa> ambo soluti. <vir comparet, negat post correctionem, purget se cum v^{ta} manu coram vicario>

424 Item quod Robyn oth' Hulle solutus adulteratur cum Agnete <suspensa> uxore Jakes Smyth conjugata. <vir comparet, negat, purget se proxima dominica cum vj^{ta} manu>

---

[1] Followed by *excommunicatus*, struck through.
[2] Followed by *abjurat*, struck through.
[3] Followed by *quam*, struck through.

413 [*in margin*]: <*he is signified*>

Next, that John Carles was and is excommunicated for one quarter of last year and is not yet absolved. <*he is signified*>

414 Next, that Sir John Harald, chaplain, is incontinent with Margaret Conyng.

LONGHOPE

415 The parishioners say that all things are well there.

416 Harriot Flesher fornicates with Alice Fox. <*suspended; the man appears, admits, abjures, to be beaten three times*>

NEWNHAM AND LITTLE DEAN

417 The parishioners say that all is well there <*except that Richard Malot fornicates with Margaret Clerkes; suspended; the man appears, admits, excommunicated because of manifest contumacy*>

418 <*John Hawekyn previously suspended, now because he does not appear is excommunicated at the instance of Joan Wyggemor, who accused him of contumacy; in a matrimonial case*>

WESTBURY-ON-SEVERN

419 The parishioners say that John Alayn has not received the Body of Christ on Easter Sunday for the past three years, as every Christian ought to etc. <*corrected and sworn to amend etc.*>

420 Next, that Walter Kadyle mistreats <*Isabel*>, his lawful wife, expelling her from his company and denying her food and clothing and other conjugal dues, by whom he fathered a son whom he refuses to support. <*it is deferred in the hope of conciliation to the consistory at Hereford*>

421 Next, that Symond oth' Hull in the same way mistreats his wife as above. <*the man appears, asserts he is ready to accept his wife properly etc., so cite the woman to the next*>

422 Next, that John Brasyer <*suspended*> and Isabel Vyell <*suspended*>, wife of William Vyell, are publicly and jointly defamed of adultery committed between them. <*the man appears, denies, to purge himself with three hands; the woman to purge herself in the same way*>

423 Next, that Walter Wodemon fornicates with Julian Arthur <*suspended*>, both single. <*the man appears, denies since correction, to purge himself with five hands before the vicar*>

424 Next, that Robin oth' Hulle, a single man, commits adultery with Agnes <*suspended*>, wife of Jakes Smyth, a married woman. <*the man appears, denies, to purge himself next Sunday with six hands*>

425   Item quod Ricardus Robyns conjugatus adulteratur cum Johanna <abs-ens est> uxore Rogeri Hikokes. <vir negat,[1] purget se coram vicario proxima dominica>

426   Item idem Ricardus committit incestum cum Elena Hotte consanguinea sua in ij° gradu. <vir negat, purget se cum iij[a] manu>

427   Item quod dominus Johannes Fawkenere monachus monasterii de Flaxley incontinens est cum Florencia Donn infra parochiam [de Ro]deford[2] commo-rante. <mulier non est citata>

428   [Item quod domin]us Johannes Carter capellanus de Parva Deen incontin-ens est cum Juliana Irych de Blechedon. <... ...[3] vir coram commissario>

[f. 9v]

429   Item quod dominus Thomas rector de Blechedon incontinens est cum Margareta Martyn uxore Johannis Martyn. <vir negat, purget se coram commis-sario generali, mulier purget se>

430   Item quod[4] Cecilia Robyns fornicata est nuper cum quodam domino Johanne Prestebur' monacho monasterii de Flaxley nuper defuncto non dum cor-recta. <vir mortuus est, mulier purgabit se coram vicario>[5]

431   Item quod dominus Willelmus at Nynde monachus incontinens est cum Elena de Pola de Blechedon alias Elena at Ʒate uxore Johannis at Ʒate. <non est citatus, ideo citetur ad proximam>

432   Item dominus Ricardus abbas de Flaxley incontinens est cum Alicia Tybur-ton uxore Colle Knafe de Lytyl Deen et continuaverunt in peccato xiiij annis. <mulier non est citata, ideo citetur ad proximam et purget se coram commissario generali>

433   Item quod Elizabeth uxor Willelmi Watkyns de Blechedon adulteratur cum eodem domino abbate. <citetur mulier ad proximam>

434   Item Johanna Gosbrok de Gloucestre soluta fornicatur cum dicto domino abbate. <mulier est extra diocesim>

435   Item Johanna Kassy uxor Walteri Kassy adulteratur cum eodem domino abbate. <mulier moratur infra scepta monasterii nec est citata, ideo citetur ad proximam>

436   Item eadem Johanna adulteratur cum domino Johanne Fawkenere mona-cho eiusdem monasterii. <ut supra proximam>

437   Item Alicia Tyburton uxor Nicholai Kolleknafe de Parva Deen adulteratur cum eodem domino Johanne monacho. <mulier non est citata, ideo citetur ad proximam>

---

[1]   Preceded by *fatetur*, struck through.
[2]   The bottom left-hand corner of the page is torn away.
[3]   The missing word(s) followed by *coram*, struck through.
[4]   Followed by *dominus*, struck through.
[5]   Preceded by *commissario*, struck through.

425   Next, that Richard Robyns, a married man, commits adultery with Joan <*she is absent*>, wife of Roger Hikokes. <*the man denies, to purge himself before the vicar next Sunday*>

426   Next, the same Richard commits incest with Helen Hotte, his blood-relative in the second degree. <*the man denies, to purge himself with three hands*>

427   Next, that Sir John Fawkenere, a monk of Flaxley monastery, is incontinent with Florence Donn, residing in the parish of Rudford. <*the woman is not cited*>

428   Next, that Sir John Carter, chaplain of Little Dean, is incontinent with Julian Irych of Blaisdon. <*... ... man before the commissary*>

[f. 9v]

429   Next, that Sir Thomas, rector of Blaisdon, is incontinent with Margaret Martyn, wife of John Martyn. <*the man denies, to purge himself before the commissary general; the woman to purge herself*>

430   Next, that Cecily Robyns lately fornicated with a certain Sir John Prestebury, a monk of Flaxley monastery lately deceased, and is not yet corrected. <*the man is dead; the woman will purge herself before the vicar*>

431   Next, that Sir William at Nynde, a monk, is incontinent with Helen de Pola of Blaisdon, otherwise Helen at Yate, wife of John at Yate. <*he is not cited, so cite to the next*>

432   Next, Sir Richard, abbot of Flaxley, is incontinent with Alice Tyburton, wife of [Nicholas][1] Colle Knafe of Little Dean, and they have continued in sin for 14 years. <*the woman is not cited, so cite to the next and to purge herself before the commissary general*>

433   Next, that Elizabeth, wife of William Watkyns of Blaisdon, commits adultery with the same lord abbot. <*cite the woman to the next*>

434   Next, Joan Gosbrok of Gloucester, a single woman, fornicates with the said lord abbot. <*the woman is outside the diocese*>

435   Next, Joan Kassy, wife of Walter Kassy, commits adultery with the same lord abbot. <*the woman lives within the monastery precinct and is not cited, so cite to the next*>

436   Next, the same Joan commits adultery with Sir John Fawkenere, a monk of the same monastery. <*as above, to the next*>

437   Next, Alice Tyburton, wife of Nicholas Kolleknafe of Little Dean, commits adultery with the same Sir John, the monk. <*the woman is not cited, so cite to the next*>

[1]   See **437**.

438   Item idem dominus Johannes monachus incontinens[1] est cum Lucia uxore Ansely Kolknafe de Parva Deen.[2]

439   Item quod Elena Byllyng fornicatur cum Waltero Hope monacho ibidem.

440   Item quod Johannes de pistrina servitor dicti abbatis adulteratur cum Johanna Cassy uxore Walteri Kassy.

441   Item Elena uxor Henrici ʒeynor de Northwode adulteratur cum dicto Waltero Hope monacho.

442   Item quod Agnes Badron uxor Reginaldi Taelour adulteratur cum domino Stephano monacho de Flaxley.

443   Item quod Johanna Rude uxor Thome Baker de Elvynton adulteratur cum Rogero Stretton monacho eiusdem monasterii.

444   Item quod Issabella Vyel uxor Willelmi Fryoll de Frodley graviter diffamatur cum Johanne Brasyour monacho eiusdem monasterii.

445   <non sunt citate mulieres, ideo citentur ad proximam>[3]

Churcham. Visitatio facta ibidem die mercurii xxiiij[4] mensis Maii anno Domini supradicto

Rodeford

446   Parochiani dicunt quod omnia bene ibidem.

Munster Worth

447   Parochiani dicunt quod Henricus Morekoce parochianus ibidem non recepit sacralia sacramentalia in ecclesia parochiali in festo Pasche nec confessus est peccata sua curato suo ut tenetur de jure semel in anno ad minus nec alibi prout scitur. <probet coram commissario et satisfaciet curato de dampnis etcetera>

448   Item quod idem Henricus subtrahit panem benedictum in cursu suo et alias oblationes et minutas decimas in magnum periculum anime sue. <negat subtractionem>

449   Item quod idem quando venit ad ecclesiam perturbat divinum officium. <negat etiam>

450   Item idem Henricus sedet in cancello invito curato suo et contra ipsius voluntatem. <inhibitum est sibi sub pena etcetera>

451   Item quod idem Henricus recusat aquam benedictam <negat> et est communis diffamator vicinorum super diversis criminibus et suscitator rixarum.[5] <negat etiam et injunctum est sibi quod non f[aciat de cetero]>[6]

---

[1]   Preceded by *adulteratur*, struck through.
[2]   **445** applies to all entries **438**–**44**.
[3]   Applies to all entries **438**–**44**.
[4]   Recte *xxiij*.
[5]   Followed by <*H juravit de parendo*>, struck through.
[6]   The bottom right-hand corner of this page is torn away.

438 Next, the same Sir John, the monk, is incontinent with Lucy, wife of Ansely Kolknafe of Little Dean.

439 Next, that Helen Byllyng fornicates with Walter Hope, a monk there.

440 Next, that John of the bakehouse, a servant of the said abbot, commits adultery with Joan Cassy, wife of Walter Kassy.

441 Next, Helen, wife of Henry Geynor of Northwode, commits adultery with the said Walter Hope, the monk.

442 Next, that Agnes Badron, wife of Reynold Taelour, commits adultery with Sir Stephen, a monk of Flaxley.

443 Next, that Joan Rude, wife of Thomas Baker of Alvington, commits adultery with Roger Stretton, a monk of the same monastery.

444 Next, that Isabel Vyel, wife of William Fryoll of Rodley, is gravely defamed with John Brasyour, a monk of the same monastery.

445 *<the women are not cited, so cite to the next>*

Churcham. Visitation made there on Wednesday, 23 May, in the year of Our Lord abovesaid

RUDFORD

446 The parishioners say that all is well there.

MINSTERWORTH

447 The parishioners say that Henry Morekoce, a parishioner there, did not receive the holy sacraments in the parish church on Easter Sunday, nor has he confessed his sins to his parish priest, as he is obliged by law to do once in a year at least, nor elsewhere, as far as is known. *<to prove before the commissary, and let him pay the parish priest for his losses etc.>*

448 Next, that the same Henry withholds the holy bread in his turn and the other offerings and small tithes, to the great danger of his soul. *<he denies withholding>*

449 Next, that when this man comes to church he disturbs the divine office. *<he denies this too>*

450 Next, the same Henry sits in the chancel, without the consent of his parish priest and against his will. *<forbidden under penalty of etc.>*

451 Next, that the same Henry refuses holy water *<he denies>* and is a habitual defamer of his neighbours over various crimes and a provoker of quarrels. *<he denies this also and is ordered not to do so in future>*

452   <Prefatus Henricus purgavit se super sibi objectis proprio juramento apud Parvam Deen et juravit ... ecclesie>

[f. 10]

Tybyrton

453   Parochiani dicunt quod Johannes Moor <de Tyberton> absentavit se a comitancia uxoris et cohabitatione uxoris sue tribus annis elapsis continue sine causa devastando bona communia et denegando eidem victum et vestitum ac alia jura conigalia et morabatur[1] apud Credenhull. <vir est extra apud Toppesley> [*in margin*] <Hereford>

454   Item quod Robertus Wynnyng nequiter et falso diffamavit dominum Walterum capellanum de Tyberton et Thomam Toky de Tyburton super homicidio propter quod iidem diffamati magnum dampnum incurrerunt. <negat diffamationem ideo probent etcetera, super quo informet se commissarius>

Churcham

455   Parochiani dicunt quod dominus Willelmus vicarius celebrat bis in die. <suspensus a celebratione>

456   Item quod dominus Walterus capellanus de Huntley incontinens est cum[2] Editha Loffe quam tenet. <vir non comparet, suspensus a celebratione divinorum, mulier suspensa>

457   <Item vicarius ibidem fornicatur cum Johanna Deny et cum Agnete Clerkes; negat quo ad primam a tempore correctionis, quo ad secundam negat, ad purgandum in proximam; vir purgavit se legitime>

Newent. Visitatio facta ibidem die jovis xxiiij mensis Maii anno Domini ut supra

Teynton

458   Parochiani dicunt quod omnia sunt bene ibidem excepto quod Jenkyn Uton senior et Johanna Tottebury uxor Willelmi Tottebury graviter sunt diffamati de adulterio commisso. <citentur ambo ad proximam>

Oxenhale

459   Parochiani dicunt quod cancellus est defectivus in muris et vitro fenestrarum in defectu parochianorum. <citentur ad proximam>

---

[1]   Corrected from *moratur* by interlineation of *ba*.
[2]   Followed by *A*, struck through.

452 *<The aforesaid Henry has purged himself in respect of the charges against him by his own oath at Little Dean and has sworn ... of the church>*

[f. 10]

TIBBERTON

453 The parishioners say that John Moor *<of Tibberton>* has, for three years past, continually absented himself from the company of his wife and from living with her, without cause, wasting their common possessions and denying her food and clothing and other conjugal rights, and he used to live at Credenhill. *<the man is outside at Tupsley>* [*in margin*]: *<Hereford>*

454 Next, that Robert Wynnyng has wickedly and falsely defamed Sir Walter, chaplain of Tibberton, and Thomas Toky of Tibberton, over a killing, because of which these men have incurred great loss. *<he denies the defamation so let them prove etc., about which the commissary to investigate>*

CHURCHAM

455 The parishioners say that Sir William, the vicar, celebrates twice in a day. *<suspended from celebration>*

456 Next, that Sir Walter, chaplain of Huntley, is incontinent with Edith Loffe whom he keeps. *<the man does not appear, suspended from the celebration of divine services; the woman suspended>*

457 *<Next, the vicar there fornicates with Joan Deny and with Agnes Clerkes; denies as to the first woman since the time of correction, he denies as to the second, to purge at the next; the man has lawfully purged himself>*

Newent. Visitation made there on Thursday, 24 May, in the year of Our Lord as above

TAYNTON

458 The parishioners say that all things are well there except that Jankin Uton the elder and Joan Tottebury, wife of William Tottebury, are gravely defamed of having committed adultery. *<to cite both to the next>*

OXENHALL

459 The parishioners say that the chancel is defective in its walls and the glass of the windows, by the fault of the parishioners. *<to cite them to the next>*

Pauntley

460   [*in margin*] \<significatum>

Parochiani dicunt quod Nicholaus Hosches in festo Pasche ultimo preterito secularibus negotiis occupatus distulit recipere sacralia sacramentalia duobus diebus
et absentat se ab ecclesia parochiali quasi per totum annum et subtrahit decimas
minutas et oblationes etcetera. \<excommunicatus est quia dixit se nolle venire>

461   Item quod Johannes Hert \<extra> non venit ad ecclesiam parochialem
diebus dominicis et festis fere per annum vix in festo Pasche. \<vir apud Newent>

462   [*in margin*] \<significatur>

Item Willelmus Carpe pari forma etcetera. \<excommunicatus quia dixit se nolle
comparere etcetera; absolutus est et dimissus>

463   Item quod babsterium¹ non \<est> seratum.

464   Item quod Johannes Compton absentat se ab ecclesia etcetera. \<citetur ad
proximam; emendabit, dimissus>

465   Item quod rector tenetur invenire duos cereos processionales in ecclesia et
non facit.²

466   Item dicunt quod mansum ecclesie est prostratum ad terram in defectu
rectoris ita quod capellanus parochialis non habet locum habitationis ibidem ad
deserviendum parochianis in necessitatis articulo. \<fructus sequestrantur, commissarius provideat in proximam de custodibus sequestratorum>

Newent

467   Parochiani³ dicunt quod cancellus est defectivus in tectura selura in
defectu rectoris. \<reparabitur>

468   Item quod aliter omnia sunt bene ibidem.

Dymmok. Visitatio facta ibidem die veneris xxv mensis Maii

Kempley

469   Parochiani dicunt quod rector subtrahit ij libras cere debitas singulis annis
ad lumen Sancti Leonardi ibidem et subtraxit decem annis elapsis. \<prosequantur
parochiani>

470   Item quod rector tenetur invenire mansum pro capellano parochiali ad
habitandum prope ecclesiam ita quod parochiani haberent recursum ad eundem
tempore necessitatis et quod domus ecclesie sunt dirute et ad terram prostrate.
\<prosequantur etiam>

471   [Ite]m⁴

---

¹   Altered from *basterium* by the interlineation of a *b*; recte *baptisterium*.
²   Followed by \<*citetur coram*>, struck through.
³   Followed by *quod*, struck through.
⁴   The bottom left-hand corner of this page is torn away, but this seems to be the only
damage to the text.

PAUNTLEY

460 [*in margin*]: <*signified*>

The parishioners say that Nicholas Hosches, last Easter Sunday, occupied with secular business, put off receiving the holy sacraments for two days, and he absents himself from the parish church for almost the whole year, and he withholds the small tithes and offerings etc. <*excommunicated because he said he would not come*>

461 Next, that John Hert <*outside*> does not come to the parish church on Sundays and feast days almost throughout the year, scarcely even on Easter Sunday. <*the man at Newent*>

462 [*in margin*]: <*he is signified*>

Next, William Cappe similarly etc. <*excommunicated because he said he would not appear etc.; he is absolved and dismissed*>

463 Next, that the font is not locked.

464 Next, that John Compton absents himself from church etc. <*cite to the next; he will amend, dismissed*>

465 Next, that the rector ought to provide two candles for processions in church and does not do so.

466 Next, they say that the church house has collapsed to the ground by the fault of the rector, so that the parish chaplain has no dwelling-place there to serve the parishioners when the need is pressing <*the revenues to be sequestrated, the commissary to make arrangements at the next for the custodians of the sequestration*>

NEWENT

467 The parishioners say that the chancel is defective in its roof [and] ceiling, by the fault of the rector. <*it will be repaired*>

468 Next, that otherwise all things are well there.

Dymock. Visitation made there on Friday, 25 May

KEMPLEY

469 The parishioners say that the rector withholds a two-pound candle owed every year for the light of St Leonard there, and has withheld it for ten years past. <*let the parishioners prosecute*>

470 Next, that the rector ought to provide a dwelling for the parish chaplain to live in near the church, so that the parishioners can have recourse to him in time of need, and that the church buildings are in ruins and have collapsed to the ground. <*let them prosecute also*>

471 Next, [*not completed*]

[f. 10v]

Bromesbarwe

472   Parochiani dicunt quod Geyles[1] Aspolon solutus et Maiota Wlyth com-
miserunt incestum. <vir comparet, excommunicatus>

473   Item quod Lorate Bade est communis diffamatrix vicinorum etcetera.
<comparet, negat, purget se coram rectore; purgavit se legitime; et dimissa est>

474[2]   Item dicunt quod Egidius Absolon tenet quandam Margeriam Oulyth
<suspensa> in amplexibus incestuosis et continuarunt xxvj annis in peccato. <vir
comparet, negat, habet diem coram commissario in proximam ad purgandum se
de peccato et loco suspecto, et hoc non obstante abjuret eam sub pena xx s>

475   Item quod Agnes Cokhull et Ricardus Tattw de parochia de Uppeleden
adulterantur adinvicem ambo conjugati. <mulier comparet, negat; purgavit se; vir
purgavit se legittime; et dimissus est>

Dymmok

476   Parochiani dicunt quod cancellus[3] est defectius in coopertura ita quod
quando pluit extra, vicarius non potest celebrare in defectu rectoris.

477   <Vicarius non comparet, suspensus et citetur ille ad proximam; vicarius
absolutus est in forma juris> [*in margin*] <dimissus>

478   Item quod ostium cancelli est defectivum in defectu rectoris.

479   Item quod rector subtrahit unum cereum ardentem ad missam diebus dominicis et festivis dum <saltim> alta missa celebraretur et subtraxit iij[bus]
annis elapsis quem ex antiqua consuetudine predecessores sui invenerunt sine
contradictione.

480   Item quod Harry Croce est communis usurarius videlicet mutuavit cuidam
Jak at Hulle xij s[4] quos recepit integros una cum iiij bussellis frumenti pro dila-
tione etcetera et mutuavit Christine Wele a qua recepit ultra sortem iij bussellos
frumenti. <ad purgandum se in proximam v manu>

481   Item quod ex antiqua consuetudine rector tenetur distribuere pauperibus
singulis septimanis ij bussellos mixtilionis quod subtractum est xx annis elapsis et
ultra.

482   Item quod Jankyn Druwe et Agnes Downe fornicantur adinvicem et sunt
in tertio gradu consanguinitatis. <vir ad purgandum>[5]

[1]   Following *Julia*, struck through.
[2]   The entry is inserted above **472**, its order and that of **473** indicated by the marginal
letters *a* and *b*.
[3]   Followed by *d*, struck through.
[4]   Followed by *et*, struck through.
[5]   Followed by *mulier suspensa*, struck through.

[f. 10v]

BROMSBERROW

472   The parishioners say that Giles Aspolon, a single man, and Maiota Wlyth commit incest. <*the man appears, excommunicated*>

473   Next, that Lorate Bade is a habitual defamer of her neighbours etc. <*appears, denies, to purge herself before the rector; she has lawfully purged herself; and is dismissed*>

474   Next, they say that Giles Absolon keeps a certain Margery Oulyth <*suspended*> in incestuous embraces and they have continued in sin for 26 years. <*the man appears, denies, has a day before the commissary at the next to purge himself of the sin and the suspicious circumstances, and this notwithstanding he is to abjure her under penalty of 20 shillings*>

475   Next, that Agnes Cokhull and Richard Tattw of the parish of Upleadon commit adultery together, both being married. <*the woman appears, denies, has purged herself; the man has lawfully purged himself; and he is dismissed*>

DYMOCK

476   The parishioners say that the chancel is defective in its roofing so that when it rains outside the vicar is not able to celebrate, by the fault of the rector.

477   <*the vicar does not appear, suspended and to be cited to the next; the vicar absolved in due form of law*> [*in margin*]: <*dismissed*>

478   Next, that the door of the chancel is defective, by the fault of the rector.

479   Next, that the rector withholds a candle that should burn at mass on Sundays and feast days, at least while high mass is being celebrated, and he has withheld it for three years past, which candle by ancient custom his predecessors provided without argument.

480   Next, that Harry Croce is a habitual usurer, that is, he lent a certain Jack at Hulle 12 shillings that he recovered in full, together with four bushels of wheat for the delay etc. and he made a loan to Christine Wele from whom he recovered over and above the original loan three bushels of wheat. <*to purge himself at the next with five hands*>

481   Next, that by ancient custom the rector ought to distribute weekly to the poor two bushels of maslin, which have been withheld for 20 years and more.

482   Next, that Jankin Druwe and Agnes Downe fornicate together and are in the third degree of blood-relationship. <*the man to purge*>

483   Item quod Ricardus Stokke nuper promotus ad sacros ordines tenet quandem Issabellam Waren[1] cum qua precontraxit ante huiusmodi ordinum susceptionem ut asserit tamen matrimonium inter eosdem non dum est solempnizatum. <suspensus> [*in margin*] <Foresta>

Ledebury <Froma>. Visitatio facta ibidem die sabbati[2] xxvj^ta^ mensis Maii anno Domini supradicto

      Parva Markyl

484   <Dominus rector ibidem suspensus>[3]

485   Parochiani dicunt quod Rogerus Solers fornicatur cum Agnete Gatley que moratur apud Ledebury. <suspensi; excommunicati>

486   Item quod cancellus est defectivus in coopertura in defectu rectoris. <differtur sub spe reedificandi usque ad festum nativitatis Sancti Johannis Baptiste>

487   Item dicunt quod rector non dicit matutinas nec vesperas in ecclesia ut tenetur. <injunctum est quod faciat de cetero>

488   Item dicunt quod die apostolorum Philippi et Jacobi et festo inventionis Sancte Crucis ultimum ad annum[4] parochiani non habuerunt neque matutinas neque missas aut vesperas in defectu rectoris.

489   Item quod prefatus Rogerus Solers recusat panem benedictum et aquam benedictam contra determinationem ecclesie etcetera.

490   Item quod ecclesia patitur defectus in tectura muris et vitro fenestrarum in defectu parochianorum. <est in emendando>

491   Item quod Jankyn Cache vadit diebus dominicis et festivis ad mercatum de Ross absentando se ab ecclesia parochiali. <juravit de emendando>

      Collewalle

492   Parochiani dicunt quod mansum rectorie patitur defectum in tectura muris clausura et aliis in defectu rectoris.

493   Item quod Johannes Monnyng <suspensus> subtrahit vj d debitos ad lumen Beate Marie. <suspensus>

494   Item quod Johannes Hoor[5] tenetur invenire unam lampadem ardentem coram crucifixo et non facit. <comparet, habet diem in proximam ad producendum evidencias hinc inde in proximam>

---

[1]   Followed by *q*, struck through.
[2]   Followed by *die*, struck through.
[3]   Written above **485**.
[4]   Followed by *non*, struck through.
[5]   Followed by *et Johannes Yonge et*, struck through.

483   Next, that Richard Stokke, lately promoted to holy orders, keeps a certain Isabel Waren, with whom he made a contract before taking this ordination as he asserts, but the marriage between them is not yet solemnised. *<suspended>* [*in margin*]: *<Forest>*

Ledbury *<Frome>*. Visitation made there on Saturday, 26 May, in the year of Our Lord abovesaid

LITTLE MARCLE

484   *<the rector there suspended>*

485   The parishioners say that Roger Solers fornicates with Agnes Gatley who lives at Ledbury. *<suspended; excommunicated>*

486   Next, that the chancel is defective in its roofing, by the fault of the rector. *<deferred in the hope of rebuilding, to the feast of the birth of St John the Baptist>*

487   Next, they say that the rector does not say matins or vespers in church as he ought to. *<ordered that he should do so in future>*

488   Next, they say that on the day of the Apostles Philip and James and on the feast of the Finding of the Holy Cross last year the parishioners did not have either matins nor masses or vespers, by the fault of the rector.

489   Next, that the aforesaid Roger Solers refuses the holy bread and holy water contrary to the direction of the church etc.

490   Next, that the church is defective in its roof, walls, and the glass of the windows, by the fault of the parishioners. *<it is being amended>*

491   Next, that Jankin Cachere goes on Sundays and feast days to Ross-on-Wye market, absenting himself from the parish church. *<he has sworn to amend>*

COLWALL

492   The parishioners say that the rectory house is defective in its roof, walls, fences, and other things, by the fault of the rector.

493   Next, that John Monnyng *<suspended>* withholds 6 pence owed to the light of the Blessed Mary. *<suspended>*

494   Next, that John Hoor ought to provide a lamp to burn before the crucifix and does not do so. *<appears, has a day at the next to produce evidence; thence to the next>*

495   Item[1] Ricardus de Reye conquestus est publice coram me registrario et parochianis quod dominus Johannes Commyn capellanus de Collewalle tenuit Johannam Baret <suspensa> uxorem suam legitimam die noctuque ipso invito, propter quod habet eos graviter suspectos de peccato commisso etcetera, et quod eadem Johanna absentat se a consortio et cohabitatione dicti mariti sui conquerentis et absentavit vj annis elapsis eo quod dictus dominus Johannes allicit eandem ad absentandum se etcetera. <vir purgavit se>

496   Item quod Cecilia de Style decessit intestata <duobus annis elapsis> et quod prefatus dominus Johannes Commyn fabricavit un[um testamentum][2] eiusdem Cecilie et constituit se ipsum executorem testamenti huiusmodi, cuius pretextu idem dominus Johannes ministravit bona dicte defuncte videlicet ix marcas argenti et alia diversa bona. <prosequ[atur cuius interest]>

497   Item quod Maiota Paty soluta adulteratur cum Thoma Monnyng conjugato; eadem Maiota fornicatur cum ... ... [prout fama] publica laborat. <vir comparet, negat, purget se in proximam cum vj^{ta} manu, mulier citetur ad proximam et dominus ... ... >

498   Item quod Alicia Barbour est suspensa ab ingressu ecclesie et denunciata et sic stetit ... ... et ultra.

499   [Item quod] Johanna <suspensa> uxor Rogeri Smyth <adulteratur cum Johanne ballivo de Berton; non noscuntur [tales] ... >[3]

500   [Item quod eadem] Johanna [graviter] diffamata est de ad[ulterio commi]sso cum Geffrey Parlour ...

501   Item quod Johannes Yong operatus est in festo Assumptionis Beate Marie per totum diem. <moneatur quod non faciat de cetero>[4]

502   Item quod Johannes Hoor et Ricardus Aleyn non veniunt ad ecclesiam diebus dominicis et festivis.

[f. 11]

Monysley

503   Parochiani dicunt quod rector non residet <et> quod servicium divinum negligitur in ecclesia in defectu rectoris. <sequestratur fructus, commissa est custodia decano, Rogero Hoor et Rogero Chebenor>

504   Item quod mansum rectoris patitur defectum in tectura muris clausura et aliis.

505   Item quod Ricardus Asshwalle fornicatur cum Elena Carles ambo conjugati.

---

[1]   Followed by *quod*, struck through.
[2]   The bottom right-hand corner of this page is torn away with a loss of up to two inches of text, and there is also slight damage along the bottom.
[3]   *adulteratur ... noscuntur* interlined above *[n]equitur, falso et maliciose diffamatur* ..., struck through.
[4]   This entry and the next are written in the margin.

495 Next, Richard de Reye has publicly complained before me, the Registrar, and the parishioners that Sir John Commyn, chaplain of Colwall, has kept Joan Baret <*suspended*>, Richard's lawful wife, by day and night, against his will, on account of which he considers them gravely suspect of committing a sin etc.; and that the same Joan absents herself from the company and home of her said husband, the complainant, and has been absent for the last six years because the said Sir John enticed her to absent herself etc. <*the man has purged himself*>

496 Next, that Cecily de Style died intestate <*two years ago*>, and that the aforesaid Sir John Commyn forged a will for this Cecily and made himself executor of this will, on which pretext the same Sir John has administered the goods of the said deceased, namely 9 marks in silver and various other goods. <*let [those concerned] prosecute*>

497 Next, that Maiota Paty, a single woman, commits adultery with Thomas Monnyng, a married man; this same Maiota fornicates with ... ... as public fame has it. <*the man appears, denies, to purge himself at the next with six hands; the woman to be cited to the next and his lordship*[1] ... ... >

498 Next, that Alice Barbour is suspended from entering the church and denounced and she had remained so for ... ... and more.

499 Next, that Joan, wife of Roger Smyth <*suspended*> commits adultery with John, the bailiff of Barton. <*they do not know these persons ... *>

500 Next, that the same Joan is gravely defamed of adultery committed with Geoffrey Parlour ...

501 Next, that John Yong worked on the feast of the Assumption of the Blessed Mary, for the whole day. <*he is warned not to do so in future*>

502 Next, that John Hoor and Richard Aleyn do not come to church on Sundays and feast days.

[f. 11]

MUNSLEY

503 The parishioners say that the rector does not reside and that divine service is neglected in the church, by the fault of the rector. <*the revenues to be sequestrated, custody committed to the dean, Roger Hoor and Roger Chebenor*>

504 Next, that the house of the rector is defective in its roof, walls, fence, and other things.

505 Next, that Richard Asshwalle fornicates with Helen Carles, both married.

---

[1] For the involvement of the bishop with this case, see **1338**.

506   Item quod dominus Walterus Broy abstulit unum portiforium de ecclesia quem recusat restituere.

507   Item quod dominus Reginaldus Monyworth rector ibidem recepit pro accomodatione xiij s iiij d per unam septimanam iij s iiij d una cum sorte.

Aelton

508   Parochiani dicunt quod omnia bene ibidem.

Ledebury

509   <Parochiani dicunt quod dominus episcopus tenetur reddere annuatim ad sustentationem unius lampadis ardentis coram summo altari pro quodam tenemento quod devenit ad manus ipsius per escetam xviij d et subtractum est etcetera; consulatur dominus super hoc>[1]

510   Parochiani <etiam> dicunt quod magister sive custos hospitalis Sancte Katerine tenetur invenire et sustentare in dicto hospitali ad deserviendum Deo quinque capellanos continue in habitu[2] a fundatione dicti hospitalis ordinato cum cruce alba ad pectus, nec invenit nisi duos capellanos tantum <inquiratur a domino remedium>

511   Item tenetur ab antiquo xiij pauperes singulis diebus in victualibus susten-tare quod subtractum est in toto.[3]

512   Item quod[4] idem custos dat omnia beneficia huiusmodi hospitali annexa laycis ad firmam ac terras et tenementa sua ubique in diocesi Heref' existentia.

513   Item quod idem custos subtrahit distributiones solitas <fieri> pauperibus bis in septimana.

514   Item quod Willelmus Davys [et] Thomas filius eiusdem jurarunt alias de stando ordinationi magistri Roberti Prys et Hugonis Carwy junioris de certis artic-ulis etcetera sub pena xl s <insolidum> solvendorum operi ecclesie de Ledebury, cuiquid ordinationi stare recusant, ideo perjuri. <comparent, habent diem Heref' in proximam ad producendum probationes adversarii>

515   Item dicunt quod dominus Willelmus Calwe obtinens officium diaconatus in ecclesia de Ledebury non jacet in thesauraria prout tenetur ad custodiendum ornamenta ecclesie. <comparet, prosequantur quorum interest>

516   <Item quod magister Robertus Prys canonicus ibidem incontinens est cum Alicia Smyth serviente sua, item cum Maiota Crommpe conjugate, item [*blank*];[5] vir comparet, negat, purget se cum vj[ta] manu, quo ad mulieres commissum est vicario>

---

[1]   Inserted above **510** and linked to the parish heading by a line.
[2]   Followed by *ab f*, struck through.
[3]   **511** runs on from **510**, and the decision is bracketed to both.
[4]   Followed by *dant*, struck through.
[5]   Followed by *Item idem Robertus*, struck through. The whole entry is added in a later hand.

506 Next, that Sir Walter Broy removed a breviary from the church that he refuses to restore.

507 Next, that Sir Reynold Monyworth, the rector there, received for lending 13 shillings and 4 pence for one week, 3 shillings and 4 pence as well as the original loan.

AYLTON

508 The parishioners say that all is well there.

LEDBURY

509 *<The parishioners say that the lord bishop ought to pay yearly 18 pence for the upkeep of a lamp to burn before the high altar, in respect of a certain tenement that fell into his hands by escheat, and it has been withheld etc.; his lordship to be consulted about this>*

510 The parishioners further say that the Master or Warden of St Katherine's Hospital ought to provide and maintain in the hospital, to serve God, five chaplains continually in a habit, as laid down at the foundation of the hospital, with a white cross at the breast, and he provides no more than two chaplains only. *<seek a remedy from his lordship>*

511 Next, he ought by ancient usage to support 13 poor people every day in food, which has been entirely withdrawn.

512 Next, that the same Warden farms out all the benefices annexed to this hospital to laymen, and their lands and tenements wherever they are in the diocese of Hereford.

513 Next, that the same Warden withholds the accustomed doles that have been made to the poor twice a week.

514 Next, that William Davys [and] his son Thomas previously took an oath to abide by the award of Master Robert Prys and Hugh Carwy the younger concerning certain articles etc., under penalty of 40 shillings in full to be paid towards the [building] work of the church of Ledbury, which award they refuse to abide by, so they are perjured. *<they appear, have a day at Hereford at the next to produce proofs to the contrary>*

515 Next, they say that Sir William Calwe, having obtained the office of deacon in the church of Ledbury, does not sleep in the treasury as he ought to, in order to guard the church's ornaments. *<appears, let those concerned prosecute>*

516 *<Next, that Master Robert Prys, a canon there, is incontinent with Alice Smyth, his servant, and further with Maiota Crommpe, a married woman, and [blank]; the man appears, denies, to purge himself with six hands; as to the women, it is committed to the vicar>*

517 Item quod Ricardus Moyses fornicatur cum Alson Tudrekes. <suspensi; absentes>

518 Item quod Johannes Cotynton junior fornicatur cum Agnete quam tenet, dicta Mayos. <vir comparet, fatetur, abjurat, fustigetur ter circa ecclesiam; mulier suspensa>

519 Item quod Thomas Braban solutus adulteratur cum Maiota Scheppert <suspensa> uxore Johannis Scheppert. <vir comparet, negat post correctionem etcetera; mulier comparet, fatetur, abjurat, fustigetur ter circa ecclesiam; mulier dimissa>

520 Item quod Tangwystel serviens Ricardi Longeford fornicatur cum eodem Thoma Braban. <vir dimissus; mulier[1] comparet, fatetur, abjurat; dimissa est quia ipsa invita concubuit cum ea semel et nunquam plus>

521 Item idem Thomas fornicatur cum Johanna nuper serviente Agnetis Combe. <vir dimissus est, mulier comparet, fatetur, abjurat, fustigetur ter circa ecclesiam; mulier egit penitenciam>

522 Item quod Thomas Braban traxit quendam Thomam Feld in causa testamentaria ad curiam secularem. <dimissus est>

523 Item dicunt Thomas Carpenter solutus adulterat cum Alicia Gryne. <citetur vir ad proximam; mulier comparet, fatetur, abjurat, fustigetur vj ante processionem et vj per forum>

Pixley

524 Parochiani dicunt quod rector celebrat bis diebus dominicis.

525 Item <quod dominus Johannes Smyth capellanus de Ledebury incontinens est cum Johanna Tyler conjugata de Ledebury;[2] vir comparet, negat, purget se cum vj^{ta} manu in proximam, mulier comparet, negat; purgavit se, commissum est vicario ad recipiendum purgationem>

[Este]nor[3]

526 Parochiani dicunt quod rector non residet et quod mansum est ruinosum. <sequestrati sunt fructus per dominum episcopum>

527 Item quod Willelmus Kete de Estenor solutus adulteratur cum Mulsaunde <suspensa> uxore Johannis[4] Hanys et cum Issabella Neel <suspensa> quam tenet[5] et Margareta Bruwer de Malvern Minor. <vir comparet, negat quo ad Mulsaunde et Isabellam, quo ad Margaretam fatetur, abjurat, fustigetur semel; quo ad Mulsaunde purgavit se>

528 Item quod dicta Alicia Brut fornicatur cum Ricardo Carter. <absentes>

---

[1]   Followed by <*suspensa*>, struck through.
[2]   Added in the hand that added **516**.
[3]   The bottom left-hand corner of this page is torn away with the loss of the margin and about an inch of the text.
[4]   Followed by *Agnes*, struck through; what follows, and the entries up to **533**, are added in the same hand as **516** and **525**.
[5]   Followed by *ac Alicia Brut*, struck through.

517   Next, that Richard Moyses fornicates with Alison Tudrekes. <*suspended; both absent*>

518   Next, that John Cotynton the younger fornicates with Agnes called Mayos whom he keeps. <*the man appears, admits, abjures, to be beaten three times around the church; the woman suspended*>

519   Next, that Thomas Braban, a single man, commits adultery with Maiota Scheppert <*suspended*> wife of John Scheppert. <*the man appears, denies since correction etc.; the woman appears, admits, abjures, to be beaten three times around the church; the woman dismissed*>

520   Next, that Tangwystl, servant of Richard Longeford, fornicates with the same Thomas Braban. <*the man dismissed; the woman appears, admits, abjures; she is dismissed because he slept with her against her will once and never more*>

521   Next, the same Thomas fornicates with Joan, lately servant of Agnes Combe. <*the man is dismissed; the woman appears, admits, abjures, to be beaten three times around the church; the woman has performed the penance*>

522   Next, that Thomas Braban took a certain Thomas Feld to a secular court in a testamentary case. <*he is dismissed*>

523   Next, they say Thomas Carpenter, a single man, commits adultery with Alice Gryne. <*the man is to be cited to the next; the woman appears, admits, abjures, to be beaten six times before the procession and six times through the marketplace*>

PIXLEY

524   The parishioners say that the rector celebrates twice on Sundays.

525   Next, <*that Sir John Smyth, a chaplain of Ledbury, is incontinent with Joan Tyler, a married woman of Ledbury; the man appears, denies, to purge himself with six hands at the next; the woman appears, denies, has purged herself; he is committed to the vicar to receive the purgation*>

EASTNOR

526   The parishioners say that the rector does not reside and that the house is in a ruinous state. <*the revenues are sequestrated by the lord bishop*>

527   Next, that William Kete of Eastnor, a single man, commits adultery with Mulsaunde <*suspended*>, wife of John Hanys, and with Isabel Neel <*suspended*>, whom he keeps, and Margaret Bruwer of Little Malvern. <*the man appears, he denies as to Mulsaunde and Isabel, as to Margaret he admits, abjures, to be beaten once, as to Mulsaunde he has purged himself*>

528   Next, that the said Alice Brut fornicates with Richard Carter. <*both absent*>

529   [Item quod] eadem Alicia fornicatur cum Johanne Cokhull. <vir citetur ad proximam>

530   [Item quod] eadem Alicia fornicatur cum Willelmo Baret conjugato. <vir comparet, negat; purgavit se>

531   [Item quod eadem] Alicia adulteratur cum Nicholao oth' Mulle conjugato. <vir comparet, negat post correctionem; purgavit se>

532   [Item quod eadem A]licia adulteratur cum Stephano Paulyn et Thoma Hulle. <Stephanus infirmus est; Thomas Hulle non noscitur talis>

533   [Item quod Tho]mas Clerk fornicatur cum Juliana Hergest et Alicia¹ Brut antedicta. <vir comparet, fatetur, abjurat, fustigetur ... ...>

[f. 11v]

Codynton

534   Parochiani dicunt quod rector est nimis tepidus et negligens in servicio divino et quod porci eiusdem deturpant cimiterium.

535   Item quod fregit clausuram cimiterii.²

536   Item quod nimis se absentat a parochia ita quod oportet parochianos ire alibi pro infantibus baptizandis.

537   Item quod retinet in domo sua publice concubinam cuius nomen non specificant.

538   Item occupat campanile cum feno et collocat suos vitulos in eodem.

539   Item quod tenetur invenire cordas campanarum et non facit.

540   Item quod idem rector occupat certas terras olim datas ad sustentationem unius lampadis in ecclesia etcetera.

541   Item quod Juliana Baret conjugata adulteratur cum <domino> Willelmo Horworth capellano. <extra diocesim commoranti>

542   Item Maiota Golthull fornicatur cum Johanne Pathere juniore.

543   Item quod eadem Maiota ivit in festo Sancti Petri ad vincula quod festum est festum illius loci extra parochiam ad operandum etcetera.

Stokydith <West'>. Visitatio facta ibidem die dominica xxvij mensis Maii

Tadynton <Weston>

544   Parochiani dicunt quod cancellus est defectius in tectura et muris et fenestris in defectu rectoris. [*in margin*] <Nota>

[*in margin*] Accusatores

545   Item dicunt quod dominus Rogerus Appelby prior de Hereford incontinens est cum Agnete uxore Thome Glasbury de Claston in parochia de Dormynton et cum Maiota uxore Johannis Scheropser et Agnete uxore Stephani de Putte de parochia de Mordeford ac cum Agnete uxore Johannis Wasbe et Maiota uxore Johannis Jutte de parochia de Okelpyschard.

---

¹   Following *Issabella*, struck through.
²   The following five entries follow without a break.

529   Next, that the same Alice fornicates with John Cokhull. *<the man to be cited to the next>*

530   Next, that the same Alice fornicates with William Baret, a married man. *<the man appears, denies; has purged himself>*

531   Next, that the same Alice commits adultery with Nicholas oth' Mulle, a married man. *<the man appears, denies since correction; has purged himself>*

532   Next, that the same Alice commits adultery with Stephen Paulyn and Thomas Hulle. *<Stephen is sick; no such person as Thomas Hulle is known>*

533   Next, that Thomas Clerk fornicates with Julian Hergest and Alice Brut, the aforenamed woman. *<the man appears, admits, abjures, to be beaten ...>*

[f. 11v]

CODDINGTON

534   The parishioners say that the rector is extremely lukewarm and negligent in divine service and that his pigs foul the churchyard.

535   Next, that he has broken the churchyard fence.

536   Next, that too frequently he absents himself from the parish so that the parishioners have to go elsewhere to have their babies baptised.

537   Next, that he publicly keeps in his house his concubine, whose name they do not state.

538   Next, he fills up the bell-tower with hay and puts his calves in it.

539   Next, that he ought to provide bell-ropes and does not do so.

540   Next, that the same rector occupies certain lands once given for the upkeep of a lamp in the church etc.

541   Next, that Julian Baret, a married woman, commits adultery with Sir William Horworth, chaplain. *<living outside the diocese>*

542   Next, Maiota Golthull fornicates with John Pathere the younger.

543   Next, that the same Maiota, on the feast of St Peter in Chains, which is the feast of this place, went outside the parish to work etc.

Stoke Edith *<Weston>*. Visitation made there on Sunday, 27 May

TARRINGTON *<Weston>*

544   The parishioners say that the chancel is defective in its roof and walls and windows, by the fault of the rector.   [*in margin*]: *<Note>*

[*in margin*]: Accusers

545   Next, they say that Sir Roger Appelby, prior of Hereford, is incontinent with Agnes, wife of Thomas Glasbury of Claston in the parish of Dormington, and with Maiota, wife of John Scheropser, and with Agnes, wife of Stephen de Putte of the parish of Mordiford, and with Agnes, wife of John Wasbe, and with Maiota, wife of John Jutte of the parish of Ocle Pychard.

Westheyde <West>

546   Parochiani dicunt quod ecclesia est defectiva in tectura in defectu parochianorum et campanile etiam.

547   Item quod Geffrey Laurens conjugatus adulteratur cum Avisia Haunte quam tenet in domo sua.

Stokydith <West>[1]

548   Parochiani dicunt quod Walterus Speyser junior tenetur pro quibusdam terris quas tenet [invenire][2] tres lampades ardentes in ecclesia dum celebrantur misse in eadem et non facit ut solitum fuit fieri. <comparet,[3] dicit quod hoc facit>

549   Item quod Ricardus Schelle et tenentes sui recusant contribuere ad reparationem ecclesie et campanilis. <dicit quod contribuit etcetera>

Magna Markel <Ross>. Visitatio facta ibidem die lune xxviij die mensis Maii

Mordeford <Ross>

550   Parochiani dicunt quod Willelmus Pytte solutus adulteratur cum Maiota Scheropser <suspensa> uxore Johannis Scheropser et fornicatur cum Ibel Bykker. <suspensa; dimissa; vir comparet, fatetur, abjurat, fustigetur ter circa ecclesiam quo ad Maiotam, quo ad aliam contractus initus est inter eosdem; mulier videlicet Maiota abjurat, fustigetur in forma>

551   Item quod Rogerus Albon <suspensus> conjugatus adulteratur cum Alicia uxore Johannis Brugemon. <mulier comparet, negat, purget se coram[4] rectore ibidem; purgavit se; vir purget se in proximam; purgavit se et dimissus est ab instancia officii etcetera>

552   Item quod Cecilia Taelour <suspensa> conjugata tenet commune burdellum ibidem pro quibuscumque. <ad purgandum se>[5]

553   Item[6]

Fownhop <Ross>

554   Parochiani dicunt quod omnia bene ibidem.

Preston <Ross>

555   Parochiani dicunt quod Harry Symondes <extra> conjugatus adulteratur cum Sibilla Portemon <extra> prout fama laborat.

556   Item[7]

---

[1]   Erroneously indicated as a centre by a box.
[2]   Omitted.
[3]   Followed by *f*, struck through.
[4]   Followed by *commissario generali*, struck through.
[5]   The three words follow <*purgavit*>, struck through.
[6]   Unfinished.
[7]   Unfinished.

WESTHIDE <*Weston*>

546   The parishioners say that the church is defective in its roof, by the fault of the parishioners, and the bell-tower too.

547   Next, that Geoffrey Laurens, a married man, commits adultery with Avice Haunte, whom he keeps in his house.

STOKE EDITH <*Weston*>

548   The parishioners say that Walter Speyser the younger, for some lands that he holds, ought to provide three lamps to burn in church while masses are celebrated in it, and he does not do it properly as it used to be done. <*appears, says that he does it*>

549   Next, that Richard Schelle and his tenants refuse to contribute to the repair of the church and bell-tower. <*he says that he has contributed*>

Much Marcle <*Ross*>. Visitation made there on Monday, 28 May

MORDIFORD <*Ross*>

550   The parishioners say that William Pytte, a single man, commits adultery with Maiota Scheropser <*suspended*>, wife of John Scheropser, and fornicates with Isabel Bykker. <*suspended; dismissed; the man appears, admits, abjures, to be beaten three times around the church as to Maiota, as to the other woman a contract between them has been entered into; the woman, that is, Maiota, abjures, to be beaten in due form*>

551   Next, that Roger Albon <*suspended*>, a married man, commits adultery with Alice, wife of John Brugemon. <*the woman appears, denies, to purge herself before the rector there; she has purged herself; the man to purge himself at the next; he has purged himself and is dismissed at the instance of the official etc.*>

552   Next, that Cecily Taelour <*suspended*>, a married woman, keeps a common brothel there for all and sundry. <*to purge herself*>

553   Next, [*not completed*]

FOWNHOPE <*Ross*>

554   The parishioners say that all is well there.

PRESTON WYNNE <*Ross*>

555   The parishioners say that Harry Symondes <*outside*>, a married man, commits adultery with Sybil Portemon <*outside*>, as fame has it.

556   Next, [*not completed*]

Hopsolers <Ross>

557　Parochiani dicunt quod omnia sunt bene ibidem.

Huwecappyl <Ross>

558　Parochiani dicunt quod omnia bene ibidem.

[f. 12]

Markyl Magna <Ross>

559　Parochiani dicunt quod Jamys Gamon[1] fornicatur cum Maiota Reyder. <absentat se mulier>

560　Item quod Willelmus Wylde <extra> conjugatus adulteratur cum[2] Avisia <extra> serviente Jankyn Deen. <inquirat commissarius de eisdem>

561　Item quod Thomas Pyers <suspensus> fornicatur cum Maiota <suspensa> serviente sua quam tenet in domo sua. <ambo comparent, negant peccatum fatentur locum suspectum, abjurant, difertur pena>

562　Item quod Phylippot Balls <extra> de Kynaston fornicatur cum Juliana de Gloucestre <suspensa> quam tenet. <mulier[3] purgavit se>

563　Item quod Margeria Lyche non tractat maritum suum affectione <conigali>[4] ut tenetur. <citetur ad proximam>

564　Item quod Rogerus Arnald non tractat uxorem suam affectione maritali denegans eidem victum et vestitum. <moratur apud Aelton>

565　Item quod cancellus est defectivus in defectu rectoris unde injunctum est rectori quod faciat reparationem cancelli citra festum Sancti Michelis proximum futurum sub pena xl s. Et dominus sequestravit fructus quousque idem rector huiusmodi cancellum repararet et etiam pro tertia parte fructuum debitorum operi ecclesie cathedralis Hereford eo quod dedit ecclesiam ad firmam sine licencia septem annis continue.[5] <consulatur dominus quia nullus audet acceptare custodiam sequestri>

Bossebury <Froma>. Visitatio facta ibidem die martis[6] xxix mensis Maii anno Domini supradicto

Donynton

566　Parochiani ibidem dicunt quod mansum rectorie fere dirutum et ad terram prostratum in defectu rectorum. <sequestrantur fructus>

---

[1]　Followed by *co*, struck through.
[2]　Followed by *Al*, struck through.
[3]　Followed by *abjurat, fustigetur in forma*, struck through.
[4]　Replacing *maritali*, struck through.
[5]　Followed by <*suspensa ecclesia*>, struck through.
[6]　Followed by *j*, struck through.

SOLLERS HOPE *<Ross>*

557   The parishioners say that all things are well there.

HOW CAPLE *<Ross>*

558   The parishioners say that all is well there.

[f. 12]

MUCH MARCLE *<Ross>*

559   The parishioners say that James Gamon fornicates with Maiota Reyder. *<the woman has absented herself>*

560   Next, that William Wylde *<outside>*, a married man, commits adultery with Avice *<outside>*, servant of Jankin Deen. *<the commissary to inquire about them>*

561   Next, that Thomas Pyers *<suspended>* fornicates with Maiota *<suspended>*, his servant, whom he keeps in his house. *<both appear, they deny the sinning, admit the suspicious circumstances, both abjure, the penalty to be deferred>*

562   Next, that Philipot Balls of Kynaston *<outside>* fornicates with Julian of Gloucester *<suspended>*, whom he keeps. *<the woman has purged herself>*

563   Next, that Margery Lyche does not treat her husband with conjugal affection as she ought to. *<to be cited to the next>*

564   Next, that Roger Arnald does not treat his wife with marital affection, denying her food and clothing. *<he lives at Aylton>*

565   Next, that the chancel is defective, by the fault of the rector, concerning which the rector is ordered to carry out the repair of the chancel before Michaelmas next, under penalty of 40 shillings, and his lordship has sequestrated the revenues until such time as the rector should repair the chancel; and further, one third part of the revenues [is made] due to the upkeep of the cathedral church at Hereford because he let the church to farm without a licence for seven years continuously. *<his lordship to be consulted because nobody dares accept the custody of the sequestration>*

Bosbury *<Frome>*. Visitation made there on Tuesday, 29 May, in the year of Our Lord abovesaid

DONNINGTON

566   The parishioners there say that the rectory house is virtually in ruins and collapsed to the ground, by the fault of the rectors. *<the revenues are sequestrated>*

567   Item dicunt quod cancellus est defectius in tectura in defectu rectorum.

568   Item quod Johanna uxor Walteri Richerdes adulteratur cum Rogero Bykerton et cum Waltero Rolffe. <mulier difertur quia graviter pregnatur, Rogerus non citatus; ideo citetur ad proximam; Walterus extra>

Bossebury

569   Parochiani dicunt quod Alson <Pompe conjugata> <que excommunicata est auctoritate ordinaria> commorans in domo Henrici Axebarn fornicatur cum quodam domino Ricardo Sterr capellano nuper[1] de Cradley. <extra>

Cowarn Magna <Froma>. Visitatio facta ibidem die mercurii xxx mensis Maii

[Cowarn Magna]

570   Parochiani ibidem dicunt quod vicarius tenetur invenire unum diaconum ad deserviendum in ecclesia quod non facit. <comparent, habent diem Hereford in proximam; concordati sunt>

571   Item dicunt quod huiusmodi diaconus qui pro tempore foret teneretur invenire cordas pro campanis quod subtractum est in defectu vicarii. <non est aliquis diaconus ibidem>

572   Item dicunt quod Andreas Homper detinet injuste iiij s legatos per Johannem Geffes nuper defunctum cuius executor idem Andreas extitit ad opus ecclesie de Cowarne. <ad probandum in proximam; postea comparuit Alicia Geffys et condempnatur in iij s solvendis ecclesie citra Pascham>

573   Item quod Johannes Walissh detinet injuste x s quod Rogerus oth' Gryn nuper defunctus legavit ad opus eiusdem ecclesie. <suspensus>

574   Item quod Johannes Walissh nuper custos bonorum ecclesie recusat reddere ratiocinationem de bonis ecclesie per eum recep[tis][2] parochianis eiusdem. <suspensus>

575   [Item quod] Lodowicus Taelour et Isbel quam tenet pro uxore ut dicitur adulterantur adinvicem quia ipse habet [legitimam uxor]em superstitem. <suspensi; vir abjurat, fustigetur in forma, mulier abjurat, fustigetur in forma>

576   [Item quod r]ector tenetur invenire unum portiforium in deserviendo[3] Deo in ecclesia quod non facit. <prosequantur>

577   [Item quod idem rector] tenetur invenire ij bussellos frumenti pro pane faciendo ad communicandum in festo Pasche quod subtractum est. <prosequantur>

---

[1]   Followed by *capellano*, struck through.
[2]   The bottom left-hand corner of this page is torn away with a loss of up to an inch of text.
[3]   Followed by *in*, struck through.

567   Next, they say that the chancel is defective in its roof, by the fault of the rectors.

568   Next, that Joan, wife of Walter Richerdes, commits adultery with Roger Bykerton and with Walter Rolffe. *<the woman to be deferred because she is heavily pregnant; Roger is not cited so to be cited to the next; Walter outside>*

BOSBURY

569   The parishioners say that Alison *<Pompe, a married woman; excommunicated on the authority of the ordinary>*, living in the house of Henry Axebarn, fornicates with a certain Sir Richard Sterr, lately chaplain of Cradley. *<outside>*

Much Cowarne *<Frome>*. Visitation made there on Wednesday, 30 May

[MUCH COWARNE]

570   The parishioners there say that the vicar ought to provide a deacon to serve in church, which he does not do. *<they appear, have a day at Hereford at the next; they have reached an agreement>*

571   Next, they say that this deacon, during his time, ought to provide bell-ropes, which provision has been withdrawn by the fault of the vicar. *<there is no such deacon there>*

572   Next, they say that Andrew Homper wrongfully withholds 4 shillings bequeathed by John Geffes, lately deceased, whose executor this Andrew is, for the benefit of the church of Cowarne. *<to bring proof at the next; later Alice Geffys appeared and is sentenced to pay 3 shillings to the church before Easter>*

573   Next, that John Walissh wrongfully withholds 10 shillings that Roger oth' Gryn, lately deceased, bequeathed for the benefit of the same church. *<suspended>*

574   Next, that John Walissh, lately keeper of the goods of the church, refuses to render an account of the church goods received by him to the parishioners of the same. *<suspended>*

575   Next, that Lewis Taelour and Isabel, whom he keeps as a wife, as is said, commit adultery together, because he has a living lawful wife. *<both suspended; the man abjures, to be beaten in due form; the woman abjures, to be beaten in due form>*

576   Next, that the rector ought to provide a breviary for the service of God in the church, which he does not do. *<let them prosecute>*

577   Next, that the same rector ought to provide two bushels of wheat to make the communion bread on Easter Sunday, which has been withheld. *<let them prosecute>*

[f. 12v]

Okelpyschard <Froma>

578 Parochiani dicunt quod omnia bene ibidem.

Asperton[1]

579 Parochiani dicunt quod dominus Robertus Roke est communis exercitor tabernarum <prout Johannes Boley, alii dicunt quod non, dimissus est>.

580 Item quod Johannes Beger solutus fornicatur cum Issabel de Cowley.

581 Item quod prefatus dominus Robertus graviter diffamatur de adulterio cum Agnete uxore Ricardi Asshewyk. <vir comparet, negat, purget se cum vj^{ta} manu>

582 Item quod Issabella Mardeston soluta fornicatur cum domino Johanne vicario de Cannon Frome. <vir comparet, negat, purget se cum vj^{ta} manu in proximam>

583 Item quod Willelmus Boley expulit dominum Robertum Roke capellanum vi et armis de ecclesia die dominica in Passione Domini ultima preterita ita quod idem capellanus non audebat celebrare ibidem illo die.

584[2] Item idem Willelmus subtrahit decimas minutas et oblationes etcetera.

Streton <Froma>

585 Parochiani dicunt quod omnia bene ibidem excepto quod non habent servicium divinum eo quod lis pendet super huiusmodi vicarium etcetera.

Stoklacy <Froma>

586 Parochiani dicunt quod cancellus est defectius et mansum rectoris in defectu rectoris. <emendentur citra festum Michelis>

587 <Thomas Cook de Stokelacy executor testamenti domini Roberti capellani ibidem condempnatur in ix s legatis ad opus pixidis pro corpore Christi in ecclesia ibidem citra festum Purificationis et ad restituendum j psalterium vel valorem ecclesie ibidem>

588 Item quod Johannes Hayward detinet injuste iiij s deputatos per communitatem parochianorum ad opus ecclesie de residuo collecte nuper facte ad solvendum[3] subsidium concessum domino regi. <negat, ad purgandum Hereford in proximam>

589 Item[4]

Felton <Froma>

590 Parochiani dicunt quod dominus Thomas vicarius ibidem celebrat bis in die videlicet apud Felton et Okel Prioris. <fatetur, inhibitum est ei ut de cetero non fiat>

---

[1] Preceded by *Stretton et*, struck through.
[2] Follows **583** on the same line.
[3] Followed by *res*, struck through.
[4] Unfinished.

[f. 12v]

OCLE PYCHARD *<Frome>*

578   The parishioners say that all is well there.

ASHPERTON

579   The parishioners say that Sir Robert Roke is a habitual frequenter of taverns *<according to John Boley; others say that this is not the case, he is dismissed>*

580   Next, that John Beger, a single man, fornicates with Isabel of Cowley.

581   Next, that the aforesaid Sir Robert is gravely defamed of adultery with Agnes, wife of Richard Asshewyk. *<the man appears, denies, to purge himself with six hands>*

582   Next, that Isabel Mardeston, a single woman, fornicates with Sir John, the vicar of Canon Frome. *<the man appears, denies, to purge himself with six hands at the next>*

583   Next, that William Boley drove Sir Robert Roke, chaplain, by force and arms from the church on Passion Sunday last, so that the same chaplain did not dare to celebrate there that day.

584   Next, the same William withholds small tithes and offerings etc.

STRETTON GRANDISON *<Frome>*

585   The parishioners say that all is well there, except that they do not have divine service because a case is pending about this vicarage etc.

STOKE LACY *<Frome>*

586   The parishioners say that the chancel is defective, and the house of the rector, by the fault of the rector. *<to be amended before the feast of St Michael>*

587   *<Thomas Cook of Stoke Lacy, executor of the will of Sir Robert, chaplain there, is sentenced in respect of 9 shillings bequeathed for making a pyx for the Body of Christ in the church there, [to be handed over] before the feast of the Purification, and is to restore one psalter or its value to the church there>*

588   Next, that John Hayward wrongfully withholds 4 shillings set aside by the community of the parishioners for the benefit of the church from the surplus of a collection lately made to pay the subsidy granted to the lord king. *<he denies, to purge at Hereford at the next>*

589   Next, [*not completed*]

FELTON *<Frome>*

590   The parishioners say that Sir Thomas, the vicar there, celebrates twice in a day, that is, at Felton and Ocle Prior. *<he admits, he is forbidden to do so in future>*

591   Item[1]

Ullynghwyk <Froma>

592   Parochiani [dicunt][2] quod rector alienavit magnum portiforium de bonis parochianorum contra voluntatem eorundem et recusat huiusmodi librum restituere seu satisfacere pro eodem. <comparet, dicit erat antiphorarius[3] et condempnatur ad restituendum vel valorem>

593   Item quod idem rector juravit alias coram magistro Reginaldo de Wolston in correctione ultime visitationis de restitutione huiusmodi libri facienda citra festum Sancti Johannis Baptiste proximum tunc futurum vel saltim satisfactione congrua quod non fecit ideo perjurus. <negat, ad purgandum in proximam>

594   Item quod quidam calix parochialis ibidem fractus est in defectu rectoris ad cuius calicis reparationem juravit ut supra nec fecit. <negat, ad purgandum>

595   Item quod idem rector asportavit hostium cancelli factum per parochianos ibidem et disposuit de eodem ad usum proprium. <negat, prosequantur quorum etcetera>

596   Item quod rector nimis tarde celebrat diebus dominicis et festivis, ut dicunt post nonam. <inhibitum est quod de cetero non fiat>

597   Item quod idem rector fregit clausuram cimiterii et quod porci sui fodiunt in eodem cimiterio in magnam dehonestatem. <dicit quod>[4]

598   Item quod ventilat blada sua ibidem et quod dimittet portam cimiterii apertam per totum annum. <inhibitum sub pena>[5]

599   Item quod idem rector subtraxit unum lapidem de muris cimiterii ad valorem xx d <et disposuit de eodem lapide ad usum suum proprium; restituatur>

600   Item idem rector alienavit unam vangam et unum bidentem de bonis parochianorum etcetera. <negat, prosequantur quorum interest>

601   Item quod Rogerus Cher ivit in festo Pasche ad ecclesiam de Preston ad recipiendum sacralia sacramentalia.

602   Item quod prefatus rector liberavit unum psalterium de bonis parochianorum cuidam famulo ad legendum, unde idem liber dehonestatur et maculatur. <negat quod est deterioratus>

Ȝarkhull <Froma>

603   Parochiani dicunt quod cancellus patitur defectum in tectura ita quod quando pluit extra capellanus non potest ibidem celebrare. <se[questrantur fructus]>[6]

---

[1]   Unfinished.
[2]   Omitted.
[3]   Recte *antiphonarius*.
[4]   Unfinished.
[5]   Followed by *excommunicationis*, struck through.
[6]   The bottom right-hand corner of this page is torn away with the loss of up to three inches of text; *sequestratur fructus* bracketed to apply to this entry and **604,** and perhaps to **605**.

591   Next, [*not completed*]

ULLINGSWICK <*Frome*>

592   The parishioners say that the rector has taken a large breviary from the goods of the parishioners against their will and refuses to restore this book or give them compensation for it. <*he appears, says it was an antiphonal, and he is sentenced to restore it or its value*>

593   Next, that the same rector previously took an oath before Master Reynold of Woolaston in the corrections of the last visitation, to return this book before the next feast of St John the Baptist then following, or at least [to give] appropriate satisfaction, which he has not done, so he is perjured. <*he denies, to purge at the next*>

594   Next, that a certain chalice belonging to the parish there is broken, by the fault of the rector, who swore to have it mended as above, and has not done so. <*he denies, to purge*>

595   Next, that the same rector carried off the door of the chancel made by the parishioners there and disposed of it for his own benefit. <*he denies, let those concerned prosecute etc.*>

596   Next, that the rector celebrates too late on Sundays and feast days, after midday, as they say. <*forbidden to do this in future*>

597   Next, that the same rector broke down the churchyard fence and that his pigs root in the churchyard, extremely disgracefully. <*he says that [unfinished]*>

598   Next, that he winnows his corn there and leaves the gate of the churchyard open all year round. <*forbidden under penalty*>

599   Next, that the same rector has taken away a stone from the walls of the churchyard worth 20 pence <*and disposed of this stone for his own benefit; it is to be restored*>

600   Next, the same rector has taken a spade and a sheep from the goods of the parishioners etc. <*he denies, let those concerned prosecute*>

601   Next, that on Easter Sunday Roger Cher went to the church of Preston [Wynne] to receive the holy sacraments.

602   Next, that the aforesaid rector has lent a psalter from the goods of the parishioners to a servant to read, as a result of which this book is soiled and stained. <*he denies that it is any the worse*>

YARKHILL <*Frome*>

603   The parishioners say that the chancel is defective in its roof so that when it rains outside the chaplain is unable to celebrate there. <*the revenues sequestrated*>

604 Item quod rector subtrahit vicario ibidem annuatim de pensione ordinata sibi ab antiquo ad victum [suum] xl s et ij lode frumenti et ij lode avene, et subtraxit toto tempore suo.

605 Item quod idem rector subtrahit stramina que deberent spargi in eadem ecclesia expensis rectoris ter in anno.

606 Item quod vicarius ibidem tenetur solvere parochianis v marcas debitas ad servicium Beate [Mari]e ibidem ... ...

607 Item quod cancellus patitur defectum in vitro fenestrarum.

608 Item quod Jamys Thomkyns conjugatus adulteratur [cum]¹ Alicia Stalworth. <extra>

609 Item Ricardus Godefrey et Felicia uxor sua receptant eosdem Jamys et Aliciam ... ...

[f.13]

610 Item dicunt quod mansum vicarii est dirutum et fere prostratum ad terram in defectu rectoris et vicarii. <asserit se non posse eo quod rector detinet sibi portionem suam ut supra etcetera>²

611 Item quod vicarius alienavit tigna de eodem manso.

612 Item quod magister Reginaldus de Wolston officialis Hereford injunxit alias vicario ibidem in partem penitencie quod inveniret unum cereum ponderis vj lb. coram³ ymagine Beati Michelis in eadem ecclesia quod non dum fecit. <fatetur, dicit se paratum si haberet portionem suam et⁴ supra>

613 Item quod Johannes Kyvo et Willelmus Merssh procuratores ecclesie⁵

Cradley <Froma>. Visitatio facta ibidem die jovis in festo Ascencionis ultimo die Maii

[Cradley]

614 Parochiani dicunt quod dominus Ricardus Sterr capellanus adulteratur cum Alicia Haket conjugata et est denunciatus excommunicatus per ministros domini episcopi qua excommunicatione non obstante celebrat in ecclesia de Scheldesley Wigorn' diocesis et quod cognovit eandem pluries ut dicitur in domo Beate Marie infra sanctuarium etcetera et quod idem dominus Ricardus fornicatur cum Isot sorore dicte Alicie. <extra>

615 Item quod idem dominus Ricardus et dominus Willelmus capellanus parochialis iverunt armati de nocte per parochiam garulando et perturbando quietem parochianorum contra honestatem ecclesiasticam.

¹ Omitted.
² Bracketed to apply to **611**.
³ Followed by *Sancto*, struck through.
⁴ Recte *ut*.
⁵ Unfinished.

604   Next, that the rector withholds from the vicar there, out of the annual salary laid down of old for his support, 40 shillings and two measures of wheat and two measures of oats and has withheld these the whole of his time.

605   Next, that the same rector withholds the straw that ought to be strewn in this church three times in the year at the expense of the rector.

606   Next, that the vicar there ought to pay the parishioners 5 marks due to the service of the Blessed Mary there ...

607   Next, that the chancel is defective in the glass of the windows.

608   Next, that James Thomkyns, a married man, commits adultery with Alice Stalworth. *<outside>*

609   Next, Richard Godefrey and his wife Felise harbour the same James and Alice ...

[f. 13]

610   Next, they say that the vicar's house is in a ruinous state and has almost collapsed to the ground, by the fault of the rector and of the vicar. *<he asserts that he is unable because the rector withholds his portion from him, as above etc.>*

611   Next, that the vicar has taken timbers from the same house.

612   Next, that Master Reynold of Woolaston, the Official of [the diocese of] Hereford, previously ordered the vicar there as part of a penance to provide a candle weighing six pounds before the image of the Blessed Michael in this church, which he has not done. *<admits, says he is ready to do so if he has his portion as above>*

613   Next, that John Kyvo and William Merssh, the proctors of the church, [*not completed*]

Cradley *<Frome>*. Visitation made there on Thursday, the feast of the Ascension, the last day of May

[CRADLEY]

614   The parishioners say *<that Sir Richard Sterr, chaplain, commits adultery>* with Alice Haket, a married woman, and has been denounced as excommunicated by the officers of the lord bishop, but despite the excommunication he celebrates in the church of Shelsley in Worcester diocese, and that he has known her [sexually] many times, so it is said, in the house of the Blessed Mary within the churchyard etc.;[1] and that the same Sir Richard fornicates with Isot, sister of the said Alice. *<outside>*

615   Next, that the same Sir Richard and Sir William, the parish chaplain, go about armed through the parish by night, chattering and disturbing the rest of the parishioners, contrary to the dignity of the church.

---

[1]   Probably the predecessor of the present Parish Hall, formerly a school, a building of c. 1500: Brooks and Pevsner, *Herefordshire*, 106.

616 Item quod idem dominus Willelmus capellanus adulteratur cum[1] Agnete Floxley prout communis fama laborat. <extra>

617 Item quod idem dominus Willelmus capellanus diffamatus est de adulterio cum Margareta þe Frunde. <extra>

618 Item quod Wilkoc Hayn son Walker fornicatur cum Lucia[2] serviente Hayn Walker. <vir comparet, fatetur, abjurat, fustigetur ter ante processionem, mulier graviter pregnatur; ideo difertur post partum>

619 Item quod Johannes Coletes fornicatur cum Agnete More. <vir comparet, fatetur, abjurat, fustigetur semel; mulier dimissa est>

620 Item quod Johannes Hulle <suspensus> conjugatus adulteratur cum Johanna Ʒoyldehalle conjugata et continuarunt in peccato xij annis elapsis. <mulier citetur ad proximam>

621 Item quod Amisia Daniel utitur sortilegio etcetera. <obiit>

Froma Episcopi. Visitatio facta ibidem die veneris primo Junii

Castell Froma

622 Parochiani dicunt quod omnia bene ibidem.

Cannon From'

623 Parochiani dicunt quod rector tenetur invenire unum portiforium ad deserviendum Deo in ecclesia et non facit.

624 <Vicarius ibidem propter incontinenciam cum Issabella Mardeston>[3]

Froma Episcopi

625 Parochiani dicunt quod rector tenetur invenire singulis annis in festo Pasche pro pane inde fiendo ad communicandum j bussellum frumenti et non facit, et subtractum est xj annis elapsis; et quod porta cimiterii cuius sustentatio pertinet ad rectorem est fracta. <premuniatur ipse vel procurator eius>

626 Item quod vicarius tenetur invenire unum diaconum ad deserviendum in ecclesia et custodiendum ornamenta et libros et non facit, et subtractum est xvj annis elapsis.

627 Item quod cancellus patitur defectum in selura et vitro fenestrarum et hostium eiusdem cancelli est nimis debile et inhonestum in defectu rectoris.

628 Item quod Ricardus Pekoke conjugatus adulteratur cum[4] Alicia Swone conjugata. <suspensi>

---

[1]   Followed by *a*, struck through.
[2]   Preceded by *Agnete Moore*, struck through.
[3]   Unfinished; see **582**.
[4]   Followed by *Alson*, struck through.

616 Next, that the same Sir William the chaplain commits adultery with Agnes Floxley, as common fame has it. *<outside>*

617 Next, that the same Sir William the chaplain is defamed of adultery with Margaret the Frunde. *<outside>*

618 Next, that Wilkoc, son of Hayn Walker, fornicates with Lucy, servant of Hayn Walker. *<the man appears, admits, abjures, to be beaten three times before the procession; the woman is heavily pregnant, so let it be deferred until after the birth>*

619 Next, that John Coletes fornicates with Agnes More. *<the man appears, admits, abjures, to be beaten once; the woman is dismissed>*

620 Next, that John Hulle *<suspended>*, a married man, commits adultery with Joan Yoyldehalle, a married woman, and they have continued in sin for the last 12 years. *<the woman to be cited to the next>*

621 Next, that Amice Daniel practises sorcery etc. *<she has died>*

Bishops Frome. Visitation made there on Friday, 1 June

CASTLE FROME

622 The parishioners say that all is well there.

CANON FROME

623 The parishioners say that the rector ought to provide a breviary for the service of God in the church and does not do so.

624 *<The vicar there on account of incontinence with Isabel Mardeston>* [*not completed*]

BISHOPS FROME

625 The parishioners say that the rector ought to provide every year on Easter Sunday, to make the communion bread, one bushel of wheat, and does not do so, and has withheld it for the last 11 years; and that the gate of the churchyard, whose upkeep is the responsibility of the rector, is broken. *<let him or his proctor be warned>*

626 Next, that the vicar ought to provide a deacon to serve in church and look after the ornaments and books, and does not do so, and has withheld it the last 16 years.

627 Next, that the chancel is defective in its ceiling and the glass of the windows, and the door of the chancel is very dilapidated and unworthy, by the fault of the rector.

628 Next, that Richard Pekoke, a married man, commits adultery with Alice Swone, a married woman. *<both suspended>*

629   Item quod Johannes Kynge conjugatus adulteratur cum Maiota Wylles. <suspensa; vir comparet, fatetur, abjurat peccatum et locum suspectum, fustigetur in forma; mulier citetur ad proximam>

630   Item David Poleyn conjugatus adulteratur cum Alicia quam tenet. <suspensi>

631   Item [quod J]ohannes[1] Taelour fornicatur cum Beton Beuchampe ambo soluti. <suspensi; mulier abjurat, fustigetur in forma>

632   Item [dicunt quod] dominus Philippus vicarius promisit alias ad constructionem campanilis C s et parochiani, illa promissione [communicata],[2] statim fecerunt huiusmodi campanile ad terram prostrari quo facto, nullum denarium dedit in prejudicium parochianorum ...oni promissionem ipsi prostrarunt campanile quod aliter non fecissent.

633   [Item dicunt quod] mansum vicarii patitur defectum in tectura muris et clausura in defectu vicarii.

634   [Item quod] vicarius accomodavit unum psalterium de bonis parochianorum sine eorum licencia unde huiusmodi [psalterium] deturpatur et plura folia abscisa in dampnum huiusmodi parochianorum.

[f. 13v]

635   Item quod rector tenetur invenire stramina expensis suis bis in anno videlicet in festo Natalis Domini et Pasche pro area ecclesie et non facit. <hoc facit>

636   Item dicunt quod vicarius dedit et vendidit arbores crescentes in cimiterio in prejudicium ecclesie quia opponebant tempestatibus etcetera. <negat>

637   I[3]

Brom3ord. Visitatio facta ibidem die dominica

Whitebarn

638   Parochiani dicunt quod Johannes Curteys tenet Johannam Mydewode non obstante divorcio alias facto et abjuratione etcetera. <absentes sunt>

639   Item quod Robertus Turnour solutus fornicatur cum Margareta Walissh. <non sunt ibidem sed apud Stanford>

Avenbury

640   Parochiani dicunt quod omnia bene ibidem.

Wacton

641   Parochiani dicunt quod omnia bene ibidem.

---

[1]   The bottom left-hand corner of the page is perished with the loss of up to two inches of text.
[2]   *communicata* seen or conjectured by Bannister.
[3]   Not finished.

629 Next, that John Kynge, a married man, commits adultery with Maiota Wylles. <*she is suspended; the man appears, admits, abjures the sin and the suspicious circumstances, to be beaten in due form; the woman to be cited to the next*>

630 Next, David Poleyn, a married man, commits adultery with Alice, whom he keeps. <*both suspended*>

631 Next, that John Taelour fornicates with Beton Beuchampe, both single. <*both suspended; the woman abjures, to be beaten in due form.*>

632 Next, they say that Sir Philip, the vicar, previously promised 100 shillings towards the building of the bell-tower and the parishioners, informed of this promise, immediately had the bell-tower taken down to the ground, which being done he gave no money, to the prejudice of the parishioners ... his promise took down the bell-tower, which otherwise they would not have done.

633 Next, they say that the vicar's house is defective in its roof, walls, and fence, by the fault of the vicar.

634 Next, that the vicar lent out a psalter from the goods of the parishioners without their permission, as a result of which this psalter has been made dirty and has many leaves cut out, to the detriment of the parishioners.

[f. 13v]

635 Next, that the rector ought to provide straw for the floor of the church at his expense twice in the year, that is, at Christmas and Easter, and does not do so. <*he does this*>

636 Next, they say that vicar gave and sold the trees growing in the churchyard to the prejudice of the church, because they protected it from storms. <*he denies*>

637 Next, [*not finished*]

Bromyard. Visitation made there on Sunday [3 June]

WHITBOURNE

638 The parishioners say that John Curteys keeps Joan Mydewode <*suspended*>, despite a divorce and abjuration previously made etc. <*they are absent*>

639 Next, that Robert Turnour, a single man, fornicates with Margaret Walissh. <*they are not there but at Stanford Bishop*>

AVENBURY

640 The parishioners say that all is well there.

WACTON

641 The parishioners say that all is well there.

Grendon Episcopi

642 Omnia bene ibidem.

Thornbury

643 Parochiani dicunt quod omnia bene ibidem.

Brokhampton

644 Parochiani dicunt quod omnia bene ibidem.

Tedest' Waffr'

645 Parochiani dicunt quod omnia bene ibidem.

Stok Blyse

646 Parochiani dicunt quod omnia bene.

Wolferlowe

647 Parochiani dicunt quod rector tenetur invenire unam lampadem ardentem coram summo altari et non facit. <sequestrantur fructus>

648 Item quod cimiterium non est clausum. <ecclesia suspendatur quousque etcetera>

649 Item quod fons baptismalis non est seratus.

650 Item quod vas olei sancti est sine cerura.

651 Item[1]

Brom3ord

652 Parochiani dicunt quod vicarius tenetur invenire unam lampadem ardentem coram summo altari die noctuque quod non facit. <condempnatur ut inveniat de nocte etcetera>

653 Item quod vicarius tenetur invenire iiij cereos processionales ardentes diebus solempnibus de quibus subtrahuntur duo cerei. <vicarius promittit de cetero etcetera>

654 Item quod Stephanus Broun subtrahit xij d debitos ad servicium Beate Marie pro una placea terre quam tenet in Brom3ord. <comparet, negat, ad probandum>

655 Item quod[2] Walterus Godyng subtrahit eidem servicio xij d. <comparet, negat, ad probandum>

656 Item quod Deyota de la Orchard subtrahit eidem servicio vj d. <comparet, negat, [ad] probandum>

657 Item quod Walterus Brugge subtrahit eidem servicio vj d. <absens>

---

[1] Unfinished.
[2] Followed by *J*, struck through.

GRENDON BISHOP

642   All is well there.

THORNBURY

643   The parishioners say that all is well there.

BROCKHAMPTON

644   The parishioners say that all is well there.

TEDSTONE WAFRE

645   The parishioners say that all is well there.

STOKE BLISS

646   The parishioners say that all is well.

WOLFERLOW

647   The parishioners say that the rector ought to provide a lamp to burn before the high altar and does not do so. *<the revenues to be sequestrated>*

648   Next, that the churchyard is not fenced. *<the church to be suspended until etc.>*

649   Next, that the baptismal font is not locked.

650   Next, that the vessel for holy oil is without a lock.

651   Next, [*not completed*]

BROMYARD

652   The parishioners say that the vicar ought to provide a lamp to burn before the high altar day and night, which he does not do. *<sentenced to provide it at night etc.>*

653   Next, that the vicar ought to provide four processional candles to burn on solemn days, of which two are withheld. *<the vicar promises in future etc.>*

654   Next, that Stephen Brome withholds 12 pence owed to the service of the Blessed Mary in respect of a plot of land he holds in Bromyard. *<he appears, denies, to prove>*

655   Next, that Walter Godyng withholds from the same service 12 pence. *<he appears, denies, to prove>*

656   Next, that Deyota of the Orchard withholds from the same service 6 pence. *<she appears, denies, to prove>*

657   Next, that Walter Brugge withholds from the same service 6 pence. *<absent>*

658   Item dicunt quod Alson Broun tenet talem opinionem quod cum ipsa maledixerit alicui homini quod [per]¹ ipsius imprecationem Deus sine mora vindictam accipiet de eo et de hoc pluries fecit p[ompam] suam quod est contra fidem catholicam et temptaret Deum.² <abjurat etcetera>

659   Item quod eadem Alson mercandizat in ecclesia vendendo canapam et liniam ...

660   Item dicunt quod clericus parochialis non pulsat campanas horis debitis etcetera. <citetur ...>

661   <Item dicunt quod capellanus Beate Marie tenetur invenire medietatem [lampadis ardentis] coram ymagine Beate Virginis in ecclesia de Brom3ord <tempore misse Beate Virginis quolibet die> et Alicia ux[or Johannis Sares tenetur] invenire alteram medietatem eiusdem, dictus Johannes Sares ...>

[f. 14]

Tedeston de la Mar

662   Parochiani dicunt quod omnia sunt bene ibidem excepto quod Meyl de Grey solutus adulteratur cum Felicia Webbe. <vir comparet, negat, ad purgandum, mulier suspensa>

Stanford Episcopi

663   Parochiani dicunt quod Thomas³ Stanford solutus fornicatur cum Margareta Herte. <vir suspensus, mulier>⁴

664   Aliter omnia bene.

Pencombe

665   Parochiani dicunt quod omnia sunt bene ibidem.

Sapy

666   Parochiani dicunt quod Ricardus Dodeshull fornicatur cum Issabella Yong quam tenet non obstante abjuratione alias facta coram commissario generali.⁵ <vir absens, mulier suspensa>

Grendone Waren

667   Nichil ibidem.

---

¹   The bottom right-hand corner of this page is torn away with the loss of up to three inches of text.
²   Followed by *negat*, struck through.
³   Preceded by *Ricardus*, struck through.
⁴   Altered from *suspensi* to *suspensus* and the insertion of *vir, mulier* unfinished.
⁵   Followed by *rectore* added and deleted.

658 Next, they say that Alison Broun maintains that when she curses any man that by her imprecation God without delay will take vengeance on him, and she has often boasted about this, which is against the catholic faith and tempts God. *<she abjures etc.>*

659 Next, that the same Alison trades in the church, selling hemp and flax ...

660 Next, they say that the parish clerk does not ring the bells at the set hours etc. *<to be cited ...>*

661 *<Next, they say that the chaplain of the Blessed Mary ought to provide half the lamp burning before the image of the Blessed Virgin in the church of Bromyard at the time of the mass of the Blessed Virgin every day and Alice, wife of John Sares, to provide the other half, the said John Sares ...>*

[f. 14]

TEDSTONE DELAMERE

662 The parishioners say that all things are well there except that Meyl de Grey, a single man, commits adultery with Felise Webbe. *<the man appears, denies, to purge; the woman suspended>*

STANFORD BISHOP

663 The parishioners say that Thomas Stanford, a single man, fornicates with Margaret Herte. *<the man suspended; the woman [not completed]>*

664 Otherwise all is well.

PENCOMBE

665 The parishioners say that all things are well there.

UPPER SAPEY

666 The parishioners say that Richard Dodeshull fornicates with Isabel Yong, whom he keeps despite an abjuration previously made before the commissary general. *<the man absent, the woman suspended>*

GRENDON WARREN

667 Nothing there.

Cowarn Parva

668   Parochiani dicunt quod dominus Mauricius rector ibidem non residet nec invenit alium capellanum ad deserviendum Deo et parochianis. <sequestrantur fructus et committitur custodia decano et rectori de Pencombe>

669   Item quod dat beneficium suum ad firma[1] cuidam Johanni Clarkston[2] layco sine licencia episcopi.

670   Item quod cancellus est ruinosus et defectius in tectura muris et vitro fenestrarum in defectu rectoris.

671   Item quod mansum rectorie est ruinosum in defectu eiusdem.

672   Item quod prefatus Johannes Clerkeston subtrahit lumini Beate Marie ibidem j d annuatim pro quadam parcella terre quam ipse tenet debiter.

673   Item quod Johannes Gaule parochianus ibidem impedivit vi et armis decanum de Frome exercere officium suum et[3] non obstante sequestro interposito per dictum decanum auctoritate domini episcopi disposuit de fructibus dicte ecclesie. <citetur> [*in margin*] <Froma>

Leom'. Visitatio facta ibidem die martis v mensis Junii anno Domini ut supra

Strateford

674   Parochiani dicunt quod ecclesia patitur defectum in muris in defectu Ricardi Kynley. <injunctum est eidem reformare citra festum Michelis sub pena xl d.; reformatum est>

675   Item quod baptisterium non est seratum in defectu parochianorum. <seratum est>

Burley

676   <Vicarius suspensus;[4] postea comparuit>

677   Parochiani dicunt quod cancellus est discoopertus in defectu rectoris.[5] <apud Leyntwardyn>[6]

678   Item quod mansum rectoris est ruinosum in defectu eiusdem et ad terram prostratum in defectu eiusdem.

679   Item quod decime reponuntur extra solum ecclesie.

---

[1]   Recte *firmam*.
[2]   Altered from *Claston* by interlineation.
[3]   Altered from *etc* by the striking through of *c*, and the rest added later.
[4]   *suspensus* struck through.
[5]   Preceded by *parochianorum*, struck through.
[6]   Bracketed to apply to entries **677**–**9**.

LITTLE COWARNE

668   The parishioners say that Sir Maurice, the rector there, does not reside nor does he provide any chaplain to serve God and the parishioners. <*the revenues to be sequestrated, custody committed to the dean and the rector of Pencombe*>

669   Next, that he farms out his benefice to a certain John Clarkston, a layman, without the bishop's licence.

670   Next, that the chancel is ruinous and defective in its roof, walls, and the glass of the windows, by the fault of the rector.

671   Next, that the rectory house is ruinous, by the fault of the same.

672   Next, that the aforesaid John Clerkeston withholds from the light of the Blessed Mary there 1 penny annually in respect of a certain parcel of land that he holds subject to that charge.

673   Next, that John Gaule, a parishioner there, by force and arms has prevented the dean of Frome from exercising his office and, despite the sequestration imposed by the said dean on the authority of the lord bishop, has disposed of the revenues of the said church. <*to be cited*> [*in margin*]: <*Frome*>

Leominster. Visitation made there on Tuesday, 5 June, in the year of Our Lord as above

STRETFORD

674   The parishioners say that the church is defective in its walls, by the fault of Richard Kynley. <*he is ordered to put it right before Michaelmas under penalty of 40 pence; it is put right*>

675   Next, that the font is not locked, by the fault of the parishioners. <*it is locked*>

BIRLEY

676   <*the vicar suspended; later he appeared*>

677   The parishioners say that the chancel is unroofed, by the fault of the rector. <*at Leintwardine*>

678   Next, that the house of the rector is ruinous, by the fault of the same, and has collapsed to the ground by the fault of the same.

679   Next, that the tithes are stored outside church land.

Hompere

680   Parochiani dicunt quod rector tenetur invenire unum capellanum divina celebrantem ibidem ac servientem Deo et parochianis ibidem die noctuque quod non facit nisi tantum diebus dominicis.[1]

681   Item dicunt quod idem capellanus non est suus set stipendarius unius parochiani de Leom'.

682   Item quod cancellus est ruinosus et tenebrosus in defectu rectoris.

683   Item quod[2]

[...][3]

684   [Paroc]hiani dicunt quod cancellus est defectius in coopertura et selura in defectu rectoris et vicarii.

685   [Item] quod campanile patitur defectum in tectura in defectu parochianorum.

[f. 14v]

Staggebach et Scharlestr'

686   Parochiani nichil dicunt.

Pudelston

687   Parochiani dicunt [quod][4] Thomas Haunton et Ibel uxor sua non cohabitant simul ut vir et uxor etcetera, aliter omnia bene. <citentur ad proximam>

Leomestr'

688   Parochiani dicunt quod rector tenetur invenire unum clericum ad deferendum tintunabulum et lumen ante vicarium deferrentem corpus Christi ad <visitandum>[5] infirmos quod non facit et subtractum est tribus annis elapsis ad cuius sustentationem consuetum est ab antiquo quod rector daret sibi annuatim viij s et aquam benedictam a ponte vulgariter nuncupato Luge Brugg ultra versus partes Lodelawe etcetera.

689   Item dicunt quod deficit in ecclesia liber pro officio sepulture in defectu rectoris quia ibi est unus liber huiusmodi vetustate quasi consumptus et aliquando ibidem tempore pestilencie sunt xvj vel xviij corpora uno et eodem die pro quibus non sufficiunt duo libri.

690   Item dicunt quod procurator rectoris non patitur aliquem communicari in ecclesia nisi facta per eum primitus oblatione unius oboli ad minus. <inhibitum est quod de cetero non fiat>

---

[1]   The next entry continues on the same line.
[2]   Unfinished.
[3]   The bottom left-hand corner of this page is torn away with the loss of up to an inch of text.
[4]   Omitted in error.
[5]   Replacing *deferendum*, struck through.

HUMBER

680 The parishioners say that the rector ought to provide a chaplain to celebrate divine services there and to serve God and the parishioners there day and night, which he does not do, other than on Sundays.

681 Next, they say that this chaplain is not his but is paid for by a parishioner of Leominster.

682 Next, that the chancel is ruinous and gloomy, by the fault of the rector.

683 Next, that [*not completed*]

[Unknown parish]

684 The parishioners say that the chancel is defective in its roofing and ceiling, by the fault of the rector and of the vicar.

685 Next, that the bell-tower is defective in its roof, by the fault of the parishioners.

[f. 14v]

STAGBATCH AND CHOLSTREY

686 The parishioners say nothing.

PUDLESTON

687 The parishioners say that Thomas Haunton and his wife Isabel do not live together as man and wife etc., otherwise all is well. <*both to be cited to the next*>

LEOMINSTER

688 The parishioners say that the rector ought to provide a clerk to carry the bell and light before the vicar when he conveys the Body of Christ to visit the sick, which he does not do, and has withheld it for three years past, for whose maintenance it was the custom of old that the rector should give him annually 8 shillings and holy water from the bridge commonly called Lugg Bridge, over towards Ludlow etc.

689 Next, they say that the church lacks a book for the office of burial, by the fault of the rector, because there is there [only] one such book virtually destroyed by age, and sometimes there, in time of plague, there are 16 or 18 bodies on one and the same day, for which [even] two books are not enough.

690 Next, they say that the rector's proctor does not allow anyone to take communion in church unless they have first, through him, made an offering of at least one halfpenny. <*forbidden to do this in future*>

691   Item quod duo antiphonaria et duo gradalia in ecclesia non sunt ydonea et sufficientia pro senibus presbiteris quia nimis obscura in defectu rectoris.

692   Item quod <simiterium>[1] deturpatur per vaccas vicarii positas ibidem ad pasturam ita quod vestimenta serica dehonestantur in processionibus.

693   Item quod dominus Willelmus Crompe est communis mercator[2] animalium et ovium emendo et vendendo ad lucrandum <et particeps lucrorum provenientium de baggerts craffte ibidem>.

694   Item quod dominus <postea dicunt quod obediens est> Willelmus capellanus Beate Marie[3] dominus Willelmus Crompe dominus Willelmus Cosyn et dominus Ricardus Pastay dominus Johannes Grasley sunt inobedientes vicario ad deserviendum Deo in divinis juxta exigenciam constitutionis etcetera. <injunctum est eis quod obediant vicario in omnibus juxta etcetera>

695   Item quod prefatus dominus Willelmus Cosyn minabatur parochianis existentibus in servicio episcopi in detegendo crimina et defectus delinquentium etcetera, eo quod detexerant crimina sua.

696   Item dicunt quod dominus Walterus Godych capellanus est communis mercator et presertim ovium qui lucratus est v s de lx ovibus emptis et postea per eum venditis. <negat; purgavit se>

697   Item quod dominus Thomas Whytebrede capellanus incontinens est cum quadam Alicia <Taelour>.[4] <suspensa; correctus est vir>

698   Item quod Willemus Doule et Alicia quam tenet adulterantur adinvicem. <vir comparet, negat post correctionem; purgavit[5] se>

699   Item quod Rogerus Wylkyns fornicatur cum Agnete quam tenet. <vir comparet, fatetur, abjurat, fustigetur ter circa ecclesiam, mulier suspensa; excommunicata>

700   Item quod Willelmus Stanway smyth adulteratur cum <Elena> uxore David Brower. <vir absens, mulier suspensa>

701   Item quod Johannes Momgomery diffamavit publice et maliciose Thomam Barbour et Thomam Wyse de Leom' super perturbatione pacis inter vicinos. <absens est>

702   Item quod Ricardus Scheppert et Johanna <suspensa; excommunicata> quam tenet adulterantur adinvicem. <vir comparet, fatetur, abjurat, fustigetur vj per forum et vj circa ecclesiam>

703   Item quod Willelmus Baldewyn et Margareta quam tenet fornicantur. <suspensi>

704   Item quod Willelmus Towne fornicatur cum Juliana quam tenet. <dimissi sunt>

---

[1]   Replacing *vicarius*, struck through.
[2]   Followed by *al*, struck through.
[3]   Followed by *et*, deleted.
[4]   Interlined, in same ink as <*suspensa*>, above *cuius cognomen ignoratur*, struck out.
[5]   Altered from *purget* by interlineation.

691   Next, that two antiphonals and two graduals in the church are not suitable and sufficient for elderly priests because they are very faded, by the fault of the rector.

692   Next, that the churchyard is fouled by the vicar's cows put there to pasture, so that the silk vestments are dirtied in processions.

693   Next, that Sir William Crompe is a habitual dealer in animals and sheep, buying and selling at a profit <*and a sharer in the profits arising from baggerts craffte there*>.[1]

694   Next, that Sir <*later they say that he is obedient*> William, chaplain of the Blessed Mary, and Sir William Crompe, Sir William Cosyn, and Sir Richard Pastay and Sir John Grasley are disobedient to the vicar in the service of God in divine matters, according to the requirement of the constitution[2] etc. <*they are ordered to obey the vicar in all matters according etc.*>

695   Next, that the aforesaid Sir William Cosyn threatened the parishioners who are in the service of the bishop in uncovering the misdeeds and defaults of delinquents etc. because they uncovered his misdeeds.

696   Next, they say that Sir Walter Godych, chaplain, is a habitual dealer and especially of sheep, on which he made a profit of 5 shillings from 60 sheep which he bought and later sold. <*he denies; has purged himself*>

697   Next, that Sir Thomas Whytebrede, chaplain, is incontinent with a certain Alice Taelour <*suspended; the man corrected*>

698   Next, that William Doule and Alice, whom he keeps, commit adultery together. <*the man appears, denies since correction; he has purged himself*>

699   Next, that Roger Wylkyns fornicates with Agnes, whom he keeps. <*the man appears, admits, abjures, to be beaten three times around the church; the woman suspended; excommunicated*>

700   Next, that William Stanway, a smith, commits adultery with Helen, wife of David Brower. <*the man absent, the woman suspended*>

701   Next, that John Momgomery has publicly and maliciously defamed Thomas Barbour and Thomas Wyse of Leominster over disturbing the peace between neighbours. <*he is absent*>

702   Next, that Richard Scheppert and Joan <*suspended; excommunicated*>, whom he keeps, commit adultery together. <*the man appears, admits, abjures, to be beaten six times through the marketplace and six times around the church*>

703   Next, that William Baldewyn and Margaret, whom he keeps, fornicate. <*both suspended*>

704   Next, that William Towne fornicates with Julian, whom he keeps. <*they are dismissed*>

---

[1]   Fraudulent beggars, as described by Langland; see introduction.

[2]   This refers to a provincial constitution on stipendiary priests, which circulated widely under an attribution to Archbishop Robert Winchelsey, though of uncertain origin: *Councils and Synods*, ed. Powicke and Cheney, 1382–5. Bishop Trefnant's resolution of the dispute at Leominster, with reference to the constitution, was entered in the register in 1397: *Register of John Trefnant*, 140–3.

705   Item quod Johannes Taelour fornicatur cum Margareta quam tenet. <vir comparet, fatetur, <abjurat>, differtur sub spe nubendi, mulier extra; vocetur ad penitenciam>

706   Item quod David de Dyngyl fornicatur cum Weirvyl quam tenet. <vir comparet, fatetur, abjurat, difertur sub spe nubendi, mulier extra; vocetur [ad penitenciam][1]

707   Item quod Willemus Mascald fornicatur cum Elena <suspensa> quam tenet. <vir comparet, negat post correctionem, purget se, mulier ..>

708   Item quod Llewelyn Flesshewer fornicatur cum Eva quam tenet. <mulier extra, vir comparet,[2] fatetur,[3] abjurat, fustigetur ..>

709   Item quod dominus Johannes Stone capellanus vadit tempore nocturno ad tabernas et alia [inhonesta loca][4] unde oritur scandalum. <moratur apud Temdebury>

710   Item quod Robet Glover junior fornicatur cum quadam serviente Stephani Dyar cuius nomen [ignorant] ... [*in margin*] Lodel' ambo.

711   Item quod Ricardus Valedewe concitavit Thomam Wyse ad iracundiam die P[asche ...] omisit recipere sacramenta sacramentalia eodem die.

712   Item quod Johannes Tylar[5] de Streteford fornicatur cum Matilda quam tenet. <s[uspensi] ..>

Item Leomestr'[6]

713   Parochiani dicunt quod clericus parochialis non potest pulsare campanas horis debitis ut tenetur eo quod monachi habent custodiam clavium.

714   Item dicunt quod rector impedit et perturbat parochianos ad reformandum et dehonestandum ecclesiam eorum parochialem prout voluntatis eorum est. [*in margin*] <Leom'>.

[f. 15][7]

Doklowe

715   Parochiani dicunt quod vicarius de Leom' tenetur invenire parochianis ibidem servicium divinum <duobus diebus>[8] sequentibus diem Natalis Domini et[9] feria iiij^ta, v^ta et vj ante festum Pasche ac feria ij^a et iij^a post Pascham et feria ij et iij^ta post Pentecostem quod non facit. <negat vicarius, prosequantur parochiani ibidem et probent>

---

[1]   The bottom right-hand corner of this page is torn away, with the loss of up to three inches of text.

[2]   Preceded by *suspensus*, struck through.

[3]   Preceded by *abjurat*, struck through.

[4]   Seen or conjectured by Bannister.

[5]   Followed by *fornicatur cum*, struck through.

[6]   These two entries are on folio 15 between **720** and **721**.

[7]   The entries on this page are amply spaced, although very few *comperta* and *correctiones* are in fact entered.

[8]   Written into a gap.

[9]   Followed by *duo*, struck through.

705   Next, that John Taelour fornicates with Margaret, whom he keeps. <*the man appears, admits, abjures, to be deferred in the hope of them marrying; the woman outside; let her be called to penance*>

706   Next, that David of Dyngyl fornicates with Gweirful, whom he keeps. <*the man appears, admits, abjures, to be deferred in the hope of them marrying; the woman outside; let her be called to penance*>

707   Next, that William Mascald fornicates with Helen <*suspended*>, whom he keeps. <*the man appears, denies since correction, to purge himself; the woman ...*>

708   Next, that Llewelyn Flesshewer fornicates with Eve, whom he keeps. <*the woman outside; the man appears, admits, abjures, to be beaten ...*>

709   Next, that Sir John Stone, chaplain, goes out at night to taverns and other improper places, from which scandal arises. <*he lives at Tenbury*>

710   Next, that Robert Glover the younger fornicates with a certain servant of Stephen Dyar whose name they do not know ... [*in margin*]: <*Ludlow both*>

711   Next, that Richard Valedewe provoked Thomas Wyse to wrath on Easter Sunday, so that he failed to receive the holy sacraments that day.

712   Next, that John Tylar of Stretford fornicates with Maud, whom he keeps. <*suspended ...*>

Next, Leominster

713   The parishioners say that the parish clerk is unable to ring the bells at the set hours as he ought to, because the monks have custody of the keys.

714   Next, they say that the rector obstructs and disturbs the parishioners from improving their parish church and making it respectable, as is their wish. [*in margin*]: <*Leominster*>

[f. 15]

DOCKLOW

715   The parishioners say that the vicar of Leominster ought to provide for the parishioners there a divine service <*on the two days*> following Christmas, and on the Thursday, Friday, and Saturday before Easter and the Monday and Tuesday after Easter, and on the Monday and Tuesday after Whitsun, which he does not do. <*the vicar denies, let the parishioners there prosecute and prove*>

Stoke

716   Parochiani dicunt quod Hugyn Mawne fornicatur cum Johanna Fawkener concubina sua. <conjugati sunt post visitationem>

717   Item quod Jankyn Taelour fornicatur cum Johanna Smyth quam tenet.[1] <vir comparet, fatetur, abjurat, fustigetur ter circa ecclesiam, mulier suspensa>

718   Item[2]

Eton Vill

719   Parochiani [dicunt][3] quod Hugyn Arnyet fornicatur cum Alicia quam tenet. <vir comparet, fatetur, abjurat, fustigetur[4] circa ecclesiam semel, mulier suspensa>

720   Item quod Johannes Taelour de Eton fornicatur cum Maiota quam tenet. <ambo suspensi>

Radenor Nova[5]

721   Parochiani dicunt quod dominus Willemus Heth capellanus incontinens est cum Eva filia y Vammeth.

722   Item dominus Johannes Discote capellanus incontinens est cum Angharat Gogh.

723   David Gadarn fornicatur [cum] Lleuky Lawen.[6] <excommunicati>

724   Rys Doppa fornicatur cum Gwenllian filia y Taelour. <excommunicati>

725   Gruffyth Says fornicatur cum Lleuky Kedewyn. <citetur; excommunicati>

726   Llewelyn Harper fornicatur cum Gwladus filia Mereduth. <citetur; mulier suspensa>

727   Jankyn Walton[7] fornicatur cum Pernella quam tenet. <commissum est magistro Rogero Andrew etcetera>

728   <Item dicunt quod non deservitur capelle Sancte Crucis debite etcetera>

729   Jak Webbe conjugatus adulteratur cum Wenllian <a> Flossy. <mulier excommunicata>

730   [A]dam[8] Webbe fornicatur Wenllian quam tenet. <excommunicati>

731   ... filius Rys Hoby fornicatur cum Dydgu quam tenet. <excommunicati>

---

[1]   Followed by *suspensi*, struck through.
[2]   Unfinished.
[3]   Omitted in error.
[4]   Followed by *ter*, struck through.
[5]   In a box, as if a centre. Written in a new hand, without the use of *Item*.
[6]   Followed by *suspensi ambo*, struck through.
[7]   Altered from *Walter*.
[8]   The bottom left-hand corner of this page is torn away with the loss of up to an inch of text.

STOKE PRIOR

716 The parishioners say that Hugyn Mawne fornicates with Joan Fawkener, his concubine. <*they were married after the visitation*>

717 Next, that Jankin Taelour fornicates with Joan Smyth, whom he keeps. <*the man appears, admits, abjures, to be beaten three times around the church; the woman suspended*>

718 Next, [*not completed*]

EATON VILL

719 The parishioners say that Hugyn Arnyet fornicates with Alice, whom he keeps. <*the man appears, admits, abjures, to be beaten around the church once; the woman suspended*>

720 Next, that John Taelour of Eaton fornicates with Maiota, whom he keeps. <*both suspended*>

NEW RADNOR

721 The parishioners say that Sir William Heth, chaplain, is incontinent with Eve, daughter of y Vammeth.[1]

722 Next, the Sir John Discote, chaplain, is incontinent with Angharad Gogh.

723 David Gadarn fornicates with Lleucu Lawen. <*both excommunicated*>

724 Rhys Doppa fornicates with Gwenllian, daughter of the tailor. <*both excommunicated*>

725 Gruffudd Says fornicates with Lleucu Kedewyn. <*to be cited; both excommunicated*>

726 Llewelyn Harper fornicates with Gwladus, daughter of Maredudd. <*to be cited; the woman suspended*>

727 Jankin Walton fornicates with Parnel, whom he keeps. <*committed to Master Roger Andrew etc.*>

728 <*Next, they say that the chapel of the Holy Cross is not served properly etc.*>

729 Jack Webbe, a married man, commits adultery with Gwenllian Flossy. <*to be cited; the woman excommunicated*>

730 Adam Webbe fornicates with Gwenllian, whom he keeps. <*both excommunicated*>

731 ..., son of Rhys Hoby, fornicates with Dyddgu, whom he keeps. <*both excommunicated*>

---

[1] Recte *y Famaeth*, the wet-nurse or foster-mother.

732 [Gru]ffuth ap Ieuan ap Mylly fornicatur cum Wenllian Monnyn. <excommunicati>

[f. 15v]
Eye. Visitatio facta ibidem die mercurii videlicet[1] vj mensis Junii anno ut supra

Mydelton

733 Parochiani dicunt quod omnia bene ibidem.

Kymbalton

734 Parochiani dicunt quod omnia bene ibidem.

Lucton

735 Parochiani dicunt quod Margareta Holle <suspensa> de Lucton receptat adulteros et fornicarios ad peccandum in domo sua et est communis diffamatrix vicinorum suorum. <committitur curato>

736 [*in margin*] <Johannes Bokynhull suspensus; comparet>

<Eyton>[2]

737 Parochiani dicunt quod omnia bene.

Croffte

738 Parochiani dicunt quod omnia bene ibidem.

Brumfeld

739 Parochiani dicunt quod Walterus Pennson fornicatur cum Issabella One-way. <conjugati sunt matrimonialiter etcetera>

740 Item quod idem Walterus fornicatur cum Matilda[3] quam tenet. <vir comparet; negat post correctionem, purget se cum v^ta manu coram curato; mulier comparet, fatetur, abjurat, fustigetur semel; dimissa est; postea vir fatetur, abjurat, fustigetur ter circa ecclesiam; peregit penitenciam>[4]

ʒarpole

741 Parochiani dicunt quod omnia bene ibidem.

Orleton

742 [*in margin*] <Willelmus Bour> <Dominus Willelmus Bour curatus suspensus>

---

[1]   Followed by *x*, struck through.
[2]   Replacing *Teynton*, struck through.
[3]   *suspensa* deleted.
[4]   *peregit penitenciam* written above *Walterus*.

732 Gruffudd ap Ieuan ap Mylly fornicates with Gwenllian Monnyn. <*both excommunicated*>

[f. 15v]
Eye. Visitation made there on Wednesday, 6 June, the year as above

MIDDLETON ON THE HILL

733 The parishioners say that all is well there.

KIMBOLTON

734 The parishioners say that all is well there.

LUCTON

735 The parishioners say that Margaret Holle <*suspended*> of Lucton takes in adulterers and fornicators to sin in her house, and she is a habitual defamer of her neighbours. <*committed to the parish priest*>

736 [*in margin*]: <*John Bokynhull suspended; he appears*>

EYTON

737 The parishioners say that all is well.

CROFT

738 The parishioners say that all is well there.

BRIMFIELD

739 The parishioners say that Walter Pennson fornicates with Isabel Oneway. <*they are joined together in matrimony etc.*>

740 Next, that the same Walter fornicates with Maud, whom he keeps. <*the man appears, denies since correction, to purge himself with six hands before the parish priest; the woman appears, admits, abjures, to be beaten once; she is dismissed; later the man admits, abjures, to be beaten three times around the church; he has completed the penance*>

YARPOLE

741 The parishioners say that all is well there.

ORLETON

742 [*in margin*]: <*William Bour*>; <*Sir William Bour, parish priest, suspended*>

743   [*in margin*] <significata>

Parochiani dicunt [quod]¹ Issabella Gose <excommunicata> uxor Jankyn Dey de Leynthale moratur ibidem et recusat cohabitare cum marito suo licet sepius per eum requisita et est communis diffamatrix et suscitatrix rixarum ibidem. <comparet; dicit quod idem pignoravit eam² etcetera; injunctum est quod tractet maritum suum etcetera, et citetur maritus coram domino; quo ad diffamationem negat, purget se cum vᵗᵃ manu; abjurat>

744   Item quod Nicholaus Turnour est communis operarius diebus festivis et quod Robertus de Wer est communis operarius in auttumpno diebus festivis. <non comparet, suspensus>

Eye

745   Parochiani dicunt quod Geffrey de Rayader solutus adulteratur cum Lleuky de Rayader quam tenet conjugaliter. <extra, citentur ad proximam; absentes>

746   Item quod Eynon Werkemon conjugatus adulteratur cum Muriele quam tenet. <vir comparet, fatetur, abjurat, fustigetur vj circa ecclesiam et vj per forum, mulier infirma, citetur ad proximam>

747   Item quod Willelmus de Maune de Asshton <suspensus> tenetur reddere ad lumen Beate Marie annuatim pro terris quas tenet xij d quod non facit et subtractum est x annis elapsis ad quorum solutionem alias juravit coram commissario generali ad sancta Dei evangelia nec fecit ideo perjurus etcetera. <dimissus>

748   Item quod Jankyn Per absentat diebus dominicis et festis ab ecclesia parochiali. <comparet, injunctum est quod exerceat de cetero>

Kyngeslon. Visitatio facta ibidem die jovis vij mensis Junii anno ut supra

[Kyngeslon]

749   Parochiani dicunt quod Jankyn de Walle de Lauton solutus et Agnes Abbat conjugata graviter diffamantur de adulterio commisso inter eos. <vir infirmus, mulier suspensa>

750   Item quod Willelmus Kemsey fornicatur cum Malkyn þe Walker ambo soluti. <vir comparet, negat, purgavit se; commissum est capellano ad recipiendum purgationem mulieris>

751   Item quod Phylipot Walker fornicatur cum Johanna quam habet et tenet. <ambo suspensi> [*in margin*] Herefordie

752   Item quod Howel clericus ecclesie adulteratur³ cum Margareta Fytheler conjugata. <ambo suspensi>

753   Item quod Johannes de Aston fornicatur cum Alicia Stafford. <ambo suspensi>

---

¹   Omitted in error.
²   Followed by *pro*, struck through.
³   Preceded by *fornicatur*, struck through.

743 [*in margin*]: <*she is signified*>

The parishioners say that Isabel Gose <*excommunicated*>, wife of Jankin Dey of Leinthall, lives there and refuses to live with her husband although frequently asked by him, and she is a habitual defamer and a provoker of quarrels there. <*appears, she says that he has pledged[1] her etc.; ordered to treat her husband etc. and the husband to be cited before his lordship; as to the defamation, she denies; to purge herself with five hands; she abjures*>

744 Next, that Nicholas Turnour is a habitual worker on feast days and that Robert of Wer is a habitual worker on feast days in harvest-time. <*he does not appear, suspended*>

EYE

745 The parishioners say that Geoffrey of Rhayader, a single man, commits adultery with Lleucu of Rhayader, whom he keeps as though they were married. <*outside, both to be cited to the next; both absent*>

746 Next, that Einion Werkemon, a married man, commits adultery with Muriel, whom he keeps. <*the man appears, admits, abjures, to be beaten six times around the church and six times through the marketplace; the woman sick, to be cited to the next*>

747 Next, that William de Maune of Ashton <*suspended*> ought to pay annually to the light of the Blessed Mary for the lands that he holds 12 pence, which he does not do, and it has been withheld for the last ten years, to the payment of which he previously swore before the commissary general on the holy Gospels of God, and he has not done so, so is perjured etc. <*dismissed*>

748 Next, that Jankin Per absents himself on Sundays and feast days from the parish church. <*appears, ordered to attend in future*>

Kingsland. Visitation made there on Thursday, 7 June, the year as above

[KINGSLAND]

749 The parishioners say that Jankin of Wales of Lawton, a single man, and Agnes Abbat, a married woman, are gravely defamed of adultery committed between them. <*the man sick; the woman suspended*>

750 Next, that William Kemsey fornicates with Malkyn the Walker, both single. <*the man appears, denies, has purged himself; committed to the chaplain to receive the purgation of the woman*>

751 Next, that Philipot Walker fornicates with Joan, whom he holds and keeps. <*both suspended*> [*in margin*]: <*at Hereford*>

752 Next, that Hywel, the clerk of the church, commits adultery with Margaret Fytheler, a married woman. <*both suspended*>

753 Next, that John of Aston fornicates with Alice Stafford. <*both suspended*>

---

[1] Perhaps by promising her labour as a means of paying off a debt.

754   Item quod Rogerus Mascald adulteratur[1] cum Agnete Vyseichere conjugata. <ambo suspensi>

755   Item quod Johannes Vysaichere maritus dicte Agnetis manutenet et sus-
tinet voluntarie huiusmodi adulterium inter uxorem suam et dictum Rogerum.
<suspensus>

756   Item quod dictus Rogerus Mascald adulteratur cum Alicia[2] <suspensa>
<V[ysai]cher;[3] ux[ore Thome London][4] ...>[5]

757   Item quod <Thomas Mouse>[6] et Maiota <suspensa> uxor sua non
cohabitant simul ut vir [et uxor et quod David Glace] et uxor sua <suspensa>
parentes dicte Maiote impediunt eandem ad cohabitandum cum eodem ...
<[David] Glace comparet, negat sibi opposita; purgavit se>

758   Item quod Johannes Penke fornicatur cum Margeria[7] Walker.[8] <vir
comparet, fatetur, abjurat, purget ...>

[f. 16]

759   Item quod Thomas Andrewes fornicatur cum Johanna quam tenet serviente nuper Thome Holgot.[9] <ambo suspensi>

760   Item quod Gwilim de Clonne qui moratur apud Aston adulteratur cum
Agnete Clerk <suspensa> quam tenet pro uxore superstite alia uxore cum qua
precontraxit apud Clonne cuius nomen ignorant.[10] <vir comparet, fatetur peccatum, abjurat, fustigetur vj[11] circa ecclesiam et ter per forum, mulier comparet,
fatetur, abjurat, dimissa est>

761   Item quod Thomas Gylle et Johanna uxor sunt illegitime copulati eo quod
attingent se in tertio gradu consanguinitatis. <difertur usque ad adventum rectoris
ad examinandum testes etcetera>

762   Item quod Vincentius Stodeherte et uxor sua sunt in eodem gradu consanguinitatis. <difertur ad idem>

763   Item quod Nicholaus Robert et Maiota Hwlle uxor sua sunt in tertio gradu
affinitatis eo quod Willelmus Hwlle consanguineus dicti Nicholai quondam habuit
eandem Maiotam in uxorem. <ad idem>

---

[1]   Preceded by *fo*, struck through.
[2]   Preceded by *Agnete*, struck through.
[3]   Preceded by *Inchelnerssh*, struck through.
[4]   Extension based on **769**, which must relate to the deleted *Inchelnerssh*.
[5]   The bottom right-hand corner of this page is torn away with the loss of up to three
inches of text.
[6]   Replacing *David Glase*, struck through.
[7]   Altered from *Maiota*.
[8]   Followed by *In*, struck through.
[9]   Preceded by *Andrewes*, struck through.
[10]   Followed by <*suspensi ambo*>, struck through.
[11]   Followed by *per*, struck through.

754   Next, that Roger Mascald commits adultery with Agnes Vyseichere, a married woman. <*both suspended*>

755   Next, that John Vysaichere, husband of the said Agnes, willingly supports and sustains this adultery between his wife and the said Roger. <*suspended*>

756   Next, that the said Roger Mascald commits adultery with Alice <*suspended*> Vysaicher, <*wife of Thomas London ...*>

757   Next, that Thomas Mouse and his wife Maiota <*suspended*> do not live together as man and wife, and that David Glace and his wife <*suspended*>, the parents of the said Maiota prevent her from living with him ... <*[David] Glace appears, denies the charge against him; he has purged himself*>

758   Next, that John Penke fornicates with Margery Walker. <*the man appears, admits, abjures, to purge ...*>

[f. 16]

759   Next, that Thomas Andrewes fornicates with Joan, lately servant of Thomas Holgot, whom he keeps. <*both suspended*>

760   Next, that Gwilym of Clun, who lives at Aston, commits adultery with Agnes Clerk <*suspended*>, whom he keeps as a wife, another wife with whom he previously made a contract being alive at Clun, whose name they do not know. <*the man appears, admits the sin, abjures, to be beaten six times around the church and three times through the marketplace; the woman appears, admits, abjures, she is dismissed*>

761   Next, that Thomas Gylle and his wife Joan are unlawfully joined, because they are related in the third degree of blood-relationship. <*to be deferred until the rector arrives to examine witnesses etc.*>

762   Next, that Vincent Stodeherte and his wife are in the same degree of blood-relationship. <*defer to the same*>

763   Next, that Nicholas Robert and his wife Maiota Hwlle are in the third degree of affinity because William Hwlle, a blood-relation of the said Nicholas, formerly had the same Maiota as his wife. <*to the same*>

764   Item quod Johannes Luger et Matilda¹ uxor sua sunt in quarto gradu consanguinitatis. <ad idem>

765   Item quod Thomas Osbarn et Alicia uxor sua sunt in eodem gradu consanguinitatis. <ad idem>

766   Item quod Johannes Kuwe et Alicia uxor sua sunt in iiij^{to} gradu consanguinitatis. <ad idem>

767   Item quod Thomas Collemon et Matilda uxor sua sunt in iiij^{to} gradu consanguinitatis. <ad idem>

768²   Item quod Thomas Pylvyche³ et Amisia uxor sua sunt in eodem gradu consanguinitatis. <ad idem>

769   Item quod Wilkoc Walker conjugatus adulteratur cum Alicia Inchemerssh uxore Thome London. <ambo suspensi>

770   Item quod eadem Alicia adulteratur cum Johanne Ledder conjugato. <absens est vir>

771   Item quod prefatus Wilkoc Walker est communis diffamator vicinorum falso et maliciose et presertim diffamavit falso Agnetem de More uxorem Willelmi More super adulterio commisso cum eodem Wilkoc.

772   Item quod dicta Alicia Inchemerssh est communis diffamatrix vicinorum suorum.

773   Item quod Howel Clerkes adulteratur cum <Maiota>⁴ Merssher. <mulier comparet, negat, purget se cum v^{ta} manu coram capellano> [*in margin*] Leom'

774   Item⁵

Dyluwe <West'>. Visitatio facta ibidem die veneris viij Junii anno ut supra

     Pyonia Regis <West>

775   Parochiani dicunt quod cancellus est ruinosus et patitur defectum in tectura et aliis in defectu rectoris. <reficiatur citra Pascham sub pena xx s>

776   Item quod Willelmus Wotton <suspensus> subtrahit viij denarios lumini Beate Marie quos parochiani recuperaverunt versus eum per sentenciam diffinitivam in consistorio Heref' et quod idem Willemus est excommunicatus ratione non solutionis huiusmodi viij d per annum iam elapsum et ultra <et quod non recepit sacramentum in festo Pasche. Comparet, fatetur se excommunicatum et non percepisse sacramentum ut articulatur, habet diem coram domino> [*in margin*] Brom3ard [die sabbati iiij]^{or6} temporum.

¹   Altered from *Maiota*.
²   This entry is followed by a gap of two inches, perhaps for the enrolment of the anticipated process in **761-8**.
³   Altered from *Pylyche* by interlineation.
⁴   Replacing *Alicia*, struck through.
⁵   Unfinished.
⁶   The bottom left-hand corner of this page has perished with the loss of the margin and up to half an inch of text; the reading is confirmed by **795**.

764 Next, that John Luger and his wife Maud are in the fourth degree of blood-relationship. *<to the same>*

765 Next, that Thomas Osbarn and his wife Alice are in the same degree of blood-relationship. *<to the same>*

766 Next, that John Kuwe and his wife Alice are in the fourth degree of blood-relationship. *<to the same>*

767 Next, that Thomas Collemon and his wife Maud are in the fourth degree of blood-relationship. *<to the same>*

768 Next, that Thomas Pylvyche and his wife Amice are in the same degree of blood-relationship. *<to the same>*

769 Next, that Wilkoc Walker, a married man, commits adultery with Alice Inchemerssh, wife of Thomas London. *<both suspended>*

770 Next, that the same Alice commits adultery with John Ledder, a married man. *<the man is absent>*

771 Next, that the aforesaid Wilkoc Walker is a habitual defamer of his neighbours falsely and maliciously, and in particular he has defamed falsely Agnes de More, wife of William More, over adultery committed with the same Wilkoc.

772 Next, that the said Alice Inchemerssh is a habitual defamer of her neighbours.

773 Next, that Hywel Clerkes commits adultery with Maiota Merssher. *<the woman appears, denies, to purge herself with five hands before the chaplain>* [*in margin*]: Leominster

774 Next, [*not completed*]

Dilwyn *<Weston>*. Visitation made there on Friday, 8 June, the year as above

KING'S PYON *<Weston>*

775 The parishioners say that the chancel is ruinous and is defective in its roof and other things, by the fault of the rector. *<to be rebuilt before Easter, under penalty of 20 shillings>*

776 Next, that William Wotton *<suspended>* withholds 8 pence from the light of the Blessed Mary that the parishioners recovered against him by a definitive sentence in the consistory at Hereford, and that the same William is excommunicated on account of not paying this 8 pence during the last year and earlier *<and that he did not receive the sacrament on Easter Sunday; appears, admits he is excommunicated and did not take the sacrament as charged, he has a day before his lordship>* [*in margin*]: *<Bromyard on Ember Saturday [16 June 1397]>*

777   Item quod idem Wilkoc Wotton <suspensus> fornicatur cum Maiota Howdy <suspensa> quam tenet in domo sua et quod abjuravit eandem alias. <vir comparet, habet diem coram domino>

778   [I]tem quod[1]

779   <[Rec]tor ibidem suspensus a celebratione divinorum; postea comparuit>[2]

[f. 16v]

Dyluwe <West'>

780   Parochiani dicunt quod vicarius de Dyluwe ordinavit in sua ultima vol-untate unum capellanum ad celebrandum ibidem pro anima sua per annum integrum et ultra si bona extenderent etcetera, et in testamento suo constituit dominum Johannem Snede <absens est> et dominum Walterum Robyns capella-nos huiusmodi testamenti executores, quiquidem dominus Johannes celebrat pro anima dicti vicarii aliquando ibidem aliquando alibi, recipiendo nomine salarii sui vij marcas nimis excessive ut credunt contra juramentum suum alias prestitum de debite exequendo dictam ultimam voluntatem. <Walterus[3] Robyns comparet, allegat quod auctoriate commissarii dictus Johannes recepit dictum salarium, et dimissus>

781   Item idem dominus Johannes Snede incontinens est cum Issabella Hannes[4] serviente Godivi de Irlond. <vir absens, mulier suspensa>

782   Item quod dominus Johannes Skylle capellanus et Johanna relicta Willelmi Snede <absens> graviter diffamantur super incontinencia commissa <vir abjurat et dimissus> et habitarunt diu in loco suspecto. [*in margin*] <v s>

783   [*in margin*] <significatum>
Item quod Willelmus of Mulle conjugatus adulteratur cum Alicia Wyrall.[5] <vir excommunicatus quia non vult etcetera, mulier suspensa; postea abjurat peccatum et locum, fustigetur vj per mercatum et vj per ecclesiam>

784   Item quod Cowesloc fornicatur cum Margareta relicta Willelmi Baylyf <que levavit filium dicti Cowesloc de sacro fonte. Vir comparet, fatetur, abjurat peccatum et locum suspectum et fustigetur vj per mercatum et ecclesiam, mulier citetur>

785   Item quod Edmundus Maen fornicatur cum Issabella serviente sua. <vir negat carnalem copulationem sed fatetur locum suspectum, abjurat et fustige-tur ter per mercatum et ecclesiam, mulier suspensa; commissum est decano ad recipiendum dictam mulierem ad correctionem; difertur penitencia viri sub spe nubendi>

[1]   Unfinished.
[2]   Perhaps a new parish, since the non-appearance of clergy is usually inserted at the head of the entry for the parish; but if so, the lack of *Parochiani dicunt* is anomalous.
[3]   Preceded by *Johannes*, struck through.
[4]   Altered from *Hannys*.
[5]   Followed by <*suspensi*>, struck through.

777   Next, that the same Wilkoc Wotton *<suspended>* fornicates with Maiota Howdy *<suspended>* whom he keeps in his house, and that he has previously abjured her. *<the man appears, has a day before his lordship>*

778   Next, that [*not completed*]

779   *<the rector there suspended from the celebration of divine services; later he appeared>*

[f. 16v]

DILWYN *<Weston>*

780   The parishioners say that the vicar of Dilwyn provided in his last will for a chaplain to celebrate there for his soul for a whole year, and longer if the resources went further etc., and in his testament he appointed Sir John Snede *<he is absent>* and Sir Walter Robyns, chaplains, the executors of this testament; which Sir John celebrates for the soul of the said vicar sometimes there, sometimes elsewhere, receiving as his salary the sum of 7 marks, which is very excessive as they believe, contrary to the oath he previously took of properly executing the said last will. *<Walter Robyns appears, alleges that by the authority of the commissary the said John received the said salary, and he is dismissed>*

781   Next, the same Sir John Snede is incontinent with Isabel Hannes, servant of Godive of Ireland. *<the man absent; the woman suspended>*

782   Next, that Sir John Skylle, chaplain, and Joan, widow of William Snede *<absent>*, are gravely defamed over incontinence *<the man abjures and is dismissed>* and they have long resided in suspicious circumstances. [*in margin*]: *<5 shillings>*

783   [*in margin*]: *<signified>*
Next, that William of Mulle, a married man, commits adultery with Alice Wyrall. *<the man excommunicated because he will not [abjure] etc.; the woman suspended; later she abjures the sin and the place, to be beaten six times through the marketplace and six times through the church>*

784   Next, that Cowesloc fornicates with Margaret, widow of William Baylyf, *<who was godmother to a son of this Cowesloc; the man appears, admits, abjures the sin and the suspicious circumstances and to be beaten six times through the marketplace and [around] the church; the woman to be cited>*

785   Next, that Edmund Maen fornicates with Isabel, his servant. *<the man denies bodily union but confesses the suspicious circumstances, he abjures and to be beaten three times through the marketplace and [around] the church; the woman suspended, commission to the dean to receive the said woman for correction; the man's penance to be deferred in the hope of them marrying>*

786 Item quod Johannes Lupeson[1] absentat se ab ecclesia parochiali diebus dominicis et festivis et fornicatur cum Johanna Hulle. <suspensi; vir comparet, purget se quo ad fornicationem post correctionem, quo ad absenciam juravit emendare, mulier fatetur, abjurat, fustigetur in forma, vir etiam> [*in margin*] <penitencia mulieris differtur usque post partum>

787 Item quod rector tenetur invenire unum par vestimentorum ad celebrandum ibidem diebus ferialibus quod non facit.

788 Item quod libri ad quorum inventionem rector tenetur sunt defectivi <et> insufficientes ad deserviendum Deo et ecclesie in defectu eiusdem rectoris.

Pennbrugg <Leom'>. Visitatio facta ibidem die sabbati nona mensis Junii anno ut supra

　　　Sarnesfeld <Leom'>

789 Parochiani dicunt quod omnia sunt bene ibidem.

　　　Staunton juxta Pennbrugg <Leom'>

790 Parochiani dicunt quod Robyn Flessewer carnifex recusat reddere decimas lucri sui de huius arte curato suo. <difertur sub spe concordie>

791 Item quod Muryel Hensor filia Willelmi Hensor fornicatur cum Ierwerth Gogh.[2] <ambo suspensi>

792 Item quod Johannes Munton <de Ereslon> impedit ultimam voluntatem Matilde Jurles <eo quod detinet ij s de bonis eiusdem licet pluries[3] requisitus per Willelmum Jurles executorem testamenti dicte Matilde ad restitutionem huiusmodi denariorum; prosequatur si velit>

　　　Pennbrugg <Leom'>

793 Parochiani dicunt quod Johannes Scheppert conjugatus adulteratur cum Alson quam tenet in domo sua, repulsa uxore. <vir comparet;[4] asserit eos matrimonialiter copulatos, interrogatus ubi, dicit quod apud Radenor, ideo denunciatus excommunicatus, mulier suspensa; denunciatus est, mulier excommunicata>

794 Item quod Lucia serviens magistri de Noke fornicatur cum Willelmo Snowe. <ambo suspensi>

795 Item quod Philippus Went et Johanna Walissh contraxerunt adinvicem per verba de presenti carnali copula subsecuta et sic non procurant matrimonium facere solempnizari inter eos. <vir comparet, asserit se cognovisse matrem eiusdem, ideo habet diem coram domino apud Brom3ard die sabbati iiij[or] temporum>

---

[1]　Altered, perhaps from *Luseson*.
[2]　Followed by *habet*, struck through.
[3]　Preceded by *plri*, struck through.
[4]　Followed by *bene*, struck through.

786   Next, that John Lupeson absents himself from the parish church on Sundays and feast days and fornicates with Joan Hulle. *<both suspended; the man appears, to purge himself as to the fornication since correction, as to the absence he has sworn to amend; the woman admits, abjures, to be beaten in due form, the man too>* [in margin]: *<the woman's penance to be deferred until after childbirth>*

787   Next, that the rector ought to provide a set of vestments to celebrate there on weekdays, which he does not do.

788   Next, that the books that the rector ought to provide are defective and insufficient to serve God and the church, by the fault of the same rector.

Pembridge *<Leominster>*. Visitation made there on Saturday, 9 June, the year as above

SARNESFIELD *<Leominster>*

789   The parishioners say that all things are well there.

STAUNTON-ON-ARROW NEAR PEMBRIDGE *<Leominster>*

790   The parishioners say that Robin Flessewer, a butcher, refuses to pay tithes from the profits of his trade to his parish priest. *<it is deferred in the hope of an agreement>*

791   Next, that Muriel Hensor, daughter of William Hensor, fornicates with Iorwerth Gogh. *<both suspended>*

792   Next, that John Munton *<of Eardisland>* obstructed the last will of Maud Jurles, *<in that he kept back 2 shillings out of her goods, although often asked by William Jurles, executor of Maud's will, to restore this money; let him prosecute if he wishes>*

PEMBRIDGE *<Leominster>*

793   The parishioners say that John Scheppert, a married man, commits adultery with Alison, whom he keeps in his house, having driven out his wife. *<the man appears, asserts that they are joined in matrimony, asked where, he says at Radnor, so is denounced excommunicate; the woman suspended; the man denounced; the woman excommunicated>*

794   Next, that Lucy, servant of the master of Noke, fornicates with William Snowe. *<both suspended>*

795   Next, that Philip Went and Joan Walissh made a contract between them in the present tense, followed by bodily union, and so have not arranged to have the marriage solemnised between them. *<the man appears, asserts that he knew her mother [sexually], so he has a day before his lordship at Bromyard on Ember Saturday [16 June 1397]>*

796   Item quod Howel Strateford <adulteratur>¹ cum Maiota Baly conjuga-
ta.² <vir comparet, negat post correctionem; purgavit se>

797   Item quod Agnes Walissh adulteratur cum Howel commorante extra
diocesim. <suspensa>

798   Item quod David Hoper conjugatus adulteratur cum Margareta Hopere.
<ambo suspensi; vir abjurat, fustigetur in forma, mulier extra>

799   Item quod Wylym of Medw fornicatur cum Gylot Swone. <ambo suspensi; vir purgavit se>

800   Item quod dominus Johannes Hopkyns capellanus incontinens est cum
Alicia Adames conjugata. <ambo suspensi; vir³ purgavit [se] ...>⁴

801   Item quod eadem Alicia adulteratur cum Waltero Carpenter de Leom'
conjugato. <mulier purget [se] ...>

802   Item quod Willelmus Screchere absentat se ab ecclesia parochiali diebus
dominicis [et festivis.]

803   Item quod Johannes Phylippes etiam absentat se ut supra et est communis
operarius [diebus dominicis et festivis.] <injunctum est quod exerceat ecclesiam de
cetero etcetera>

804   Item quod Gybon Brimley diffamavit maliciose Agnetem uxorem ... ...
super adulterio commisso cum Thoma Gomond et sic suscitavit ... <vir comparet,
negat; purgavit se>

[f. 17]

805   Item quod Gruffuth serviens Rogeri Clerkes fornicatur cum quadam quam
tenet. <suspensi; extra>

Almaly <Webley>. Visitatio facta ibidem die lune xj Junii anno Domini⁵ ut supra

        Wynforton <Webley>

806   +Parochiani dicunt quod Jankyn Malmeshull <extra>⁶ fornicatur cum
Maiota Baldenhale. <citentur ad proximam; citentur per edictum>

807   +Item quod Reynald Taelour fornicatur cum Letitia quam tenet. <non
reperiuntur ideo citentur ad proximam; citentur>

808   Item quod dominus Johannes Ely capellanus commorans in diocesi Wigorn' incontinens est cum Johanna de la Hay. <ambo extra>

---

¹   Replacing *fornicatur*, struck through.
²   Followed by <*suspensi ambo*>, struck through.
³   Altered from *mulier*.
⁴   The bottom right-hand corner of this page is perished with the loss of up to three
inches of text.
⁵   *Domini* repeated in error.
⁶   Deleted, then reinstated.

796 Next, that Hywel Strateford commits adultery with Maiota Baly, a married woman. <*the man appears, denies since correction; he has purged himself*>

797 Next, that Agnes Walissh commits adultery with Hywel, who lives outside the diocese. <*she is suspended*>

798 Next, that David Hoper, a married man, commits adultery with Margaret Hopere. <*both suspended; the man abjures, to be beaten in due form; the woman outside*>

799 Next, that William of Medw fornicates with Gylot Swone. <*both suspended; the man has purged himself*>

800 Next, that Sir John Hopkyns, chaplain, is incontinent with Alice Adames, a married woman. <*both suspended; the man has purged himself ...*>

801 Next, that the same Alice commits adultery with Walter Carpenter of Leominster, a married man. <*the woman to purge herself ...*>

802 Next, that William Screchere absents himself from the parish church on Sundays and feast days.

803 Next, that John Phylippes also absents himself as above and is a habitual worker on Sundays and feast days. <*ordered to attend church in future etc.*>

804 Next, that Gybon Brimley has maliciously defamed Agnes the wife ... ..., over adultery committed with Thomas Gomond, and so has provoked ... <*the man appears, denies; has purged himself*>

[f. 17]

805 Next, that Gruffudd, servant of Roger Clerkes, fornicates with a certain woman whom he keeps. <*both suspended; outside*>

Almeley <*Weobley*>. Visitation made there on Monday, 11 June, in the year of Our Lord as above

WINFORTON <*Weobley*>

806 +The parishioners say that Jankin Malmeshull <*outside*> fornicates with Maiota Baldenhale. <*to be cited to the next; to be cited by edict*>

807 +Next, that Reynold Taelour fornicates with Lettice, whom he keeps. <*they are not found, so cite both to the next; both to be cited*>

808 Next, that Sir John Ely, chaplain, residing in the diocese of Worcester, is incontinent with Joan de la Hay. <*both outside*>

809   Item quod dominus Robertus Tymmys commorans apud Clyfford incontinens est [cum][1] Juliana Baker conjugata de Wynforton. <vir comparet, negat,
purget se cum vj[ta] manu; mulier[2] comparet, negat, habet ad purgandum coram
curato; vir purgavit se>

Whiteney <Webley>

810   Parochiani dicunt quod Llewelyn Gronwe[3] conjugatus adulteratur cum
Angharat Bach. <ambo suspensi; vir excommunicatus quia etcetera, mulier etiam
excommunicata quia etcetera> [*in margin*] <+ fiat executio quia etcetera>

811   Item quod Howel Says non recepit sacralia sacramentalia in ecclesia parochiali in festo Pasche ultimo preterito, an alibi vel ne ipsi nesciunt. <dimissus est>

812   <Willelmus Carpenter fornicatur cum Johanna Hoby. Vir comparet; fatetur, abjurat, fustigetur ter circa ecclesiam parochialem et ter ante processionem
Heref'>[4]

Erdesley <Webley>

813   Parochiani dicunt quod cancellus patitur defectum in tectura et aliis in
defectum[5] rectoris. <injunctum est quod faciat reparari>

814   Item quod idem rector tenetur invenire unum portiforium in choro ad
deserviendum Deo et ecclesie quod non facit.

815   Item quod vicarius tenetur invenire unum clericum ad deserviendum Deo
in ecclesia qui sciat[6] legere et cantare pulsare campanas ire ante eundem ad
visitandum infirmos et alia facienda quod non facit. <differuntur omnia conter-
vencia[7] vicarii sub spe concordie etcetera>

816   Item quod Agnes Knethur et Issabella servientes dicti vicarii pulsant
campanas et juvant ipsum vicarium ad celebrandum quod est contra honestatem
ecclesiasticam.

817   Item dicunt scandalum et sinistra suspicio est inter parochianos de cohabitatione <dicti vicarii> cum eisdem mulieribus.

818   Item quod Walterus Grobbe mortuus fuit sine sacramentis et confessione
in defectu vicarii.

819   Item quod Rogerus filius Walteri Wardrop mortuus est pari forma in
defectu vicarii.[8]

---

[1]   Omitted in error.
[2]   Followed by *suspensa*, struck through.
[3]   Altered from *Gronue*.
[4]   Whole entry added.
[5]   Recte *defectu*.
[6]   Altered from *scit* by a superscribed *a*.
[7]   Recte *contraventia*.
[8]   Preceded by *rectoris*, struck through.

809   Next, that Sir Robert Tymmys, residing at Clifford, is incontinent with Julian Baker of Winforton, a married woman. <*the man appears, denies, to purge himself with six hands; the woman appears, denies, she has [a day] to purge [herself] before the parish priest; the man has purged himself*>

WHITNEY <*Weobley*>

810   The parishioners say that Llewelyn Gronwe, a married man, commits adultery with Angharad Bach. <*both suspended; the man excommunicated because etc., the woman also excommunicated because etc.*> [*in margin*]: <*+sentence to be carried out because etc.*>

811   Next, that Hywel Says did not receive the holy sacraments in the parish last Easter Sunday, and whether or not anywhere else they do not know. <*he is dismissed*>

812   <*William Carpenter fornicates with Joan Hoby; the man appears, admits, abjures, to be beaten three times around the parish church and three times before the procession at Hereford*>

EARDISLEY <*Weobley*>

813   The parishioners say that the chancel is defective in its roof and other things, by the fault of the rector. <*ordered to have it repaired*>

814   Next, that the same rector ought to provide a breviary in the choir to serve God and the church, which he does not do.

815   Next, that the vicar ought to provide a clerk, for the service of God in the church, who knows how to read and sing, to ring the bells, go before him when visiting the sick, and carry out other duties, which he does not do. <*all contraventions by the vicar to be deferred in the hope of agreement etc.*>

816   Next, that Agnes Knethur and Isabel, servants of the said vicar, ring the bells and help the vicar to celebrate, which is against ecclesiastical decency.

817   Next, they say that there is scandal and sinister suspicion among the parishioners about the vicar's living with these women.

818   Next, that Walter Grobbe died without the sacraments and confession, by the fault of the vicar.

819   Next, that Roger, son of Walter Wardrop, died in the same way, by the fault of the vicar.

820 Item quod Ricardus Bady[1] et Alicia Barbour obierunt sine extrema unctione in defectu vicarii.

821 Item quod quidam infans Thome Correyour baptizato[2] fuit sine crismate in defectu vicarii.

822 Item quod idem vicarius dum humaret Johannem Boley in cimiterio publice dixit in audiencia plurium ibidem existentium 'jace ibi excommunicate' in magnum opprobrium etcetera.

823 Item quod in festo Pasche ultimo preterito idem vicarius recusavit ministrare sacramenta Waltero Jewe seniori quousque concordaret cum eo super certis decimis quas[3]

824 Item quod recusat ministrare sacramenta in festo Pasche servientibus dicte parochie quousque concordaverint cum eo de decima salarii eorundum.

825 Item quod idem vicarius[4] est communis mercator diversorum bonorum bladorum et aliorum et est usurarius.

826 Item quod idem vicarius celebravit clamdestinum matrimonium inter Jankyn Colle et Margaretam uxorem suam bannis non editis nisi semel constito sibi de reclamatione fienda secundo die bannorum etcetera.

827 Item quod idem vicarius celebrat bis in die.

828 Item quod Wilkoc Vachan conjugatus adulteratur cum Cecilia Besaunde repulsa uxore sua ligitima. <vir comparet, negat, purget se cum v^ta manu coram vicario, mulier comparet, negat, purget se similiter; purgarunt se coram vicario>

829 [Ite]m[5] quod Andrewe Walteri Wardrop son fornicatur cum Matilda[6] Carpenter. <suspensa; vir comparet,[7] fatetur, abjurat, fustigetur [t]er circa ecclesiam, mulier comparet, fatetur, abjurat, fustigetur ter circa ecclesiam; excommunicati quia non egerunt penitenciam>

830 [Ite]m quod Johannes filius eiusdem Walteri fornicatur cum Juliana Baron. <suspensa; vir comparet, fatetur, abjurat, fustigetur ter etcetera, mulier comparet, fatetur, abjurat, [fu]stigetur[8] circa ecclesiam semel>

831 [Item] quod Willelmus Jewe et Juliana Lather[9] fornicantur adinvicem. <vir comparet, fatetur, abjurat, fustigetur ter circa ecclesiam, mulier suspensa; [vir] excommunicatus quia non fecit penitenciam et denunciatus est excommunicatus; mulier abjurat, fustigetur in forma>

---

[1] Preceded by *Baylyf*, struck through.
[2] Recte *baptizatus*.
[3] Unfinished.
[4] Preceded by *mer*, struck through.
[5] The bottom left-hand corner of this page is perished with the loss of up to half an inch of text.
[6] Altered from *Maiota*.
[7] Followed by *excommunicatus propter contumaciam*, struck through.
[8] Followed by *ter*, deleted.
[9] Altered from *Lath*.

820 Next, that Richard Bady and Alice Barbour died without extreme unction, by the fault of the vicar.

821 Next, that a certain infant of Thomas Correyour was baptised without chrism, by the fault of the vicar.

822 Next, that the same vicar, while he was burying John Boley in the church-yard, publicly said in the hearing of many people there, 'Lie there, you excommunicate!', to the great scandal etc.

823 Next, that last Easter Sunday the same vicar refused to administer the sacraments to Walter Jewe the elder until he came to an agreement with him about certain tithes that [*not finished*]

824 Next, that he refuses to administer the sacraments on Easter Sunday to servants of the parish, until they have come to an agreement with him about the tithes on their wages.

825 Next, that the same vicar is a habitual dealer in various goods, corn, and other things, and is a usurer.

826 Next, that the same vicar celebrated a clandestine marriage between Jankin Colle and his wife Margaret, the banns not having been given out more than once, he being aware that a challenge would be made on the second day of the banns etc.

827 Next, that the same vicar celebrates twice in a day.

828 Next, that Wilkoc Vachan, a married man, commits adultery with Cecily Besaunde, having driven out his lawful wife. <*the man appears, denies, to purge himself with five hands before the vicar; the woman appears, denies, to purge herself similarly; they have purged themselves before the vicar*>

829 Next, that Andrew, Walter Wardrop's son, fornicates with Maud Carpenter. <*suspended; the man appears, admits, abjures, to be beaten ... around the church; the woman appears, admits, abjures, to be beaten three times around the church; excommunicated because they have not carried out the penance*>

830 Next, that John, son of the same Walter, fornicates with Julian Baron. <*suspended; the man appears, admits, abjures, to be beaten three times etc.; the woman appears, admits, abjures, to be beaten around the church once*>

831 Next, that William Jewe and Julian Lather fornicate together. <*the man appears, admits, abjures, to be beaten three times around the church; the woman suspended; the man excommunicated because he has not done the penance and is denounced as excommunicated; the woman abjures, to be beaten in due form*>

[f. 17v]

832   Item quod vicarius noluit ministrare sacramenta in festo Pasche ultimo preterito Amisie filie Johannis Baker.

833   Item quod Mylo Webbe fornicatur cum Alicia Syre. <vir comparet, fatetur, abjurat, fustigetur vj^{es} per forum et circa ecclesiam; mulier¹ comparet, fatetur, abjurat, fustigetur vj per ecclesiam et forum; vir dimissus; mulier etiam>

834   Item quod Davy Thresser fornicatur cum Johanna Specerer. <vir extra, mulier in carcere; mulier suspensa>

835   Item quod vicarius tenetur invenire unam lampadem ardentem in ecclesia die noctuque et non facit.

836   Item quod Johannes Baker non venit ad ecclesiam diebus dominicis et festivis. <dimissus est>

837   Item quod Isota Lather non venit ad ecclesiam ut supra.

838   Item quod vicarius juratus est alias coram domino episcopo de inveniendo unum capellanum ad celebrandum in capella de Bolynghull quod non facit ideo perjurus.

839   Item quod unus calix furatus est in ecclesia de bonis parochianorum ad valorem xl s in defectu vicarii quia tenetur ad custodiam.

840   Item quod tenetur pulsare ante missam omni die quod non facit idem vicarius.

841   Item quod dehonesta² ecclesiam cum lino et canapo etcetera.

842   Item quod tenetur invenire cordas pro campanis quod non facit.

843   Item quod Jankyn Baelyf³ et Amisia uxor sua non cohabitant simul. <vir obiit>

844⁴   Item conquesti sunt Johannes Baker de Erdesley et Margeria uxor sua penes officium quod vicarius de Erdesley in quadragesima ultima preterito⁵ ad annum recusavit expresse absolvere dictam Margeriam habita ipsius confessione nisi vellet dare xij denarios ad reparationem librorum ecclesie ut asseruit; quequidem Margeria ivit Herefordiam pro absolutione obtinenda et ibidem confessa est et absoluta ibidem per dominum Johannem Mawdelen. Demum in festo Pasche tunc proximo sequenti eadem Margeria accessit ad mensam Domini cui idem vicarius recusavit ministrare sacramenta nisi iterum confiteretur sua peccata sibi etcetera.⁶

¹   Followed by *suspensa*, struck through.
²   Recte *dehonestat*.
³   Altered from *Baley*.
⁴   A heading *Wyllardesley*, opposite the beginning of **844**, is struck through.
⁵   Recte *preterita*.
⁶   The next entry continues on the same line.

[f. 17v]

832   Next, that the vicar would not administer the sacraments last Easter Sunday to Amice, daughter of John Baker.

833   Next, that Miles Webbe fornicates with Alice Syre. *<the man appears, admits, abjures, to be beaten six times through the marketplace and around the church; the woman appears, admits, abjures, to be beaten six times through the church and marketplace; the man dismissed; the woman too>*

834   Next, that Davy Thresser fornicates with Joan Specerer. *<the man outside, the woman in prison; the woman suspended>*

835   Next, that the vicar ought to provide a lamp burning in church day and night and does not do so.

836   Next, that John Baker does not come to church on Sundays and feast days. *<he is dismissed>*

837   Next, that Isot Lather does not come to church as above.

838   Next, that the vicar previously swore before the lord bishop that he would provide a chaplain to celebrate in the chapel of Bollingham, which he does not do, so is perjured.

839   Next, that a chalice worth 40 shillings was stolen in the church from the goods of the parishioners by the fault of the vicar because he was responsible for its safekeeping.

840   Next, that he ought to ring [a bell] before mass every day, which the same vicar does not do.

841   Next, that he makes the church unseemly with flax and hemp etc.

842   Next, that he ought to provide ropes for the bells, which he does not do.

843   Next, that Jankin Baelyf and his wife Amice do not live together. *<the man has died>*

844   Next, John Baker of Eardisley and his wife Margery have complained to the Official that a year last Lent the vicar of Eardisley expressly refused to absolve the said Margery having taken her confession unless she would give 12 pence towards the repair of the church books, as she alleged; Margery went to Hereford to obtain absolution and there confessed and was absolved there by Sir John Mawdelen. Then the following Easter Sunday the same Margery went to the Lord's table and the same vicar refused to administer the sacraments to her unless she again confessed her sins to him etc.

845   Item quadragesima ultima idem vicarius noluit ministrare eisdem sacra-menta[1] quia noluerunt dimittere cuidam Ricardo Wilson baker occisionem Wal-teri filii dictorum Johannis et Margerie et etiam dimittere prosecutionem suam contra eundem Ricardum.

Wyllardesley <Web'>

846   Parochiani dicunt quod Meuric Walishmon adulteratur cum Eva uxore cuiusdam cuius nomen ignorant etcetera.

Kynarsley <Web'>

847   Parochiani dicunt quod dominus Walterus Ondys capellanus cohabitat cum Agnete quondam concubina sua, dicunt tamen quod credunt eos immunes de peccato commisso a tempore correctionis excepta cohabitatione tantum.

848   Item quod Johanna Coward de Kynarsley conjugata adulteratur cum domino Johanne Somerton rectore de Letton et non cohabitat cum marito suo licet sepius requisita <et cum Agnete Walter; quo ad Johannam negat, ambo pur-gent se, quo ad Agnetem fatentur, abjurant peccatum et locum suspectum>

849   Item quod Alicia Mayard est communis diffamatrix et suscitatrix brigarum inter vicinos. <negat, injunctum est quod non faciat de cetero>

850   Item quod Ieuan Taelour fornicatur cum Margareta Clanvowe quam tenet. <matrimonialiter copulati sunt>

Almaly <Web'>

851   Parochiani dicunt quod omnia sunt bene ibidem excepto quod portio vicarii ibidem est nimis exilis ad sustentationem ipsius et onera sibi incumbentia supportanda.

[f. 18]

Lunhales <Web'>

852   <Vicarius quia non comparet ideo suspensus et citatus quod compareat coram domino die sabbati iiij^{or} temporum>

853   Parochiani habent diem apud Kynton ubi dicunt quod Philippus Lurke et Juliana Godrych <suspensa> contraxerunt adinvicem carnali copula subsecuta nec faciunt huiusmodi matrimonium solempnizari et hoc in defectu dicte Juliane. <vir comparet, asserit se paratum>

854   Item quod Johannes Hopley <junior> est communis operarius diebus dominicis et festivis.

855   Item quod rector tenetur invenire unam lampadem ardentem coram summo altari quod non facit.

856   Item quod <Jankyn Lullewal adulteratur cum Juliana Moor; vir comparet, habet diem coram domino die sabbati iiij^{or} temporum; mulier suspensa>

---

[1]   Followed by *nisi v*, struck through.

845   Next, last Lent the same vicar would not administer the sacraments to them because they would not release a certain Richard Wilson, baker, for the killing of Walter, the son of the said John and Margery, and also to release their prosecution against the same Richard.

WILLERSLEY *<Weobley>*

846   The parishioners say that Meurig Walishmon commits adultery with Eve, the wife of someone whose name they do not know etc.

KINNERSLEY *<Weobley>*

847   The parishioners say that Sir Walter Ondys, chaplain, lives with Agnes, his former concubine, but they say that they believe that they have been free from sin since the time of correction, other than cohabitation alone.

848   Next, that Joan Coward of Kinnersley, a married woman, commits adultery with Sir John Somerton, the rector of Letton, and does not live with her husband although often called on to do so *<and with Agnes Walter; as to Joan he denies it, both to purge themselves; as to Agnes, both admit it, both abjure the sin and the suspicious circumstances>*

849   Next, that Alice Mayard is a habitual defamer and provoker of brawls between neighbours. *<she denies, ordered not to do so in future>*

850   Next, that Ieuan Taelour fornicates with Margaret Clanvowe, whom he keeps. *<they are joined in marriage>*

ALMELEY *<Weobley>*

851   The parishioners say that all things are well there except that the portion of the vicar there is too small to sustain him and to support the burdens incumbent upon him.

[f. 18]

LYONSHALL *<Weobley>*

852   *<the vicar, because he does not appear, is therefore suspended, and cited that he appear before his lordship on Ember Saturday [16 June 1397]>*

853   The parishioners have a day at Kington where they say that Philip Lurke and Julian Godrych *<suspended>* contracted together, with bodily union following, and did not have their marriage solemnised, by the fault of the said Julian. *<the man appears, asserts that he is ready>*

854   Next, that John Hopley *<the younger>* is a habitual worker on Sundays and feast days.

855   Next, that the rector ought to provide a lamp to burn before the high altar, which he does not do.

856   Next, that *<Jankin Lullewal commits adultery with Julian Moor; the man appears, he has a day before his lordship on Ember Saturday [16 June 1397]; the woman suspended>*

857   \<Willelmus Holom fornicatur cum Johanna Deveros; vir comparet, negat, purget se coram commissario apud Webley; mulier[1] comparet, negat ad idem; vir purgavit se; mulier purgavit se>[2]

Clyfford \<Web'>. Visitatio facta ibidem die martis xij die[3] Junii anno Domini supradicto

[Clyfford]

858   Parochiani dicunt quod cancellus patitur defectum in tectura in defectu rectoris. \<emendabitur>

859   +Item quod Philipot Mulward et Lleuky filia Ieuan Hir post divorcium habitum inter eos cohabitant simul in eadem domo quod suspectum est. \<ambo suspensi; vir abjurat, fustigetur in forma et mulier similiter eadem forma>

860   Item dicunt quod parochiani de Curshop tenentur ad contribuendum reparationi ecclesie de Clyfford campanilis et aliorum ornamentorum ut matrici ecclesie quod non faciunt etcetera. \<prosequantur parochiani>

861[4]   \<+Johannes ap Robyn Jekes fornicatur cum Nest verch Ieuan, vir indictatus est, et Isabell Tewe alias verch Meredyd; Isabell dicit quod vicarius recepit juramentum ipsius et abjurat, fustigetur in forma>

862   \<+Alicia Belmar \<incestat>[5] cum Johanne Gomme; mulier excommunicata; vir indictus; mulier abjurat, fustigetur in forma>

863   \<+David ap Iorwerth incestat cum Dedgu quam tenet, suspensi>

864   \<+ Ieuan Kevyn adulteratur cum Alicia Brydd, suspensi>

865   \<+Philippus Frer adulteratur cum Margareta Oldeacre;[6] mulier suspensa; vir apud abbatiam de Wygmour>

Curshop \<Web'>

866   \<Dominus Owynus capellanus ibidem suspensus a celebratione divinorum>

867   Parochiani dicunt quod cancellus est ruinosus et defectius in tectura muris et fenestris in defectu rectoris.

868   Item quod non habent nec missas nec alia divina servicia nisi missam tantum diebus dominicis et hoc expensis eorum propriis in defectu rectoris.

869   Item quod infantes non baptizantur ibidem in defectu rectoris.

870   Item quod Ieuan Gwyn conjugatus adulteratur cum Nest filia Howel repulsa uxore legitima.

---

[1]   Followed by *suspensa*, struck through.
[2]   Whole entry added.
[3]   Followed by *lun*, struck through.
[4]   Entries **861–5** added in the annotating hand.
[5]   Replacing *fornicatur*, struck through; the process in **861** was added after the insertion of *incestat*.
[6]   Followed by \<*suspensi*>, struck through.

857 <*William Holom fornicates with Joan Deveros; the man appears, denies, to purge himself before the commissary at Weobley; the woman appears, denies as to the same; the man has purged himself; the woman has purged herself*>

Clifford <*Weobley*>. Visitation made there on Tuesday, 12 June, in the year of Our Lord abovesaid

[CLIFFORD]

858 The parishioners say that the chancel is defective in its roof, by the fault of the rector. <*it will be put right*>

859 +Next, that Philipot Mulward and Lleucu, daughter of Ieuan Hir, after their divorce, lived together in the same house, which is suspect. <*both suspended; the man abjures, to be beaten in due form and the woman similarly in the same form*>

860 Next, they say that the parishioners of Cusop ought to contribute to the repair of the church of Clifford, of the bell-tower, and of the other ornaments, as to the mother church, which they do not do etc. <*let the parishioners prosecute*>

861 <+*John ap Robin Jekes fornicates with Nest verch Ieuan (the man is indicted) and Isabel Towe, otherwise verch Maredudd; Isabel says that the vicar has received her oath and she abjures, to be beaten in due form*>

862 <+*Alice Belmar commits incest with John Gomme; the woman excommunicated; the man indicted; the woman abjures, to be beaten in due form*>

863 <+*David ap Iorwerth commits incest with Dedgu, whom he keeps; both suspended*>

864 <+*Ieuan Kevyn commits adultery with Alice Brydd; both suspended*>

865 <+*Philip Frer commits adultery with Margaret Oldeacre; the woman suspended; the man at the abbey of Wigmore*>

CUSOP <*Weobley*>

866 <*Sir Owain, chaplain there, suspended from the celebration of divine services*>

867 The parishioners say that the chancel is in a ruinous state and defective in its roof, walls, and windows, by the fault of the rector.

868 Next, that they have neither masses nor other divine services, but only mass on Sundays and this at their own expense, by the fault of the rector.

869 Next, that infants are not baptised there, by the fault of the rector.

870 Next, that Ieuan Gwyn, a married man, commits adultery with Nest, daughter of Hywel, having driven out his lawful wife.

871   Item quod Ieuan ap Philip fornicatur cum Johanna[1] filia Hoedlywe quam tenet.

872   Item quod dominus Owain capellanus ibidem incontinens est cum quadam Wladus filia Jokkyn.

[f. 18v]
Kynton <Web'>. Visitatio facta ibidem die mercurii xiij mensis Junii

     Huntynton <Web'>

873   Parochiani dicunt quod Howel ap y Penlloyt fornicatur cum Dydgu filia David ap Meilir. <ambo extra>

874   +Item quod Llewelyn Bannour fornicatur cum Gweirvyl verch Lwgyr y Coet <et Angharat filia Gronwy; suspensi ambo; excommunicati>

875   +Item quod Ricard ap Howel fornicatur cum Margret filia Gwilim ap Gruffuth. <ambo suspensi; mulier excommunicata; vir recusat abjurare, excommunicatus; vir abjurat, fustigetur in forma; mulier committitur curato>

876   +Item quod Ieuan ap Philip Derroc <adulteratur;[2] conjugatus est> cum Eva filia Eynon. <citetur ad proximam; suspensa; vir citetur ad proximam>

877   [*in margin*] <significatum>
+Item quod Rogerus Gogh <suspensus> fornicatur cum Angharat filia David.[3] <mulier comparet; excommunicata; denunciata est; vir abjurat, fustigetur in forma>

878   [*in margin*] <significatum>
+Item quod David ap Eynon Dilest fornicatur cum Angharat filia Gruffuth. <ambo comparent, abjurant, fustigentur ter circa ecclesiam; denunciati sunt>

879   [*in margin*] <significavit>
+Item quod Llewelyn Bryton fornicatur cum Mald filia Ieuan. <ambo suspensi; excommunicati; denunciati sunt; vir abjurat peccatum et locum suspectum, fustigetur in forma>

880   <+Item Meuric ap Eynon fornicatur cum Angharat filia David; ambo suspensi; excommunicati; vir abjurat, fustigetur in forma>

     Brimley <Web'>

881   Parochiani dicunt quod rector tenetur invenire unum portiforium ad deserviendum Deo et ecclesie in eadem quod non facit. <sequestrantur fructus>

---

[1]   Followed by *qu*, struck through.
[2]   Replacing *fornicatur*, struck through.
[3]   Followed by <*ambo suspensi*>, struck through.

871 Next, that Ieuan ap Philip fornicates with Joan, daughter of Hoeddlyw, whom he keeps.

872 Next, that Sir Owain, chaplain there, is incontinent with a certain Gwladus, daughter of Jokkyn.

[f. 18v]
Kington <*Weobley*>. Visitation made there on Wednesday, 13 June

HUNTINGTON <*Weobley*>

873 The parishioners say that Hywel ap y Penlloyt[1] fornicates with Dyddgu, daughter of David ap Meilyr. <*both outside*>

874 +Next, that Llewelyn Bannour fornicates with Gweirful verch Lwgyr y Coet[2] <*and with Angharad, daughter of Goronwy; both suspended; both excommunicated*>

875 +Next, that Richard ap Hywel fornicates with Margaret, daughter of Gwilym ap Gruffudd. <*both suspended; the woman excommunicated; the man refuses to abjure, excommunicated; the man abjures, to be beaten in due form; the woman to be committed to the parish priest*>

876 +Next, that Ieuan ap Philip Derroc <*he is a married man*> commits adultery with Eve, daughter of Einion. <*to be cited to the next, suspended; the man to be cited to the next*>

877 [*in margin*]: <*signified*>
+Next, that Roger Gogh <*suspended*> fornicates with Angharad, daughter of David. <*the woman appears, excommunicated; she is denounced; the man abjures, to be beaten in due form*>

878 [*in margin*]: <*signified*>
+Next, that David ap Einion Dilest fornicates with Angharad, daughter of Gruffudd. <*both appear, both abjure, both to be beaten three times around the church; they are denounced*>

879 [*in margin*]: <*signification*>
+Next, that Llewelyn Bryton fornicates with Mald, daughter of Ieuan. <*both suspended; both excommunicated; they are denounced; the man abjures the sin and the suspicious circumstances, to be beaten in due form*>

880 <+*Next, Meurig ap Einion fornicates with Angharad, daughter of David; both suspended; both excommunicated; the man abjures, to be beaten in due form*>

BRILLEY <*Weobley*>

881 The parishioners say that the rector ought to provide a breviary to serve God and the church in the same, which he does not do. <*the revenues to be sequestrated*>

---

[1]   Possibly for *ap y Penllwyd*, son of the grey-haired one.
[2]   Recte *verch Llwgr y Coed*, daughter of the Coward of the Woods.

882   Item quod dat fructus ecclesie ad firmam laycis licencia non petita nec obtenta et quod huiusmodi fructus non reponuntur in solo ecclesie. <sequestrati sunt fructus, commissa est custodia decano de Webley>

883   +Item quod Johannes ap Ivor fornicatur cum Erdudvyl¹ filia Gwilim. <ambo suspensi;² excommunicati; mulier abjurat, fustigetur ter>

884   Item quod Ieuan ap Eynon fornicatur cum Angharat filia Gruffuth. <ambo suspensi; absentes>

885   +Item quod Gruffuth Lloyt ap Llewelyn Doppa conjugatus adulteratur cum Gwenllian Duy. <vir³ absens, mulier suspensa; excommunicata; denunciata est; mulier abjurat, fustigetur in forma>

886   +Item quod Gruffuth ap Rys <conjugatus adulteratur>⁴ cum Eva Duy. <mulier suspensa; vir comparet, fatetur, abjurat, fustigetur ter per forum et ter circa ecclesiam; denuncietur excommunicatus; mulier excommunicata; mulier comparet, abjurat, fustigetur in forma>

887   Item quod Howel Kycheynokes et Gwenllian filia Ieuan uxor sua sunt illegitime copulati eo quod Gwilim ap Howel quondam maritus dicte Gwenllian attingebat dictum Howel infra iiijᵗᵘᵐ gradum affinitatis et prefatus Howel adulteratur cum Matilda filia David. <mulier extra, vir et uxor citentur ad proximam; vir abjurat, fustigetur in forma; denuncietur, vocetur ad penitenciam; mulier citetur>

888   +Item quod Rys ap Howel fornicatur cum Angharat verch Wilym. <suspensa; vir comparet, fatetur, abjurat, fustigetur ter circa ecclesiam; difertur sub spe nubendi; vir excommunicatus, mulier abjurat, fustigetur ter>

889   +Item quod Howel Wyne fornicatur cum Eva filia Ivor. <suspensi; vir comparet,⁵ excommunicatus quia renuit etcetera, mulier citetur publice; vir abjurat, fustigetur vj et per mercatum Heref'; mulier abjurat, fustigetur semel>

890   Item quod Ieuan ap Llewelyn Veddik fornicatur cum Nest filia Ieuan. <suspensa mulier, vir extra; mulier committitur decano>

891   Item quod Gruffuth⁶ ap Rys conjugatus adulteratur cum Eva filia Llewelyn. <superius est nominatus> [*in margin*] quia supra⁷

892   +Item quod Gruffuth ap Llewelyn Whith fornicatur cum Eva filia Jak. <suspensi; vir fatetur, abjurat, fustigetur in forma, mulier excommunicata; vocetur ad penitenciam; mulier abjurat, fustigetur ter>

893   Item quod Roger ap Gwallder et Llewelyth <suspensa> uxor sua sunt illegitime copulati quia sunt infra iiijᵗᵘᵐ gradum consanguinitatis. <juravit quod nescit impedimentum>

---

¹   The initial letter corrected from a D.
²   Followed by *excommunicati*, struck through.
³   Interlined above *mulier*, struck through.
⁴   Interlined above *fornicatur*, struck through.
⁵   Followed by *abjurat sub pena xl s*, struck through.
⁶   *Item quod Gruffuth* struck through, in lieu of the whole entry.
⁷   At **886**.

882   Next, that he farms out the revenues of the church to laymen without a licence being sought or obtained and that these revenues are not stored on church land. <*the revenues are sequestrated, the custody is committed to the dean of Weobley*>

883   +Next, that John ap Ifor fornicates with Erdudful, daughter of Gwilym. <*both suspended; both excommunicated; the woman abjures, to be beaten three times*>

884   Next, that Ieuan ap Einion fornicates with Angharad, daughter of Gruffudd. <*both suspended; absent*>

885   +Next, that Gruffudd Lloyt ap Llewelyn Doppa, a married man, commits adultery with Gwenllian Duy. <*the man absent; the woman suspended; excommunicated, she is denounced; the woman abjures, to be beaten in due form*>

886   +Next, that Gruffudd ap Rhys, <*a married man, commits adultery*> with Eve Duy. <*the woman suspended; the man appears, admits, abjures, to be beaten three times through the marketplace and three times around the church; to be denounced as excommunicated; the woman excommunicated; the woman appears, abjures, to be beaten in due form*>

887   Next, that Hywel Kycheynokes and his wife Gwenllian, daughter of Ieuan, are unlawfully joined because Gwilym ap Hywel, formerly the husband of the said Gwenllian, was related to the said Hywel within the fourth degree of affinity, and the aforesaid Hywel commits adultery with Maud, daughter of David. <*the woman outside; the man and wife to be cited to the next; the man abjures, to be beaten in due form; to be denounced, to be called to penance; the woman to be cited*>

888   +Next, that Rhys ap Hywel fornicates with Angharad verch Gwilym. <*suspended; the man appears, admits, abjures, to be beaten three times around the church; to be deferred in the hope of them marrying; the man excommunicated; the woman abjures, to be beaten three times*>

889   +Next, that Hywel Wyne fornicates with Eve, daughter of Ifor. <*both suspended; the man appears; excommunicated because he refused etc.; the woman to be cited publicly; the man abjures, to be beaten six times and through the marketplace at Hereford; the woman abjures, to be beaten once*>

890   Next, that Ieuan ap Llewelyn Veddik[1] fornicates with Nest, daughter of Ieuan. <*the woman suspended; the man outside; the woman to be committed to the dean*>

891   [*the entry deleted*] Next, that Gruffudd ap Rhys, a married man, commits adultery with Eve, daughter of Llewelyn. <*mentioned earlier*> [*in margin*]: <*because above*>[2]

892   +Next, that Gruffudd ap Llewelyn Whith[3] fornicates with Eve, daughter of Jakes. <*both suspended; the man admits, abjures, to be beaten in due form; the woman excommunicated; to be called to penance; the woman abjures, to be beaten three times*>

893   Next, that Roger ap Gwallter and his wife Llywelyth <*suspended*> are unlawfully joined because they are within the fourth degree of blood-relationship. <*he has sworn that he was unaware of the impediment*>

---

[1]   Recte *Feddyg*, the doctor.
[2]   **886**, where she is called Eve Duy.
[3]   Possibly for *chwith*, left-handed.

894   +Item quod Iorwerth ap Rys fornicatur cum Gwenllian filia Madoc. <suspensi; vir abjurat, fustigetur in forma; excommunicata mulier; mulier denunciata est>

895   Item quod Howel ap Ieuan ap David fornicatur cum Margareta filia Gwilim. <suspensi; vir <purget a tempore correctionis>; mulier abjurat et fustigetur in forma; differ penitenciam super gestura>

896   +Item quod Howel ap Gwilim ap Cad' fornicatur cum Nest filia y taelour.[1] <ambo suspensi; mulier excommunicata; absentes sunt; vir abjurat, differ etcetera>

897   Item quod dominus Gruffuth capellanus de Castell Maen incontinens est cum Eva Moel. <v[ir comparet],[2] negat, purget se [coram] commissario, mulier extra>

898   Item dicunt quod ecclesia patitur diversos defectus et cimiterium in defectu parochianorum. <emendetur [citra festum P]asche s[ub] pena x s>

899   Item quod[3] ordinatum est ab antiquo quod mulieres non sederent in ecclesia ultra ... ... ecclesie sub pena vj s et viij d quod non est observatum etcetera. <injunctum est quod n[on] ...>

900   Item quod laici sedent in cancello contra ordinationem ecclesie.

[f. 19]

          Mychelchurch <Webley>

901   Parochiani dicunt quod cancellus patitur defectum in tectura in defectu rectoris et in vitro fenestrarum et quod ostium fractum est.

902   Item quod Gwilim ap Philip et Nest filia Howel sunt illegitime copulati eo quod sunt in iiij^to gradu consanguinitatis. <vir comparet, credit accusationem veram>[4] [*in margin*] <fiat de novo>

903   Item quod Philippus ap Llewelyn fornicatur cum[5] Margareta filia David. <vir comparet, fatetur, abjurat, differtur sub spe nubendi, mulier infirma>

904   Item quod Angharat filia David receptat adulteros et fornicarios in domo sua. <citetur ad proximam>

905   Item quod Nest filia Ieuan fornicatur cum Rys Duy. <ambo extra>

906   Item quod dominus Johannes dormit de nocte extra parochiam. <dimissus est>

---

[1]   Followed by *l*, struck through.
[2]   The bottom right-hand corner of this page is torn away with the loss of up to three inches of text.
[3]   Followed by *mul*, struck through.
[4]   Followed by <*suspensus*>, struck through.
[5]   Followed by *A*, struck through.

894 +Next, that Iorwerth ap Rhys fornicates with Gwenllian, daughter of Madog. <*both suspended; the man abjures, to be beaten in due form; the woman excommunicated; the woman denounced*>

895 Next, that Hywel ap Ieuan ap David fornicates with Margaret, daughter of Gwilym. <*the woman suspended; the man to purge since the time of correction; the woman abjures and to be beaten in due form; defer the penance on condition of good behaviour*>

896 +Next, that Hywel ap Gwilym ap Cadwgan[1] fornicates with Nest, daughter of the tailor. <*both suspended; the woman excommunicated; they are absent; the man abjures, defer etc.*>

897 Next, that Sir Gruffudd, chaplain of Castell Maen [in Huntington], is incontinent with Eve Moel. <*the man appears, denies, to purge himself before the commissary; the woman outside*>

898 Next, they say that the church and the churchyard suffer from various defects, by the fault of the parishioners. <*to be put right before Easter, under penalty of 10 shillings*>

899 Next, that it has been laid down of old that women should not sit in church beyond ... ... of the church, under penalty of 6 shillings and 8 pence, which is not observed etc. <*ordered not ...*>

900 Next, that laymen sit in the chancel contrary to the rule of the church.

[f. 19]

MICHAELCHURCH-ON-ARROW <*Weobley*>

901 The parishioners say that the chancel is defective in its roof, by the fault of the rector, and in the glass of the windows, and that the door is broken.

902 Next, that Gwilym ap Philip and Nest, daughter of Hywel, are unlawfully joined, because they are in the fourth degree of blood-relationship. <*the man appears, he believes the accusation true*> [*in margin*]: <*to be done again*>

903 Next, that Philip ap Llewelyn fornicates with Margaret, daughter of David. <*the man appears, admits, abjures, to be deferred in the hope of them marrying; the woman sick*>

904 Next, that Angharad, daughter of David, receives adulterers and fornicators in her house. <*to be cited to the next*>

905 Next, that Nest, daughter of Ieuan, fornicates with Rhys Duy. <*both outside*>

906 Next, that Sir John sleeps at night outside the parish. <*he is dismissed*>

---

[1]   *Cadwaladr* would be an alternative extension of the MS *Cad'*.

907   Item quod Gwenllian filia Madoc fornicatur cum Iorwerth ap Rys. <ambo suspensi>

908   Item quod David ap Llewelyn male decimat bona sua. <suspensus>

909   Item¹

Kynton <Webley>

910   Parochiani dicunt quod rector tenetur invenire unum portiforium in ecclesia pro servicio divino quod non facit.

911   Item quod Willelmus Hunte non tractat uxorem suam affectione maritali et adulteratur cum Wladus <extra> concubina sua que moratur apud Webley. <vir moratur apud Garwy> [*in margin*] Garwy

912   Item quod Symon Lulewale fornicatur cum Margareta Brimley. <suspensa; vir excommunicatus propter suam contumaciam; absolutus est et dimissus>

913   Item quod Gruffuth Hir male tractat uxorem suam denegando sibi victualia et alia jura conigalia et adulteratur cum Matilda Here. <ambo extra; cesset quo ad Rys quousque dominus episcopus fuerit consultus super hoc>²

914   Item quod Jankyn Knolle fornicatur cum Matilda Leythe. <suspensi>

915   Item quod Wenhoyvar filia David soluta adulteratur cum Ivor Geneppyn. <ambo extra, citentur; absentes>

916   Item quod Rys Hergest et Eva uxor sua non cohabitant simul ut vir et uxor tenentur et quod idem Rys adulteratur cum <Dydgu>³ Boche. <ambo suspensi>

917   Item quod Johannes Caradoc <obiit> conjugatus adulteratur cum Margareta Schorthose <que moratur apud Penbrug>.

918   Item quod Willemus Trosse⁴ et Maiota uxor sua non cohabitant simul ut vir et uxor in defectu uxoris et tenet quandam⁵ Margaretam nuper concubinam suam in domo sua unde oritur sinistra suspicio. <vir et dicta Margareta comparent, negant post correctionem, purget se coram vicario die dominica proxima cum vᵗᵃ manu; purgavit se> [*in margin*] <purgatio>

919   Item quod Johannes Cokton fornicatur cum Issabella Hoper conjugata. <vir comparet, fatetur, abjurat, mulier comparet, fatetur, excommunicata; vir fustigetur ter per mercatum et ecclesiam, idem injunctum est mulieri; egunt penitenciam>

920   Item quod idem Johannes absentat se ab ecclesia parochiali diebus dominicis et festivis. <negat; injunctum est quod faciat de cetero etcetera>

921   Item quod Johannes Scherosbury fornicatur cum Katerina <suspensa> quam tenet. <vir comparet, fatetur, abjurat, fustigetur ter circa ecclesiam; injunctum est eidem quod faciat diligenciam suam de impetrando litteras testimoniales pro parte mulieris etcetera>

¹ Unfinished.
² Seemingly misplaced and probably referring to **916**.
³ Replacing *Eva*, struck through.
⁴ *conjugatus* interlined and then struck through.
⁵ Followed by *q*, struck through.

907 Next, that Gwenllian, daughter of Madog, fornicates with Iorwerth ap Rhys. *<both suspended>*

908 Next, that David ap Llewelyn wrongly tithes his goods. *<suspended>*

909 Next, [*not completed*]

KINGTON *<Weobley>*

910 The parishioners say that the rector ought to provide a breviary in church for divine service, which he does not do.

911 Next, that William Hunte does not treat his wife with marital affection and commits adultery with Gwladus *<outside>*, his concubine, who lives at Weobley. *<the man lives at Garway>* [*in margin*]: *<Garway>*

912 Next, that Simon Lulewale fornicates with Margaret Brimley. *<suspended; the man excommunicated on account of his contumacy; he is absolved and dismissed>*

913 Next, that Gruffudd Hir treats his wife badly, denying her food and other conjugal rights, and he commits adultery with Maud Here. *<both outside; to cease as to Rhys until the lord bishop has been consulted about this>*

914 Next, that Jankin Knolle fornicates with Maud Leythe. *<both suspended>*

915 Next, that Gwenhwyfar, daughter of David, a single woman, commits adultery with Ifor Geneppyn. *<both outside, to be cited; both absent>*

916 Next, that Rhys Hergest and his wife Eve do not live together as a man and wife ought to, and that the same Rhys commits adultery with Dyddgu Boche. *<both suspended>*

917 Next, that John Caradoc *<he has died>*, a married man, commits adultery with Margaret Schorthose *<who lives at Pembridge>*.

918 Next, that William Trosse and his wife Maiota do not live together as man and wife, by the fault of the wife, and he keeps a certain Margaret, lately his concubine, in his house, as a result of which sinister suspicion arises. *<the man and the said Margaret appear, both deny since correction, he is to purge himself before the vicar next Sunday with five hands; he has purged himself>* [*in margin*]: *<purgation>*

919 Next, that John Cokton fornicates with Isabel Hoper, a married woman. *<the man appears, admits, abjures; the woman appears, admits, excommunicated; the man to be beaten three times through the marketplace and the church; the same ordered for the woman; they have carried out the penance>*

920 Next, that the same John absents himself from the parish church on Sundays and feast days. *<he denies, ordered to do so in future etc.>*

921 Next, that John Scherosbury fornicates with Katherine *<suspended>*, whom he keeps. *<the man appears, admits, abjures, to be beaten three times around the church, ordered that he do his best to obtain letters testimonial on behalf of the woman etc.>*

922   [Ite]m[1] quod Philipot Turnour fornicatur cum Lucia quam tenet. <ambo suspensi>

923   [Ite]m quod Philippus de Weyndehull[2] non tractat uxorem suam affectione maritali. <vir non comparet; suspensus>

924   [Item] quod Willelmus Walker et Johanna uxor sua sunt illegitime copulati eo quod sunt infra quartum [grad]um <affinitatis>[3] ut sequitur <eo quod Rys consanguineus dicti Willelmi precognovit eandem>.

... verch David fuit stirps qui genuit

   Howel qui genuit Johannam qui genuit Johannem qui genuit Rys.

   David Vychan qui genuit Issabellam qui genuit Aliciam que genuit Willelmum Walker.

<dimissi sunt etcetera>

[f. 19v]

Presteinde <Leom'>. Visitatio ibidem die jovis xiiij Junii anno Domini ut supra

   Knulle <Web'>

925   Parochiani dicunt quod omnia sunt bene ibidem.

   Tytley <Leom'>[4]

926   Parochiani dicunt quod Ricardus Noys non tractat uxorem suam affectione maritali et quod adulteratur cum quadam Issota <suspensa> Uchdrete[5] quam tenet in domo sua infra parochiam de Oldradenor. <vir comparet, negat post correctionem, nichilominus abjurat locum suspectum et purget>

927   Item quod Iorwerth Goch fornicatur cum Muryel quam tenet. <mulier suspensa, vir non citatus et citentur quod sint apud Leyntwardyn; vir comparet, fatetur, abjurat, fustigetur[6] circa ecclesiam <semel>; mulier extra, citetur cum venerit; dimissi sunt> [*in margin*] <dimissi>

   Bewton[7] <Leom'>

928   Parochiani dicunt quod Willelmus Gryne fornicatur cum Johanna <ap> Rykker.[8] <extra; vir suspensus; excommunicatus; vir comparet, non vult, excommunicatus; abjurat, fustigetur>

---

[1]   The bottom left-hand corner of this page is torn away with the loss of up to half an inch of text.
[2]   Followed by *fornicatur cum*, struck through.
[3]   Replacing *consanguinitatis*.
[4]   Preceded by *W*, struck through.
[5]   Preceded by *Lyghdrete*, struck through.
[6]   Followed by *ter*, struck through.
[7]   Corrected from *Beyton*.
[8]   Corrected from *Prykker*.

922　　Next, that Philipot Turnour fornicates with Lucy, whom he keeps. <*both suspended*>

923　　Next, that Philip de Weyndehull does not treat his wife with marital affection. <*the man does not appear; suspended*>

924　　Next, that William Walker and his wife Joan are unlawfully joined because they are within the fourth degree <*of affinity, because Rhys, a blood-relation of the said William, previously knew her [sexually]*> as follows:

... verch David was the progenitor, who produced:

　　　Hywel, who produced Joan, who produced John, who produced Rhys

　　　David Vychan, who produced Isabel, who produced Alice, who produced William Walker

<*they are dismissed etc.*>

[f. 19v]

Presteigne <*Leominster*>. Visitation there on Thursday, 14 June, in the year of Our Lord as above

　　　KNILL <*Weobley*>

925　　The parishioners say that all things are well there.

　　　TITLEY <*Leominster*>

926　　The parishioners say that Richard Noys does not treat his wife with marital affection and that he commits adultery with a certain Isot <*suspended*> Uchdrete, whom he keeps in his house in the parish of Old Radnor. <*the man appears, denies since correction, nevertheless abjures the suspicious circumstances and to purge*>

927　　Next, that Iorwerth Goch fornicates with Muriel, whom he keeps. <*the woman suspended, the man not cited, and they are to be cited to be at Leintwardine; the man appears, admits, abjures, to be beaten around the church once; the woman outside, to be cited when she comes back; they are dismissed*> [*in margin*]: <*dismissed*>

　　　BYTON <*Leominster*>

928　　The parishioners say that William Gryne fornicates with Joan ap Rhicer. <*outside; the man suspended; excommunicated; the man appears, he will not [abjure], excommunicated; abjures, to be beaten*>

929   Item dicunt quod habitatores de Nether Keynsham[1] exceptis Waltero Neweton Ricardo Tanner et Johanne filio eiusdem recusant contribuere reparationi ecclesie de Beyton ut parochiani.

930   Item quod Howel Dewe conjugatus adulteratur cum Johanna Howel. <ambo extra, citentur nichilominus si possint apprehendi>

Norton <Leom'>

931   Parochiani dicunt quod rector tenetur invenire duos cereos ardentes coram summo altari diebus dominicis et festivis dum misse fiunt quod non facit.

932   Item quod rector tenetur invenire unum par vestimentorum ad celebrandum ibidem diebus ferialibus et non facit.

933   Item quod Ieuan Bola adulteratur cum Elena Lippa repulsa uxore legitima. <vir extra, mulier suspensa>

934   Item quod Lleuky verch y Vicary adulteratur cum Ieuan ap Eynon conjugato de parochia de Knyghton. <extra>

935   Item quod rector tenetur invenire lumen ad celebrandum in capella de Dischecote et unum par vestimentorum pro diebus ferialibus que non facit.

936   Item quod cancellus ibidem est discoopertus in defectu rectoris.

937   Item quod quidem Ieuan Salw est lepra percussus qui debet separari a communione populi ne inficiat etcetera. <citetur ad proximam>

938   Item quod David ap Jankyn fornicatur cum Angharat filia Llewelyn ap Gronwe. <ambo suspensi; vir abjurat, fustigetur; mulier recessit> [*in margin*] ... °

939   Item quod Harry Game fornicatur cum Wenllian quam tenet. <contraxerunt etcetera>

Prestheinde <Leom'>

940   [*in margin*] <significatum>[2]

Parochiani dicunt quod Walterus Boscher conjugatus adulteratur cum Alicia quam tenet. <ambo suspensi; excommunicati; excommunicati denunciati>

941   Item quod Lewys Taelour fornicatur cum Matilda quam tenet. <contraxerunt et recesserunt etcetera>

942   [*in margin*] °

Item quod Ieuan Taelour fornicatur cum Matilda Coly. <suspensi ambo; excommunicati>[3]

---

[1]   Corrected from *Keynham*.
[2]   The *s* of *significatum* written over a circle similar to those in entries **938** and **942**.
[3]   Preceded by *r*, struck through. The marginal circle is preceded by another circle, struck through.

929   Next, they say that the inhabitants of Nether Kinsham, other than Walter Neweton, Richard Tanner, and John his son, refuse to contribute to the repairs of the church of Byton as parishioners.

930   Next, that Hywel Dewe, a married man, commits adultery with Joan Howel. *<both outside, nevertheless to be cited if they can be apprehended>*

NORTON *<Leominster>*

931   The parishioners say that the rector ought to provide two candles to burn before the high altar on Sundays and feast days during masses, which he does not do.

932   Next, that the rector ought to provide a set of vestments for celebrating there on weekdays and does not do so.

933   Next, that Ieuan Bola commits adultery with Helen Lippa, his lawful wife having been driven away. *<the man outside, the woman suspended>*

934   Next, that Lleucu daughter of the vicar commits adultery with Ieuan ap Einion, a married man from the parish of Knighton. *<outside>*

935   Next, that the rector ought to provide a light for celebrating in the chapel of Discoed and a set of vestments for weekdays, which he does not do.

936   Next, that the chancel there is unroofed, by the fault of the rector.

937   Next, that a certain Ieuan Salw is smitten by leprosy and ought to be separated from the company of people lest he infect etc. *<to be cited to the next>*

938   Next, that David ap Jankin fornicates with Angharad, daughter of Llewelyn ap Goronwy. *<both suspended; the man abjures, to be beaten; the woman has gone away>* [*in margin*]:[1] ... °

939   Next, that Harry Game fornicates with Gwenllian, whom he keeps. *<they have made a contract etc.>*

PRESTEIGNE *<Leominster>*

940   [*in margin*]: *<signified>*

The parishioners say that Walter Boscher, a married man, commits adultery with Alice, whom he keeps. *<both suspended; both excommunicated; both denounced as excommunicated>*

941   Next, that Lewis Taelour fornicates with Maud, whom he keeps. *<they have made a contract and gone away etc.>*

942   [*in margin*]: °

Next, that Ieuan Taelour fornicates with Maud Coly. *<both suspended; both excommunicated>*

---

[1]   The marginal annotations to entries **938**, **940**, and **942** probably relate to stages in the process leading to excommunication.

943 Item quod Ieuan Saer fornicatur cum Maiota concubine; vir <et mulier> habent diem apud Leyntwardyn. <ambo comparent, fatentur, abjurant, peniten- cia respectuatur sub spe nubendi quia jurarunt ad hoc citra festum Purificationis Beate Marie proximum futurum; vocentur ad penitenciam>

944 Item quod Jankyn þe Reyder et Maiota uxor sua sunt illegitime copulati eo quod sunt in iiij^to gradu consanguinitatis. <vir prosequatur etcetera>

Radenor Vetus <Leom'>. Visitatio facta ibidem die veneris xv die mensis Junii anno Domini u[t supra]¹

[Radenor Vetus]

945 Parochiani dicunt quod Ricardus Noes conjugatus adulteratur cum Issota Uchdrute. <mulier suspensa; mandet[ur] ... [su]b p[ena] ... idem² Ricardus habeat uxorem suam in sua comitancia infra decem dies proximos futuros al[iter] ...>

946 Item quod Thomas Heilin et Issot uxor sua sunt infra iiij^tum gradum con- sanguinitatis. <mande[tur] ... gradu assistente sibi magistro Rogero Andrewe>

947 Item quod altare capelle de Adenwale non est sacratum et capellanus ibidem hoc [sciente] ... < ... sciatur etcetera>.

[f. 20]

Elynton³ <Leom'>

948 Parochiani⁴ dicunt quod cancellus est discoopertus in defectu rectoris.

949 Item quod capellanus ibidem, videlicet vicarius de Buraton, celebrat bis in die.

950 Item quod Jankyn serviens Petri Parker fornicatur cum Tybota Banastre. <citentur quod sint apud Leyntwardyn; vir comparet, fatetur, abjurat, fustige- tur ter circa ecclesiam; mulier comparet, fatetur, abjurat, fustigetur semel circa ecclesiam>

Wyggemor <Leom'>

951 Parochiani dicunt quod rector tenetur invenire unum diaconum ad deser- viendum Deo et ecclesie et unum clericum quod non facit.

952 Item quod clericus⁵ qui pretendit se clericum ibidem non pulsat ca[m]- panas ut tenetur, videlicet in aurora unam pulsationem vocatam daybelle et ignite- gium de nocte.

---

¹ The bottom right-hand corner of this page is torn away with the loss of up to three inches of text.
² Preceded by *he*, struck through.
³ Altered from *Elton* by interlineation.
⁴ Preceded by *par* in the margin, struck through.
⁵ Preceded by *m*, struck through.

943   Next, that Ieuan Saer fornicates with Maiota, his concubine. *<the man and the woman have a day at Leintwardine; both appear, both admit, both abjure, penance respited in the hope of them marrying because they have sworn to do this by the next feast of the Purification of the Blessed Mary; they are called to penance>*

944   Next, that Jankin the Reyder and his wife Maiota are unlawfully joined because they are in the fourth degree of blood-relationship. *<the man to be prosecuted etc.>*

Old Radnor *<Leominster>*. Visitation made there on Friday, 15 June, in the year of Our Lord as above

[OLD RADNOR]

945   The parishioners say that Richard Noes, a married man, commits adultery with Isot Uchdrute. *<the woman suspended, ordered ... under penalty of ... the same Richard to admit his wife to his company within the next ten days otherwise ...>*

946   Next, that Thomas Heilin and his wife Isot are within the fourth degree of blood-relationship. *<ordered ... degree with Master Roger Andrewe helping him>*

947   Next, that the altar of the chapel of Ednol is not consecrated and the chaplain there [knowing] this ... *< ... let it be known etc.>*

[f. 20]

ELTON *<Leominster>*

948   The parishioners say that the chancel is unroofed, by the fault of the rector.

949   Next, that the chaplain there, that is, the vicar of Burrington, celebrates twice in a day.

950   Next, that Jankin, the servant of Peter Parker, fornicates with Tybota Banastre. *<cited to be at Leintwardine; the man appears, admits, abjures, to be beaten three times around the church; the woman appears, admits, abjures, to be beaten once around the church>*

WIGMORE *<Leominster>*

951   The parishioners say that the rector ought to provide a deacon to serve God and the church and a clerk, which he does not do.

952   Next, that a clerk, who claims to be the clerk there, does not ring the bells as he ought to, that is, at dawn a ring called day bell and the curfew at night.

953 Item quod idem rector tenetur invenire unam lampadem ardentem coram summo altari expensis suis die noctuque quod non facit debite.

954 Item quod idem rector tenetur invenire libros pro matutinis, horis et vesperis ad honorem Dei dicendo, quod non facit quia deficiunt psaltaria et libri ympnorum.

955 Item quod Ricardus Stanway fornicatur cum Johanna Lyngen non obstante abjuratione alias per eos facta coram commissario generali et etiam non obstante quod ille contraxit cum alia et ipsa cum alio. <ambo comparent, fatentur, abjurant; fustigentur ter circa ecclesiam parochialem>

956 Item quod Eva Lloyt cum qua dictus Ricardus contraxit fornicatur cum Gruffuth serviente Thome le Fox. <mulier comparet, fatetur, abjurat, fustigetur ter circa ecclesiam parochialem; vir suspensus>

957 Item quod Agnes Deryn fornicatur cum Johanne Onybury <Hibernie est> et cum Ieuan serviente David Reynald. <mulier comparet, fatetur, abjurat;[1] quo ad Johannem fustigetur ter circa ecclesiam, quo ad Ieuan negat; purgarunt se adinvicem>

958 Item quod Thomas Hopkyns[2] fornicatur cum Alison Balle. <vir comparet, excommunicatus propter manifestam contumaciam; mulier suspensa>

959 Item[3]

Schobdon <Leom'>

960 Parochiani dicunt [quod][4] Willelmus Leyntwardyn detinet de bonis ecclesie unam patellam valoris v s legatam alias per Walterum Leyntwardyn nuper defunctum ad opus ecclesie predicte. <concordes sunt partes>

961 Item detinet idem Willelmus unam cistam precii ij s vj d legatam per dictum Walterum ad opus campanilis ibidem etcetera. <concordes ut supra>

962 Item quod Jankyn Donne conjugatus adulteratur cum Agnete Walissh. <vir comparet, fatetur, abjurat, fustigetur vj per forum, vj circa ecclesiam parochialem et vj ante processionem in ecclesia cathedrali, mulier suspensa; dimissi sunt>

963 Item quod Willelmus Thomkyns fornicatur cum Alson quam tenet. <ambo comparent, fatentur, abjurant, fustigentur ter circa ecclesiam parochialem; fecerunt penitenciam ut dicunt>

964 Item quod clausura cimiterii est defectiva in defectu rectoris.

---

[1] Followed by *excommunicatus propter contumaciam*, struck through.
[2] Preceded by *Hosky*, struck through.
[3] Unfinished.
[4] Omitted in error.

953   Next, that the same rector ought to provide at his expense a lamp to burn before the high altar day and night, which he does not do properly.

954   Next, that the same rector ought to provide books for saying matins, the hours, and vespers to the honour of God, which he does not do because psalters and hymnbooks are lacking.

955   Next, that Richard Stanway fornicates with Joan Lyngen despite an abjuration previously made by them before the commissary general, and also despite the fact that he has made a contract with another woman and she with another man. *<both appear, both admit, both abjure, both to be beaten three times around the parish church>*

956   Next, that Eve Lloyt, with whom the said Richard made a contract, fornicates with Gruffudd, servant of Thomas le Fox. *<the woman appears, admits, abjures, to be beaten three times around the parish church; the man suspended>*

957   Next, that Agnes Deryn fornicates with John Onybury *<he is in Ireland>* and with Ieuan, servant of David Reynald. *<the woman appears, as to John admits, abjures, to be beaten three times around the church, as to Ieuan denies; they have purged themselves jointly>*

958   Next, that Thomas Hopkyns fornicates with Alison Balle. *<the man appears, excommunicated because of his manifest contumacy; the woman suspended>*

959   Next, [*not completed*]

SHOBDON *<Leominster>*

960   The parishioners say that William Leyntwardyn withholds from the goods of the church a bowl worth 5 shillings previously bequeathed by Walter Leyntwardyn, lately deceased, for the benefit of the aforesaid church. *<the parties are agreed>*

961   Next, the same William withholds a chest worth 2 shillings and 6 pence bequeathed by the said Walter for the benefit of the bell-tower there etc. *<they are agreed as above>*

962   Next, that Jankin Donne, a married man, commits adultery with Agnes Walissh. *<the man appears, admits, abjures, to be beaten six times through the marketplace, six times around the parish church, and six times before the procession in the cathedral church; the woman suspended; they are dismissed.>*

963   Next, that William Thomkyns fornicates with Alison, whom he keeps. *<both appear, both admit, both abjure, both to be beaten three times around the parish church; they have done the penance as they say>*

964   Next, that the fence of the churchyard is defective, by the fault of the rector.

Leynthalle Starkares <Leom'>

965 Parochiani dicunt quod Hugo Orleton fornicatur cum Issabella Dewkes. <vir comparet, fatetur, abjurat, fustigetur ter circa ecclesiam parochialem; mulier suspensa>

966 Item quod Willelmus Stury <suspensus> fornicatur cum Alicia Perkys non obstante abjuratione. <mulier comparet, fatetur, abjurat, fustigetur semel; vir comparet, fatetur, abjurat, fustigetur ter circa ecclesiam>

967 Item Willelmus Harpere fornicatur cum Emota Sweyn. <ambo suspensi>

Aelmes[tre][1] <Leom'>

968 Parochiani dicunt quod Jak Walissh et Lucia Norshe contraxerunt adin-vicem de presenti nec faciunt huiusmodi matrimonium solempnizari in defectu dicte mulieris. <vir absens;[2] prosequantur si velint>

969 Item quod eadem Lucia fornicatur cum Jankyn Copener junior. <suspen-sus; mulier comparet, fatetur, abjurat, fustigetur ter circa ecclesiam; vir comparet, fatetur, abjurat, fustigetur ter circa ecclesiam>

970 Item quod Jankyn Wykes <obiit> fornicatur cum Margeria Thony. <mulier apud Lodel'>

971 [I]tem quod Jankyn Phileppes fornicatur et[3] Agnete Yngeson. <ambo comparent, negant; purgarunt se>

972 [Ite]m Rogerus Wykes fornicatur cum Agnete <Deyvykes> <suspensa> de Worcetre[4] quam tenet. <vir comparet, negat post correctionem, purget se>

973 <[Item] quod habitatores ville Lyngen recusant reparare clausuram cimit-erii saltim partem eos concernentem; ... [diff]ertur sub spe concordie>

[f. 20v]

974 Item quod Willelmus <suspensus> filius Johannis Paty fornicatur cum Iss-abella Ragedon <suspensa> non obstante abjuratione alias facta quod nunquam committerent peccatum inter se nisi in matrimonio.

975 Item quod Jankyn Paty executor Thome Bore detinet ix d legatos ad opus ecclesie ibidem. <excommunicatus propter manifestam contumaciam>

---

[1]   The bottom left-hand corner of this page is torn away with the loss of up to half an inch of text.

[2]   Followed by *mulier comparet*, struck through.

[3]   Recte *cum*.

[4]   Altered from *Agnete de Worcetre* by interlineation, the caret placed incorrectly after *de*.

LEINTHALL STARKES <*Leominster*>

965   The parishioners say that Hugh Orleton fornicates with Isabel Dewkes. <*the man appears, admits, abjures, to be beaten three times around the parish church; the woman suspended*>

966   Next, that William Stury <*suspended*> fornicates with Alice Perkys despite an abjuration. <*the woman appears, admits, abjures, to be beaten once; the man appears, admits, abjures, to be beaten three times around the church*>

967   Next, William Harpere fornicates with Emota Sweyn. <*both suspended*>

AYMESTREY <*Leominster*>

968   The parishioners say that Jack Walissh and Lucy Norshe made a contract together in the present tense and have not had the marriage solemnised, by the fault of the said woman. <*the man absent; let them prosecute if they wish*>

969   Next, that the same Lucy fornicates with Jankin Copener the younger. <*suspended; the woman appears, admits, abjures, to be beaten three times around the church; the man appears, admits, abjures, to be beaten three times around the church*>

970   Next, that Jankin Wykes <*he has died*> fornicates with Margery Thony. <*the woman at Ludlow*>

971   Next, that Jankin Phileppes fornicates with Agnes Yngeson. <*both appear, they deny; they have purged themselves*>

972   Next, Roger Wykes fornicates with Agnes Deyvykes <*suspended*> of Worcester, whom he keeps. <*the man appears, denies since correction, to purge himself*>

973   <*Next, that the inhabitants of the vill of Lingen refuse to repair the fence of the church-yard, especially the part for which they are responsible; to defer in the hope of agreement*>

[f. 20v]

974   Next, that William <*suspended*>, son of John Paty, fornicates with Isabel Ragedon <*suspended*> despite an abjuration previously made to the effect that they would never commit the sin between them except in marriage.

975   Next, that Jankin Paty, executor of Thomas Bore, withholds 9 pence bequeathed for the benefit of the church there. <*excommunicated because of manifest contumacy*>

Lyngen <Leom'>

976 Parochiani dicunt quod Jankyn Knyke et Alson de Orcobe sunt illegitime copulati eo quod dicta Alson precontraxit cum quodam Willelmo Smyth ad huc superstite. <citentur quod sint apud Leyntwardyn; comparent, commissum est magistro R[ogero] Andrewe ad examinandum testes super primo contractu et carnali copula inter ipsam mulierem et dictum Willelmum Smyth post huiusmodi contractum subsequta;[1] habent diem apud Hereford etcetera>

Castrum Ricardi <Lodel'>. Visitatio facta ibidem die lune xviij mensis Junii anno Domini supradicto ut supra

[Castrum Ricardi]

977 Parochiani dicunt quod Johannes Frer, Johannes Gogh, Johannes Dobles et Ricardus frater suus ac Ricardus Cheylde vadunt diebus dominicis et festivis ad villam de Lodelawe cum focalibus et aliis vendendis contempnendo ecclesiam parochialem et subtrahendo ecclesie[2] sua jura. <comparent omnes, dimissi sunt>

978 Item quod Johannes Estham et Agnes pretensa uxor sua sunt illegitime copulati eo quod idem Johannes habet aliam uxorem superstitem nomine Cristinam filiam Ade Mason cum qua precontraxit. <vir negat, difertur>

979 Item quod Walterus Watkyn fornicatur cum Margareta Brugge Water. <vir comparet, fatetur,[3] abjurat, fustigetur ter circa ecclesiam; mulier suspensa>

980 Item quod Sibilla Hannys fornicatur cum Johanne Bue[4] <suspensus> et dicunt quod eadem est communis fornicatrix cum quibuscumque. <mulier comparet, negat post correctionem; purgavit>

981 Item quod idem Johannes Buwe adulteratur[5] cum Margeria de Medewe[6] uxore Rogeri Medewe prout communis fama laborat. <vir comparet, negat, purget se cum vj^{ta} manu>

982 Item quod Maiota Evyote <suspensa> non recepit sacralia sacramentalia in festo Pasche ultimo preterito in ecclesia parochiali nec alibi prout ipsi sciunt.

983 Item quod dictus Johannes Buwe injecit manus violentas in quendam dominum Hugonem <capellanum> usque ad sanguinis effusionem et econtrario idem dominus Hugo in dictum Johannem clericum.

984 Item quod <Hugo>[7] Coly et Johannes frater eius, Willelmus Pyeres non veniunt ad ecclesiam parochialem diebus dominicis et festivis.[8]

985 Item Hugyn Smyth et uxor sua non veniunt ut supra. <dimissi sunt>

---

[1] Recte *subsecuta*.
[2] Altered from *ecclesiam*.
[3] Preceded by *negat*, struck through.
[4] Preceded by *Boe*, struck through.
[5] Preceded by *fornicatur*, struck through.
[6] Preceded by *n*, struck through.
[7] Replacing *Ricardus*, struck through.
[8] The next entry follows on the same line; *dimissi sunt* applies to both.

LINGEN <*Leominster*>

976 The parishioners say that Jankin Knyke and Alison of Orcop are unlawfully joined because the said Alison made a previous contract with a certain William Smyth who is still alive. <*both to be cited to attend at Leintwardine; they appear, committed to Master Roger Andrewe to examine witnesses about the first contract and the bodily union between this woman and the said William Smyth after this contract; they have a day at Hereford etc.*>

Richards Castle <*Ludlow*>. Visitation made there on Monday, 18 June, in the year of Our Lord as above

[RICHARDS CASTLE]

977 The parishioners say that John Frer, John Gogh, John Dobles and his brother Richard, and Richard Cheylde go on Sundays and feast days to the town of Ludlow with firewood and other things for sale, disdaining the parish church and withholding from the church its rights. <*all appear, they are dismissed*>

978 Next, that John Estham and Agnes, his pretended wife, are unlawfully joined because the same John has another wife living named Christine, daughter of Adam Mason, with whom he made a previous contract. <*the man denies, to be deferred*>

979 Next, that Walter Watkyn fornicates with Margaret Brugge Water. <*the man appears, admits, abjures, to be beaten three times around the church; the woman suspended*>

980 Next, that Sybil Hannys fornicates with John Bue <*suspended*> and they say that she is a habitual fornicator with any man. <*the woman appears, denies since correction; she has purged*>

981 Next, that the same John Buwe commits adultery with Margery de Medewe, wife of Roger Medewe, as common fame has it. <*the man appears, denies, to purge himself with six hands*>

982 Next, that Maiota Evyote <*suspended*> did not receive the holy sacraments last Easter Sunday in the parish church or anywhere else, as far as they know.

983 Next, that the said John Buwe violently laid hands on a certain Sir Hugh, <*a chaplain*>, to the extent of spilling blood, and in return the same Sir Hugh on the said John, a clerk.

984 Next, that Hugh Coly, his brother John, and William Pyeres do not come to the parish church on Sundays and feast days.

985 Next, Hugyn Smyth and his wife do not come, as above. <*they are dismissed*>

986　Item Johannes Gilleson fornicatur cum Editha filia Willelmi de Feld. <vir comparet, negat post correctionem; purgavit se; mulier extra>

Wystanstowe <Lodel'>. Visitatio facta ibidem die mercurii xx^{mo} die Junii

[Wystanstowe]

987　Parochiani dicunt quod Llewelyn Carwet <suspensus> conjugatus adulteratur cum Wenllian <suspensa> quam tenet repulsa uxore. <vir[1] habet diem apud Castrum Episcopi>[2] [*in margin*] <Citatus ad Castrum Episcopi>

988　Item quod rector tenetur invenire unum diaconum ad deserviendum in ecclesia quod non facit. <citetur ad proximam>

989　Item quod clausura cimiterii est defectiva et injunctum est parochianis quod faciant reparari citra festum sancti Michelis proximum futurum. <sub pena x [s]>[3]

990　Item quod Nicholaus Gryne[4] fornicatur cum Matilda <suspensa> relicta Janyn Herdwyk. <[vir comparet,] fatetur, abjurat, fu[stigetur] ... ...>

991　Item quod dominus Johannes Brokton capellanus domini Hugonis Cheyny militis [incontinens est] cum Issota[5] filia Thome Taelour. <ambo extra>

992　Item quod Ricardus Matys fornicatur cum Margareta Postarn. <vir Hibernie; m[ulier] ... ...>

993　Item quod dominus Rogerus Reynald capellanus incontinens est cum Johan[na] ... .noroh que iam moratur apud Mydelton in decanatu de Leom' ... ... iiij^{or} filios et adhuc est pregnans cum eodem. <vir infirmus est, citetur ad ...>

[f. 21]
Staunton Lacy. Visitatio facta ibidem die jovis xxj mensis Junii anno Domini ut supra

[Staunton Lacy]

994　Parochiani dicunt quod Adam Bragge <excommunicatus> nuper serviens Philippi Collebage adulteratur cum Juliana uxore Johannis Lake de Sparteresmull. <mulier extra>

995　Item quod idem Johannes Lake conjugatus adulteratur cum Alicia quam tenet conjugater.[6] <vir comparet, negat; purgavit se>

---

[1]　Preceded by *h*, struck through.
[2]　Preceded by *Lydebury in*, struck through.
[3]　The bottom right-hand corner of this page is perished with the loss of up to three inches of text.
[4]　<*suspensus*> struck through.
[5]　Followed by *T*, struck through.
[6]　Recte *conjugaliter*; followed by <*ambo extra*>, struck through.

986   Next, John Gilleson fornicates with Edith, daughter of William de Feld. *<the man appears, denies since correction, has purged himself; the woman outside>*

Wistanstow *<Ludlow>*. Visitation made there on Wednesday, 20 June

[WISTANSTOW]

987   The parishioners say that Llewelyn Carwet *<suspended>*, a married man, commits adultery with Gwenllian *<suspended>*, whom he keeps, having driven out his lawful wife. *<the man has a day at Bishops Castle>* [*in margin*]: *<to be cited to Bishops Castle>*

988   Next, that the rector ought to provide a deacon to serve in church, which he does not do. *<to be cited to the next>*

989   Next, that the fence of the churchyard is defective, and the parishioners are ordered to have it repaired before Michaelmas next. *<under penalty of 10 shillings>*

990   Next, that Nicholas Gryne fornicates with Maud *<suspended>*, widow of Janyn Herdwyk. *<the man appears, admits, abjures, to be beaten ... ...>*

991   Next, that Sir John Brokton, the chaplain of Sir Hugh Cheyny, knight, is incontinent with Isot, daughter of Thomas Taelour. *<both outside>*

992   Next, that Richard Matys fornicates with Margaret Postarn. *<the man in Ireland; the woman ... ...>*

993   Next, that Sir Roger Reynald, chaplain, is incontinent with Joan ... ...noroh who now lives at Middleton on the Hill in the deanery of Leominster ... four children and again is pregnant by him. *<the man is sick, to be cited to ...>*

[f. 21]
Stanton Lacy. Visitation made there on Thursday, 21 June, in the year of Our Lord as above

[STANTON LACY]

994   The parishioners say that Adam Bragge *<excommunicated>*, lately a servant of Philip Collebage, commits adultery with Julian, wife of John Lake of Sparteres-mull. *<the woman outside>*

995   Next, that the same John Lake, a married man, commits adultery with Alice, whom he keeps as though they were married. *<the man appears, denies; has purged himself>*

996 Item quod dominus Ricardus Frayn <suspensus> incontinens est cum Agnete Chaundler. <suspensa; vir purgavit se et dimissus est>

997 Item quod idem dominus Ricardus est communis mercator emendo et vendendo pro lucro inde captando.

Buterley. Visitatio facta in ecclesia de Buterley die martis xix mensis Junii anno ut supra post prandium

[Buterley]

998 Parochiani dicunt quod Issabella Ondys uxor Johannis Strawe et falso et maliciose diffamavit Margaretam filiam Willelmi Caleys super adulterio commisso cum dicto Johanne Strawe. <mulier prosequatur pars>

999 Item Walterus Smyth solutus fornicatur cum Emota quam tenet. <ambo extra>

1000 Item quod habitatores villarum de Cluton et Ledewych tenentur ad contribuendum reparationi[1] matricis ecclesie de Buterley, campanilis eiusdem et clausure cimiterii quod non faciunt.[2] <ambe partes ibidem comparentes diu certarunt et judex assignavit ambabus partibus ad producendum probationes coram commissario generali in proximo consistorio generali>

Ledewych

1001 Dicunt quod bene per omnia.

Stokmylburgh

1002 Dicunt quod bene per omnia <excepto quod Philippus Bysshop <suspensus> firmarius ibidem conjugatus adulteratur cum Maiota Scheppert <suspensa> de Bokylton conjugata>

Hop' Bagard

1003 Idem dicunt.

Sylveton

1004 Idem dicunt.

Caynham <Lodelawe>

1005 Idem dicunt[3] quod dominus Johannes Porslowe vicarius de Kynlet <in decanatu de Stodeston> incontinens est cum Emota filia Johannis Leper. <citentur ad proximam> [*in margin*] <Stodeston>

---

[1] Followed by *ecc*, struck through.
[2] Followed by <*prosequantur l*>, struck through.
[3] *excepto* has perhaps been omitted in error.

996 Next, that Sir Richard Frayn *<suspended>* is incontinent with Agnes Chaundler. *<the woman suspended; the man has purged himself and is dismissed>*

997 Next, that the same Sir Richard is a habitual dealer, buying and selling for the profit to be gained from it.

Bitterley. Visitation made in the church of Bitterley on Tuesday, 19 June, the year as above, after lunch

[BITTERLEY]

998 The parishioners say that Isabel Ondys, wife of John Strawe, has both falsely and maliciously defamed Margaret, daughter of William Caleys, over committing adultery with the said John Strawe. *<let the woman prosecute as a party>*

999 Next, Walter Smyth, a single man, fornicates with Emota, whom he keeps. *<both outside>*

1000 Next, that the inhabitants of the vills of Cleeton and Ledwyche ought to contribute to the repairs of the mother church of Bitterley, its bell-tower, and the fence of the churchyard, which they do not do. *<both parties appearing there argued for a long time, and the judge required both parties to produce proofs before the commissary general at the next general consistory>*

LEDWYCHE

1001 They say that everything is well.

STOKE ST MILBOROUGH

1002 They say that everything is well *<except that Philip Bysshop <suspended>, the farmer there, a married man, commits adultery with Maiota Scheppert of Bockleton <suspended>, a married woman>*

HOPE BAGOT

1003 They say the same.

SILVINGTON

1004 They say the same.

CAYNHAM *<Ludlow>*

1005 They say the same except that Sir John Porslowe, the vicar of Kinlet *<in the deanery of Stottesdon>*, is incontinent with Emota, daughter of John Leper. *<both to be cited to the next>* [in margin]: *<Stottesdon>*

Leyntwardyn <Clone>. Visitatio facta ibidem die sabbati xxiij Junii

Brompton <Clone>

1006 <Dicunt quod dominus Brianus Brompton capellanus celebrans divina apud Lodel' incontinens est cum Margareton Puton;[1] mulier suspensa; excommunicata>

1007 Parochiani dicunt quod David Gwynnyon fornicatur cum <Johanna ap Crech> concubina sua quam tenet. <suspensi; excommunicati>

1008 Item quod Llewelyn[2] morans apud Revys fornicatur cum Dydgu quam tenet. <suspensi; vir extra, mulier excommunicata>

1009 Item quod Nicholaus Hosches fornicatur cum Johanna Patys. <suspensi; excommunicati; mulier abjurat, fustigetur in forma>

1010 Item quod Rogerus de Neweton nequiter diffamavit Willelmum Lloyt super furto falso et maliciose. <comparet, negat, prosequatur pars>

1011 Item quod idem Rogerus fornicatur cum Maiota Tylar. <vir comparet, fatetur, abjurat, fustigetur ter circa;[3] mulier comparet, fatetur, abjurat, fustigetur ter circa ecclesiam; non fecerunt penitenciam, ideo excommunicati>

1012 Item quod Gruffuth Fermour conjugatus adulteratur cum eadem Maiota. <ambo[4] comparent, negant; purgarunt se>

1013 Item quod Rogerus Neweton perturbat divinum officium in ecclesia.

[Kn]ighto[n][5]

1014 [Par]ochiani dicunt quod David Vawr et Wenllian filia David iverunt extra diocesim pro matrimonio clamdestino [cel]ebrando inter eos non obstante reclamatione facta per Eva Bach propter precontractum cum dicta Eva. <extra>

1015 [Item] quod dictus David cognovit dictam Eva carnaliter. <infirma mulier; suspensa>

1016 [Item quod] Dawkoc et Wenllian quam tenet fornicantur adinvicem non obstante divorcio et abjuratione [facta] etcetera. <suspensi; excommunicati; dimissi sunt>

1017 [Item quod D]avid Lloydach fornicatur cum Eva Schappester. <extra>

1018 [Item quod Nic]holaus Webbe fornicatur cum Dydgu verch Ragor. <suspensi; excommunicati; vir fustigetur in forma>

[f. 21v]

1019 Item quod Llewelyn ap Ieuan fornicatur cum Wenllian filia Ieuan Taelour. <extra, vir apud Brompton>

---

[1]   Altered from *Preton*.
[2]   Preceded by *Mereduth*, struck through.
[3]   *ecclesiam* omitted in error.
[4]   Preceded by <*mulier comparet*>, struck through.
[5]   The bottom left-hand corner of this page is perished with the loss of up to an inch of text.

Leintwardine <*Clun*>. Visitation made there on Saturday, 23 June

BRAMPTON BRYAN <*Clun*>

1006 <*They say that Sir Brian Brompton, a chaplain celebrating services at Ludlow, is incontinent with Margaret Puton; the woman suspended; excommunicated*>

1007 The parishioners say that David Gwynnyon fornicates with <*Joan ap Crech*>,[1] his concubine, whom he keeps. <*both suspended; both excommunicated*>

1008 Next, that Llewelyn, living at Reeves Hill, fornicates with Dyddgu, whom he keeps. <*suspended; the man outside; the woman excommunicated*>

1009 Next, that Nicholas Hosches fornicates with Joan Patys. <*both suspended; both excommunicated; the woman abjures, to be beaten in due form*>

1010 Next, that Roger of Newton has wickedly defamed William Lloyt over a theft, falsely and maliciously. <*appears, denies, let the party prosecute*>

1011 Next, that the same Roger fornicates with Maiota Tylar. <*the man appears, admits, abjures, to be beaten three times around the church; the woman appears, admits, abjures, to be beaten three times around the church; she has not performed the penance, so excommunicated*>

1012 Next, that Gruffudd Fermour, a married man, commits adultery with the same Maiota. <*both appear, deny; they have purged themselves*>

1013 Next, that Roger Neweton disturbs the divine office in church.

KNIGHTON

1014 The parishioners say that David Vawr and Gwenllian, daughter of David, went outside the diocese to have a clandestine marriage celebrated between them, despite a challenge made by Eve Bach on account of a previous contract with the said Eve. <*outside*>

1015 Next, that the said David knew the said Eve carnally. <*the woman is sick, suspended*>

1016 Next, that Dawkoc and Gwenllian, whom he keeps, fornicate together despite a divorce and abjuration made etc. <*both suspended; both excommunicated; they are dismissed*>

1017 Next, that David Lloydach fornicates with Eve Schappester. <*outside*>

1018 Next, that Nicholas Webbe fornicates with Dyddgu verch Ragor. <*suspended; excommunicated; the man to be beaten in due form*>

[f. 21v]

1019 Next, that Llewelyn ap Ieuan fornicates with Gwenllian, daughter of Ieuan Taelour. <*outside; the man at Brampton*>

---

[1]　Recte *Crych*, the wrinkled one.

1020 Item quod Ieuan ap Eynon conjugatus adulteratur cum Lleuky[1] filia y vicar de diocese Men'. \<citentur; vir suspensus; vir fustigetur\>

1021 Item quod Eynon Daelour conjugatus adulteratur cum Eva filia Ieuan ap Madoc Coch. \<suspensi; excommunicatus vir\>

1022 Item Jak[2] Gronno fornicatur cum Wenllian Webbe. \<vir apud Leom', mulier suspensa\>

Clongyneford \<Clone\>

1023 Parochiani dicunt quod Thomas Atkys fornicatur cum Constancia Note. \<concitentur ad proximam; suspensi; committitur decano\> [*in margin*] \<committitur decano\>

1024 Item quod David Taelour adulteratur cum Alson[3] quam tenet conjugaliter ut dicitur. \<vir comparet, asserit eos conjugatos, mulier asserit idem, habent diem ad producendum litteras testimoniales citra festum Pasche\>

1025 Item quod Reynald Thresser fornicatur cum Katerina quam tenet. \<extra\>

1026 Item quod Henricus Collyng decessit intestatus et officiarii comitis Arrundell ministrarunt bona dicti defuncti eo quod fuit nativus suus sine auctoritate ordinarii. \<citentur ministri etcetera\>

1027 Item quod Isbel Harrys conjugata adulteratur cum Bady serviente rectoris. \<citentur ad proximam; suspensi\>

Stowe \<Clone\>

1028 Parochiani dicunt quod David Benhir \<excommunicatus\> reclamavit banna inter Gruffuth ap Gwilim et Gwenllian verch[4] Iorwerth maliciose ad extorquendum munera ab eisdem quominus matrimonium inter eos posset solempnizari. \<citetur ad proximam\>

1029 Item quod rector tenetur invenire duos cereos[5] processionales ardentes etiam ad missam ibidem diebus dominicis et festivis quod non facit et subtractum est xij annis elapsis. \<prosequantur parochiani et deceant\>

1030 Item dicunt [quod][6] clausura cimiterii est defectiva in defectu parochianorum, unde habent diem ad reparandum citra festum Pasche proximum futurum, sub pena ad arbitrium ministrorum domini episcopi limitanda. \<reparatur etcetera\>

1031 Item[7]

---

[1]　Preceded by *A*, struck through.
[2]　Preceded by *Jq*, struck through.
[3]　Preceded by *Ma*, struck through.
[4]　Preceded by *ei*, struck through.
[5]　Altered from *cerros*.
[6]　Omitted in error.
[7]　Unfinished.

1020 Next, that Ieuan ap Einion, a married man, commits adultery with Lleucu, daughter of the vicar of the diocese of St David's. *<both to be cited; the man suspended; the man to be beaten>*

1021 Next, that Einion Daelour, a married man, commits adultery with Eve, daughter of Ieuan ap Madog Coch. *<they are suspended; the man excommunicated>*

1022 Next, Jack Gronno fornicates with Gwenllian Webbe. *<the man at Leominster; the woman suspended>*

CLUNGUNFORD *<Clun>*

1023 The parishioners say that Thomas Atkys fornicates with Constance Note. *<cite together to the next; both suspended; it is committed to the dean>* [*in margin*]: *<it is committed to the dean>*

1024 Next, that David Taelour commits adultery with Alison, whom he keeps as though they were married, as is said. *<the man appears, asserts they are married; the woman asserts the same; they have a day to produce letters testimonial before Easter>*

1025 Next, that Reynold Thresser fornicates with Katherine, whom he keeps. *<outside>*

1026 Next, that Henry Collyng died intestate and the officers of the earl of Arundel administered the estate of the said deceased, because he was his bondman, without the authority of the ordinary. *<the officers to be cited etc.>*

1027 Next, that Isabel Harrys, a married woman, commits adultery with Bady, the rector's servant. *<both to be cited to the next; both suspended>*

STOW *<Clun>*

1028 The parishioners say that David Benhir *<excommunicated>* maliciously challenged the banns between Gruffudd ap Gwilym and Gwenllian verch Iorwerth in order to extort money from them before the marriage between them could be solemnised. *<to be cited to the next>*

1029 Next, that the rector ought to provide two processional candles, to burn also at mass there on Sundays and feast days, which he does not do and has withheld them for the last 12 years. *<let the parishioners prosecute, and they ought to>*

1030 Next, they say that the fence of the churchyard is defective, by the fault of the parishioners, so they have to repair it by next Easter, under a penalty to be set by the judgement of the officers of the lord bishop. *<it is repaired etc.>*

1031 Next, [*not completed*]

Villata de Atteforton <Clone>

1032 Villani dicunt quod Wilkoc Meuric manutenet fornicarios et adulteros in domo sua ad peccandum, videlicet Johannem <suspensus> filium suum et Johannam <suspensa> concubinam eiusdem, item Jankyn Chaumbereresmon et eandem Johannam, item eandem Johannam et Hopkyn Boly. <extra; Johanna comparet, correcta; vir nupsit, alii etcetera>

1033 Item quod Geffrey Taelour fornicatur cum Elena concubina sua, quos Lleuky Llannddewy receptat in domo sua. <vir comparet, fatetur, abjurat, fustigetur ter circa ecclesiam, respectuatur sub spe nubendi>

1034 Item quod Gryge Moel <suspensus> vendit bona sua in cariori foro quam valent propter dilationem etcetera. <excommunicatus>

1035 Item quod Wilkoc North Forlong et Issabella quam tenet pro uxore ut communis fama laborat ibidem non sunt matrimonialiter copulati. <citentur ad proximam; excommunicati>[1]

Boryton[2] <Clon>

1036 Parochiani dicunt quod campanile est discoopertum in defectu parochianorum. <reformatum est>

1037 Item quod Willelmus Adames et Issabella <suspensa> uxor sua non cohabitant simul nec communicant ut vir et uxor in defectu uxoris. <vir asserit se paratum; mulier monita est ad tractandum maritum suum sub pena excommunicationis; excommunicata est propter suam contumaciam; postea paruit etcetera>

1038 Item quod Willelmus Vicarys et Alson Schepmon <suspensa> fornicantur adinvicem. <vir est Hibernie; mulier dimissa>

1039 Item quod vicarius celebrat bis in die. <difertur>

1040 Item quod Johannes Malyar et Willelmus Adames et Wilkoc Spyney sunt communes operarii diebus dominicis et fest[ivis].[3]

1041 [*in margin*] <significatum Wyggmor>

<Item quod Johannes Watys[4] fornicatur cum muliere quam tenet et continuarunt xx annis etcetera; nomine Maiota; vir comparet, negat post correctionem, [abjurat] peccatum et locum suspectum; excommunicatus>

Bokenhull <Clone>

1042 Parochiani dicunt quod Issabella Hoke[5] fornicatur cum domino Johanne Schippe capellano p[arochiali qui morat]ur apud Glouc'. <vir comparet, negat post correctionem, purget se cum v^{ta} manu in proxima; mulier[6] ...us>

---

[1] Preceded by *suspensi*, struck through.
[2] Altered from *Bodyton*.
[3] The bottom right-hand corner of this page has perished with the loss of up to three inches of text.
[4] <*suspensus*> struck through.
[5] Preceded by *Hu*, struck through.
[6] Preceded by *mrl*, struck through.

VILL OF ADFORTON <*Clun*>

1032 The villeins say that Wilkoc Meuric harbours fornicators and adulterers in his house so that they can sin, that is, his son John <*suspended*> and Joan <*suspended*>, the latter's concubine, next Jankin Chaumbereresmon and the same Joan, next the same Joan and Hopkyn Boly. <*outside; Joan appears, corrected; the man has married, the others etc.*>

1033 Next, that Geoffrey Taelour fornicates with Helen, his concubine, both of whom Lleucu Llanddewy receives in her house. <*the man appears, admits, abjures, to be beaten three times around the church; to be postponed in the hope of them marrying*>

1034 Next, that Grug Moel[1] <*suspended*> sells his goods at a higher price than they are worth by delaying etc. <*excommunicated*>

1035 Next, that Wilkoc North Forlong and Isabel, whom he keeps as a wife, as common fame has it there, are not joined in marriage. <*both to be cited to the next; both excommunicated*>

BURRINGTON <*Clun*>

1036 The parishioners say that the bell-tower is unroofed, by the fault of the parishioners. <*it has been put right*>

1037 Next, that William Adames and his wife Isabel <*suspended*> do not live together nor do they behave as man and wife, by the fault of the wife. <*the man asserts that he is ready; the woman is warned to treat her husband [better], under penalty of excommunication; she is excommunicated on account of her contumacy; later she gave birth etc.*>

1038 Next, that William Vicarys and Alison Schepmon <*suspended*> fornicate together. <*the man is in Ireland; the woman dismissed*>

1039 Next, that the vicar celebrates twice in a day. <*deferred*>

1040 Next, that John Malyar, William Adames, and Wilkoc Spyney are habitual workers on Sundays and feast days.

1041 [*in margin*]: <*signified Wigmore*>

<*Next, that John Watys fornicates with a woman whom he keeps, and they have done this for 20 years etc.; her name is Maiota; the man appears, denies since correction, abjures the sin and the suspicious circumstances; excommunicated*>

BUCKNELL <*Clun*>

1042 The parishioners say that Isabel Hoke fornicates with Sir John Schippe, the parish chaplain who lives at Gloucester. <*the man appears, denies since correction, to purge himself with six hands at the next; the woman ...*>

---

[1] A name implying a bald or barren man (*moel*) who stammers (*cryg*).

1043 Item Rogerus Wodeward et Alicia uxor sua sunt illegitime copulati eo [quod contraxerunt adinvicem] vivente quadam alia <Agnete que mora<ba>tur apud Atteforton>[1] cum qua precontraxerat carnal[i copula subsecuta] que tamen obiit post matrimonium contractum inter ipsos Rogerum et Aliciam. <dimissi [sunt]>

1044 Item quod idem Rogerus adulteratur cum Tangwystel Goch. <vir comparet, fatetur, ... ; mulier comparet, negat; purgavit se>

1045 Item quod Nest Ivor alias filia Ieuan ap Ivor soluta adulteratur cum Hu[gone] ... <[negat post] correctionem;[2] postea fatetur, abjurat, fustigetur vj circa ecclesiam; difer usque post partum; m[ulier] ...>

1046 Item quod dominus Ricardus vicarius ibidem incontinens est cum Maiota Cle[rke].[3] <[negat, purget se coram] consistorio cum vj manu; mulier suspensa; defecit in purgatione, abjurat peccatum et locum suspectum ...>

1047 Item quod vicarius non deservit laudabiliter in divinis quia absentat se alibi ... ... negligendo servicium divinum etcetera. <negat>

[f. 22]

1048 Item quod abbas de Wygg' subtrahit decimas de Cokkeshalle debitas ab antiquo portioni vicarii ibidem. <prosequatur vicarius>

1049 Item quod abbas subtrahit panem benedictum in cursu suo pro grangia sua ibidem et elemosinam pro cereo paschali, videlicet unum denarium pro aratro.

Bedeston <Clone>

1050 <Dominus Walterus>

1051 Parochiani dicunt quod non habent lanternam ad visitandum infirmos et quod basteristerium[4] non est clausum in defectu parochianorum. <habent diem ad reparandum huiusmodi defectus citra festum Natalis Domini quia pauperes>

1052 Item quod Reginaldus[5] Penymawe alias Collynge incontinens est cum Johanna Boterell et continuarunt in peccato xx annis in peccato. <apud Bromfeld>

1053 Item quod Iorwerth Daldrayn fornicatur cum Erdudvyl[6] Knollyn non obstante abjuratione etcetera. <suspensi>

1054 Item quod Wenllian Botterell <extra> alias Johanna superius nominata diffamavit maliciose et falso Aliciam Aleyn super furto CCCCC fili lini etcetera.

1055 Item quod eadem Johanna <extra> diffamavit maliciose Walterum Davys super adulterio cum Alicia Aleyn.

[1]   Replacing *cuius nomen ignorant*, struck through.
[2]   Followed by *excommunicata*, struck through.
[3]   *Clerke* seen or conjectured by Bannister.
[4]   Recte *baptisterium*.
[5]   Preceded by *ca*, struck through.
[6]   Preceded by *D*, struck through.

1043 Next, Roger Wodeward and Alice his wife are unlawfully joined because [they contracted together] in the lifetime of a certain woman, <*Agnes who lived at Adforton*>, with whom he made a previous contract, followed by bodily union, who however died after the marriage contracted between Roger and Alice. <*they are dismissed*>

1044 Next, that the same Roger commits adultery with Tangwystl Goch. <*the man appears, admits, ...; the woman appears, denies; she has purged herself*>

1045 Next, that Nest Ifor otherwise the daughter of Ieuan ap Ifor, a single woman, commits adultery with Hugh ... <*she denies after correction; later admits, abjures, to be beaten six times around the church; defer until after birth; the woman ...*>

1046 Next, that Sir Richard, the vicar there, is incontinent with Maiota Clerke <*denies, to purge himself before the consistory with six hands; the woman suspended; he has failed in purgation, abjures the sin and the suspicious circumstances ...*>

1047 Next, that the vicar does not serve his divine duties in a praiseworthy manner because he absents himself elsewhere ... ... neglecting divine service etc. <*he denies*>

[f. 22]

1048 Next, that the abbot of Wigmore withholds the tithes of Coxall, from of old due to the portion of the vicar there. <*let the vicar prosecute*>

1049 Next, that the abbot withholds the holy bread, when it comes to the turn of his grange there, and the alms for the Easter candle, that is, 1 penny for each plough.

BEDSTONE <*Clun*>

1050 <*Sir Walter*> [*not completed*]

1051 The parishioners say that they do not have a lantern for visiting the sick and that the font is not closed, by the fault of the parishioners. <*they have a day to put right this defect before Christmas because they are poor people*>

1052 Next, that Reynold Penymawe otherwise Collynge is incontinent with Joan Boterell and they have continued in sin, 20 years in sin. <*at Bromfield*>

1053 Next, that Iorwerth Daldrayn fornicates with Erdudful Knollyn despite an abjuration etc. <*both suspended*>

1054 Next, that Gwenllian Botterell <*outside*> otherwise Joan, the woman named above, has maliciously and falsely defamed Alice Aleyn over a theft of 500 linen threads etc.

1055 Next, that the same Joan <*outside*> has maliciously defamed Walter Davys over adultery with Alice Aleyn.

1056 Item quod[1]

Dounton[2] <Clone>

1057 Parochiani dicunt quod cancellus est defectius in tectura in defectu parochianorum.

Dudelbury <Lodel'>. Visitatio facta ibidem die dominica xxiiij^to die mensis Junii anno Domini ut supra

Culmyton <Lodel'>

1058 Parochiani dicunt quod Walterus Wodeward fornicatur cum Johanna Horde quam tenet. <ambo extra; mulier suspensa>

1059 Item quod Jankyn Tasger <suspensus> et Katerina <suspensa> quam tenet pro uxore fornicantur adinvicem <quia> ut creditur non sunt matrimonialiter copulati.

1060 [*in margin*] <Dominus Ricardus Carter[3] incontinens est cum>[4]

1061 Item quod Mathewe Taelour <tenens Philippi Bakon> et Agnes quam tenet ut creditur etiam non sunt copulati matrimonialiter. <ambo suspensi>

1062 Item quod Wilkoc de Dounton et Maiota uxor sua non cohabitant simul in defectu mulieris. <dimissi sunt>[5]

1063 Item quod cimiterium non est debiter clausum in defectu habitatorum ville <de> Syvyton.

1064 Item in defectu habitatorum de Culmyton similiter clausura cimiterii patitur defectum.

1065 Item quod Issabella de Wallia <fornicatur cum uno Wallico cuius nomen ignorant; set ut credunt Jankyn Taelour; extra ambo>

D[ud]elbury <[Lode]l'>[6]

1066 Parochiani dicunt quod selura cancelli est defectiva in defectu rectoris et vicarii. <reformata est>

1067 [Item] quod vicarius tenetur invenire unum capellanum ad celebrandum in capella de Mydelhop [sing]ulis diebus dominicis et festis solempnibus etiam feria iiij^ta et vj^ta quod non facit, et subtractum [est vii]j annis elapsis. <prosequantur parochiani>

1068 [Item quod] Willelmus de Lowe conjugatus adulteratur cum Agnete <Naylard> serviente ipsius[7] Willelmi. <ambo suspensi>

---

[1]   Unfinished.
[2]   Interlined above *Donyton*, struck through.
[3]   Altered from *Carpenter*.
[4]   Unfinished.
[5]   Preceded by <*suspensi*>, struck through.
[6]   The bottom left-hand corner of this page is torn away with the loss of up to two inches of text.
[7]   Preceded by *W*, struck through.

1056 Next, that [*not completed*]

DOWNTON <*Clun*>

1057 The parishioners say that the chancel is defective in its roof, by the fault of the parishioners.

Diddlebury <*Ludlow*>. Visitation made there on Sunday, 24 June, in the year of Our Lord as above

CULMINGTON <*Ludlow*>

1058 The parishioners say that Walter Wodeward fornicates with Joan Horde, whom he keeps. <*both outside; the woman suspended*>

1059 Next, that Jankin Tasger <*suspended*> and Katherine <*suspended*>, whom he keeps as a wife, fornicate together, <*because*> as it is believed they are not joined in marriage.

1060 [*in margin*]: <*Sir Richard Carter is incontinent with*> [*not completed*]

1061 Next, that Matthew Taelour, <*tenant of Philip Bakon*>, and Agnes, whom he keeps, are also not, as is believed, joined in marriage. <*both suspended*>

1062 Next, that Wilkoc of Downton and his wife Maiota do not live together, by the fault of the woman. <*they are dismissed*>

1063 Next, that the churchyard is not properly fenced, by the fault of the inhabitants of the vill of Siefton.

1064 Next, by the fault of the inhabitants of Culmington, the fence of the churchyard is similarly defective.

1065 Next, that Isabel of Wales <*fornicates with a Welshman whose name they do not know; but as they believe it is Jankin Taelour; both outside*>

DIDDLEBURY <*Ludlow*>

1066 The parishioners say that the ceiling of the chancel is defective, by the fault of the rector and of the vicar. <*it has been put right*>

1067 Next, that the vicar ought to provide a chaplain to celebrate in the chapel of Middlehope every Sunday and solemn feast day, also on Wednesdays and Fridays, which he does not do, and he has withheld this for the past eight years. <*let the parishioners prosecute*>

1068 Next, that William de Lowe, a married man, commits adultery with Agnes <*Naylard*>, servant of the same William. <*both suspended*>

1069　[Item] quod Willelmus Mersshton fornicatur cum Margareta Broun. <vir extra, mulier suspensa>

1070　[Item quod] Ieuan Tasgor conjugatus adulteratur cum Margareta, quam tenet. <vir comparet, negat post correctionem; purgavit se>

1071　[Item quod] Willelmus Kyde ivit de parochia de Dudelbury ad ecclesiam de …we pro matrimonio clamdestino solempnizando ibidem post reclamationem etcetera. <citetur ad proximam>

1072　[Item quod Willelmus][1] Maylard conjugatus adulteratur cum Agnete Lyche. <vir comparet, negat; purgavit[2] se; mulier purgavit se>

[f. 22v]

1073　Item quod Juliana uxor Johannis Lake non tractat maritum suum affectione conjugali. <extra>

1074　Item quod Willelmus Laurens cocus domine de Corffham fornicatur cum Matilda quam tenet. <non citati, ideo citentur>

1075　Item quod Willelmus Polley fornicatur cum Johanna filia Johannis Leye qui quidem Willelmus abjuravit eandem sub pena matrimonii et postea procreavit de eadem duos filios. <non citati; sunt>

1076　Item quod Hopkyn Baker qui moratur cum Thoma[3] Yong contraxit matrimonium per verba de presenti cum quadam Johanna filia Alicie Mersshton et postea non obstante huiusmodi contractu idem Hopkyn duxit quandam sibi in uxorem de facto in parochia de Clonbury.

1077　Item[4]

Stoksay <Lodel'>. Visitatio facta ibidem die lune xxv mensis Junii anno ut supra

　　　[Stoksay]

1078　Parochiani dicunt quod vicarius celebrat bis in die singulis diebus dominicis et festivis, videlicet primo apud Aldon et postea in ecclesia de Stok, ita quod parochiani non habent tantam devotionem in secunda missa ac si esset prima ut dicunt. <allegat tolleranciam per dominum episcopum sibi concessam>

1079　Item quod non habent matutinas diebus dominicis et festivis in defectu vicarii. <allegat impotenciam etcetera>

1080　Item quod idem vicarius vel rector tenetur invenire unum capellanum ad celebrandum in dicta capella diebus dominicis et festivis ac singulis feriis iiij[ta] et vj[ta] per annum quod non facit. <allegat impotenciam propter exilitatem portionis>

---

[1]　　*Willelmus* supplied from Bannister.
[2]　　Altered from *purget*, followed by *coram curato*, struck through.
[3]　　Preceded by *H*, struck through.
[4]　　Unfinished.

1069   Next, that William Mersshton fornicates with Margaret Broun. *<the man outside; the woman suspended>*

1070   Next, that Ieuan Tasgor, a married man, commits adultery with Margaret, whom he keeps. *<the man appears, denies since correction; he has purged himself>*

1071   Next, that William Kyde went from the parish of Diddlebury to the church of ...we to solemnise a clandestine marriage there after a challenge etc. *<to be cited to the next>*

1072   Next, that William Maylard, a married man, commits adultery with Agnes Lyche. *<the man appears, denies; he has purged himself; the woman has purged herself>*

[f. 22v]

1073   Next, that Julian, wife of John Lake, does not treat her husband with conjugal affection. *<outside>*

1074   Next, that William Laurens, the cook of the lady of Corfham, fornicates with Maud, whom he keeps. *<they have not been cited, so to be cited>*

1075   Next, that William Polley fornicates with Joan, daughter of John Leye, which William abjured her under penalty of marriage and later he fathered two children with her. *<they have not been cited; they are>*

1076   Next, that Hopkyn Baker who lives with Thomas Yong contracted marriage in the present tense with a certain Joan, daughter of Alice Mersshton, and later, despite this contract, the same Hopkyn actually made a certain woman his wife in the parish of Clunbury.

1077   Next, [*not completed*]

Stokesay *<Ludlow>*. Visitation made there on Monday, 25 June, the year as above

STOKESAY

1078   The parishioners say that the vicar celebrates twice in a day every Sunday and feast day, namely first at Aldon and later in the church of Stokesay, so that the parishioners do not have as much devotion at the second mass as they would if it were the first, as they say. *<he alleges permission granted to him by the lord bishop>*

1079   Next, that they do not have matins on Sundays and feast days, by the fault of the vicar. *<he alleges inability etc.>*

1080   Next, that the same vicar, or the rector, ought to provide a chaplain to celebrate in the said chapel on Sundays and feast days and every Wednesday and Friday throughout the year, which he does not do. *<he alleges inability because of the meagreness of the portion>*

1081 Item quod Rogerus Rowton fornicatur cum Sibilla Onwyn[1] quam tenet. <suspensi>

1082 Item quod idem Rogerus non venit ad ecclesiam parochialem diebus dominicis et festivis.

1083 Item quod Wilim Rwth conjugatus adulteratur cum Juliana filia Ricardi Pengule. <vir comparet, fatetur, abjurat, fustigetur vj circa ecclesiam parochialem et vj per forum de Lodel', absolutus est a sentencia excommunicationis etcetera; mulier pregnans est ideo respicitur usque post partum>

1084 Item quod Johannes Hir <conjugatus> fornicatur cum Dydgu Wallica quam tenet conjugaliter. <vir extra, mulier suspensa; mulier abjurat peccatum et locum suspectum, fustigetur in forma>

1085 Item quod Jankyn Penngul adulteratur cum Agnete Baron conjugata. <vir comparet, negat post correctionem; purgavit se; mulier dimissa est>

1086 Item quod Thomas Frenssh fornicatur cum Maiota Madok. <vir extra, mulier suspensa>

Bromfeld <Lodel'>. Visitatio facta ibidem die martis xxvj Junii anno domini ut supra

Onybury
1087 Parochiani [dicunt] quod omnia sunt bene ibidem.

Capelle de Lodeford et Syde
1088 Parochiani dicunt quod omnia bene ibidem.

Dodynȝob
1089 Dicunt quod dominus Willelmus Westhop incontinens est cum quadam Johanna Stake <suspensa, citetur> quam tenet in domo sua continue. <vir comparet, negat, habet diem ad purgandum se in proxima cum vj^{ta} manu; vir monitus est ad ammovendum eam de cohabitatione et loco suspecto infra sex dies [sub p] ena[2] excommunicationis>

Bromfeld <Lodel'>
1090 Parochiani dicunt quod habitatores villarum de Lodeford, Syde et Assheford [recusan]t contribuere reparationi campanilis ecclesie matricis videlicet de Bromfeld et quod idem campanile p[atitur defectum i]n tectura in eorum defectu.

1091 Item quod clausura cimiterii patitur defectum in defectu parochianorum.

---

[1]   Preceded by *V*, struck through.
[2]   The bottom right-hand corner of this page is perished with the loss of up to three inches of text.

1081   Next, that Roger Rowton fornicates with Sybil Onwyn, whom he keeps. <*both suspended*>

1082   Next, that the same Roger does not come to the parish church on Sundays and feast days.

1083   Next, that Wilim Rwth, a married man, commits adultery with Julian, daughter of Richard Pengule. <*the man appears, admits, abjures, to be beaten six times around the parish church and six times through the marketplace of Ludlow, he is absolved from the sentence of excommunication etc.; the woman is pregnant so postpone until after birth*>

1084   Next, that John Hir <*a married man*> fornicates with Dyddgu the Welsh woman, whom he keeps as though they were married. <*the man outside; the woman suspended; the woman abjures the sin and the suspicious circumstances, to be beaten in due form*>

1085   Next, that Jankin Penngul commits adultery with Agnes Baron, a married woman. <*the man appears, denies since correction, has purged himself; the woman is dismissed*>

1086   Next, that Thomas Frenssh fornicates with Maiota Madok. <*the man outside; the woman suspended*>

Bromfield <*Ludlow*>. Visitation made there on Tuesday, 26 June, the year as above

ONIBURY

1087   The parishioners say that all things are well there.

CHAPELS OF LUDFORD AND SYDE

1088   The parishioners say that all is well there.

DINCHOPE

1089   They say that Sir William Westhop is incontinent with a certain Joan Stake <*suspended, to be cited*>, whom he keeps in his house continuously. <*the man appears, denies, he has a day to purge himself with six hands at the next; the man is warned to remove her from cohabitation and the suspect place within six days, under penalty of excommunication*>

BROMFIELD <*Ludlow*>

1090   The parishioners say that the inhabitants of the vills of Ludford, Syde, and Ashford refuse to contribute to the repairs of the bell-tower of the mother church, namely of Bromfield, and that the same bell-tower has defects in its roof, by their fault.

1091   Next, that the fence of the churchyard is defective, by the fault of the parishioners.

1092 Item quod Johanna Penymawe <suspensa; excommunicata> fornicatur cum domino Reginaldo Penymawe <suspensus> d.. ... <vir comparet apud Lodel' xx°; reddit se reverenter>

1093 Item quod Margareta Scheppert <suspensa, citetur> fornicatur cum quodam cuius nomen ignorant ... ... de quo procreavit unum filium.

1094 <Item quod frater Johannes Yeton canonicus regularis qui moratur apud Leyn... [incontinens est] cum quadam Emlyn filia cuiusdam mulieris de Bromfeld et cum Johanna ... ... Hugonis Partrich ac¹ cum Agnete uxore Johannis Bulleston de A... ... Connar serviente Ricardi Marlowe>. <vir purgavit se> [*in margin*] <Nota>

1095 <Thomas Reynald de Halton fornicatur cum Agnete quam tenet; ambo suspensi; mulier ...>

1096 [*in margin*] <Dominus Thomas vicarius de Bromfeld incontinens est cum Issabella Baylyf et cum Elynor uxore Willelmi Clerk; vir purget se sola manu>

1097 [*in margin*] <Dominus Willelmus Westhop incontinens est cum Margret Scheppert; vir comparet, negat, purget se in proxima cum vjᵗᵃ manu>

[f. 23]

Aston visitata apud Leyntwardyn <Clone>

1098 Parochiani dicunt quod ecclesia patitur defectum in tectura in defectu parochianorum.

1099 Item quod quedam Alicia Bernard nuper defuncta legavit in suo testamento unam ollam eneam rectori nuper ibidem et suis successoribus successive, tandem dominus Johannes Knyghton rector ibidem alienavit huiusmodi ollam in prejudicium successorum suorum huiusmodi.

1100 Item idem rector alienavit unum pannum qui solebat pendere supra magnum altare legatum ad huiusmodi usum per dictam Aliciam.

1101 Item quod Johannes Swayn recusat ministrare panem benedictum in cursu suo.

1102 Item²

Lydebury North <Clone> Visitatio facta ibidem die mercurii xxvij die Junii etcetera

Castrum Episcopi <Clone>

1103 <Dominus Jacobus vicarius ibidem incontinens est cum Issabella concubina sua et serviente; vir comparet, negat, purget se cum vᵗᵃ manu in proxima; purgavit se>

¹ Preceded by *et*, struck through.
² Unfinished.

1092   Next, that Joan Penymawe <*suspended; excommunicated*> fornicates with Sir Reynold Penymawe <*suspended*> ... ... <*the man appears at Ludlow on the 20th; he submits himself respectfully*>

1093   Next, that Margaret Scheppert <*suspended, to be cited*> fornicates with a certain man whose name they do not know ... ... by whom she has had a child.

1094   <*Next, that Brother John Yeton, a canon regular who lives at Leintwardine, ... is incontinent with a certain Emlyn, daughter of some woman of Bromfield, and with Joan ... ... [wife of] Hugh Partrich, and with Agnes, wife of John Bulleston of A... [and with] ... Connar, servant of Richard Marlowe; the man has purged himself*> [in margin]: <*note*>

1095   <*Thomas Reynald of Halton fornicates with Agnes, whom he keeps; both suspended; the woman ...*>

1096   [in margin]: <*Sir Thomas, the vicar of Bromfield, is incontinent with Isabel Baylyf and with Eleanor, wife of William Clerk; the man to purge himself with a single hand*>

1097   [in margin]: <*Sir William Westhop is incontinent with Margaret Scheppert; the man appears, denies, to purge himself at the next with six hands*>

[f. 23]

ASTON visited at Leintwardine <*Clun*>

1098   The parishioners say that the church is defective in its roof, by the fault of the parishioners.

1099   Next, that a certain Alice Bernard, lately deceased, in her will bequeathed a brass vessel to the late rector there and to his successors in turn, however Sir John Knyghton, the [present] rector there, has taken this vessel, to the prejudice of his successors.

1100   Next, the same rector has taken a cloth that used to hang over the high altar bequeathed for this purpose by the said Alice.

1101   Next, that John Swayn refuses to provide the holy bread in his turn.

1102   Next, [*not completed*]

Lydbury North <*Clun*> Visitation made there on Wednesday, 27 June, etc.

BISHOPS CASTLE <*Clun*>

1103   <*Sir James, the vicar there, is incontinent with Isabel, his concubine and servant; the man appears, denies, to purge himself with six hands at the next; he has purged himself*>

1104 Parochiani dicunt quod cancellus est ruinosus et male discoopertus in defectu rectoris. <est in reparando>

1105 Item quod idem rector tenetur invenire portiforium vocatum lyger[1] ad deserviendum Deo in ecclesia quod non facit.

1106 Item quod idem rector tenetur invenire unum par vestimentorum ad celebrandum ad summum altare quod non facit.

1107 Item quod Johannes Robyns incontinens est cum Dydgu quam tenet. <vir absens, citetur cum venerit; mulier suspensa>

1108 Item quod Willelmus Herdewyk fornicatur cum Agnete quam tenet.[2] <mulier suspensa; vir citetur ad proximam>

1109 Item quod Owein ap Gruffuth constabularius ibidem fornicatur cum Alson quam tenet. <suspensi>

1110 Item quod Ricardus[3] Collynge fornicatur cum Maiota quam tenet. <mulier apud Temdebury; vir comparet, fatetur, abjurat, fustigetur ter etcetera>

1111 Item quod Gruffuth frater Jowkys Duy fornicatur cum Wenllia filia Johannis Bwgys. <suspensi>

1112 Item quod Jankyn Smyth junior fornicatur cum Angharat quam tenet.[4] <vir comparet, fatetur, abjurat; ter circa ecclesiam, mulier idem>[5]

1113 Item quod Philippus Brugge fornicatur cum Issabella Duy quam tenet.[6] <ambo comparent, fatentur peccatum, asserunt se matrimonialiter copulatos>

1114 Item quod Jankyn Schappemon fornicatur cum eadem Issabella. <suspensi>

1115 Item quod Philippus Jakkes fornicatur cum Wenllian Kyde. <vir comparet, fatetur, abjurat, fustigetur vj[7] per forum et vj circa ecclesiam et jejunet omni feria vj per vij^m [septimanam], mulier comparet, fatetur, abjurat, fustigetur ter circa ecclesiam>

1116 Item quod idem Philippus fornicatur[8] cum Johanna relicta Johannis Hikkokes. <mulier comparet, fatetur, abjurat, fustigetur ter circa ecclesiam>

1117 Item quod David Gethin fornicatur cum Lleuky Gylbert.[9] <vir comparet, negat post correctionem, purget se cum v^ta manu in proxima, mulier comparet, negat; purgavit se>

1118 Item quod Cadogyn ap Madoc fornicatur cum Mably quam tenet. <suspensi>

[1] Preceded by *lytl*, struck through.
[2] Followed by <*suspensi*>, struck through.
[3] Preceded by *Rogerus*, struck through.
[4] Followed by <*suspensi*>, struck through.
[5] Preceded by *f*, struck through.
[6] Followed by <*suspensi*>, struck through.
[7] Altered from *ter*.
[8] Preceded by *fornicatur, adulteratur*, both struck through.
[9] Followed by <*suspensi*>, struck through.

1104   The parishioners say that the chancel is in a ruinous state and badly unroofed, by the fault of the rector. <*it is being repaired*>

1105   Next, that the same rector ought to provide a breviary called a 'ledger' to serve God in the church, which he does not do.

1106   Next, that the same rector ought to provide a set of vestments to celebrate at the high altar, which he does not do.

1107   Next, that John Robyns is incontinent with Dyddgu, whom he keeps. <*the man absent, to be cited when he comes; the woman suspended*>

1108   Next, that William Herdewykes fornicates with Agnes, whom he keeps. <*the woman suspended; the man to be cited to the next*>

1109   Next, that Owain ap Gruffudd, the constable there, fornicates with Alison, whom he keeps. <*both suspended*>

1110   Next, that Richard Collynge fornicates with Maiota, whom he keeps. <*the woman at Tenbury; the man appears, admits, abjures, to be beaten three times etc.*>

1111   Next, that Gruffudd, brother of Jowkys Duy, fornicates with Gwenllian, daughter of John Bwgys. <*both suspended*>

1112   Next, that Jankin Smyth the younger fornicates with Angharad, whom he keeps. <*the man appears, admits, abjures; [to be beaten] three times around the church; the woman the same*>

1113   Next, that Philip Brugge fornicates with Isabel Duy, whom he keeps. <*both appear, they admit the sin, they assert that they are married*>

1114   Next, that Jankin Schappemon fornicates with the same Isabel. <*both suspended*>

1115   Next, that Philip Jakkes fornicates with Gwenllian Kyde. <*the man appears, admits, abjures, to be beaten six times through the marketplace and six times around the church and to fast every Friday weekly; the woman appears, admits, abjures, to be beaten three times around the church*>

1116   Next, that the same Philip fornicates with Joan, widow of John Hikkokes. <*the woman appears, admits, abjures, to be beaten three times around the church*>

1117   Next, that David Gethin fornicates with Lleucu Gylbert. <*the man appears, denies since correction, to purge himself with six hands at the next; the woman appears, denies; she has purged herself*>

1118   Next, that Cadwgan ap Madog fornicates with Mably, whom he keeps. <*both suspended*>

1119 Item quod Howel filius Johannis Bygwth fornicatur cum serviente Jankyn Falke. <suspensi>

1120 Item quod Willelmus Dogans fornicatur cum Matilda[1] filia Thome Taelour. <alias contraxerunt volentes facere solempnizari rite etcetera, set accidit interim quod vir subito captus est adeo gravi infirmitate quod deficiunt sibi sensus gressus et loquela; considerandum quid sit agendum>

1121 [Ite]m[2] quod Johanna uxor Gruffuth de Ley non tractat dictum maritum suum affectione conigali [ne]c cohabitat cum eo. <extra>

1122 [Ite]m quod David Willes non venit ad ecclesiam parochialem diebus dominicis et festivis. <comparet, negat, dimissus est>

1123 [Ite]m quod Gruffuth ap Iorwerth contraxit cum Agnete Dogans quam tenet in domo sua nec volunt matrimonium facere [sole]mpnizari etcetera. <com­parent, negant post correctionem usque ad solempnizationem matrimonii; dimissi sunt>

1124 [Item] quod Mereduth <ap Eignon> de Ley fornicatur cum Angharat quam tenet. <ambo comparent, fatentur, abjurant, fustigentur ter circa ecclesiam>

1125 [Item quod] Eignon Gwyned <suspensus> fornicatur cum Alson quam Owein tenet.

1126 [Item quod Henricus][3] clericus ecclesie fornicatur cum eadem Alson. <vir comparet, negat post porrectionem,[4] purget se>

1127 [Item quod] Johannes Juwes capellanus incontinens cum Johanna Mael <suspensa> uxore Willelmi de Eton. <vir comparet, ...>

1128[5] Ieuan ap David <Duy> fornicatur cum Jonet filia Rogeri Jakkes de Colbach. <vir comparet, sunt matrimonialiter copulati>

[f. 23v]

Lyddom <Clone>

1129 Parochiani dicunt quod Meuric ap Meuric Vychan subtrahit decimas suas rationales. <suspensus; excommunicatus>

1130 Item quod Gwilim ap Ieuan ap Gwilim etiam subtrahit decimas. <suspensus>

1131 [*in margin*] .e.
Item quod prefatus Meuric et Eva <suspensa> filia <David ap Eignon Vychan>[6] fornicantur adinvicem et continuaverunt in peccato xxx annis <et ultra; excom­municati; et eadem Eva est communis usuratrix, videlicet, recepit de Gwilim ap Ieuan Hensor pro xx s, xxxij s ij d>

---

[1] Preceded by *Maiota*, struck through.
[2] The bottom left-hand corner of this page is perished with the loss of up to an inch of text.
[3] Supplied from Bannister.
[4] Recte *correctionem*.
[5] Apparently continued on the same line as the last entry.
[6] Replacing *Mereduth*, struck through.

1119   Next, that Hywel, son of John Bygwth, fornicates with a servant of Jankin Falke. <*both suspended*>

1120   Next, that William Dogans fornicates with Maud, daughter of Thomas Taelour. <*they previously made a contract wishing to have it properly solemnised etc., but in the meantime it happened that the man was suddenly overcome by so serious an illness that he lost his senses, motion, and speech; to consider what should be done*>

1121   Next, that Joan, wife of Gruffudd of Lea, does not treat her said husband with conjugal affection and does not live with him. <*outside*>

1122   Next, that David Willes does not come to the parish church on Sundays and feast days. <*appears, denies, he is dismissed*>

1123   Next, that Gruffudd ap Iorwerth made a contract with Agnes Dogans, whom he keeps in his house, but they will not have the marriage solemnised etc. <*they appear, deny since correction, up to the solemnisation of marriage; they are dismissed*>

1124   Next, that Maredudd ap Einion of Lea fornicates with Angharad, whom he keeps. <*both appear, both admit, both abjure, both to be beaten three times around the church*>

1125   Next, that Einion Gwyned <*suspended*> fornicates with Alison, whom Owain keeps.

1126   Next, that Henry, the clerk of the church, fornicates with the same Alison. <*the man appears, denies since correction, to purge himself*>

1127   Next, that John Juwes, chaplain, is incontinent with Joan Mael <*suspended*>, wife of William of Eaton. <*the man appears, ...*>

1128   Ieuan ap David Duy fornicates with Jonet, daughter of Roger Jakkes of Colebatch. <*the man appears, they are married*>

[f. 23v]

LYDHAM <*Clun*>

1129   The parishioners say that Meurig ap Meurig Vychan withholds his reasonable tithes. <*suspended; excommunicated*>

1130   Next, that Gwilym ap Ieuan ap Gwilym also withholds tithes. <*suspended*>

1131   [*in margin*]: .e.

Next, that the aforesaid Meurig and Eve <*suspended*>, daughter of David ap Einion Vychan, fornicate together and have continued in sin for 30 years <*and more; both excommunicated; and the same Eve is a habitual usurer, that is, she received £1 12s 2d from Gwilym ap Ieuan Hensor for 20 shillings*>.

1132 [*in margin*] <significantur>

Item quod Ieuan ap David ap Adda fornicatur cum Eva <suspensa; excommunicata> quam tenet.[1] <vir comparet, fatetur; excommunicatus; denunciatus est; abjurat, fustigetur in forma; mulier suspensa; excommunicata>

1133　Item quod ecclesia patitur defectum in tectura in defectu parochianorum.

　　　Wentenor <Clone>

1134　Parochiani dicunt quod rector non deservit laudabiliter in divinis dicendo missas et alia servicia. <difertur sub spe emendationis>

1135　Item quod mansum rectoris patitur ruinam in defectu eiusdem rectoris. <dicit quod non fuit ibidem nisi per unum annum et vult emendare>

1136　Item quod idem rector exercet tabernas die ac nocte contra honestatem ecclesiasticam. <negat>

1137　Item quod dominus Johannes Bent detinet injuste diversa ornamenta ecclesie predicte[2] et detinuit a tempore quo fuit capellanus parochialis ibidem.

1138　Item quod rector dat ecclesiam suam ad firmam dicto domino Johanni Bent capellano inhonesto et insufficienti ad deserviendum Deo et parochianis. <emendatum est>

1139　Item quod idem dominus Johannes Bente <suspensus> incontinens est cum Meueddus <suspensa> quam tenet. <vir ad purgandum>

1140　Item quod rector tenetur invenire unum par vestimentorum pro diebus ferialibus quod non facit. <dicit quod non tenetur>

1141　Item quod Willelmus Godewote <suspensus> detinet iij s iiij d deputatos ad opus ecclesie.

1142　Item quod idem Willelmus Godewot graviter diffamatur cum Cecilia uxore Willelmi Wade <mulier suspensa>, ut idem Willelmus queritur etcetera. <vir comparet, negat>

1143　Item quod idem Willemus Godewote diffamavit dictum Willelmum Wade falso, nequiter et injuste super furto bestiarum etcetera.

1144　Item quod cimiterium non est clausum in defectu parochianorum et habent diem circa festum Sancti Michelis proximum futurum. <difertur ad Pentecostem>

1145　<Item parochiani non inveniunt superpellicium pro capellano ad visitandum infirmos et baptizandum infantes nec lumen pro visitatione infirmorum; baptisterium non est seratum>

　　　Norbury <Clone>

1146　Parochiani dicunt quod cancellus est male coopertus et patitur defectum in vitro fenestrarum in defectu rectoris. <difertur sub spe emendationis>

---

[1]　Followed by *amb*, struck through.
[2]　Followed by *a te*, struck through.

1132 [*in margin*]: <*they are signified*>

Next, that Ieuan ap David ap Adda fornicates with Eve <*suspended; excommunicated*>, whom he keeps. <*the man appears, admits; excommunicated; denounced; abjures, to be beaten in due form; the woman suspended; excommunicated*>

1133 Next, that the church is defective in its roof, by the fault of the parishioners.

WENTNOR <*Clun*>

1134 The parishioners say that the rector does not serve in a praiseworthy manner in divine matters when saying masses and other services. <*it is deferred in the hope of amendment*>

1135 Next, that the house of the rector is ruinous, by the fault of the same rector. <*he says that he has been there only one year and wants to repair*>

1136 Next, that the same rector frequents taverns day and night, contrary to church decency. <*he denies*>

1137 Next, that Sir John Bent wrongfully withholds various ornaments of the aforesaid church and has withheld them since the time he was parish chaplain there.

1138 Next, that the rector farms out his church to the said Sir John Bent, an unworthy chaplain and one inadequate to serve God and the parishioners. <*it is put right*>

1139 Next, that the same Sir John Bente <*suspended*> is incontinent with Meueddus[1] <*suspended*>, whom he keeps. <*the man to purge*>

1140 Next, that the rector ought to provide a set of vestments for weekdays, which he does not do. <*he says that he is not obliged to*>

1141 Next, that William Godewote <*suspended*> withholds 3 shillings and 4 pence assigned for the benefit of the church.

1142 Next, that the same William Godewot is gravely defamed with Cecily, wife of William Wade, as the same William [Wade] complains etc. <*the woman suspended; the man appears, denies*>

1143 Next, that the same William Godewote has falsely, wickedly, and wrongfully defamed the said William Wade over the theft of animals etc.

1144 Next, that the churchyard is not fenced, by the fault of the parishioners, and they have a day around Michaelmas next. <*it is deferred to Whitsun*>

1145 <*Next, the parishioners have not provided a surplice for the chaplain to visit the sick and baptise infants nor a light for visiting the sick; the font is not locked*>

NORBURY <*Clun*>

1146 The parishioners say that the chancel is badly roofed and is defective in the glass of the windows, by the fault of the rector. <*it is deferred in the hope of amendment*>

---

[1] An adjective meaning *rich*.

1147 Item quod Philippus Rogeres[1] subtrahit decimas rationales etcetera. <concordes sunt rector et idem Philippus>

Maenston <Clone>

1148 Parochiani dicunt quod navis ecclesie patitur defectum in coopertura et quod clausura cimiterii patitur defectum in defectu parochianorum; ibi nullus gerit curam. <parochiani habent diem ad reparandum citra festum Pasche>

1149 Item quod cancellus est defectius in tectura in defectu rectoris. <cancellus est in emendatione> [*in margin*] <Nota contra abbatem de Wyggemor>

1150 Item[2]

More <Clone>

1151 Parochiani dicunt quod omnia sunt bene ibidem.

Lydeburynorth <Clone>

1152 Parochiani dicunt quod cancellus est defectius in tectura in defectu rectoris et injun[ctum] ... ...[3] citra festum Sancti Michelis proximum futurum sub pena C s. <difertur pena usque ad festum ...>

1153 Item quod rector tenetur invenire unum par vestimentorum pro diebus ferialibus et non [facit] ... ...

1154 Item quod campane non pulsantur debitis horis videlicet de mane in a[urora] ... ... in defectu diaconi tempore quadragesimali.

1155 Item quod Willelmus Walkot graviter diffamatur super adulterio commisso ... ... Juwes. <vir comparet, fatetur; committitur commissario>

1156 Item quod vicarius absentavit se a festo Sancti Michelis ultimo preterito usque ... ... etcetera et quod recepit salarium apud Leyntwardyn toto tempore predicto ... ...

[f. 24]

1157 Item quod Elena filia Willelmi Hankokes de Eyton fornicatur cum Jankyn filio domini Willelmi de Egydon. <mulier purgavit se>

1158 Item quod Thomas <extra> filius Rogeri de Neweton de Donne <serviens Walteri Coykyn> et Issote filia Ricardi Longe contraxerunt adinvicem carnali copula subsecuta nec faciunt huiusmodi matrimonium solempnizari. <mulier constituit Johannem Went procuratorem suum ad prosequendum cum clausula substituendi>

1159 Item quod unus calix perditus est in defectu domini Johannis Montisgomeri nuper diaconi ibidem. <non est citatus>

---

[1] Preceded by *H*, struck through.
[2] Unfinished.
[3] The bottom right-hand corner of this page is perished with the loss of up to three inches of text.

1147 Next, that Philip Rogeres withholds reasonable tithes etc. <*the rector and the same Philip are agreed*>

MAINSTONE <*Clun*>

1148 The parishioners say that the nave of the church is defective in its roofing and that the fence of the churchyard is defective, by the fault of the parishioners; nobody performs the cure of souls there. <*the parishioners have a day to repair before Easter*>

1149 Next, that the chancel is defective in its roofing, by the fault of the rector. <*the chancel is being improved*> [*in margin*]: <*note against the abbot of Wigmore*>

1150 Next, [*not completed*]

MORE <*Clun*>

1151 The parishioners say that all things are well there.

LYDBURY NORTH <*Clun*>

1152 The parishioners say that the chancel is defective in its roofing, by the fault of the rector, and he is ordered ... ... before Michaelmas, under penalty of 100 shillings. <*the penalty is deferred to the feast ...*>

1153 Next, that the rector ought to provide a set of vestments for weekdays and does not do so ...

1154 Next, that the bells are not rung at the proper hours, namely in the early morning at dawn ... ..., by the fault of the deacon, during Lent.

1155 Next, that William Walkot is gravely defamed over adultery committed [with] ... ... Juwes. <*the man appears, admits; it is committed to the commissary*>

1156 Next, that the vicar absented himself from Michaelmas last until ... ... etc. and that he received a salary at Leintwardine for the whole of that time ... ...

[f. 24]

1157 Next, that Helen, daughter of William Hankokes of Eyton, fornicates with Jankin, son of Sir William of Edgton. <*the woman has purged herself*>

1158 Next, that Thomas <*outside*>, son of Roger de Neweton of Lower Down, a servant of Walter Coykyn, and Isot, daughter of Richard Longe, made a contract together, followed by bodily union, and have not had this marriage solemnised. <*the woman has appointed John Went her proctor to prosecute, with a clause of substitution*>

1159 Next, that a chalice has been lost by the fault of Sir John Montgomery, lately deacon there. <*he has not been cited*>

1160 Item quod dominus Rogerus vicarius graviter diffamatur super adulterio commisso cum Johanna uxore Rogeri[1] Staltagh. <vir purgavit se>

1161 Item quod eadem Johanna diffamavit Emlyn servientem vicarii super fornicatione commissa cum priore de Lanthon' de Wallia falso et maliciose. <prosequatur>

1162 Item quod Jankyn Hurste adulteratur cum Cecilia Phylippes non obstante divorcio habito inter eos. <vir comparet, negat, purget se coram curato cum v^{ta} manu>

1163 Item quod portio <cimiterii> concernens abbatem de Wygg' patitur defectum in clausura in defectu Jankyn Hay, Rogeri Wilkokes, Reginaldi Walisshmon et Willelmi Kyvernowe et aliorum tenentium dicti abbatis et Thome Juwes. <injunctum <est> quod reformetur citra Annunciationis dominicam sub pena x s>

Hopsay <Clone>

1164 Parochiani dicunt quod rector tenetur invenire unum clericum ad deserviendum in ecclesia quod non facit.

1165 Item quod Willelmus <Bragger alias> Thomkys fornicatur cum Maiota Toppe quam tenet affine sua in iiij^{to} gradu. <suspensi>

1166 Item quod Ricardus Taelour de Aston perturbat servicium divinum in ecclesia. <citetur ad proximam; committitur domino Johanni capellano ibidem ad corrigendum eundem etcetera propter impotenciam dicti Ricardi etcetera>

1167 Item quod prefatus Willelmus Thomkys non recepit sacramenta sacramentalia in ecclesia parochiali in festo Pasche per tres annos continuos nec alibi prout ipsi sciunt.

Clone. Visitatio facta ibidem die jovis xxviij Junii

[Clone]

1168 Parochiani dicunt quod quidam qui nuncupatur Mab Philkyn <suspensus> contraxit per verba de presenti cum Wenllian[2] Gogh <suspensa> filia y Mab Pwl qui quidem Mab Philkyn divertit ab ea et nubsit alteri.

1169 Item quod y Mab Pwl conjugatus adulteratur cum Lleuky Bach. <vir comparet, fatetur, abjurat, fustigetur ter circa ecclesiam; mulier fatetur, abjurat, fustigetur ter>

Clunbury

1170 Parochiani dicunt quod dominus Edwardus capellanus parochialis non deservit parochianis debite prout decet ymmo suscitat rixas et contentiones inter parochianos et alia detestabilia facit in scandalum etcetera.

---

[1]   Preceded by *Jo*, struck through.
[2]   Altered from *Lleu...* .

1160   Next, that Sir Roger, the vicar, is gravely defamed over adultery committed with Joan, wife of Roger Staltagh. <*the man has purged himself*>

1161   Next, that the same Joan falsely and maliciously defamed Emlyn, servant of the vicar, over committing fornication with the prior of Llanthony in Wales. <*let her prosecute*>

1162   Next, that Jankin Hurste commits adultery with Cecily Phylippes, despite a divorce made between them. <*the man appears, denies, to purge himself before the parish priest with five hands*>

1163   Next, that the portion <*of the churchyard*> for which the abbot of Wigmore is responsible is defective in its fence, by the fault of Jankin Hay, Roger Wilkokes, Reynold Walisshmon, William Kyvernowe, and the other tenants of the said abbot and of Thomas Juwes. <*ordered to be put right before Annunciation Sunday, under penalty of 10 shillings*>

HOPESAY <*Clun*>

1164   The parishioners say that the rector ought to provide a clerk to serve in church, which he does not do.

1165   Next, that William <*Bragger otherwise*> Thomkys fornicates with Maiota Toppe, whom he keeps, a relative of his in the fourth degree of affinity. <*both suspended*>

1166   Next, that Richard Taelour of Aston disturbs divine service in church. <*to be cited to the next; committed to Sir John, the chaplain there, to correct it etc. on account of the incapacity of the said Richard etc.*>

1167   Next, that the aforesaid William Thomkys has not received the holy sacraments in the parish church on Easter Sunday for three years in succession, nor anywhere else, as far as they know.

Clun. Visitation made there on Thursday, 28 June

[CLUN]

1168   The parishioners say that a certain man who is called Mab Philcyn <*suspended*> made a contract in the present tense with Gwenllian Goch <*suspended*>, daughter of y Mab Pwl, and this Mab Philcyn turned aside from her and married another.

1169   Next, that y Mab Pwl, a married man, commits adultery with Lleucu Bach. <*the man appears, admits, abjures, to be beaten three times around the church; the woman admits, abjures, to be beaten three times*>

CLUNBURY

1170   The parishioners say that Sir Edward, the parish chaplain, does not serve the parishioners properly as is fitting, but rather provokes quarrels and disputes between the parishioners and does other vile things, to the scandal etc.

1171 Item quod idem dominus Edwardus fuit requisitus ad ministrandum Ricardo Crowe in extremis laboranti extremam unctionem[1] quod recusavit expresse et sic prefatus Ricardus sine huiusmodi sacramento decessit in defectu dicti capellani. [*in margin*] <Dominus Edwardus capellanus ibidem excommunicatus est propter manifestam contumaciam apud Lodel'; absolutus est in forma juris>

1172 Item quod quidam parochiani venerunt cum uno infante Willelmi Corvyger pro baptismo[2] in articulo mortis nec potuerunt reperire dictum capellanum et ideo oportuit eos ire ad ecclesiam de Clongonford pro baptismo etcetera.

1173 Item quod idem dominus Edwardus absentavit se ab ecclesia in festo corporis Christi ita quod parochiani non habuerunt servicium divinum in defectu ipsius domini Edwardi.

1174 I[tem quod][3] Willelmus filius Johannis Phyppes nuper defunctus fuit sepultus sine missa et obsequio mortuorum [in defectu ei]usdem capellani.[4]

1175 Item quod filius Willelmi Webbe similiter sine missa et obsequio ut supra.

1176 [Item quod idem domi]nus Edwardus recusavit recipere Maiotam uxorem Johannis Crowe ad purgationem suam in [ecclesia faciendam po]st partum nisi offerret ad libitum suum.

1177 [Item quod idem] dominus Edwardus incontinens est cum Alicia <suspensa> filia Thome Eynones qui etiam baptizavit [filium suum prop]rium ex ea procreatum et postea cognovit eandem carnaliter et procreavit ex eadem alium infantem...<...post correctionem purget>

1178 [Item quod] .... Byllyng impetravit litteras domini archiepiscopi Cantuar' et domini episcopi Heref' continentes indulgencias ... ... benefactoribus pontis <de> Porslowesbrug quarum vigore collegit in partibus valorem xx ... ... exponit ad usum suum proprium <nichil expendendo ad reparationem dicte pontis; citetur ad proximam; ad purgandum; purgavit se, dimissus est>

1179 [Item quod ... ... est] communis usurarius. <excommunicatus; abjurat, dimissus est>

1180 [Item quod ... ...]s est communis usurarius. <ad purgandum in proximam; abjurat, dimissus est>

1181 [Item quod ...] prior de Wenlok recusat se habere curam animarum ibidem dicens curam pertinere ad vicarium ... <... [vicarius] dicit se non habere curam animarum ibidem set quod prior habet>

1182 [Item quod rector tenetur invenire] unum diaconum ad deserviendum in ecclesia quod non facit.

---

[1] Preceded by *ux*, struck through.
[2] Followed by *etc.*, struck through.
[3] The bottom left-hand corner of this page is perished with the loss of up to two inches of text.
[4] The next entry continues on the same line.

1171 Next, that the same Sir Edward was asked to minister extreme unction to Richard Crowe as he lay dying, which he expressly refused to do, and so the aforesaid Richard died without this sacrament, by the fault of the said chaplain. [*in margin*]: <*Sir Edward, chaplain there, is excommunicated because of manifest contumacy at Ludlow; he is absolved in form of law*>

1172 Next, that certain parishioners came with an infant of William Corvyger for baptism at the point of death, but could not find the said chaplain, and so they had to go to the church of Clungunford for the baptism etc.

1173 Next, that the same Sir Edward absented himself from church on the feast of Corpus Christi so that the parishioners did not have divine service, by the fault of the same Sir Edward.

1174 Next, that William, son of John Phyppes, lately deceased, was buried without a mass and the service for the dead, by the fault of the same chaplain.

1175 Next, that the son of William Webbe [was treated] similarly, [buried] without mass and a service, as above.

1176 Next, that the same Sir Edward refused to allow Maiota, wife of John Crowe, to perform her purgation in church after giving birth unless she offered what he wanted.

1177 Next, that the same Sir Edward is incontinent with Alice <*suspended*>, daughter of Thomas Eynones, and he has even baptised his own child fathered with her, and later he knew her carnally and fathered with her another infant ... < ... *since correction, to purge*>

1178 Next, that [Peter][1] Byllyng obtained letters of the lord archbishop of Canterbury and the lord bishop of Hereford containing indulgences ... ... to the benefactors of Purslow Bridge, on the strength of which letters he collected in the neighbourhood to the value of 20 ... ... which he laid out for his own benefit, spending nothing on the repair of the said bridge. <*to be cited to the next; to purge; he has purged himself, he is dismissed*>

1179 Next, that ... ... is a habitual usurer. <*excommunicated; abjures, he is dismissed*>

1180 Next, that ... ... is a habitual usurer. <*to purge at the next; abjures, he is dismissed*>

1181 Next, that ... the prior of Wenlock denies that he has the cure of souls there, saying that the cure belongs to the vicar ... <*... the vicar says that he does not have the cure of souls there but that the prior has*>

1182 Next, that the rector ought to provide a deacon to serve in church, which he does not do.

---

[1]   By reference to **1185**; the name could apply to **1179** or **1180**.

[f. 24v]

1183 Item quod rector tenetur invenire unum par vestimentorum pro diebus ferialibus.

1184 Item quod rector tenetur invenire unum ordinale et non facit.

[*in margin*] <require tale signum + in proximo folio>[1]

1185 Item quod Juliana[2] uxor dicti Petri[3] detinet j towall legatum ad maius altare per matrem suam nuper defunctam.

1186 Item quod injunctum est eidem Petro in correctionibus ultime visitationis offerre ij libras cere ad maius altare quod non <dum> fecit.

1187 Item quod uxor dicti Petri est communis operatrix diebus dominicis et festivis.

1188 Item quod Gwilim ap David ap Gruffuth conjugatus adulteratur cum quadam Agnete quam tenet apud Kyngeslon.

1189 Item quod Ieuan Heine est communis usurarius.

1190 Item[4]

1191 Item quod Ricardus Davys de Clunton est communis operarius diebus dominicis et festivis. <dimissus est>

1192 Item quod Johannes de Lowe non venit ad ecclesiam diebus dominicis et festivis. <dimissus est>

   Villa de Cloune

1193 Parochiani dicunt quod Jankyn Webbe fornicatur cum Wenllian Wehed-des.[5] <sunt matrimonialiter copulati>

1194 Item quod Johannes Elvel junior fornicatur cum Eva Bolleston.[6] <vir comparet, fatetur, abjurat, fustigetur ter circa ecclesiam; mulier suspensa et citata ad proximam>

1195 <Item idem Johannes fornicatur cum Agnete Murydon>.

1196 Item quod Gruffuth ap Ieuan Lloyt conjugatus adulteratur cum Gweirvyl filia Ieuan Hyr. <vir extra, mulier suspensa>

1197 Item quod Howel Ragor <fornicatur> cum Mariona quam tenet. <suspensi>

---

[1] Written opposite a gap of two inches, before and after which are two entries, all of which presumably belong with Clunbury. Entries **1185–90**, bracketed together and identified with the same mark, are to be found at the top of folio 25v. The division may be the result of the clerk having mistakenly turned over two folios, then returned to the original place for two extra entries. The reference to *dicti Petri* in the separated entries may suggest that they were written before **1183–4** and possibly after **1181–2**, the insertions at the foot of folio 24.

[2] Preceded by *Marg*, struck through.

[3] Peter was presumably the name of one of the men whose names are missing in **1178–80**.

[4] Unfinished.

[5] Altered from *veheddes*.

[6] Followed by <*suspensi*>, struck through.

[f. 24v]

1183   Next, that the rector ought to provide a set of vestments for weekdays.

1184   Next, that the rector ought to provide an ordinal and does not do so.
[*in margin*]: <*look for this sign + in the next folio*>

1185   Next, that Julian, wife of the said Peter, withholds one towel bequeathed for the high altar by her mother, lately deceased.

1186   Next, that the same Peter was ordered in the corrections of the last visitation to donate a two-pound candle to the high altar, which he has not <*yet*> done.

1187   Next, that the wife of the said Peter is a habitual worker on Sundays and feast days.

1188   Next, that Gwilym ap David ap Gruffudd, a married man, commits adultery with a certain Agnes, whom he keeps at Kingsland.

1189   Next, that Ieuan Heine is a habitual usurer.

1190   Next, [*not completed*]

1191   Next, that Richard Davys of Clunton is a habitual worker on Sundays and feast days. <*he is dismissed*>

1192   Next, that John de Lowe does not come to church on Sundays and feast days. <*he is dismissed*>

VILL OF CLUN

1193   The parishioners say that Jankin Webbe fornicates with Gwenllian Weheddes. <*they are married*>

1194   Next, that John Elvel the younger fornicates with Eve Bolleston. <*the man appears, admits, abjures, to be beaten three times around the church; the woman suspended and cited to the next*>

1195   <*Next, the same John fornicates with Agnes Murydon*>

1196   Next, that Gruffudd ap Ieuan Lloyt, a married man, commits adultery with Gweirful, daughter of Ieuan Hyr. <*the man outside; the woman suspended*>

1197   Next, that Hywel Ragor fornicates with Marion, whom he keeps. <*both suspended*>

1198   Item quod y Bongam Kynyd fornicatur cum Johanna quam tenet. <extra>

1199   Item quod David ap <Ieuan ap> Mereduth fornicatur cum Emota <suspensa> quam tenet. <vir comparet, fatetur, abjurat, fustigetur ter circa ecclesiam;[1] absolutus est, difer penitenciam sub spe nubendi>

1200   Item quod Johannes Parkes fornicatur cum Amisia quam tenet.[2] <vir comparet, negat; purgavit se>

1201   Item quod Eva filia Johannis Blake fornicatur cum filio vicarii de Boryton. <mulier comparet, fatetur, abjurat, fustigetur ter circa ecclesiam; vir in Hibernia; postea mulier purgavit se post correctionem>

1202   Item quod Howel filius Gwilim Cwtte fornicatur cum Gwenlli quam tenet. <suspensi>

Waterden

1203   Parochiani dicunt quod ab antiquo fuit[3] vicaria in ecclesia de Waterden solita per clericum secularem gubernari, qui per diocesenarium institui deberet in eadem, quibus non obstantibus prior de Wenlok tenet dictam ecclesiam in proprios usus cui facit deserviri per capellanum parochialem subtrahendo vicarium et eius portionem sine auctoritate sufficienti ut credunt, unde petunt quod idem rector exhibeat titulum suum etcetera.

1204   Item quod idem rector ad minus solebat invenire duos capellanos ad deserviendum ibidem et non invenit nisi unum tantum.

1205   Item quod cancellus est defectius in tectura, selura et vitro in defectu rectoris, etiam descos et scabellum pro libris.

1206   Item quod idem rector tenetur invenire unum antiphonarium et unum psaltarium quod non facit.

1207   Item quod unum vestimentum pro diebus ferialibus quod non facit.

1208   Item quod Gwenllian <suspensa> filia Mereduth Gogh fornicatur cum fratre Johanne ap Ieuan ap Llewelyn monacho monasterii de Cumhir.

1209   Item quod Angharat filia David ap Gwrgene fornicatur cum Mereduth Taelour. <suspensi>

1210   Item quod Howel ap Eudos adulteratur cum Dydgu Gall conjugata. <suspensi>

1211   Item quod Llewelyn Cledde et dicta Dydgu iverunt extra diocesim pro matrimonio solempnizando etcetera. <suspensi>

1212   Item quod Ieuan ap Iorwerth ap Eignon magister[4] forestarius adulteratur cum Gwenllian filia David. <vir extra; mulier suspensa>

---

[1]   Followed by *excommunicatus*, struck through.
[2]   Followed by <*suspensi*>, struck through.
[3]   Preceded by *soli*, struck through.
[4]   Preceded by *f*, struck through.

1198 Next, that y Bongam Kynyd[1] fornicates with Joan, whom he keeps. <*outside*>

1199 Next, that David ap <*Ieuan ap*> Maredudd fornicates with Emota <*suspended*>, whom he keeps. <*the man appears, admits, abjures, to be beaten three times around the church; he is absolved, defer the penance in the hope of them marrying*>

1200 Next, that John Parkes fornicates with Amice, whom he keeps. <*the man appears, denies; he has purged himself*>

1201 Next, that Eve, daughter of John Blake, fornicates with the son of the vicar of Burrington. <*the woman appears, admits, abjures, to be beaten three times around the church; the man in Ireland; later the woman has purged herself since correction*>

1202 Next, that Hywel, son of Gwilym Cwtte,[2] fornicates with Gwenlli, whom he keeps. <*both suspended*>

LLANFAIR WATERDINE

1203 The parishioners say that of old there was a vicarage in the church of Waterdine accustomed to be governed by a secular clerk, who ought to be instituted in it by the diocesan bishop; despite which, the prior of Wenlock holds the said church to his own benefit, and he has it served by a parish chaplain, taking away the vicar and his portion without sufficient authority, as they believe, whence they ask that the same rector exhibit his title etc.

1204 Next, that the same rector used at least to provide two chaplains to serve there, and provides but one only.

1205 Next, that the chancel is defective in its roof, ceiling, and glass, by the fault of the rector, also [in its] desks and a bench for books.

1206 Next, that the same rector ought to provide an antiphonal and a psalter, which he does not do.

1207 Next, that [he ought to provide] a vestment for weekdays, which he does not do.

1208 Next, that Gwenllian <*suspended*>, daughter of Maredudd Gogh, fornicates with Brother John ap Ieuan ap Llewelyn, a monk of the monastery of Cwmhir.

1209 Next, that Angharad, daughter of David ap Gwrgan, fornicates with Maredudd Taelour. <*both suspended*>

1210 Next, that Hywel ap Eudos commits adultery with Dyddgu Gall, a married woman. <*both suspended*>

1211 Next, that Llewelyn Cledde and the said Dyddgu went outside the diocese to solemnise a marriage etc. <*both suspended*>

1212 Next, that Ieuan ap Iorwerth ap Einion, master forester, commits adultery with Gwenllian, daughter of David. <*the man outside; the woman suspended*>

---

[1] Recte *y bongam cynydd*, the bandy-legged huntsman.

[2] Recte *Gwilym Cwta*, short Gwilym.

Villata de Bugunton

1213 Dicunt quod omnia bene ibidem.

Villata de Spode

1214 Dicunt quod Lleuku filia Gwilim Bach conjugata adulteratur cum <Mereduth> mab y Keissiat Gwyll...¹

1215 Item quod Philippus Whith ap Llewelyn ap Philip et Gwladus filia Philippi uxor sua non [cohabitant simul] ut vir et uxor etcetera. <suspensi>

1216 Item quod Gwilim ap Cad' Lloyt conjugatus adulteratur cum Angharat filia Llewelyn² ap ...

1217 Item quod³

[f. 25]

Monsgomeri <Ponsbury>. Visitatio facta ibidem die veneris xxix die Junii

[Monsgomeri]

1218 Parochiani dicunt quod Ricardus Alesaundr' <nuper decessit cuius bona>⁴ et Johannes Mongomery et Willelmus filius Johannis Hikkokes ministrarunt bona dicti defuncti sine auctoritate ordinarii in magnum prejudicium ecclesie et debitorum quibus ipse tenebatur. <dimissus est>

1219 Item quod Johannes Momgomery detinet injuste xxv s legatos per Alson Skynner uxorem Johannis Gruffuth ad opus unius calicis ad celebrandum in ecclesia. <recognovit debitum, condempnatus ad solvendum huiusmodi xxv s citra Pascha>

1220 Item quod idem Johannes Gruffuth detinet v s < x d> ad opus eiusdem calicis per eandem Alson legatos. <recognovit ut supra, habet eundem diem>

1221 Item quod David Deheubarth male tractat uxorem suam et adulteratur cum Margareta Edyth. <vir comparet, negat post correctionem, purgavit se; mulier⁵ non comparet, commissum est rectori ad recipiendum purgationem; purgavit coram eodem>

1222 Item quod Johannes Saer animo malignandi irruit in quendam dominum Johannem Gylbert capellanum volens ipsum verberare. <correctus est>

1223 [*in margin*] <fiat significavit contra virum>

Item quod Willelmus Webbe conjugatus adulteratur [cum]⁶ Maiota filia Willelmi de Riston repulsa uxore. <mulier suspensa>

---

¹ The bottom right-hand corner of this page is perished with the loss of up to two inches of text.
² Preceded by *David ap*, struck through.
³ Unfinished.
⁴ Replacing *decessit intestatus* struck through; *cuius bona* redundant.
⁵ Followed by *suspensa*, struck through.
⁶ Omitted in error.

VILL OF BICTON

1213 They say that all is well there.

VILL OF SPOAD

1214 They say that Lleucu, daughter of Gwilym Bach, a married woman, commits adultery with *<Maredudd>* son of y Keissiat[1] Gwyll...

1215 Next, that Philip Whith[2] ap Llewelyn ap Philip and his wife Gwladus, daughter of Philip, do not live together as man and wife etc. *<both suspended>*

1216 Next, that Gwilym ap Cadwgan[3] Lloyt, a married man, commits adultery with Angharad, daughter of Llewelyn ap ...

1217 Next, that [*not completed*]

[f. 25]

Montgomery *<Pontesbury>*. Visitation made there on Friday, 29 June

MONTGOMERY

1218 The parishioners say that Richard Alesaundre *<lately died>*, and John Mongomery and William, son of John Hikkokes, administered the estate of the said deceased without the authority of the ordinary, to the great prejudice of the church and the creditors to whom he was obliged. *<it is dismissed>*

1219 Next, that John Momgomery wrongfully withholds 25 shillings bequeathed by Alison Skynner, wife of John Gruffudd, for making a chalice for celebrating in church. *<he has acknowledged the debt, sentenced to pay this 25 shillings before Easter>*

1220 Next, that the same John Gruffudd withholds 5 shillings *<and 10 pence>* for making the same chalice bequeathed by the same Alison. *<he has acknowledged as above, he has the same day>*

1221 Next, that David Deheubarth mistreats his wife and commits adultery with Margaret Edyth. *<the man appears, denies since correction, has purged himself; the woman does not appear, it is committed to the rector to receive the purgation; she has purged before him>*

1222 Next, that John Saer, with evil intent, rushed at a certain Sir John Gylbert, chaplain, trying to beat him. *<he is corrected>*

1223 [*in margin*]: *<let there be a signification against the man>*

Next, that William Webbe, a married man, commits adultery with Maiota, daughter of William of Rhiston, having driven out his lawful wife. *<the woman suspended>*

---

1   Recte *y Ceisiad*, the serjeant of the peace or bailiff.
2   Possibly for *chwith*, left-handed.
3   *Cadwaladr* would be an alternative extension of the MS *Cad'*.

1224 Item quod <Willelmus>[1] Bredleder conjugatus adulteratur cum Jonet Warde repulsa uxore violenter. <suspensi>

1225 Item quod Johannes Bowedeler <suspensus> male tractat uxorem suam et adulteratur cum quadam <Matilda quam tenet>[2] in parochia de Chirbury. <mulier suspensa>

1226 Item quod Madoc Carne fornicatur cum Gweirvyl quam tenet. <suspensi>

1227 Item quod Howel Goygyn fornicatur cum Eva filia Gruffuth. <suspensi>

1228 Item quod Llewelyn Bach fornicatur cum Dydgu quam tenet. <suspensi>

1229 Item quod Willelmus Collefaste fornicatur cum Gwervill[3] filia Madoc Duy. <vir comparet, negat post correctionem; purgavit se>

1230 Item quod Madoc ap Cad' exequitur testamentum Amisie[4] infrascripte; <prosequatur cuius interest>

1231 Item quod Johannes Howel executor Amisie Peny non exequitur ultimam voluntatem dicte Amisie. <prosequatur cuius interest>

1232 Item quod rector dat ecclesiam suam ad firmam. <negat>

1233 <Item Willelmus Collefaste adulteratur cum Roseta uxore David Deheubarth; ambo comparent, fatentur, fustigentur vj ante processionem et vj per forum cum j candela>

Chirbury <Ponsbury>. Visitatio facta ibidem die sabbati ultima mensis Junii anno Domini ut supra

Fordon

1234 Parochiani dicunt quod omnia bene ibidem.

Chirstoke

1235 Parochiani dicunt quod Ieuan ap David ap Iorwerth de Ucheldref recepit pro xv s mutuatis Madoc ap David annuatim v s in usura et hoc vj annis continue ita quod ipse recepit in claro de usura xxx s. <obiit>

1236 Item quod Johannes ap Thomas <suspensus> recepit de Adam ap Seysyvaunte pro v s mutuatis eidem x s in usura in processu temporis.

1237 Item quod idem Johannes recepit de dicto Madoc ap David pro viij s mutuatis eidem xx s et ultra.

1238 Item idem Johannes recepit de eodem pro v s, viij s viij d et duos vitulos.

---

[1] Original *Willelmus* replaced by <*Johannes*>, itself struck through and <*Willelmus*> reinstated.

[2] Replacing *Margeria Brut*; *G* interlined and struck through.

[3] Altered from *Gwenllian*.

[4] Preceded by *dicte*, struck through.

1224   Next, that William Bredleder, a married man, commits adultery with Jonet Warde, having violently driven out his lawful wife. <*both suspended*>

1225   Next, that John Bowedeler <*suspended*> mistreats his wife and commits adultery with a certain <*Maud, whom he keeps*> in the parish of Chirbury. <*the woman suspended*>

1226   Next, that Madog Carne fornicates with Gweirful, whom he keeps. <*both suspended*>

1227   Next, that Hywel Goygyn fornicates with Eve, daughter of Gruffudd. <*both suspended*>

1228   Next, that Llewelyn Bach fornicates with Dyddgu, whom he keeps. <*both suspended*>

1229   Next, that William Collefaste fornicates with Gweirful, daughter of Madog Duy. <*the man appears, denies since correction; he has purged himself*>

1230   Next, that Madog ap Cadwgan[1] executes the will of the below-mentioned Amice. <*let whoever is concerned prosecute*>

1231   Next, that John Howel, executor of Amice Peny, does not execute the last will of the said Amice. <*let whoever is concerned prosecute*>

1232   Next, that the rector farms out his church. <*he denies*>

1233   <*Next, William Collefaste commits adultery with Rosetta, wife of David Deheubarth; both appear, both admit, both to be beaten six times before the procession and six times through the marketplace with one candle*>

Chirbury <*Pontesbury*>. Visitation made there on Saturday, the last day of June, in the year of Our Lord as above

FORDEN

1234   The parishioners say that all is well there.

CHURCHSTOKE

1235   The parishioners say that Ieuan ap David ap Iorwerth of the high town received for 15 shillings lent to Madog ap David 5 shillings a year in usury, and this for six consecutive years, so that he received clear from usury 30 shillings. <*he has died*>

1236   Next, that John ap Thomas <*suspended*> received from Adam ap Seysy-vaunte, for 5 shillings lent to him, 10 shillings in usury in the course of time.

1237   Next, that the same John received from the said Madog ap David for 8 shillings lent to him 20 shillings and more.

1238   Next, the same John received from him 8 shillings and 8 pence and two calves, for 5 shillings.

---

[1]   *Cadwaladr* would be an alternative extension of the MS *Cad'*.

1239 [Item quod]¹ David ap Ieuan Bole recepit de dicto Madoc ap David pro vj
s viij d sibi mutuatis [ad ultimum] xl s.² <comparet, negat, purget se coram curato
cum vᵗᵃ manu>

1240 [Item quod] Eignon ap Eignon ap Adda recepit de Llewelyn ap Cad' pro
v s³ mutuatis vj s viij[d.] [<purgavit se>]

1241 [Item quod Gwi]lim ap Grono ap Henry <suspensus> recepit de⁴ eodem
Llewelyn pro v s mutuatis sibi xx s ... ... Howel ap David ap Gwyn.

1242 [Item quod David] ap Ieuan Bole recepit pro vj s viij d [de eodem decem s
vj d] in usura. <purget ut supra>

1243 [Item quod David] Hir recepit de eodem Llewelyn pro [xv s, viij s x d in
usura] ...

1244 [Item quod Philippus] Kady conjugatus adulteratur [cum Dydgu filia
Gwilim] ...

[f. 25v]

1245 Item⁵ quod Lleuku filia Meuric et Ieuan ap Philip ap Meuric sunt illegitime conjugati eo quod attingunt in iiijᵗᵒ gradu affinitatis. <divorciati sint habitis
probationibus>

1246 Item quod Ieuan ap David ap Madoc et David ap Ieuan Vychan recusant
contribuere reparationi ecclesie.⁶ <dimissi sunt>

1247 Item quod Howel ap Gruffuth ap Adda fornicatur cum Gweirvyl <sus-
pensa> filia Llewelyn.⁷ <vir comparet; fatetur, abjurat, fustigetur ter circa ecclesiam et ter per forum>

1248 Item quod Ieuan ap Ieuan Ddewis <suspensus> conjugatus adulteratur
cum Gwenllian filia Llewelyn Lloyt.⁸ <mulier comparet; fatetur, abjurat, fustigetur vj per forum et vj ante processionem>

1249 Item quod dominus Johannes Lloyt capellanus incontinens est cum Angharat filia Howel ap Eignon conjugata. <vir est in carcere, mulier suspensa>

1250 Item quod David ap Ieuan ap Philip fornicatur cum Gwenllian y Dail. <vir
Hibernie, mulier suspensa>

1251 Item quod David ap Ieuan ap Iorwerth et Gwenllian filia Gwilim uxor sua
non cohabitant simul. <suspensi>

¹ The bottom left- and right-hand corners of this page are torn away with the loss of
up to two inches on the left and six inches on the right. Much of the material within [ ] in
entries **1239–44** has been recovered from the text read or conjectured by Bannister.
² Followed by <*suspensus*>, struck through.
³ Followed by *vi*, struck through.
⁴ Preceded by *dicti*, struck through.
⁵ Follows the six Clunbury entries (**1185–90**) at the top of this page.
⁶ Followed by *Je*, struck through.
⁷ Followed by <*suspensi*>, struck through.
⁸ Followed by <*suspensi*>, struck through.

1239 Next, that David ap Ieuan Bole received from the said Madog ap David, for 6 shillings and 8 pence lent to him, in the end 40 shillings. <*appears, denies, to purge himself before the parish priest with five hands*>

1240 Next, that Einion ap Einion ap Adda received from Llewelyn ap Cadwgan,[1] for 5 shillings lent, 6 shillings and 8 pence. <*he has purged himself*>

1241 Next, that Gwilym ap Goronwy ap Henry <*suspended*> received from the same Llewelyn, for 5 shillings lent to him, 20 shillings. ... ... Hywel ap David ap Gwyn.

1242 Next, that David ap Ieuan Bole received for 6 shillings and 8 pence, 10 shillings and 6 pence in usury. <*to purge as above*>

1243 Next, that David Hir received from the same Llewelyn for 15 shillings, 8 shillings and 10 pence in usury.

1244 Next, that Philip Kady, a married man, commits adultery with Dyddgu, daughter of Gwilym ...

[f. 25v]

1245 Next, that Lleucu, daughter of Meurig, and Ieuan ap Philip ap Meurig are unlawfully married because they are related in the fourth degree of affinity. <*to be divorced, given proofs*>

1246 Next, that Ieuan ap David ap Madog and David ap Ieuan Vychan refuse to contribute to the repair of the church. <*they are dismissed*>

1247 Next, that Hywel ap Gruffudd ap Adda fornicates with Gweirful <*suspended*>, daughter of Llewelyn. <*the man appears, admits, abjures, to be beaten three times around the church and three times through the marketplace*>

1248 Next, that Ieuan ap Ieuan Ddewis <*suspended*>, a married man, commits adultery with Gwenllian, daughter of Llewelyn Lloyt. <*the woman appears, admits, abjures, to be beaten six times through the marketplace and six times before the procession*>

1249 Next, that Sir John Lloyt, chaplain, is incontinent with Angharad, daughter of Hywel ap Einion, a married woman. <*the man is in prison, the woman suspended*>

1250 Next, that David ap Ieuan ap Philip fornicates with Gwenllian y Dail.[2] <*the man in Ireland, the woman suspended*>

1251 Next, that David ap Ieuan ap Iorwerth and his wife Gwenllian, daughter of Gwilym, do not live together. <*both suspended*>

---

[1] *Cadwaladr* would be an alternative extension of the MS *Cad'*.

[2] Gwenllian of the leaves.

1252 Item quod David ap Gruffuth Lloyt fornicatur cum Eva filia Griffri. <suspensi>

1253 Item quod David ap Ieuan ap David fornicatur cum Gwirvil filia Ieuan.[1] <vir comparet, fatetur, abjurat, fustigetur ter circa ecclesiam; mulier suspensa>

1254 Item quod Janyn ap y Toppa et Matilda filia Llewelyn uxor sua sunt illegitime copulati eo quod Cadwaladr ap John consanguineus dicti Janyn in iij° gradu precognovit dictam Matildam.[2] <dimissi sunt>

1255 Item quod Llewelyn ap Howel fornicatur cum Maruret filia Ricardi. <mulier comparet, fatetur, abjurat, difertur penitencia sub spe nubendi; moneatur vir sub pena excommunicationis quod non commisceat se cum eadem etiam sub pena matrimonii>

1256 Item quod David ap Ieuan ap Gwyl et Gwenllian filia Gwilim contraxerunt adinvicem nec faciunt huiusmodi matrimonium solempnizari inter se. <suspensi>

1257 [*in margin*] <fiat significavit contra virum>
Item quod Llewelyn Gamme fornicatur cum Eva filia Madoc et quod idem Llewelyn non venit ad ecclesiam diebus dominicis et festivis. <suspensi>

1258 Item quod Ieuan Velinyd fornicatur cum Alicia quam tenet. <suspensi>

1259 Item quod Dydgu filia David fornicatur cum David de Arwystly. <suspensus; mulier comparet, fatetur, abjurat; difertur sub spe nubendi>

1260 Item quod Howel ap David ap Howel fornicatur cum Maruret filia Gruffuth ap Iorwerth. <suspensi>

1261 Item quod clausura cimiterii est defectiva in defectu parochianorum. <habent diem ad reparandum citra festum Sancti Michelis sub pena [*blank*]; habent diem usque ad Pascha sub pena xx s>

1262 Item quod Jowkys Gogh fornicatur cum <Wenllian Hir filia>[3] David ap Llywarch. <mulier comparet, fatetur, abjurat, fustigetur ter circa ecclesiam; vir suspensus>

1263 Item quod Maruret filia Llewelyn fornicatur cum Madoc Wehyd. <ambo comparent, fatentur, fustigentur ter circa ecclesiam de Chirbury vir, mulier Arrystok'>

1264 Item quod Ieuan ap Philip ap Meuric conjugatus adulteratur cum Gwenllian filia Ieuan Ddewys. <vir comparet, fatetur, abjurat, fustigetur vj ante processionem apud Chirbury et vj per forum de Montisgomeri>

1265 Item quod Gruffuth ap Eignon ap Tudur conjugatus adulteratur cum Gwenllian filia Eignon Dynlas[4] conjugata. <suspensi>

---

[1] Followed by <*suspensi*>, struck through.
[2] Followed by <*suspensi*>, struck through.
[3] Replacing *filia*, struck through.
[4] Preceded by *Ddilesk conjugata*, struck through.

1252   Next, that David ap Gruffudd Lloyt fornicates with Eve, daughter of Griffri. <*both suspended*>

1253   Next, that David ap Ieuan ap David fornicates with Gweirful, daughter of Ieuan. <*the man appears, admits, abjures, to be beaten three times around the church; the woman suspended*>

1254   Next, that Janyn ap y Toppa and his wife Maud, daughter of Llewelyn, are unlawfully joined because Cadwaladr ap John, a blood-relation of the said Janyn in the third degree, previously knew the said Maud [sexually]. <*they are dismissed*>

1255   Next, that Llewelyn ap Hywel fornicates with Maruret, daughter of Richard. <*the woman appears, admits, abjures; the penance is deferred in the hope of them marrying; the man to be warned that, under penalty of excommunication, he is not to consort with her; also under penalty of marriage*>

1256   Next, that David ap Ieuan ap Gwyl and Gwenllian, daughter of Gwilym, have made a contract together and have not had this marriage solemnised between them. <*both suspended*>

1257   [*in margin*]: <*let there be a signification against the man*>
Next, that Llewelyn Gamme fornicates with Eve, daughter of Madog, and that the same Llewelyn does not come to church on Sundays and feast days. <*both suspended*>

1258   Next, that Ieuan Velinyd[1] fornicates with Alice, whom he keeps. <*both suspended*>

1259   Next, that Dyddgu, daughter of David, fornicates with David of Arwystli. <*suspended; the woman appears, admits, abjures; it is deferred in the hope of them marrying*>

1260   Next, that Hywel ap David ap Hywel fornicates with Maruret, daughter of Gruffudd ap Iorwerth. <*both suspended*>

1261   Next, that the fence of the churchyard is defective, by the fault of the parishioners. <*they have a day until Michaelmas to repair under penalty of [blank]; they have until Easter, under penalty of 20 shillings*>

1262   Next, that Jowkys Gogh fornicates with Gwenllian Hir, daughter of David ap Llywarch. <*the woman appears, admits, abjures, to be beaten three times around the church; the man suspended*>

1263   Next, that Maruret, daughter of Llewelyn, fornicates with Madog Wehyd.[2] <*both appear, both admit, both to be beaten three times around the church of Chirbury; the man, the woman at Harry Stoke*>

1264   Next, that Ieuan ap Philip ap Meurig, a married man, commits adultery with Gwenllian, daughter of Ieuan Ddewys. <*the man appears, admits, abjures, to be beaten six times before the procession at Chirbury and six times through the marketplace of Montgomery*>

1265   Next, that Gruffudd ap Einion ap Tudur, a married man, commits adultery with Gwenllian, daughter of Einion Dynlas, a married woman. <*both suspended*>

---

[1]   Recte *Felinydd*, the miller.
[2]   Recte *Wehydd*, the weaver.

Chirbury

1266 Parochiani dicunt quod dominus Ricardus Gledwyn et Nest nuper concubina sua cohabit[ant simul in]¹ una et eadem domo et mensa ut vir et uxor.

1267 Item quod Jankyn Wynsbury senior fornicatur cum Issabella <suspensa> filia Willelmi W... <... expediendum et corrigendum virum>

1268 Item quod Ricardus Streton fornicatur cum Issabella Croke. <suspensi>

1269 Item quod Philippus de prioratu fornicatur cum Margareta Spermon relicta Johannis ... <vir comparuit, fatetur, promisit sub pena vj s viij d operi ecclesie Heref' dimittere p[eccatum] ...> [*in margin*] <[vj]s. viij d>

1270 Item quod Madoc ap y Cogh Hir <suspensus> fornicatur cum Wenllian Gornyoc <s[uspensa] ... >

1271 [Item quod Thomas Dudeston] fornicatur cum Amisia filia Willelmi Schepper[t] ...

1272 [Item quod Nicholaus Coke fornicatur cum] Alicia Spermon.² <vir apud Wort[hyn] ...

1273 [Item quod Tangwystel filia Ieuan et David a]p Ieuan de Akelle sunt [infra iiijᵗᵘᵐ gradum consanguinitatis] ...³

1274 [Item quod Gruffuth Saer de Brompton conjugatus adulteratur cum] <Matilda>⁴ filia Llewelyn ...

[f. 26]

Husynton

1275 <Dominus Gruffinus capellanus ibidem>

1276 Parochiani dicunt quod Sibilla de Broke fornicatur cum Willelmo Broun. <suspensi; mulier fustigetur in forma>

1277 Item quod Philippus filius Willelmi Phippe fornicatur cum eadem Sibilla. <suspensi; mulier purget a tempore correctionis>

1278 Item quod David Taelour fornicatur cum Gwenllian filia Ieuan ap Madoc. <mulier excommunicata, vir suspensus>

1279 Item quod Ieuan ap Howel fornicatur cum Gwenllian filia Ieuan ap Hilder. <mulier comparet, fatetur, abjurat, fustigetur ter circa ecclesiam, vir citetur>

---

¹ The bottom left- and right-hand corners of this page are perished with the loss of up to four inches on the left and three inches on the right. Much of the material within [ ] in entries **1266**–**74** has been recovered from the text read or conjectured by Bannister.
² For what is apparently the same charge, which Nicholas called *Flesshewer*, see **1290**.
³ The surviving part of the page shows, at this point, a gap in writing of perhaps two lines, which might indicate another presenting district, but since only one charge follows this is not very likely.
⁴ Replacing *Marret*, struck through.

CHIRBURY

1266   The parishioners say that Sir Richard Gledwyn and Nest, lately his concubine, live together in one and the same house and at the same table as man and
wife.

1267   Next, that Jankin Wynsbury the elder fornicates with Isabel *<suspended>*,
daughter of William ... *<... to deal with and correct the man>*

1268   Next, that Richard Streton fornicates with Isabel Croke. *<both suspended>*

1269   Next, that Philip of the priory fornicates with Margaret Spermon, widow
of John ... *<the man appeared, admits, has promised, under penalty of 6 shillings and 8 pence to
the upkeep of the church of Hereford, to leave off the sin ...>* [*in margin*]: *<6 shillings 8 pence>*

1270   Next, that Madog ap y Cogh Hir¹ *<suspended>* fornicates with Gwenllian
Gornyoc² *<suspended>* ...

1271   Next, that Thomas Dudeston fornicates with Amice, daughter of William
Schepper[t] ...

1272   Next, that Nicholas Coke fornicates with Alice Spermon. *<the man at
Worthen ...>*

1273   Next, that Tangwystl, daughter of Ieuan and David ap Ieuan of Ackley are
within the fourth degree of blood-relationship ...

1274   Next, that Gruffudd Saer of Brompton, a married man, commits adultery
with Maud, daughter of Llewelyn ...

[f. 26]

HYSSINGTON

1275   *<Sir Gruffudd chaplain there>*

1276   The parishioners say that Sybil of Brook fornicates with William Broun.
<both suspended; the woman to be beaten in due form>

1277   Next, that Philip, son of William Phippe, fornicates with the same Sybil.
<both suspended; the woman to purge since the time of correction>

1278   Next, that David Taelour fornicates with Gwenllian, daughter of Ieuan ap
Madog. *<the woman excommunicated, the man suspended>*

1279   Next, that Ieuan ap Hywel fornicates with Gwenllian, daughter of Ieuan
ap Hilder. *<the woman appears, admits, abjures, to be beaten three times around the church, the
man to be cited>*

---

¹   Recte *ap y Coch Hir*, son of the tall redhead.
²   Recte Gwenllian *Gorniog*, frowning Gwenllian.

1280 Item quod dominus Gruffuth capellanus parochialis ibidem incontinens est cum Agnete Colyn quam tenet. <vir comparet, negat post correctionem, purget se cum v^ta manu in proximo consistorio>

Worthyn. Visitatio facta ibidem die lune secundo die julii anno ut supra

Schelfe

1281 Parochiani dicunt quod omnia bene ibidem.

Worthyn

1282 Parochiani dicunt quod Llian Duy fornicatur cum Jankyn[1] ap Ieuan ap Madoc conjugato. <vir in Hibernia>

1283 Item quod Philippus serviens Gruffuth Baker fornicatur cum Dwgys serviente eiusdem Gruffuth. <vir citetur ad proximam; mulier comparet,[2] fatetur, abjurat, fustigetur ter circa ecclesiam>

1284 Item quod Gruffuth Taelour fornicatur cum Lleuku quam tenet. <dimissi sunt quia matrimonialiter copulati xxiiij annis>

1285 Item quod Georgius Waethe[3] serviens filii Thome Corbet de Lye adulteratur cum Cecilia uxore Rogeri Bullok. <mulier comparet, fatetur, abjurat, fustigetur vj circa ecclesiam et vj per forum; vir absens>

1286 Item quod Ricardus Lye conjugatus adulteratur cum Margareta relicta Rogeri Madokes. <correcti sunt per decanum>

1287 Item quod dominus de Lye quondam dedit certas terras in eadem villa ad sustentandum lampadem ardentem coram summo altari quas quidem terras rector tenet nec invenit huiusmodi lampadem.

1288 Item quod Ricardus Horde de Salop tenetur reddere annuatim ad sustentationem luminis Beate Marie ibidem pro terris quas tenet in Aston Bygot viij d vel j librum cere quod non facit et subtractum est toto tempore suo.

1289 Item quod Gruffuth Baker detinet ij s debitos <annuatim> servicio Beate Marie pro tenemento Galfridi Soweter quod tenet idem Gruffuth.

1290 <Item quod Nicholaus Flesshewer <suspensus> conjugatus adulteratur cum Alicia Spermon de Chirbury;[4] mulier comparet, fatetur, abjurat, fustigetur vj ante processionem et vj per forum de Montisgomeri et jejunet in pane et aqua omni feria vj ad festum Sancti Michelis; vir>[5]

1291 Item quod Hawisia Porssell detinet eidem servicio annuatim iiij d.

---

[1] Preceded by *Gruffuth Taelour*, struck through.
[2] Preceded by *suspensa*, struck through.
[3] Altered from *Wage*.
[4] For what is apparently the same charge, which Nicholas called *Coke*, see **1272**.
[5] Unfinished.

1280 Next, that Sir Gruffudd, parish chaplain there, is incontinent with Agnes Colyn, whom he keeps. <*the man appears, denies since correction, to purge himself with five hands at the next consistory*>

Worthen. Visitation made there on Monday, 2 July, the year as above

SHELVE

1281 The parishioners say that all is well there.

WORTHEN

1282 The parishioners say that Llian Duy fornicates with Jankin ap Ieuan ap Madog, a married man. <*the man in Ireland*>

1283 Next, that Philip, servant of Gruffudd Baker, fornicates with Dwgys, servant of the same Gruffudd. <*the man to be cited to the next; the woman appears, admits, abjures, to be beaten three times around the church*>

1284 Next, that Gruffudd Taelour fornicates with Lleucu, whom he keeps. <*they are dismissed because they have been married for 24 years*>

1285 Next, that George Waethe, servant of the son of Thomas Corbet of Leigh, commits adultery with Cecily, wife of Roger Bullok. <*the woman appears, admits, abjures, to be beaten six times around the church and six times through the marketplace; the man absent*>

1286 Next, that Richard Lye, a married man, commits adultery with Margaret, widow of Roger Madokes. <*they have been corrected by the dean*>

1287 Next, that the lord of Leigh formerly gave certain lands in the same vill to maintain a lamp to burn before the high altar, which lands the rector holds and does not provide this lamp.

1288 Next, that Richard Horde of Shrewsbury ought to pay annually for the upkeep of the light of the Blessed Mary there, for the lands he holds in Aston Pigott, 8 pence or a one-pound candle, which he does not do, and he has withheld it for all his time.

1289 Next, that Gruffudd Baker withholds 2 shillings due <*annually*> to the service of the Blessed Mary for the tenement of Geoffrey Soweter that the same Gruffudd holds.

1290 <*Next, that Nicholas Flesshewer <suspended>, a married man, commits adultery with Alice Spermon of Chirbury; the woman appears, admits, abjures, to be beaten six times before the procession and six times through the marketplace of Montgomery and to fast on bread and water each Friday until Michaelmas; the man [not completed]*>

1291 Next, that Hawise Porssell withholds from the same service annually 4 pence.

1292   Item quod Adam Corbet detinet eidem servicio vj d annuatim.

1293   <Item quod Johannes Fyssher adulteratur cum Agnete Scheppert; non noscuntur tales>

Westbury. Visitatio facta ibidem die martis[1] tertio Julii anno Domini ut supra

> [Westbury]

1294   [Pa]rochiani[2] dicunt quod Edmundus Burley fornicatur cum Margeria quam tenet. <mandatur domino Willelmo Brune capellano ad citandum [eosdem] E et M ad comparendum apud Wenlok die lune proximo et ad comparendum ibidem; etiam ad respondendum super contemptu; vir comparet, abjurat; difer penitenciam; mulier citetur>

1295   [Item] quod Hugo Croke fornicatur cum Issabella relicta Robyn Bourderbir. <suspensi; mulier comparet, abjurat et fustigetur etcetera; ... fustigetur in forma; vir purget se>

1296   [Item] quod Willelmus Croke fornicatur cum Sibilla filia Willelmi Jones. <suspensi; mulier abjurat, fustigetur in forma; vir apud Shelf' et ... ... citandum eundem>

1297   [Item quod Jo]hannes filius Johannis Geffes fornicatur cum Issabella serviente patris sui. <mulier suspensa;[3] vir abjurat et purget se a tempore correctionis ...>

1298   [Item quod] ... Lynne fornicatur cum Gwenllian quam tenet. <comparent, allegunt quod sunt vir et uxor, vir abjurat quous[que] ...; ... testes de solempnizatione matrimonii>

1299   [Item quod] dominus Rogerus rector capelle de Caos dat dictam capellam de Caos ad firmam sine [auctoritate ordin]arii. <sequestrantur fructus>

1300   [Item quod] ... [a]p Howel fornicatur cum Sibilla filia[4] Hikemones de Caos. <comparent, ...>

1301   [Item quod] ... [Bu]rnell de Streton fornicatur cum Johanna nuper serviente Jacobi <Borl[ey]>[5] ...

1302   [Item quod ... filius Johann]is Mylde graviter diffamatur de adulterio cum Johanne ...

1303   [Item quod] ... ... [tenetur] invenire duos capellanos ad celebrandum singulis diebus ... ... celebrandum tempestive pro servitoribus et altam[6] m[issam] ... ... tantum. <contrarium invenitur quia ibi sunt duo qu[orum] ... ... est nescitur eis.

---

[1]   Followed by *anno*, struck through.
[2]   The bottom left-hand and right-hand corners of this page are perished with the loss of up to two inches on the left and three inches on the right.
[3]   Altered from *suspensi* by the interlineation of mulier above *sus'*.
[4]   Preceded by *f*, struck through.
[5]   Replacing *Burnell*, expunged.
[6]   Preceded by *mag*, struck through.

1292 Next, that Adam Corbet withholds from the same service annually 6 pence.

1293 *<Next, that John Fyssher commits adultery with Agnes Scheppert; such people are unknown>*

Westbury. Visitation made there on Tuesday, 3 July, in the year of Our Lord as above

WESTBURY

1294 The parishioners say that Edmund Burley fornicates with Margery, whom he keeps. *<Sir William Brune, chaplain, is ordered to cite the same Edmund and Margery to appear at Much Wenlock next Monday and to appear there; also to answer over contempt; the man appears, abjures; defer the penance; the woman to be cited>*

1295 Next, that Hugh Croke fornicates with Isabel, widow of Robin Bourderbir. *<both suspended; the woman appears, abjures, and to be beaten etc.; [the man] to be beaten in due form; the man to purge himself>*

1296 Next, that William Croke fornicates with Sybil, daughter of William Jones. *<both suspended; the woman abjures, to be beaten in due form; the man at Shelve and ... ... cite him>*

1297 Next, that John, son of John Geffes, fornicates with Isabel, the servant of his father. *<the woman suspended; the man abjures and to purge himself since the time of correction ...>*

1298 Next, that ... Lynne fornicates with Gwenllian, whom he keeps. *<they appear, allege that they are man and wife; the man abjures up to [marriage] ... ... witnesses of the marriage having been solemnised>*

1299 Next, that Sir Roger, rector of the chapel of Caus, lets the said chapel of Caus to farm without the authority of the ordinary. *<the revenues to be sequestrated>*

1300 Next, that ... ap Hywel fornicates with Sybil, daughter of Hikemones of Caus. *<they appear, ...>*

1301 Next, that ... [Bu]rnell of Stretton fornicates with Joan, lately the servant of James *<Borley>* ...

1302 Next, that ... son of John Mylde is gravely defamed of adultery with Joan ...

1303 Next, that ... ... ought to provide two chaplains to celebrate every day ... ... celebrate at a convenient time for those serving and a high mass ... ... only. *<the opposite is found because there are two there of whom ... ... is, is not known to them>*[1]

---

[1]   Relates almost certainly to the chantry of St Margaret at Caus, established for two priests by Thomas Corbet by a charter of 25 March 1272: *Register of Richard Swinfield*, 162–4.

[f. 26v]

Albyrbury. Visitatio facta ibidem die mercurii iiij^to mensis Julii anno ut supra

[Albyrbury]

1304 Parochiani dicunt quod Iorwerth ap Heilin ap David et Dydgu filia Ieuan ap Griffri sunt illegitime copulati eo quod sunt infra iiij^tum gradum consanguinitatis et quod fecerunt clamdestine solempnizari matrimonium inter eos in alia diocesi. <vir excommunicatus, mulier suspensa>

1305 Item quod Ieuan ap <Ieuan ap> David ap Gruffuth et Gweirvyl quam tenet sunt illegitime copulati eo quod idem Ieuan habet aliam uxorem superstitem videlicet nomine Gwladus filiam David. <suspensi>

1306 Item quod dominus Johannes Yale incontinens est cum Agnete serviente sua et quod celebrat bis in die et quod vadit ad visitandum infirmos absque lumine et superpellicio. <committitur decano>

1307 Item quod dominus Philippus Momgomery incontinens est cum Dillen filia Eignon ap David. <vir ad purgandum vj manu in proximo [consistorio] generali, etiam mulier ad purgandum>

1308 Item quod Deyo serviens rectoris de Cardeston conjugatus adulteratur [cum]¹ Eva filia Llewelyn conjugata. <vir absens, mulier suspensa; mulier purget>

1309 Item quod Madoc Saer conjugatus adulteratur cum Lleuky quam tenet. <suspensi>

1310 [*in margin*] <significatum>

Item quod <Petrus>² Pygot et uxor sua non cohabitant simul et quod idem Petrus³ adulteratur cum Lleuky quam tenet. <suspensi; excommunicati>

1311 Item dicunt quod Gruffuth ap Tudur <et Jankyn Huwet ac Willelmus Feynsbury Thomas Nessh> falso et maliciose indictaverunt⁴ Howel de Bradeshull super receptatione bonorum furatorum etcetera. <purgant se et dimissi sunt>

1312 Item quod Gwilim <ap Iorwerth> ap Eignon <suspensus> ballivus domini de Mouthwy conjugatus adulteratur cum Eva <Hir> <suspensa> quam tenuit et cum Malli Pehenne <mortua> ac Juliana serviente Issabelle Gonion <absens> et Eva filia Llewelyn et Maiota sorore sua. <suspensi; vir comparet, fatetur de Eva, fustigetur in forma>

1313 Item quod Wilkoc Veynsbury et Sibilla uxor sua non cohabitant simul ut vir et uxor. <vir infirmus, mulier citetur; excommunicata>

¹ Omitted in error.
² Replacing *Philippus*, struck through.
³ Preceded by *Ph*, struck through.
⁴ Altered from *indictavit*.

[f. 26v]

Alberbury. Visitation made there on Wednesday, 4 July, the year as above

ALBERBURY

1304 The parishioners say that Iorwerth ap Heilyn ap David and Dyddgu, daughter of Ieuan ap Griffri, are unlawfully joined because they are within the fourth degree of blood-relationship and that they had a clandestine marriage solemnised between them in another diocese. *<the man excommunicated, the woman suspended>*

1305 Next, that Ieuan ap *<Ieuan ap>* David ap Gruffudd and Gweirful, whom he keeps, are unlawfully joined because the same Ieuan has another wife surviving, that is, one named Gwladus, daughter of David. *<both suspended>*

1306 Next, that Sir John Yale is incontinent with Agnes, his servant, and that he celebrates twice in a day and goes to visit the sick without a light and a surplice. *<it is committed to the dean>*

1307 Next, that Sir Philip Momgomery is incontinent with Dillen, daughter of Einion ap David. *<the man to purge with six hands at the next general consistory; the woman also to purge>*

1308 Next, that Deio, servant of the rector of Cardeston, a married man, commits adultery with Eve, daughter of Llewelyn, a married woman. *<the man absent, the woman suspended; the woman to purge>*

1309 Next, that Madog Saer, a married man, commits adultery with Lleucu, whom he keeps. *<both suspended>*

1310 [*in margin*]: *<signified>*

Next, that Peter Pygot and his wife do not live together and that the same Peter commits adultery with Lleucu, whom he keeps. *<both suspended; both excommunicated>*

1311 Next, they say that Gruffudd ap Tudur, and Jankin Huwet, and William Feynsbury and Thomas Nessh falsely and maliciously indicted Hywel of Bretchel for receiving stolen goods etc. *<they purge themselves and are dismissed>*

1312 Next, that Gwillm *<ap Iorwerth>* ap Einion *<suspended>*, bailiff of the lord of Mawddwy, a married man, commits adultery with Eve Hir *<suspended>*, whom he kept, and with Malli Pehenne *<dead>*, and with Julian, servant of Isabel Gonion *<absent>*, and with Eve, daughter of Llewelyn, and her sister Maiota. *<they are suspended; the man appears, admits in respect of Eve, to be beaten in due form>*

1313 Next, that Wilkoc Veynsbury and his wife Sybil do not live together as man and wife. *<the man sick, the woman to be cited; excommunicated>*

1314 Item quod dominus Johannes rector de Cardeston vadit ad domum Con-
stancie nuper concubine sue et ipsam ad domum habitationis dicti domini Johannis quod suspectum est etcetera. <citentur per edictum in capella de Cardeston;
excommunicatus uter>

1315 Item quod cancellus est defectivus in tectura et vitro fenestrarum in defectu
rectoris.

1316 Item quod rector et vicarius tenentur invenire unum clericum vulgariter
nuncupatum sexten sumptibus suis videlicet de rectore annuatim xiij s iiij d quod
rector non facit. Vicarius tamen paratus est portionem ipsum contingentem
exhibere.

> Scrawrthy

1317 Parochiani dicunt quod Madoc ap Ririt et Lucia filia Ieuan ap David contraxerunt adinvicem et quod non faciunt huiusmodi matrimonium solempnizari
inter eos.[1]

1318 <Dominus Johannes Jonson suspensus a celebratione>

1319 Item quod Jankyn clericus ecclesie ibidem fornicatur cum dicta Lucia.

1320 Item quod Howel Pyse fornicatur cum Amisia Mulward.

1321 Item quod Jankyn Webbe et Johannes Webbe sunt communes operarii
diebus festivis[2] <quibus operandum est caritative>.

Pontesbury. Visitatio facta ibidem die jovis v julii anno Domini ut supra

> [Pontesbury]

1322 Parochiani dicunt quod deficit unus diaconus sive clericus ad legendum
epistolas et pulsandum ignitegium et daybelle ac horas in quadragesima in defectu
rectorum ibidem, ad cuius clerici sustentationem solebant rectores ministrare j
quarterium frumenti singulis septem septimanis per annum quod non faciunt.
<prosequantur quorum interest>

1323 Item quod dominus Thomas Sturr capellanus incontinens est cum Margareta Wyllemote. <vir absens, mulier abjurat>

1324 Item quod dominus Robertus Colle capellanus incontinens est cum Margareta Hunte. <vir ad purgandum, mulier citetur in [par]ochia[3] de Westbury>

> Hannewode

1325 Parochiani dicunt quod ecclesia patitur defectum in tectura in defectu
parochianorum.

---

[1]   The next entry follows on the same line.
[2]   Preceded by *dominicis et*, struck through.
[3]   The bottom left-hand corner of this page is torn away with the loss of up to an inch
from four lines of text; the right-hand corner is perished, with the loss of up to three inches
from 14 lines.

1314   Next, that Sir John, rector of Cardeston, goes to the house of Constance, his late concubine, and she to the dwelling-house of the said Sir John, which is suspicious etc. *<both to be cited by edict in the chapel of Cardeston; both excommunicated>*

1315   Next, that the chancel is defective in its roofing and the glass of the windows, by the fault of the rector.

1316   Next, that the rector and the vicar ought to provide a clerk, commonly called a sexton, at their expense, that is, from the rector yearly 13 shillings and 4 pence, which the rector does not do; the vicar, however, is prepared to provide his share.

SHRAWARDINE

1317   The parishioners say that Madog ap Rhiryd and Lucy, daughter of Ieuan ap David, made a contract together and that they have not had this marriage solemnised between them.

1318   *<Sir John Jonson suspended from celebrating>*

1319   Next, that Jankin, clerk of the church there, fornicates with the said Lucy.

1320   Next, that Hywel Pyse fornicates with Amice Mulward.

1321   Next, that Jankin Webbe and John Webbe are habitual workers on feast days, *<on which working is well-paid>*.[1]

Pontesbury. Visitation made there on Thursday, 5 July, in the year of our Lord as above

PONTESBURY

1322   The parishioners say that they lack a deacon or clerk to read the epistles and ring the curfew and day bell, and the hours in Lent, by the fault of the rectors there, to the support of which clerk the rectors used to supply one quarter of wheat every seven weeks throughout the year, which they do not do. *<let those concerned prosecute>*

1323   Next, that Sir Thomas Sturr, chaplain, is incontinent with Margaret Wyllemote. *<the man absent; the woman abjures>*

1324   Next, that Sir Robert Colle, chaplain, is incontinent with Margaret Hunte. *<the man to purge; the woman to be cited in the parish of Westbury>*

HANWOOD

1325   The parishioners say that the church is defective in its roofing, by the fault of the parishioners.

---

[1]   The Latin *caritative* means *charitably*, but we assume the clerk intended it as a derivative of *carus* and have translated it accordingly.

1326 Item quod cimiterium non est clausum in defectu eorundem et injunctum est parochianis quod faciant r[eparari] citra festum Omnium Sanctorum[1] sub pena j marce. <inquiratur si inciderunt in penam>

[P]ollerbache

1327 Parochiani dicunt quod mansum ecclesie est ad terram prostratum in defectu rectoris. <sequestrantur fructus>

1328 Item quod rector dat ecclesiam suam ad firmam domino Ricardo Combley. <ab[sens] ...>

1329 Item quod cimiterium non est bene clausum in defectu Johannis Adames de ... <suspensus> et abbatis de Hamond. <clausum est ut dicitur; comparent et dicunt ..>

1330 Item quod Gruffuth Schepert conjugatus adulteratur cum Margareta Tranter. <absens ...>

[?]

1331 Parochiani dicunt quod rector celebrat super superaltare ibidem eo quod summum a[ltare ...]

1332 Item quod medietas cancelli est male cooperta in defectu rectoris de W...

1333 Item quod Willelmus Bent conjugatus adulteratur cum Johanna Wylkes douȝter J...

[Meole Brace]

1334 Parochiani dicunt quod cancellus est ruinosus in defectu abbatis de ...

1335 [Item] quod idem rector tenetur [invenire][2] xlviij garbarum annuatim ad stram[inandum] ...

1336 [Item quod] orreum rectoris est ruinosum; injunctum est rectori reparare [citra festum ... proximum fut]urum sub pena xl s. <inquiratur etcetera>

---

[1] *citra ... Sanctorum* repeated in error.
[2] Omitted in error.

1326   Next, that the churchyard is not fenced, by the fault of the same, and the parishioners are ordered to make repairs before the feast of All Saints, under penalty of 13 shillings and 4 pence. *<inquiry to be made whether they have incurred the penalty>*

CHURCH PULVERBATCH

1327   The parishioners say that the church house has collapsed to the ground, by the fault of the rector. *<the revenues to be sequestrated>*

1328   Next, that the rector farms out his church to Sir Richard Combley. *<absent ...>*

1329   Next, that the churchyard is not well fenced, by the fault of John Adames of ... *<suspended>* ... and the abbot of Haughmond. *<it is fenced as it is said; they appear and say ...>*

1330   Next, that Gruffudd Schepert, a married man, commits adultery with Margaret Tranter. *<absent ...>*

[unknown parish, perhaps a continuation of Westbury][1]

1331   The parishioners say that the rector celebrates on a portable altar there because the high altar ...

1332   Next, that half of the chancel is badly roofed, by the fault of the rector of W...

1333   Next, that William Bent, a married man, commits adultery with Joan Wylkes, daughter of J...

[MEOLE BRACE]

1334   The parishioners say that the chancel is in a ruinous state, by the fault of the abbot of [Wigmore].[2]

1335   Next, that the same rector ought to provide annually 48 sheaves to strew straw ...

1336   Next, that the rector's barn is in a ruinous state; the rector is ordered to repair it before the feast of ... next, under penalty of 40 shillings. *<to make inquiry etc.>*

---

[1]   These three entries may be a continuation from the recto of the same folio of Westbury, which had two rectors, named by Ecton as *dextra et sinistra partes*, implying divided responsibility for the chancel and its roof: *Taxatio ecclesiastica Angliae et Walliae auctoritate P. Nicolai IV circa A.D. 1291* (Record Commission, 1802), 166; John Ecton, *Thesaurus rerum ecclesiasticarum: Being an Account of the Valuations of All the Ecclesiastical Benefices in the Several Dioceses in England and Wales*, 3rd edition (London, 1783), 168.
[2]   *Taxatio*, 167; Ecton, *Thesaurus*, 169.

[Notes entered on the inside of the parchment cover of MS 1779]

1337 Nota indulgencia ... processa est ... Cisterciensibus in provinciis Cant' et Ebor' imposterum infra confirmationem per Urbanum V episcopum Romanum [quod rectores] in quorum parochiis oves [eorum] pascuntur non possunt exigere ab eis decimas de lana lacte et de agnis earundem ovium. Item Bonifacius confirmavit alias indulgencias infrascriptas et concessit ... ut de terris suis cultis et incultis ad suum ordinem spectantibus quas aliis [concesserunt vel] concedent imposterum excolendas de quibus tamen aliquis decimas seu primicias non percepit. Nullus ab eis seu cultoribus ipsarum terrarum aut quibuscumque aliis decimas seu primicias exigere vel extorquere presumat decernetur irritum et inane quicquid etcetera [contra tenorem huiusmodi indulgencie fuerit attemptatum].[1]

1338 Veniant apud Bodenham secundo die mensis Maii proxima futura persone infrascripte; quam diem dominus continuavit ad xxx diem proximam futuram si dies ipsa xxx^{ma} juridica juridictum fuerit sinautem proxima die juridica extra immedietate sequentem compareant coram eodem domino ubicumque fuerit infra suam diocesim quod erit apud Froma Episcopi primo die Junii. Quo die advento dominus continuavit quo ad decanum Hereforden' et vicarium altaris Sancti Johannis usque ad 3^m diem mensis Octobris proximam futuram si juridicam fuerit apud Whiteborn et quo ad alios de Monte Gomeri usque ad vigiliam Trinitatis proximam futuram apud Wygemore. Quo die advento continuata est usque ad Montem Gomeri, videlicet [*blank*]. Magister Johannes Prophet decanus Hereforden', Dominus Johannes Baker vicarius altaris Sancti Johannis in ecclesia Hereforden'; Dominus Robertus Moyl rector de Montegomeri; Johannes Says de Mongomery; Gruffuth ap Gwilim de Chirbury; Johannes Monnyng de Collewalle.

1339 Memorandum quod dominus Willelmus Lude capellanus constituit Walterum Kay procuratorem suum in causa vertente inter Robertum Juweson ex una et eundem dominum Walterum ex altera meliori modo etcetera cum potestate substituendi.

[1]   The text of this badly damaged entry has been partially reconstructed with reference to the two indulgences enrolled in several Cistercian cartularies, for example *The Coucher Book of Furness Abbey: Part III*, ed. J. C. Atkinson, Chetham Society, second series 14 (1887), 595–6. Urban V's bull of 2 September 1364 was a confirmation of indulgences of Innocent IV issued on 11 February 1244 and of Boniface VIII on 18 December 1302.

[Notes entered on the inside of the parchment cover of MS 1779]

1337 Note the indulgence issued to the Cistercians in the provinces of Canterbury and York that in future according to the confirmation by Urban V bishop of Rome that the rectors in whose parishes their ewes are pastured may not demand from them tithes of the wool, milk, and lambs of the same ewes. Next Boniface [VIII] confirmed other indulgences that from the lands, cultivated and uncultivated, relating to their order, which they had granted to others to be cultivated in future, provided that no one has taken tithes or first fruits, no one should presume to demand or extort tithes or first fruits from them or the cultivators of the same lands or from anyone else; and that anything attempted against the tenor of this indulgence should be deemed void and of no effect.

1338 Let there come to Bodenham on the second day of the month of May next coming the underwritten persons; on which day his lordship adjourned to the 30th day next coming, if that 30th day be a juridical day; otherwise let them appear on the next juridical day before him wherever he might be within his diocese, which will be at Bishops Frome on the first day of June. Which day having come, his lordship adjourned, respecting the dean of Hereford and the vicar of the altar of St John, until the 3rd day of the month of October next coming, if it be a juridical day, at Whitbourne, and respecting the others from Montgomery to the eve of Trinity next coming [16 June 1397] at Wigmore. Which day having come, it was adjourned to Montgomery, namely [*blank*]. Master John Prophet dean of Hereford, Sir John Baker vicar of the altar of Saint John in the church of Hereford; Sir Robert Moyl rector of Montgomery [**1232**]; John Says of Montgomery; Gruffudd ap Gwilym of Chirbury; John Monnyng of Colwall [**493**].

1339 Memorandum that Sir William Lude chaplain appointed Walter Kay his proctor in the case in progress between Robert Juweson on one side and the same Sir Walter on the other, in the best way etc., with a power of substitution.

1340 Memorandum quod die mercurii xij die mensis Junii anno Domini M°
CCC^{mo} nonagesimo vij° dominus Adam vicarius de Erdesley ex parte una et paro-
chiane[1] ibidem parte ex altera[2] de et super omnibus et singulis controversiis litibus
seu querelis motis inter easdem partes compromiserunt in alto et basso in quatuor
bonos viros tanquam amicabiles compositores, videlicet duos pro parte una et duos
ex parte altera; pro parte dicti vicarii magistrum Philippum Grym et Rogerum de
la Hay, si idem magister Philippus huiusmodi onus acceptaverit, sinautem loco eius
<in> magistrum Philippum Lyppa; et pro parte parochianorum <in> magistrum
Rogerum Andrewe et Johannem Halle; et si huiusmodi amicabiles compositores
non poterint huiusmodi litibus finem imponere, voluerunt ambe partes quod rev-
erendus in Christo pater dominus Johannes episcopus Heref' discutiet et terminet
omnem ambiguitatem inter eosdem compositores, ita tamen quod hoc fecit citra
sex septimanas proximas sequentes continue numerandas sub pena xx librarum
per partem non parentem arbitrio dictorum compositorum, applicandarum ad
opus ecclesie cathedralis Hereforden' et ecclesie de Erdesley, videlicet ad opus
ecclesie cathedralis xv libre et ecclesie de Erdesley v libre.

1341 Magister Thomas Neweport portionarius.

1342 Magister Thomas Neweport secundus portionarius de Pontesbury habet
diem apud Wenlake.

1343 Parochiani de Burghull habent diem apud Wormesley. <non comparent>

1344 Dominus Philippus rector de Llanwaran habet diem crastinum diem apud
[Deu]church.

1345 Abbas et conventus Gl[ouc'] habent diem apud Churcham ad exhibendum titulum suum quo ad Homlacy. <exhibitum est ibidem>

1346 ... ... Dineriri[3] solvet feodum apud Sellak. <solutum est ibidem>

1347 [Parochiani] de Llangaran habent diem apud Sellak. <comparuerunt
ibidem>

1348 [Parochiani] de Bykenor Walissh[4] habent diem apud Bykenor Englissh.
<ibidem comparuerunt>

1349 [Rector] ibidem habet diem ad exhibendum titulum suum apud Sellak.
<quia non comparuit suspensus est a celebratione divinorum>

1350 [Recto]r et parochiani de Hop Maloysel habent diem apud Ross. <compa-
ruerunt ibidem>

1351 [Rector] de Staunton habet diem apud Ross. <ibidem comparuit cum
parochianis>

1352 [Apud] Newent vocatus est frater Johannes Brugg[5] ordinis predicatorum.
<non comparet, ideo suspensus; habet diem apud Markel>

---

[1] Recte *parochiani*.
[2] Preceded by *v*, struck through.
[3] Reading uncertain.
[4] Preceded by *Englissh*, struck through.
[5] Interlined, preceded by *Broun*, struck through.

1340 Memorandum that on Wednesday 12 June 1397 Sir Adam vicar of Eardisley on one side and the parishioners there on the other side concerning and upon
all and singular disagreements, suits, or quarrels moved between the same parties
have agreed in every respect on four good men as friendly arbitrators, namely two
for one side and two on the other side; on the side of the said vicar Master Philip
Grym and Roger de la Hay, if the same Master Philip will accept this charge,
otherwise in his place Master Philip Lyppa; and for the side of the parishioners
Master Roger Andrewe and John Halle; and if these friendly arbitrators cannot
put an end to these suits, both sides wish that the reverend father in Christ John
[Trefnant] lord bishop of Hereford should examine and end all doubtful points
between the same arbitrators, so that they should do this within six weeks next following, to be counted continuously, under penalty of £20 for the side not obeying
the arbitration of the said arbitrators, to be applied to the use of the cathedral
church of Hereford and the church of Eardisley, namely £15 to the use of the
cathedral church and £5 to the use of the church of Eardisley [**815**].

1341 Master Thomas Neweport portioner.

1342 Master Thomas Neweport second portioner of Pontesbury has a day at
Much Wenlock.

1343 The parishioners of Burghill have a day at Wormsley. <*they do not appear*>
[**7**]

1344 Sir Philip rector of Llanwarne has a day on the next day [10 May 1397] at
Much Dewchurch.

1345 The abbot and convent of Gloucester have a day at Churcham to show
their title regarding Holme Lacy. <*it was shown there*>

1346 ... ... should pay the fee at Sellack. <*it was paid there*>

1347 The parishioners of Llangarron have a day at Sellack. <*they appeared there*>
[**326**]

1348 The parishioners of Welsh Bicknor have a day at English Bicknor. <*they
appeared there*> [**249**]

1349 The rector there has a day to show his title at Sellack. <*because he did not
appear he was suspended from divine celebration*>.

1350 The rector and parishioners of Hope Mansell have a day at Ross-on-Wye.
<*they appeared there*>

1351 The rector of Staunton has a day at Ross-on-Wye. <*he appeared there with the
parishioners*>

1352 To Newent was called Brother John Brugg of the Order of Preachers. <*he
does not appear, so suspended; he has a day at Much Marcle*> [**373**]

1353 [Dominus] assignavit magistro Johanni Malverne custodi hospitalis Sancte Katerine ad exhibendum titulum suum de huiusmodi hospitali die [martis] videlicet quinto Junii proximo futuro apud Leomestr'.

1354 [Memorandum quod] magister Johannes Prophet portionarius de Overha[ll] in Ledebury habet diem apud Pennbrug ix die Junii proximo futuro ad ostendendum titulum suum super huiusmodi beneficio et aliis que tenet in diocese Heref' ac omnibus aliis et singulis quorum sua crediderint interesse in huiusmodi beneficio ad comparendum ibidem et opponendum. <quando cesset>

1355 Rector de Mordeford habet diem apud Leom' ad exhibendum titulum beneficii et litteras ordinum quas ... <ibidem exhibuit>

1356 Prior Sancti Guthlaci Herefordie habet diem apud Leom' ad exhibendum titulum si quem habet in illis decimis quas percipit infra parochiam de Stoklacy, <videlicet quintum diem mensis Junii>.

1357 Memorandum quod discretus vir magister Ricardus Whylar procurator constitutus venerabilis viri magistri Johannis Prophet portionarii de Overhall in ecclesia de Ledebury habentis hos diem at locum videlicet novum diem mensis Junii anno Domini M° CCC^{mo} nonagesimo septimo et consecrationis nostri anno viij° in ecclesia de Pennbrugg nostre diocesis ad exhibendum titulum suum super dicta portione ex assignatione nostra sibi alias apud Ledebury ac omnibus aliis et singulis quorum sua in hac parte crediderint interesse facit titulum eiusdem domini sui, nobis ibidem judicaliter sedentibus. Quo facto fecimus ibidem preconizari si quis sit qui velit aliquid dicere seu opponere in huiusmodi materia et nullus comparuit.

1358 Memorandum quod Johannes Estham constituit magistrum David ap Kynwric procuratorem suum apud actionem in causa matrimoniali etcetera ac in omnibus causis et negotiis xxvj die Junii anno Domini M° CCC^{mo} nonagesimo septimo.

Acta in ecclesia de Chirbury die Sabbati ultimo Junii anno Domini M° CCC^{mo} nonagesimo vij:

1359 In causa matrimoniali et divorcii inter Rogerum ap Ieuan ap Llewellyn et Sibillam Herdemon partem actricem ex una et Maiotam filiam David Deheubarth partem ream ex altera partibus comparentibus personaliter lite continuato affirmative juratis partibus de calumpnia dicta pars actrix produxit Johannem Saer et David ap Ieuan ap Llewellyn ad probandum precontractum inter dictos Rogerum et Sibillam initum; item produxit Sibillam Coly cuius examinatio commissa est rectori Montis Gomeri.

1353 His lordship assigned to Master John Malverne, warden of the hospital of St Katherine [of Ledbury], to show his title of that hospital on Tuesday, namely 5 June next coming at Leominster [**510–13**].

1354 Memorandum that Master John Prophet, portionary of Overhall in Ledbury, has a day at Pembridge on 9 June next coming to show his title to that benefice and to the others which he holds in the diocese of Hereford, and [to warn] all and singular who believe themselves to have an interest in that benefice to appear there and object. <*when it ceased*>

1355 The rector of Mordiford has a day at Leominster to show the title of the benefice and the letters of [his] orders, which ... <*he showed there*>

1356 The prior of St Guthlac at Hereford has a day at Leominster to show the title if he has any in the tithes that he takes within the parish of Stoke Lacy, <*namely on 5 June*>.

1357 Memorandum that the distinguished man Master Richard Whylar the appointed proctor of the venerable man Master John Prophet portionary of Overhall in the church of Ledbury, having this day and place, namely 9 June 1397 and the eighth year of our consecration in the church of Pembridge in our diocese to show his title to the said portion, by our assignment to him on another occasion at Ledbury, to all and singular others who believe themselves to have an interest in this regard, makes the title of his same client to us, there sitting in judgement. Which done, we there gave notice whether there was anyone who wished to say or object anything in this matter, and nobody appeared.[1]

1358 Memorandum that John Estham appointed Master David ap Kynwric his proctor at a session in a matrimonial case etc. and in all cases and business on 26 June 1397 [**978**].

Proceedings in the church of Chirbury on Saturday, 30 June 1397

1359 In a case of marriage and divorce between Roger ap Ieuan ap Llewelyn and Sybil Herdemon plaintiff on the one side and Maiota daughter of David Deheubarth defendant on the other side; the parties appearing in person, the case having continued affirmatively [and] the parties sworn concerning the claim, the said plaintiff produced John Saer and David ap Ieuan ap Llewelyn to prove a pre-contract entered into between the said Roger and Sybil; next she produced Sybil Coly, whose examination was committed to the rector of Montgomery.[2]

---

[1] The adjournment of the process from Ledbury to Pembridge and the proceedings there on 8 June 1397, together with John Prophet's title to the prebend dated 28 October 1390 and other documents relating to it, were enrolled in *Register of John Trefnant*, 138–40.

[2] The bishop's sentence in this case, annulling the marriage of Roger with Maiota, there called Margery, on account of a pre-contract with Sybil, there called the daughter of Robert Herdemoun of Montgomery, given at Much Wenlock on 9 July 1397, was enrolled in *Register of John Trefnant*, 143–4.

1360 In causa matrimoniale vertente inter Elenam filiam Gruffuth ap Jonas partem actricem ex una et Ririt ap Ieuan Gogh ex [parte] altera; partibus personaliter comparentibus lite continuato negative habent diem apud Worthyn die Martis proximo futuro videlicet iij° die Julii [anno domini millesimo] CCC^mo nonagesimo septimo.

1361 ... [R]irit ap Ieuan Gogh ad probandum materiam contrariam etcetera.

1362 ... David ap Madoc, Gwilim ap Madoc, Gruffuth ap David, ... ap Llewellyn, Llewellyn ap Madoc.

1363 ... ... [constituit magistrum] Rogerum Andrewe procuratorem suum apud actionem ... ... apud Clubry Mortemere contra abbatem [et conventum de] Wygg' cum potestate substituendi.

1364 ... Leghton, Hawkeyn, Hawelyn.[1]

1365 Dormyton, Molmeshull Gamage, Homlacy, Deuchurche, Kilpek, Byrch Sancti Thome, Foy, Churcham: abbas et conventus de Glouc' est rector earundem ecclesiarum.

1366 In causa de Streton et Asperton ... inter ... ... dominus visa huiusmodi inhibitione ... ... lite pendente in curia regis.

1367 Memorandum quod dominus Edwardus rector de Buterley constituit [magistros Johannem] Gryn, Johannem Went et Rogerum [H]oore procuratores suos ... ... actionem etcetera.

---

[1]   These three words are written on separate lines and may be the last words of three separate entries, since any text to their left has been obliterated by damage to the parchment.

1360 In a case of marriage in progress between Helen daughter of Gruffudd ap Jonas plaintiff on the one side and Rhiryd ap Ieuan Gogh on the other side; the parties appearing in person, the case having continued negatively, they have a day at Worthen on Tuesday next, namely 3 July 1397.

1361 ... Rhiryd ap Ieuan Gogh to prove the opposing material.

1362 ... David ap Madoc, Gwilym ap Madog, Gruffudd ap David, ... ap Llewelyn, Llewelyn ap Madog.[1]

1363 ... ... appointed Master Roger Andrew his proctor at a session ... ... at Cleobury Mortimer against the abbot and convent of Wigmore with the power of substitution.

1364 ... Leghton, Hawkeyn, Hawelyn.

1365 Dormington, Mansell Gamage, Holme Lacy, Much Dewchurch, Kilpeck, Much Birch, Foy, Churcham: the abbot and convent of Gloucester is rector of these churches.

1366 In the case of Stretton and Ashperton ... between ... ... his lordship, having seen this inhibition ... ... a case pending in the king's court [**585**].[2]

1367 Memorandum that Sir Edward, rector of Bitterley appointed Masters John Gryn, John Went, and Roger Hoore their proctors ... ... action etc.

---

[1]   Perhaps Rhiryd's witnesses and so related to **1360** and **1361**.
[2]   The resolution of this dispute between Roger Wodewalle and Thomas Pekke, dating back to 1379, with a list of evidences produced by both parties before the bishop at Hereford on 23 April 1397, was enrolled in *Register of John Trefnant*, 152–5.

Index of place-names

Notes: Roman numerals refer to pages in the Introduction. The text is indexed by item number; references to notes there are to the translation. Locators in bold type indicate the main entry for each place. County names refer to the period before local government reorganisation in 1974. Deaneries are indexed in the Introduction only.

Abenhall (Glos.)   **408**
Ackley (in Forden) (Montgomerys.)   1273
Adforton (Herefs.)   xxvi, **1032–5**, 1043
Alberbury (Salop)   **1304–16**
   visitation held at   1304–21
     map of route   xxii–xxiii
Aldon (in Stokesay) (Salop)   1078
Almeley (Herefs.)   134, **851**
   visitation held at   806–57
     map of route   xxii–xxiii
Alvington (Glos.)
   chapel   379
   chaplain of   390
   see also Woolaston and Alvington
Archenfield deanery   xxxviii
Arwystli (Montgomerys.)   xxxviii, 1259
Ashford (Bowdler or Carbonell)
   (Salop)   1090
Ashperton (Herefs.)   **579–84**, 1366
Ashton (in Eye) (Herefs.)   747
Aston (in Kingsland) (Herefs.)   753, 760
Aston (Salop)   **1098–102**, 1166
Aston on Clun (Montgomerys.)   xxxviii
Aston Ingham (Herefs.)   **330**
Aston Pigott (in Worthen) (Salop)   1288
Avenbury (Herefs.)   **640**
Awre (Glos.)   **403–6**
   visitation held at   403–6
     map of route   xxii–xxiii
Aylton (Herefs.)   **508**, 564
Aymestrey (Herefs.)   **968–75**

Bacton (Herefs.)   **44–9**
Ballingham (Herefs.)   **159**
Barton (in Colwall) (Herefs.), bailiff
   of   499

Beachley (Glos.)   372
Bedstone (Salop)   **1050–6**
Bicknor, English (Glos.)   xxviii, 249,
   345–9, 1348
   visitation held at   345–9
     map of route   xxii–xxiii
Bicknor, Welsh (Herefs.)   xxviii, xxxii–
   xxxiii, **249**, 345, 1348–9
Bicton (in Clun) (Salop)   xxvi, **1213**
Biddlestone (in Llangarron)
   (Herefs.)   310
Birch, Much (Birch St Thomas)
   (Herefs.)   179, **197–201**, 1365
Birley (Herefs.)   **676–9**
Bishops Castle (Salop)   987, **1103–28**
Bishops Frome *see* Frome, Bishops
Bishopstone (Herefs.)   **133–4**
Bitterley (Salop)   xxix, **998–1000**, 1367
   visitation held at   998–1005
     map of route   xxii–xxiii
   see also Ledwyche
Blaisdon (Glos.)   **407**, 428, 429, 431, 433
Bockleton (Worcs.)   1002
Bodenham (Herefs.)   **39–40**, 1338
   visitation held at   39–40
     map of route   xxii–xxiii
Bolstone (Herefs.)   **161**
Bosbury (Herefs.)   **569**
   visitation held at   xxiv, 566–9
     map of route   xxii–xxiii
Brampton Abbotts (Herefs.)   **343**
Brampton Bryan (Herefs.)   **1006–13**,
   1019
Bredwardine (Herefs.)   **92–105**
Bretchel (in Alberbury) (Salop)   1311
Bridge Sollers (Herefs.)   **126**

Bridstow (Herefs.) **306**
Brilley (Herefs.) xxxvii, **881–900**
Brimfield (Herefs.) **739–40**
Brinsop (Herefs.) **1–5**
Brobury (Herefs.) **124**
Brockhampton (Herefs.) **644**
Bromfield (Salop) xxvi, 1052, **1090–7**
    Bromfield Priory xviii
    visitation held at xxvi, 1087–97
        map of route xxii–xxiii
    see also Dinchope
Brompton (in Churchstoke)
    (Salop) 1274
Bromsberrow (Glos.) **472–5**
Bromyard (Herefs.) xl–xli, 95, **652–61**,
    776, 795
    visitation held at xxiv, 638–73
        map of route xxii–xxiii
Bucknell (Salop) **1042–9**
Bullinghope (Herefs.), prebend xix
Burford deanery, omitted from
    visitation xxiv–xxv, xxxi
Burghill (Herefs.) xxviii–xxix, **7–24**,
    1343
    visitation held at xxiv, 1–24
        map of route xxii–xxiii
Burrington (Herefs.) xviii n.31, 949,
    1036–41
Byford (Herefs.) **116–20**
Byton (Herefs.) **928–30**

Canon Frome *see* Frome, Canon
Canterbury, archbishops of xix–xxi,
    xxvii, 329, 694 n.2, 1178
Caple, King's (Herefs.) **314**
Cardeston (Salop) 1308, 1314
Castell Maen (Herefs.) *see* Huntington
Castle Frome *see* Frome, Castle
Caus (in Westbury) (Salop) 1300
    chantry of St Margaret 1299, 1303
    n.1
Caynham (Salop) xxiv n.48, **1005**
Chirbury (Salop) xxix, xxxix, 1225, 1263,
    1264, **1266–74**, 1290, 1338, 1359
    visitation held at xxiv, 1234–80
        map of route xxii–xxiii
Cholstrey (Herefs.) *see* Stagbatch and
    Cholstrey
Church Pulverbatch (Salop) **1327–30**

Churcham (Glos.) **455–7**, 1345, 1365
    visitation held at 446–57
        map of route xxii–xxiii
Churchstoke (Montgomerys.) xviii
    n.31, xxxviii, xxxix, **1235–65**
    see also Brompton; Rhiston
Claston (in Dormington) (Herefs.) 545
Cleeton (in Bitterley) (Salop) 1000
Cleobury Mortimer (Salop) 1363
    see also Doddington
Clifford (Herefs.) 809, **858–65**
    visitation held at 858–72
        map of route xxii–xxiii
Clun (Salop) xxvi, 760, **1168–9**,
    1193–202
    visitation held at 1168–217
        map of route xxii–xxiii
    see also Bicton; Spoad
Clunbury (Salop) xviii, xxx n.68, 1076,
    1170–92
Clungunford (Salop) **1023–7**, 1172
Clunton (in Clunbury) (Salop) 1191
Coddington (Herefs.) xxxiii, **534–43**
Colebatch (in Bishops Castle)
    (Salop) 1128
Colwall (Herefs.) **492–502**, 1338
Coombe (Herefs., location
    unknown) 307
Corfham (in Diddlebury) (Salop) 1074
Cowarne, Little (Herefs.) **668–73**
Cowarne, Much (Herefs.) **570–7**
    visitation held at 570–613
        map of route xxii–xxiii
Cradley (Herefs.) xxxiv, **614–21**
    visitation held at 614–21
        map of route xxii–xxiii
Credenhill (Herefs.) **110**, 453
Croft (Herefs.) xxxix, **738**
Culmington (Salop) xxxviii, **1058–65**
Cusop (Herefs.) xxxiii, 91, 860,
    866–72
Cwmhir Abbey (Radnors.) 1208

Dean, Forest of xxiv
    see also Tidenham and Lancaut;
        Woolaston and Alvington
Dean, Little (Glos.) 428, 432, 437–8,
    452
    see also Newnham and Little Dean

Deheubarth xxxviii
Dewchurch, Little (Herefs.) **160**, 307
Dewchurch, Much (Herefs.) **188–95**,
   1344, 1365
  visitation held at 181–201
    map of route xxii–xxiii
Diddlebury (Salop) **1066–77**
  visitation held at 1058–77
    map of route xxii–xxiii
Dilwyn (Herefs.) xxxiii, 151, **780–8**
  visitation held at 775–88
    map of route xxii–xxiii
Dinchope (in Bromfield) (Salop) **1089**
Discoed (in Presteigne)
   (Radnors.) 935–6
Dixton (Monmouths.) xxviii, **293–5**
Docklow (Herefs.) **715**
Doddington (in Cleobury Mortimer)
   (Salop) xxiv
Donnington (Herefs.) **566–8**
Dormington (Herefs.) **26–30**, 1365
  see also Claston
Dorstone (Herefs.) 42, **72–91**
  visitation held at 72–106
    map of route xxii–xxiii
Down, Lower (in Lydbury North)
   (Salop) 1158
Downton (Herefs.) **1057**, 1062
Dymock (Glos.) xxxiv, **476–83**
  visitation held at 469–83
    map of route xxii–xxiii

Eardisley (Herefs.) xxx, xl, xli, **813–45**,
   844, 1340
Eastnor (Herefs.) **526–33**
Eaton (in Leominster) (Herefs.) xxvi,
  719–20
Edgton (Salop) 1157
Ednol (in Old Radnor) (Radnors.) 947
Elfael xxxviii
Elton (Herefs.) **948–50**
English Bicknor *see* Bicknor, English
Ergyng, Welsh kingdom of xxxviii
Eye (Herefs.) **745–8**
  visitation held at xxvi, 733–48
    map of route xxii–xxiii
Eyton (Herefs.) **737**, 1157

Felton (Herefs.) **590–1**

Flanesford Priory (Herefs.) 233
Flaxley Abbey (Glos.) 427, 430–44
Forden (Montgomerys.) **1234**
  see also Ackley
Forest of Dean *see* Dean, Forest of
Fownhope (Herefs.) **554**
Foy (Herefs.) **323–5**, 1365
Frome, Bishops (Herefs.) **625–37**, 1338
  visitation held at 622–37
    map of route xxii–xxiii
Frome, Canon (Herefs.) 582, **623–4**
Frome, Castle (Herefs.) **622**
Frome deanery 673

Ganarew (Herefs.) 252, **255–6**
Garway (Herefs.) xxxviii, **217–25**, 911
  visitation held at 202–29, 229 n.1
    map of route xxii–xxiii
Gloucester 434, 562, 1042
  Gloucester Abbey 1345, 1365
Goodrich (Herefs.) **230–48**
  Goodrich Castle 236–7, 240
Grendon Bishop (Herefs.) **642**
Grendon Warren (Herefs.) **667**

Halton (in Bromfield) (Salop) 1095
Hanwood (Salop) **1325–6**
Harry Stoke (in Stoke Gifford)
   (Glos.) xxxix, 1263
Hendre (in Sellack) (Herefs.) 309
Hentland (Herefs.) **315–18**
Hereford
  absolution received at 844
  archiepiscopal visitation proposed
   (1396) xx
  archives of the dean and chapter xii
  bishop's consistory *see* subject index
   under church tribunals
  bishops of *see personal names index*
  cathedral
   altar of St John 1338
   money for upkeep as
     penalties 565, 1269, 1340
  cathedral library xii
  dean of *see* Prophet, Master John *in*
   personal names index
  deanery estates xix, xxxv
  penances at
   beating around the church 107

beating before the
    procession   107, 812, 962
beating through the
    marketplace   107, 889
people to 'have a day' at   2, 67, 137,
    292, 514, 570, 976
    to purge themselves   122, 588
persons of   91, 107
St Guthlac's Priory   545, 1356
Hereford diocese, extent   xxiv
Hewelsfield (Glos.)   **402**
Holme Lacy (Herefs.)   **162–8**, 1345,
    1365
    visitation held at   159–68
    map of route   xxii–xxiii
Hope Bagot (Salop)   **1003**
Hope Mansell (Herefs.)   1350
Hopesay (Salop)   **1164–7**
How Caple (Herefs.)   **558**
Humber (Herefs.)   **680–3**
Huntington (Herefs.)   **873–80**
    Castell Maen   897
Huntley (Glos.)   **409–10**, 456
Huntsham (in Goodrich)
    (Herefs.)   236–7
Hyssington (Montgomerys.)   **1275–80**

Ireland, expeditionary force to   xviii,
    xxxviii, 957, 992, 1038, 1201, 1250,
    1282

Kempley (Glos.)   **469–71**
Kenchester (Herefs.)   xxxi, **121–2**
Kenderchurch (Herefs.)   **181**
Kentchurch (Herefs.)   **202–5**
Kilpeck (Herefs.)   xxxix, **182–7**, 1365
Kimbolton (Herefs.)   **734**
King's, place-names beginning with, *see
    under second element*
Kingsland (Herefs.)   **749–74**, 1188
    visitation held at   749–74
    map of route   xxii–xxiii
Kington (Herefs.)   853, **910–24**
    visitation held at   873–924
    map of route   xxii–xxiii
Kinlet (Salop)   xxiv n.48, 1005
Kinnerley (Salop) *see* Kynaston
Kinnersley (Herefs.)   **847–50**
Kinsham, Nether (Herefs.)   929

Knighton (Radnors.)   934, **1014–22**
Knill (Herefs.)   **925**
Kynaston (in Kinnerley) (Salop)   562

Lancaut (Glos.)   376
    see also Tidenham and Lancaut
Lawton (in Kingsland) (Herefs.)   749
Lea (in Bishops Castle) (Salop)   1121,
    1124
Ledbury (Herefs.)   485, **509–23**, 525
    St Katherine's Hospital,
        warden   510–13, 1353
    visitation held at   xxiv, 484–543
        map of route   xxii–xxiii
    see also Overhall
Ledwyche (in Bitterley) (Salop)   1000,
    1001
Leigh (in Worthen) (Salop)   1285, 1287
Leinthall (unspecified) (Herefs.)   743
Leinthall Starkes (Herefs.)   **965–7**
Leintwardine (Herefs.)   677, 1094, 1156
    persons to appear at   927, 943, 950,
        976
    visitation held at   1006–57, 1098–102
        map of route   xxii–xxiii
Leominster (Herefs.)   xxxiii, xxxv,
    688–714, 715, 773, 1022
    bishop dictates letter from   xxvi
    Leominster Priory   xvii, xxix, xxxv,
        688–97, 713–14
    Lugg Bridge   688
    persons of   681, 801, 1022
    persons to appear at   152, 1353, 1355–6
    visitation held at   xxiv, xxvi, 674–732
        map of route   xxii–xxiii
    see also Eaton; Stagbatch and
        Cholstrey
Letton (Herefs.)   848
Lingen (Herefs.)   973, **976**
Linton (Herefs.)   **340–2**
Little, place-names beginning with, *see
    under second element*
Llandaff, bishop and diocese of   253–4,
    287, 350
Llandinabo (Herefs.)   **169**, 175
Llanfair Waterdine (Salop)   **1203–12**
Llangarron (Herefs.)   xxix, **229**,
    326–8, 1347
    see also Biddlestone

Llanrothal (Herefs.) **206–12**

Llanthony Priory (Monmouths.) 1, 171, 1161

Llanwarne (Herefs.) xxix, xxxii–xxxiii, **170–3**, 179, 1344
  visitation held at 169–80
    map of route xxii–xxiii

Longhope (Glos.) **415–16**

Lower Down *see* Down, Lower

Lucton (Herefs.) **735–6**

Ludford (Salop) 1090
  chapel of Ludford and Syde xxvi, **1088**, 1090

Ludlow (Salop) 710, 970, 977, 1006, 1083, 1092, 1171
  deanery xxiv, xxvi

Lugwardine (Herefs.) **33–4**, 213
  visitation held at 25–38
    map of route xxii–xxiii
  see also Llangarron

Lydbury North (Salop) **1152–63**
  visitation held at 1103–67
    map of route xxii–xxiii

Lydham (Salop) **1129–33**

Lydney (Glos.) **390–3**, 406
  visitation held at 390–402
    map of route xxii–xxiii

Lyonshall (Herefs.) **852–7**

Madley (Herefs.) 306

Mainstone (Salop) **1148–50**

Malvern, Little (Worcs.) 527

Mansell Gamage (Herefs.) xxvi n.58, **112–15**, 1365

Mansell Lacy (Herefs.) **125**

Marcle, Little (Herefs.) **484–91**

Marcle, Much (Herefs.) **559–65**, 1352
  visitation held at 550–65
    map of route xxii–xxiii

Marstow (Herefs.) **321**

Meole Brace (Salop) **1334–6**

Michaelchurch-on-Arrow (Radnors.) **901–9**

Middlehope (in Diddlebury) (Salop) 1067

Middleton on the Hill (Herefs.) **733**, 993

Minsterworth (Glos.) **447–52**

Mitcheldean (Glos.) xxxii, **411–14**

Moccas (Herefs.) **106**

Monmouth xxviii, 252, **257–92**, 285
  Monmouth Priory xviii, 210, 262, 291
  St Thomas, Overwye 291
  visitation held at xxviii, 230–95
    map of route xxii–xxiii

Monnington (Herefs.) 58, **107–9**

Montgomery xxix n.67, **1218–33**, 1264, 1290, 1338, 1359
  visitation held at 1218–33
    map of route xxii–xxiii

Mordiford (Herefs.) 323, 545, **550–3**, 1355

More (Salop) **1151**

Much, place-names beginning with, *see under second element*

Munsley (Herefs.) **503–7**

Nether Kinsham *see* Kinsham, Nether

New Radnor *see* Radnor, New

Newent (Glos.) **467–8**, 1352
  visitation held at 458–68
    map of route xxii–xxiii

Newland (Glos.) xxxi, **350–2**, **356–64**
  visitation held at xxxi, 350–64
    map of route xxii–xxiii

Newnham and Little Dean (Glos.) **417–18**

Newton, Welsh (Herefs.) **226–8**, 327

Norbury (Salop) **1146–7**

Norton (Radnors.) xxxix, 87, **931–9**

Ocle Pychard (Herefs.) 351, 545, **578**
  Ocle Prior 590

Old Radnor *see* Radnor, Old

Onibury (Salop) **1087**

Orcop (Herefs.) xxx n.68, **174–9**, 976

Orleton (Herefs.) **742–4**

Overhall, prebend xxxv, 1354, 1357

Oxenhall (Glos.) **459**

Oxford, Bodleian Library xii

Pauntley (Glos.) **460–6**

Pembridge (Herefs.) **793–805**, 917, 1354, 1357
  Court of Noke Farm 794
  visitation held at 789–805
    map of route xxii–xxiii

Pencombe (Herefs.) **665**, 668
Pencoyd (Herefs.) **319–20**
Penderyn (Brecons.) 253
Penn-y-Clawdd (Monmouths.) 254
Penrose (in St Weonards) (Herefs.),
  chapel of 213
Peterchurch (Herefs.) xxxii, xxxvi, **59–71**
  visitation held at 41–71
    map of route xxii–xxiii
  see also Snodhill
Peterstow (Herefs.) **322**
Pixley (Herefs.) **524–5**
Pontesbury (Salop) xxiv n.48, **1322–4**,
  1342
  visitation held at xxiv, xxv, 1322–30
    map of route xxii–xxiii
Presteigne (Radnors.) **940–4**
  visitation held at 925–44
    map of route xxii–xxiii
  see also Discoed
Preston Wynne (Herefs.) **555–6**, 601
Pudleston (Herefs.) **687**
Purslow Bridge (in Clunbury)
  (Salop) 1178
Pyon (unspecified) (Herefs.) 9, 153
Pyon, King's (Herefs.) **775–9**

Radnor (unspecified) 793
Radnor, New (Radnors.) **721–32**
Radnor, Old (Radnors.) 926, **945–7**
  visitation held at 945–76
    map of route xxii–xxiii
Reeves Hill (in Brampton Bryan)
  (Herefs.) 1008
Rhayader (Radnors.) xxxviii, 745
Rhiston (in Churchstoke) (Salop) 1223
Richards Castle (Salop) xxix, **977–86**
  visitation held at 977–86
    map of route xxii–xxiii
Rome, papal court 261
Ross-on-Wye (Herefs.) **331–9**
  market 491
  people to 'have a day' at 238, 364,
    1350–1
  visitation held at 329–44
    map of route xxii–xxiii
Ruardean (Glos.) xxxix, 248, **299–305**
Rudford (Glos.) 427, **446**
Rushbury (Salop) xxiv

St Asaph, bishops of xxxviii
St Briavels (Glos.) **394–401**
St David's, diocese 43, 74, 253, 1020
St Devereux (Herefs.) **196**
St Weonards (Herefs.) **213–16**
  Glangarren Farm 229 n.1
Sapey, Upper (Herefs.) **666**
Sarnesfield (Herefs.) 154, **789**
Sellack (Herefs.) 229 n.1, **307–13**,
  1346–7, 1349
  visitation held at 306–28
    map of route xxii–xxiii
Shelsley (Worcs.) 614
Shelve (Salop) **1281**, 1296
Shobdon (Herefs.) **960–4**
Shrawardine (Salop) **1317–21**
Shrewsbury (Salop) 1288
Siefton (in Culmington) (Salop) 1063
Silvington (Salop) **1004**
Snodhill (in Peterchurch) (Herefs.) 66,
  83, 89
Sollers Hope (Herefs.) **557**
Sparteresmull (in Stanton Lacy)
  (Salop) 994
Spoad (in Clun) (Salop) xxvi, **1214–17**
Stagbatch and Cholstrey (in Leominster)
  (Herefs.) **686**
Stanford Bishop (Herefs.) 639, **663–4**
Stanton Lacy (Salop) **994–7**
  visitation held at 994–7
    map of route xxii–xxiii
Staunton (Glos.) **353–5**, 1351
Staunton-on-Arrow (Herefs.) xxix,
  790–2
Staunton-on-Wye (Herefs.) 9, 69, **123**
  visitation held at 107–34
    map of route xxii–xxiii
Stoke Bliss (Worcs.) **646**
Stoke Edith (Herefs.) **548–9**
  visitation held at 544–9
    map of route xxii–xxiii
Stoke Gifford (Glos.) *see* Harry Stoke
Stoke Lacy (Herefs.) **586–9**, 1356
Stoke Prior (Herefs.) **716–18**
Stoke St Milborough (Salop) **1002**
Stokesay (Salop) xxxviii, **1078–86**
  visitation held at 1078–86
    map of route xxii–xxiii

Stottesdon deanery, omitted from
  visitation xxiv, 1005
Stow (Salop) **1028–31**
Stretford (Herefs.) **674–5**, 712
Stretton Grandison (Herefs.) **585**, 1366
Stretton Sugwas (Herefs.) **111**
Sutton St Michael (Herefs.) **25**
Sutton St Nicholas (Herefs.) **31–2**
Syde (Salop) *see* Ludford

Talgarth (Brecons.) 78
Tarrington (Herefs.) **544–5**
Taynton (Glos.) **458**
Tedstone Delamere (Herefs.) **662**
Tedstone Wafre (Herefs.) **645**
Tenbury (Worcs.) xxiv, 709, 1110
Thornbury (Herefs.) **643**
Tibberton (Glos.) **453–4**
Tidenham and Lancaut
  (Glos.) **365–76**
  visitation held at 365–76
    map of route xxii–xxiii
Titley (Herefs.) **926–7**
Treferanon (in St Weonards) (Herefs.),
  chapel of 213
Tretire (Herefs.) **180**, 311
Tupsley (Herefs.) 453
Turnastone (Herefs.) **41–3**

Ullingswick (Herefs.) xviii, xxxii–xxxiii,
  592–602
Upleadon (Glos.) 475
Upper Sapey *see* Sapey, Upper
Urishay (in Peterchurch) (Herefs.) 65

Vowchurch (Herefs.) **50–8**

Wacton (Herefs.) **641**
Walford (Herefs.) **296–8**
  visitation held at 296–305
    map of route xxii–xxiii
Waterdine (Salop) *see* Llanfair Waterdine
Wellington (Herefs.) **6**, 108
Welsh, place-names beginning with, *see
  under second element*
Wenlock, Much (Salop) xxiv, xxiv n.48,
  1294, 1342, 1359 n.2
  deanery, omitted from
    visitation xxiv–xxv

Wenlock Priory 1181, 1203–7
Wentnor (Salop) xxxiii, **1134–45**
Weobley (Herefs.) xxix, 9, **135–57**, 857,
  911
  visitation held at 135–58
    map of route xxii–xxiii
Westbury (Salop) xxiv, xxiv n.48,
  1294–303, 1324, **1331–3**
  visitation held at 1294–303
    map of route xxii–xxiii
Westbury-on-Severn (Glos.) xxxvii,
  419–45
  visitation held at 407–45
    map of route xxii–xxiii
Westhide (Herefs.) **546–7**
Weston Beggard (Herefs.) xxviii, **35–8**
Weston-under-Penyard (Herefs.) **344**
Whitbourne (Herefs.) xl–xli, **638–9**,
  1338
Whitchurch (Herefs.) **250–4**
Whitney (Herefs.) xl, 220, **810–12**
Wigmore (Herefs.) xviii n.31, xxxii,
  951–9, 1338
  Wigmore Abbey 101, 865, 1048–9,
    1163, 1334, 1363
Willersley (Herefs.) **846**
Winforton (Herefs.) **806–9**
Wistanstow (Salop) xviii n.31, **987–93**
  visitation held at 987–93
    map of route xxii–xxiii
Wolferlow (Herefs.) **647–51**
Woolaston (Glos.) xxxiv, 376, **377–89**
  Reynold of *see personal names index*
Woolaston and Alvington
  visitation held at 377–89
    map of route xxii–xxiii
Worcester, diocese of 614, 808
Wormbridge (Herefs.) 221
Wormsley (Herefs.) xxviii, 7, **158**, 1343
Worthen (Salop) **1282–93**
  visitation held at xxv, 1281–93, 1360
    map of route xxii–xxiii

Yarkhill (Herefs.) **603–13**
Yarpole (Herefs.) **741**
Yarsop (in Yazor) (Herefs.) 132
Yazor (Herefs.) **129–32**

Index of personal names

Abbat, Agnes   749
Absolon (Aspolon), Giles   472, 474
Adam ap Seysyvaunte   1236
Adames
    Alice   800–1
    John   1329
    William   1040
        and his wife Isabel   1037
Aelward, Hik   369
Agnes ap Pye   xxxvi, 67–8
Agyns, Wilkok   297
Alayn *see* Aleyn
Albon, Roger   551
Aldeford, Walter   33
Alesaundre, Richard   1218
Aleyn (Alayn)
    Alice   1054–5
    John   419
    Richard   502
Alrete, John   122
Amney, Thomas   367
Andrew(e), Master Roger, notary
    public   727, 946, 976, 1340, 1363
Andrewes, Thomas   759
Angharad verch Gwilym   888
Appelby, Sir Roger, prior of
    Hereford   545
Arnald, Roger   564
Arnyet, Hugyn   719
Arthur, Julian   423
Arundel, Thomas, archbishop of
    Canterbury   xx–xxi, xxvii
Arundel, earls of *see* Fitzalan

Arwystli, David of   1259
Aspolon *see* Absolon
Asshewyk, Richard, his wife Agnes   581
Asshwalle, Richard   505
Aston, John of   753
Atkys, Thomas   1023
Axebarn, Henry   569

Bach
    Angharad   810
    Eve   1014–15
    Gwilym, his daughter Lleucu   1214
    Gwladus   223
    Lleucu (Clun)   1169
    Lleucu (Welsh Newton), wife of
        David Paty   228
    Llewelyn   1228
Bade, Lorate   473
Badron, Agnes, wife of Reynold
    Taelour   442
Bady, Richard   820
Baelyf *see* Baylyf
Baker
    Adam, his wife Emota   107–8
    Gruffudd   1289
        his servants Philip and
            Dwgys   1283
    Hopkyn   1076
    Joan   382, 390
    John (Eardisley)   836, 844–5
        his daughter Amice   832
        his son Walter   845
        his wife Margery   844–5

Sir John (Hereford)   1338
Julian   809
Lucy   303
Thomas, his wife Joan Rude   443
Bakon, Philip   1061
Baldenhale, Maiota   806
Baldewyn, William   703
Ballard, Joan   302
Balle, Alison   958
Balls, Philipot   562
Baly, Maiota   796
Banastre, Tybota   950
Bannister, Arthur Thomas   xiii, xiv
Bannour, Llewelyn   874
Barbour
   Alice (Colwall)   498
   Alice (Eardisley)   820
   Thomas   701
Baret
   Joan, wife of Richard de Reye   495
   Julian   541
   William   530
Barne
   Isabel   392
   John   412
Baron
   Agnes   1085
   Julian   830
Barton, Ralph   147
Bayly, John   305
Baylyf (Baelyf)
   Isabel   1096
   Jankin, and his wife Amice   843
   Margaret   2
   Thomas   3
   William, his widow Margaret   784
Been, Margaret   15
Beger, John   580
Belmar, Alice   862
Bengrych (Pengrych)
   Meurig   212, 218
   Thomas   218
Benhir, David   1028
Bent, William   1333
Bent(e), Sir John   1137–9
Berde, Jankin   126
Bernard, Alice   1099–100
Berwalle, Walter   165
Berwe, Thomas   332

Besaunde, Cecily   828
Beuchampe, Beton   631
Beveney, Roger   246
Blake, John   20
   his daughter Eve   1201
Blakemon, Maiota   362
Blakney, Richard, his wife Julian   316
Blusy, Isabel ap Wylim, otherwise
   Blusy   69
Boche, Dyddgu   916
Bokynhull, John   736
Bola, Ieuan   933
Boley
   John (Ashperton)   579
   John (Eardisley)   xl, 822
   William   583–4
Bolleston, Eve   1194
Bollynghop, Roger   351
Bolt, John   7
Bolte, Joan   15
Boly, Hopkyn   1032
Bongam Kynyd, y (the bandy-legged
   huntsman)   1198
Bore, Thomas   975
Borl..., James, his servant Joan   1301
Boscher, Walter   940
Botemon, Thomas   248
Boterell (Botterell), Joan, otherwise
   Gwenllian   1052, 1054–5
Bounde, Wilkoc   284
Bour, Sir William   742
Bourderbir, Robin, his widow
   Isabel   1295
Bowedeler, John   1225
Boweton, Nicholas   301
Braban, Thomas   519–22
Bragge, Adam   994
Bragger, William, otherwise
   Thomkys   1165, 1167
Brasyer (Brasyour), John   422, 444
Bredleder, William   1224
Bretchel, Hywel of   1311
Bridgewater (Brugge Water),
   Margaret   979
Brimley
   Gybon   804
   Margaret   912
Brokton, Sir John   991
Brome, Stephen   654

Brompton, Sir Brian   1006
Brook, Sybil de   1276–7
Broun (Brune)
    Alison   xl, 658–9
    Margaret   1069
    William (Hyssington)   1276
    Sir William (Tidenham and
        Lancaut)   372
    Sir William (Westbury)   1294
Brower, David, his wife Helen   700
Broy, Sir Walter   506
Brugemon, John, his wife Alice   551
Brugg, Brother John   373, 1352
Brugge
    Philip   1113
    Walter   657
Brune *see* Broun
Brut
    Alice   527 n.5, 528–33
    Margery   1225 n.2
    Walter   xix, xxxix, xl
Brute, William   351
Bruwer, Margaret   527
Brydd, Alice   864
Bryde, Parnell   283
Brykkon, Robin   98
Bryngwyn, Alice   332
Bryton, Llewelyn   879
Bue *see* Buwe
Bugeyl, Sir John   179
Bulleston, John, his wife Agnes   1094
Bullok, Roger, his wife Cecily   1285
Bunte, Sir Walter   49
Burchull, Roger   7
Burley, Edmund   1294
[Bu]rnell, ___   1301
Burton
    Agnes   152
    Maiota   151
Burych, Jack   351
Buwe (Bue), John   980–1, 983
Bwgys, John, his daughter
    Gwenllian   1111
Bygwth, John, his son Hywel   1119
Bykerton, Roger   568
Bykker, Isabel   550
Byllyng
    Helen   439
    Peter   1178, 1186

his wife Julian   1185, 1187
Byrche, William   179
Bysshop, Philip   1002
Byterlowe (Bytyrlowe), Sir John   236,
    240, 249

Cachere, Jankin   491
Cadwaladr ap John   1254
Cadwgan ap Madog   1118
Caldecote (Caldekot), Richard   162, 167
Caleys, William, his daughter
    Margaret   998
Calwe, Sir William   515
Canterbury, archbishops of *see* Arundel;
    Courtenay; Winchelsey
Cantilupe, Thomas, bishop of
    Hereford   xvii, xviii, xxxviii
Capes, William Wolfe   xii, xiii
Capestre, Margaret   298
Cappe, William   462
Caradoc, John   917
Carles
    Helen   505
    John   413
Carne, Madog   1226
Carpenter
    John   191
    Maud   829
    Thomas   523
    Walter   801
    William   812
Carter
    Sir John   428
    Richard   528
    Sir Richard   1060
Carwet, Llewelyn   987
Carwy, Hugh   514
Cassy *see* Kassy
Catell, Walter   258
Caus, Hikemones of, his daughter
    Sybil   1300
Charlton, Thomas, bishop of
    Hereford   xvii
Chaumbereresmon, Jankin   1032
Chaundler, Agnes   996
Chebenor, Roger   503
Chepestere, Margaret   88
Cher, Roger   601
Cherwynd, Richard   194

Cheylde, Richard 977
Cheyny, Sir Hugh 991
Chiltenham, William 333
Clanvowe, Margaret 850
Clarkston *see* Clerkeston
Cledde, Llewelyn 1211
Clenston, Gwenllian 191
Clerk
    Agnes 760
    Alice 380
    Maiota 1046
    Thomas 533
    William, his wife Eleanor 1096
Clerkes
    Agnes 457
    Hywel 773
    Margaret 417
    Roger, his servant Gruffudd 805
Clerkeston (Clarkston), John 669, 672
Clun, Gwilym of 760
Clyfdon, Alison 400
Clyffe, Sir William 388
Cockes, Hugh, and his wife Isabel 63
Cogh, Ieuan 213
Coke *see* Cook
Cokhull
    Agnes 475
    John 529
Cokton, John 919–20
Coletes, John 619
Colle
    Jankin, and his wife Margaret 826
    Sir Robert 1324
Colle Knafe *see* Kolleknafe
Collebage, Philip 994
Collefaste, William 1229, 1233
Collemon, Thomas, and his wife
    Maud 767
Collyng(e)
    Henry 1026
    Reynold *see* Penymawe
    Richard 1110
Coly
    Hugh 984
    John 984
    Maud 942
    Sybil 1359
Colyer, Stephen 166

Colyn, Agnes 1280
Combe, Agnes, her servant Joan 521
Combley, Sir Richard 1328
Commyn, Sir John 495–6
Compton, John 464
Conyng
    Isabel 387
    Margaret 414
Cook (Coke, Cookes)
    Jack (Llanwarne) 171
    Jack (Monmouth) 276
    Jankin 272
    Nicholas 1272
    Thomas 587
Copener, Jankin 969
Coppe, Agnes 15
Corbet
    Adam 1292
    Thomas, and chantry of St Margaret
        at Caus 1303 n.1
    Thomas, of Lye (Leigh) 1285
Correyour, Thomas 821
Corvyger
    Morys 267
    William 1172
Corvyser, Grug (recte *Cryg* – defective of
    speech, stammering) 266
Cosyn, Sir William 694–5
Cotynton, John 518
Courte, William 351
Courtenay, William, archbishop of
    Canterbury xix–xxi
Coward, Joan 848
Cowley, Isabel de 580
Coykyn, Walter 1158
Cravel
    Jankin 79–80
    John 81
Croce, Harry 480
Croke
    Hugh 1295
    Isabel 1268
    John 372
    William (Tidenham and
        Lancaut) 374
    William (Westbury) 1296
Crokenek, Sir Walter 171
Crommpe, Maiota 516

Crompe, Sir William   xxxv, 693–4

Crowe
  John, his wife Maiota   1176
  Richard   1171

Curteys, John   638

Cuthler, Nicholas   xxxix, 300

Cwtte, Gwilym (recte *Gwilym Cwta* –
    short Gwilym), his son Hywel   1202

Daelour, Einion   1021

Dail, Gwenllian y (Gwenllian of the
    leaves)   1250

Daldrayn, Iorwerth   1053

Danger, Jack   360

Daniel
  Amice   621
  Rose   133

Daunderfeld (Daundevyl), Harry   9,
    148

David ap Einion Dilest   878

David ap Einion Vychan, his daughter
    Eve   1131

David ap Gruffudd Lloyt   1252

David ap Gwrgan, his daughter
    Angharad   1209

David ap Ieuan (Ackley)   1273

David ap Ieuan ap David   1253

David ap Ieuan ap Gwyl   1256

David ap Ieuan ap Iorwerth, and his wife
    Gwenllian   1251

David ap Ieuan ap Llewelyn   1359

David ap Ieuan ap Maredudd   1199

David ap Ieuan ap Philip   1250

David ap Ieuan Bole   1239, 1242

David ap Ieuan Vychan   1246

David ap Iorwerth   863

David ap Jankin   938

David ap Kynwric, Master   1358

David ap Llewelyn   908

David ap Llywarch, his daughter
    Gwenllian Hir   1262

David ap Madoc   1362

David ap Meilyr, his daughter
    Dyddgu   873

Davy, Sir William   350

Davys
  Sir John   91
  Richard   1191

Thomas   514

Walter   1055

William   514

Dawe, John   338

Daykys, Jack   173

Ddewys, Ieuan, his daughter
    Gwenllian   1264

Deen, Jankin, his servant Avice   560

Deheubarth, David
    (Montgomery)   xxix n.67, 1221
  his daughter Maiota
    (Margery)   xxix, 1359
  his wife Rosetta   1233

Dellok, Joan   69, 83, 89

Deny, Joan   457

Denys, Philip   362

Deryn, Agnes   957

Deveros
  Elizabeth   190
  Joan   857

Dewall, Walter   146

Dewe
  Hywel   930
  Llewelyn, his daughter Beton   78
  see also Duy

Dewkes, Isabel   965

Dey, Jankin, and his wife Isabel
    Gose   743

Deyvykes, Agnes   972

Discote, Sir John   722

Dobles
  John   977
  Richard   977

Dodeshull, Richard   666

Dogans
  Agnes   1123
  William   1120

Dolle, Maiota   361

Donn, Florence   427

Donne, Jankin   962

Doppa, Rhys   724

Doule, William   698

Dounwode
  John   151
  William   152

Downe, Agnes   482

Downton, Wilkoc of, and his wife
    Maiota   1062

Druwe
  Jankin 482
  Thomas 351
Dudeston, Thomas 1271
Duffyll, Joan 391
Duglace, John 360
Durandus, William, *Speculum iuris* xvi
Duy
  Alice 363
  Eve 886, 891
  Gwenllian 885
  Isabel 1113–14
  Jowkys, his brother Gruffudd 1111
  Llian 1282
  Madog, his daughter Gweirful 1229
  Rhys (Llanrothal/Garway) 212, 218
  Rhys (Michaelchurch-on-
    Arrow) 905
  see also Dewe
Dyar, Stephen 710
Dyddgu verch Ragor 1018
Dyer, David 290
Dyngyl, David de 706
Dynlas, Einion, his daughter
    Gwenllian 1265

Edgton, Sir William of, his son
    Jankin 1157
Edyth, Margaret 1221
Einion ap David, his daughter
    Dillen 1307
Einion ap Einion ap Adda 1240
Elvel (Elvael, Elvell)
  Davy 10
  Eve (Kentchurch) 204
  Eve (Kilpeck) 185
  John 1194–5
Ely
  Jankin 351
  Sir John 808
  Mark de 363
  Thomas 351
Estham, John 978, 1358
  his wife Christine and his pretended
    wife Agnes 978
Eton, William de, his wife Joan
    Mael 1127
Ever, Thomas 285–6
  his wife Elizabeth 285

Evyote, Maiota 982
Eynones, Thomas, his daughter
    Alice 1177

Falke, Jankin 1119
Fawkener(e)
  Joan 716
  Sir John 427, 436–8
Feld
  Thomas 522
  William de, his daughter Edith 986
Fermour, Gruffudd 1012
Feynsbury (Veynsbury)
  Wilkoc, and his wife Sybil 1313
  William 1311
Fifield, Leslie Frank xii
Fitzalan
  Richard, 3rd earl of Arundel xx
  Richard, 4th earl of Arundel 1026
  see also Arundel
Flesher (Flessewer, Flessher,
    Flesshewer) 790
  Harriot 416
  Llewelyn 708
  Mark 85
  Maud 353
  Nicholas 1290
Flossy, Gwenllian 729
Floxley, Agnes 616
Folyot
  Thomas 399
  Sir Thomas 219
Fourches, Philip 7
Fowyer, Sir John 350
Fox
  Alice 416
  Richard 107
  Thomas le 956
  William 250–1
Frayn, Sir Richard 996–7
Frens(s)h
  Alice 18–19
  Thomas 1086
Frer
  John 977
  Philip 865
Frunde
  Agnes 287
  Harry 392

Margaret the   617
Fryer, John   179
Fryoll *see* Vyell
Fyssher
   Agnes   412
   John   329
   John (Worthen)   1293
Fytheler (Fythler)
   Margaret   752
   Tybota   119

Gadarn, David   723
Gall
   Dyddgu   1210–11
   John   157
Game (Gamme)
   Harry   939
   Llewelyn   1257
   Nicholas   211
Gamon, James   559
Gardenere, William   247
Gatley, Agnes   485
Gaule, John   673
Geffes (Geffys)
   Alice   572
   John (Much Cowarne)   572
   John (Westbury), his son John and his
      servant Isabel   1297
Gelyf, William   245
Geneppyn, Ifor   915
Gergeamide, Joan   272
Gethin, David   1117
Geynor, Henry, his wife Helen   441
Gilbert (Gylbert)
   John, bishop of Hereford   xvii
   Sir John   1222
   Lleucu   1117
Gilleson, John   986
Glace (Glase), David   757
Glasbury
   Hugyn   168
   Thomas, his wife Agnes   545
Glase *see* Glace
Gledwyn, Sir Richard   1266
Gloucester, Julian of   562
Gloucester, abbot of   1345, 1365
Glover(e)
   Cecily   16
   Robert   710

Goch *see* Gogh
Godefrey, Richard, and his wife
   Felise   609
Godemon, Davy, his daughter Joan   317
Godewot(e), William   1141–3
Godrych, Julian   853
Godych
   Jankin   14
   Sir Walter   696
Godyng, Walter   655
Gogh (Goch)
   Angharad   722
   David   254
   Gwenllian   1168
   Ieuan   339
   Iorwerth   791, 927
   John   977
   Jowkys   1262
   Maredudd, his daughter
      Gwenllian   1208
   Richard   41–2, 73
   Roger   877
   Tangwystl   1044
Golthull, Maiota   542–3
Gomme, John   862
Gomond
   John   123
   Thomas   804
Gonion, Isabel, her servant Julian   1312
Gorde, John   31
Gornyoc, Gwenllian (recte *Gwenllian
   Gorniog* – frowning Gwenllian)   1270
Gorpa, Sir Roger   180
Gosbrok, Joan   434
Gose, Isabel, wife of Jankin Dey   743
Goygyn, Hywel   1227
Grange, William   337
Grasley, Sir John   694
Graunte, Walter   131
Grey, Meyl de   662
Grobbe, Walter   818
Gronno, Jack   1022
Gronwe, Llewelyn   810
Gruffudd, John, his wife Alison
   Skynner   1219–20
Gruffudd ap David   1362
Gruffudd ap Einion ap Tudur   1265
Gruffudd ap Gwilym (Chirbury)   1338
Gruffudd ap Gwilym (Stow)   1028

Gruffudd ap Ieuan ap Mylly   732
Gruffudd ap Ieuan Lloyt   1196
Gruffudd ap Iorwerth (Bishops
    Castle)   1123
Gruffudd ap Iorwerth (Churchstoke), his
    daughter Maruret   1260
Gruffudd ap Jonas, his daughter
    Helen   1360
Gruffudd ap Llewelyn Whith (?*Chwith*,
    left-handed)   892
Gruffudd ap Madog   76
Gruffudd ap Rhys   886, 891
Gruffudd ap Tudur   1311
Gruffudd Lloyt ap Llewelyn
    Doppa   885
Grym, Master Philip   1340
Gryn (Gryne)
    Alice   523
    Master John   1367
    Nicholas   990
    Roger oth'   573
    William   928
Gurney, Henry   191
Gweirful verch Lwgyr y Coet (recte *Llwgr
    y Coed* – daughter of the Coward of
    the Woods)   874
Gwenllian verch Hoesgyn   76
Gwenllian verch Iorwerth   1028
Gwillm ap Iorwerth ap Einion   1312
Gwilym ap Cadwgan Lloyt   1216
Gwilym ap David ap Gruffudd   1188
Gwilym ap Goronwy ap Henry   1241
Gwilym ap Gruffudd, his daughter
    Margaret   875
Gwilym ap Hywel   887
Gwilym ap Ieuan ap Gwilym   1130
Gwilym ap Ieuan Hensor   1131
Gwilym ap Madog   1362
Gwilym ap Philip   902
Gwtta, Hywel   186
Gwyn, Ieuan   870
Gwyned, Einion   1125
Gwynnyon, David   1007
Gyffe, David   58
Gylbert *see* Gilbert
Gylle, Thomas, and his wife Joan   761

Hadyrley, Sir Walter   352
Hair, Paul   xiv

Haket, Alice, and her sister Isot   614
Halle, John   1340
Hamond(e), Richard   xxxvi, 67
Hankokes
    Philip   244
    William, his daughter Helen   1157
Hannes, Isabel   781
Han(n)ys
    John, his wife Mulsaunde   527
    Sybil   980
Harald, Sir John   414
Hardyng, Joan   250
Harper(e)
    Llewelyn   726
    William   967
Harrys, Isabel   1027
Haughmond, abbot of   1329
Haunte, Avice   547
Haunton, Thomas, and his wife
    Isabel   687
Hawekyn, John   418
Hawys, Alice   271
Hay
    Jankin   1163
    Joan de la   808
    Roger de la   1340
Haydon, John   361
Hayn, William   370
Hayward, John   588
Heilin
    Sir Philip   153
    Thomas, and his wife Isot   946
Heine, Ieuan   1189
Held, Cecily   105
Hely, Margaret   248
Hensor, William, his daughter
    Muriel   791
Herdemo(u)n, Robert, his daughter
    Sybil   xxix, 1359
Herdewykes (Herdwyk)
    Janyn, his widow Maud   990
    William   1108
Here, Maud   913
Hereford
    bishops of *see* Cantilupe; Charlton;
        Gilbert; Orleton; Swinfield;
        Trefnant; Trillek
    canons of *see* Hoor(e)
    deans of *see* Prophet

priors of *see* Appelby
Hergest
    Julian 533
    Rhys, and his wife Eve 916
Hert(e)
    John 461
    Margaret 663
    Sir William 410
Heryng, Walter 11
Hetey, John 279
Heth, Sir William 721
Heyde, Thomas 305
Hik(k)okes
    John (Bishops Castle), his widow
        Joan 1116
    John (Montgomery), his son
        William 1218
    Roger, his wife Joan 425
Hir (Hyr)
    David 1243
    Eve 1312
    Gruffudd 913
    Gwenllian 1262
    Ieuan (Clifford), his daughter
        Lleucu 859
    Ieuan (Clun), his daughter
        Gweirful 1196
    John (Dorstone) 90
    John (Stokesay) xxxviii, 1084
Hoby
    Joan 812
    Rhys 731
Hobys, Margaret 301
Hoke, Isabel 1042
Holder, Agnes 20
Holgot, Thomas, his servant Joan 759
Holle, Margaret 735
Holom, William 857
Home, Cecily oth' 31
Homper, Andrew 572
Hoor(e)
    John 494, 502
    Master Roger, canon of
        Hereford 503, 1367
Hope, Walter 439, 441
Hoper(e)
    David 798
    Isabel 919
    Margaret 798

Hopkyns
    Sir John 800
    Thomas 958
Hopley, John 854
Horde
    Joan 1058
    Richard 1288
Horworth, Sir William 541
Hosches
    Nicholas (Brampton Bryan) 1009
    Nicholas (Pauntley) 460
Hotte, Helen 426
Howdy, Maiota 777
Howel
    Annot xxxi–xxxii, 386
    Joan 930
    John 1231
Huges (Huggys)
    John 341
    Richard 26–8
        his wife Agnes 28
Hull (Hulle, Hwlle)
    Hugyn 14
    Jack at 480
    Joan 786
    John (Cradley) 620
    John (Kilpeck) 184
    Maiota, wife of Nicholas
        Robert 763
    Robin oth' 424
    Symond oth' 421
    Thomas 532
    William 763
Hunte
    Agnes, wife of John Smyth 220
    Margaret (Pontesbury) 1324
    Margaret (Turnastone) 41
    William 911
Huntelowe, Robert 105
Hurste, Jankin 1162
Huwet, Jankin 1311
Hwkesmon, Hik 303
Hwlle *see* Hull
Hyr *see* Hir
Hywel ap David ap Gwyn 1241
Hywel ap David ap Hywel 1260
Hywel ap Einion, his daughter
    Angharad 1249
Hywel ap Eudos 1210

Hywel ap Gruffudd ap Adda 1247
Hywel ap Gwilym ap Cadwgan 896
Hywel ap Ieuan ap David 895
Hywel ap John 202
Hywel ap y Penlloyt (?*ap y penllwyd* – son
of the grey-haired one) 873

Ieuan, Rhys 120
Ieuan ap David, his daughter
Lucy 1317, 1319
Ieuan ap David ap Adda 1132
Ieuan ap David ap Iorwerth 1235
Ieuan ap David ap Madog 1246
Ieuan ap David Duy 1128
Ieuan ap Einion (Brilley) 884
Ieuan ap Einion (Knighton) 934, 1020
Ieuan ap Griffri, his daughter
Dyddgu 1304
Ieuan ap Gwyn
his daughter Eve 74
his daughter Gwenllian 77
Ieuan ap Hilder, his daughter
Gwenllian 1279
Ieuan ap Hywel 1279
Ieuan ap Ieuan ap David ap Gruffudd,
and his wife Gwladus 1305
Ieuan ap Ieuan Ddewis 1248
Ieuan ap Ifor, his daughter Nest 1045
Ieuan ap Iorwerth ap Einion 1212
Ieuan ap Llewelyn Veddik (recte *Feddyg* –
the doctor) 890
Ieuan ap Madog, his daughter
Gwenllian 1278
Ieuan ap Madog Coch, his daughter
Eve 1021
Ieuan ap Philip (Cusop) 871
Ieuan ap Philip (Monmouth) 260
Ieuan ap Philip (Orcop), his daughter
Margaret 178
Ieuan ap Philip ap Meurig 1245, 1264
Ieuan ap Philip Derroc 876
Ifor, Nest 1045
Inchemerssh, Alice Vysaicher, otherwise
Inchemerssh, wife of Thomas
London 756, 769–70, 772
Iorwerth ap Heilyn ap David, and his
wife Dyddgu 1304
Iorwerth ap Rhys 894, 907
Ireland, Godive of 781

Irych, Julian 428
Isabel ap Wylim, otherwise Blusy 69
Isabel verch Maredudd, otherwise Isabel
Towe 861

Jack ap Roger, his daughter Alice 75
Jak, Michael 179
Jakkes
Philip 1115–16
Roger, his daughter Jonet 1128
Jankin ap Gwilym 274
Jankin ap Ieuan, otherwise Wlan (?*Wlân*
– wool) 316
Jankin ap Ieuan ap Llewelyn 74–5
Jankin ap Ieuan ap Madog 1282
Janyn ap y Toppa, and his wife
Maud 1254
Jerwerth, Thomas, his wife Perwar 211
Jevanes, Dynys 246
Jewe
Walter 823
William 831
Joan ap Crech (recte *Crych* – the wrinkled
one) 1007
Joan ap Rhicer 928
Johenes, Roger 399
John, Jankin 264
John ap Adam, Sir 172
John ap Gwilym ap Rhys, Sir 182–3,
187
John ap Ieuan ap Llewelyn,
Brother 1208
John ap Ifor 883
John ap Robin Jekes 861
John ap Thomas 1236–8
John ap Tommi (Tommy) xxxvi, 67–8
Jones
Agnes 401
William, his daughter Sybil 1296
Jonson, Sir John 1318
Jurles
Maud 792
William 792
Justyn, Thomas 269
Jutte, John, his wife Maiota 545
Juwes
John 1127
Thomas 1163
Juweson, Robert 1339

Kady, Philip 1244
Kadyle, Walter, and his wife Isabel 420
Kassy (Cassy), Walter, his wife
    Joan 435–6, 440
Kay, Walter 1339
Kedewyn, Lleucu 725
Kedy, Lleucu 41
Keissiat Gwyll..., y (recte *y Ceisiad* – the
    serjeant of the peace or bailiff), his
    son Maredudd 1214
Kemsey, William 750
Kete, William 527
Kevyn, Ieuan 864
Knethur, Agnes 816
Knolle, Jankin 914
Knollyn, Erdudful 1053
Knyght, John 280
    his servant Joan 281
    his son Jankin 281
Knyghton, Sir John 1099–100
Knyke, Jankin 976
Kolleknafe (Colle Knafe, Kolknafe)
    Ansely, his wife Lucy 438
    Nicholas, his wife Alice
        Tyburton 432, 437
Kuwe, John, and his wife Alice 766
Kycheynokes, Hywel, and his wife
    Gwenllian 887
Kyde
    Gwenllian 1115
    William 1071
Kydes, Robert, his wife Felise 247
Kyfflyhode, Ieuan 14
Kynge, John 629
Kynley, Richard 674
Kyvernowe, William 1163
Kyvo, John 613

Lake
    John (Diddlebury), his wife
        Julian 1073
    John (Stanton Lacy) 995
        his wife Julian 994
Langeston, Nicholas 328
Lather
    Isot 837
    Julian 831
Laurens
    Geoffrey 547

Jack 288
    William 1074
Lawen, Lleucu 723
Lawton, Jankin of Wales of 749
Lea, Gruffudd of, and his wife
    Joan 1121
Ledder, John 770
Leduart, Maiota 182
Leper
    John, his daughter Emota 1005
    William 11
Leye, John, his daughter Joan 1075
Leyntwardyn
    Walter 960–1
    William 960–1
Leythe, Maud 914
Lippa (Lyppa)
    Helen 933
    Master Philip 1340
Llandaff, bishop of 350
Llanddewy, Lleucu 1033
Llanthony, prior of 1161
Llewelyn ap Cadwgan 1240–1, 1243
Llewelyn ap Goronwy, his daughter
    Angharad 938
Llewelyn ap Hywel 1255
Llewelyn ap Ieuan 1019
Llewelyn ap Ieuan ap Madog 223
Llewelyn ap Madog 1362
Lloydach, David 1017
Lloyt
    David, his wife Joan 328
    Eve 956
    Sir John 1249
    Llewelyn, his daughter
        Gwenllian 1248
    Margaret 194
    William 1010
Loffe, Edith 456
London, Thomas, his wife
    Alice Vysaicher otherwise
    Inchemerssh 756, 769–70, 772
Longe
    John 368
    Richard, his daughter Isot 1158
Longeford, Richard, his servant
    Tangwystl 520
Longhop, Sir Geoffrey 367
Lotmon, Annot 383

Lowe
John de 1192
William de 1068
Lude, Sir William 1339
Luger, John, and his wife Maud 764
Lulewale (Lullewal)
Jankin 856
Simon 912
Lunteley
Hugh 149
Richard 146
Lupeson, John 786
Lurke, Philip 853
Lybykes, John 288
Lyche
Agnes 1072
Margery 563
Lye, Richard 1286
Lyngen, Joan 955
Lynne, ___ 1298
Lyppa *see* Lippa

Mab Pwl, y 1169
his daughter Gwenllian Goch 1168
Madog ap Cadwgan 1230
Madog ap David 1235, 1237–9
Madog ap Rhiryd 1317
Madog ap y Cogh Hir (recte *ap y Coch Hir* – son of the tall redhead) 1270
Madog Wehyd (recte *Wehydd* – the weaver) 1263
Madok, Maiota 1086
Madokes, Roger, his widow Margaret 1286
Mael, Joan, wife of William de Eton 1127
Maen, Edmund, and his servant Isabel 785
Malmeshull, Jankin 806
Malot, Richard 417
Malverne, Master John, Warden of St Katherine's Hospital, Ledbury 510–13, 1353
Malyar, John 1040
March, earl of *see* Mortimer
Mardeston, Isabel 582, 624
Maredudd ap Einion of Lea 1124
Marlowe, Richard, his servant Connar 1094

Martyn
Ieuan 328
John, his wife Margaret 429
Mascald
Roger 754–6
William 707
Mason
Adam, his daughter Christine 978
Jankin 289
Joan 405
Thomas 405
Mathewe, Sir John 87
Matys
Davy 12
Richard 992
Maunce, John, escheator of Herefordshire xxvi, 114
Maune (Mawne)
Hugyn 716
William de 747
Maurice ap Ieuan ap Iorwerth, Sir 253
Mawddwy, lord of *see* Pole, John de la
Mawdelen, Sir John 844
Mawne *see* Maune
Mayard, Alice 849
Maylard, William 1072
Mayos, Agnes called 518
Mede, Sir Nicholas 350
Medewe (Medw)
Roger, his wife Margery de Medewe 981
William de 799
Merssh, William 613
Merssher, Maiota 773
Mersshton
Alice, her daughter Joan 1076
William 1069
Meuric, Wilkoc, and his son John 1032
Meurig ap Einion 880
Meurig ap Gwilym 179
Meurig ap Meurig Vychan 1129, 1131
Moel
Eve 897
Grug (name implying a bald or barren man (*moel*) who stammers (*cryg*)) 1034
Mongomery *see* Montgomery
Monkes, Sir Roger 292
Monnyn(g)

Gwenllian 732
John 493, 1338
Thomas 497
Montayn, William, and his wife
Isabel 375
Montgomery (Momgomery,
Mongomery)
John (Leominster) 701
John (Montgomery) 1218–19
Sir John (Lydbury North) 1159
Sir Philip 1307
Monyworth, Sir Reynold 507
Moor (More)
Agnes (Cradley) 618 n.2, 619
John 453
Julian 856
Philipot oth' 283
William, his wife Agnes de
More 771
Morekoce, Henry 447–52
Mortimer, Roger, 4th earl of
March xviii
Morys, Richard, and his wife
Agnes 353
Morys ap Ifor 177
Mouse, Thomas, and his wife
Maiota 757
Moyl, Sir Robert 1338
Moyses, Richard 517
Mulle
Nicholas oth' 531
William de 783
Mulward
Amice 1320
Joan 85
Philipot 859
Walter 52
Munton, John 792
Mury, Sir Roger 406
Murydon, Agnes 1195
Mychel
Philip 351
Thomas 349
Mydewode, Joan 638
Mylde, John 1302

Naylard, Agnes 1068
Neel, Isabel 527
Nessh, Thomas 1311

Nest verch Ieuan 861
Neubry, William 34
Neweport, Master Thomas 1341–2
Newton (Neweton)
Roger de (Brampton Bryan) 1010–
11, 1013
Roger de (Lower Down), his son
Thomas 1158
Walter 929
Nichols (Nychol)
Jack 348
Joan 94
John 99
Noes (Noys), Richard 926, 945
Noke
master of, his servant Lucy 794
Robin oth', his daughter
Margaret 183
Norshe, Lucy 968–9
North Forlong, Wilkoc 1035
Northyn, Margaret 29
Norton
Harry 351
Jankin 351
Norys
Agnes 290
John de, his wife Sybil 133
Note, Constance 1023
Noys *see* Noes
Nychol *see* Nichols
Nynde, Sir William at 431

Okel, Wate of 351
Oldeacre, Margaret 865
Ondys
Isabel, wife of John Strawe 998
Katherine 154
Sir Walter 847
Oneway, Isabel 739
Onwyn, Sybil 1081
Onybury, John 957
Orchard
Deyota of the 656
Sir Thomas 402
Orcop, Alison of 976
Orleton
Adam, Bishop of Hereford xxxi
Hugh 965
Ornel, Jankin 271

Osbarn, Thomas, and his wife
    Alice 765
Oulyth (Wlyth), Margery (Maiota) 474
Owain ap Gruffudd 1109
Owein, Wilkok 311

Parker, Peter, his servant Jankin 950
Parkes, John 1200
Parlour, Geoffrey 500
Parnell, Philip 86
Partrich(e)
    Hugh, his wife Joan 1094
    Thomas, his servant Agnes 90
Pastay, Sir Richard 694
Pathere, John 542
Paty
    David, and his wife Lleucu Bach 228
    Jankin 975
    John, his son William 974
    Maiota 497
Patys, Joan 1009
Paulyn, Stephen 532
Peer
    Sir John 95
    Sir Richard 350
Pehenne, Malli 1312
Pekke, Thomas 1366 n.2
Pekoke, Richard 628
Pengrych *see* Bengrych
Pengule (Penngul)
    Jankin 1085
    Richard, his daughter Julian 1083
Penke, John 758
Penngul *see* Pengule
Pennson, Walter 739–40
Peny
    Amice 1230–1
    Sir William 5
Penymawe
    Joan 1092
    Sir Reynold 1092
    Reynold, otherwise Collynge 1052
Per, Jankin 748
Perkys, Alice 966
Philcyn, Mab 1168
Phileppes (Phylippes)
    Cecily 1162
    Jankin 971
    John 803

Philip ap Llewelyn
    (Michaelchurch-on-Arrow) 903
Philip ap Llewelyn (Orcop) 178
Philip Whith ap Llewelyn ap Philip
    (possibly for *Chwith* – left-handed),
    and his wife Gwladus 1215
Phippe (Phyppes)
    John, his son William 1174
    William, his son Philip 1277
Phylippes *see* Phileppes
Phyppes *see* Phippe
Pluntyng, Richard 18
Pola, Helen de (Helen atte Yate), wife of
    John atte Yate 431
Pole
    Sir John 35–8
    John de la (lord of Mawddwy) 1312
Poleyn, David 630
Polley, William 1075
Pollyrbache, John xl
Pompe, Alison 569
Porslowe, Sir John 1005
Porssell, Hawise 1291
Portemon, Sybil 555
Postarn, Margaret 992
Prat, Thomas 88
Prestebury, Sir John 430
Preston, Isabel 12–13
Prior, Alice 274
Prophet, Master John, dean of
    Hereford xix, xxxv, 1338, 1354,
    1357
Prophete, Thomas, and his servant
    Maiota 278
Prustes, Isabel xl–xli
Prykes, Sir Richard 32
Pryll, Thomas 122
Prys, Master Robert 514, 516
Pullesdon, Alexander 347
Puton, Margaret 1006
Putte, Stephen de, his wife Agnes 545
Pye, Agnes (Agnes ap) xxxvi, 67–8
Pyer(e)s
    Thomas, and his servant
        Maiota 561
    William 984
Pygot, Peter 1310
Pylvyche, Thomas, and his wife
    Amice 768

Pyper, Margery 157
Pyschard, Agnes 131
Pyse, Hywel 1320
Pytte, William 550

Ragedon, Isabel 974
Raglyn, Robin 381
Ragor, Hywel 1197
Raker, John 378
Reyder
 Jankin the, and his wife Maiota 944
 Maiota 559
Reye, Richard de, and his wife Joan
  Baret 495
Reynald
 David, his servant Ieuan 957
 Sir Roger 993
 Thomas 1095
Rhayader
 Geoffrey of 745
 Lleucu of 745
Rhiryd ap Ieuan Gogh 1360–1
Rhiston, William of, his daughter
  Maiota 1223
Rhys, Margaret 334
Rhys ap Hywel 888
Richard ap Hywel 875
Richerdes, Walter, his wife Joan 568
Robert
 Nicholas, and his wife Maiota
  Hwlle 763
 William 351
Robyn (Robynes, Robyns)
 Agnes xxxvi, 67
 Cecily 430
 John (Bishops Castle) 1107
 John (Llanwarne) 173, 1107
 John (Monmouth), his daughter
  Lucy 259
 Richard 425–6
 Thomas 243
 Sir Walter 780
Roger ap Gwallter, and his wife
  Llywelyth 893
Roger ap Gwatkyn 205
Roger ap Ieuan ap Llewelyn xxix, 1359
Rogeres, Philip 1147
Roke, Sir Robert 579, 581, 583

Rolffe
 Walter 568
 William 351
Rowton, Roger 1081–2
Rude
 Jankin 391
 Joan, wife of Thomas Baker 443
Rutherford, Margaret *see* Whittick
Rwth, Wilim 1083
Rydemarley, John 119
Rype, Roger 371
Ryve, Philipot 400

Saer
 Gruffudd 1274
 Ieuan 943
 John 1222, 1359
 Madog 1309
St Asaph, bishops of xxxviii
Salw, Ieuan 937
Sares, John, and his wife Alice 661
Sarney, Joan 352
Saundrys, William 155–6
Saweterer, Roger 382
Sawyer, Gruffudd, and his wife
  Maiota 306
Says
 Dyddgu 95
 Gruffudd 725
 Hywel xl, 811
 John 1338
Schappemon, Jankin 1114
Schappester, Eve 1017
Schelle, Richard 549
Schepmon, Alison 1038
Schep(p)ert
 Agnes 1293
 Gruffudd 1330
 Joan 224
 John (Ledbury), his wife Maiota 519
 John (Pembridge) 793
 Maiota 1002
 Margaret 1093, 1097
 Richard 702
 Robert 219
 Stephen 372
 William (Chirbury), his daughter
  Amice 1271
 William (Lydney) 393

Scheropser, John, his wife Maiota   545,
      550
Scherosbury, John   921
Schippe, Sir John   1042
Schorn
      Sir John   345
      William   335
Schorthose, Margaret   917
Schyryton, Ieuan   323
Scote
      Agnes   15
      Isabel   46
      Richard   265
      Robert   94
Screchere, William   802
Sholdewyk, John   1
Skylle, Sir John   782
Skynner
      Alison, wife of John
            Gruffudd   1219–20
      Richard   263
Slefmaker, Ieuan   141
Smyth
      Alice   516
      David, and his wife Gwenllian   252
      Edward, his wife Alice   133
      Hugyn   985
      Isabel   297
      Jakes, his wife Agnes   424
      Jankin   1112
      Joan (Staunton-on-Wye)   123
      Joan (Stoke Prior)   717
      John (Dorstone), and his wife
            Tibota   91
      John (Garway), and his wife Agnes
            Hunte   220
      Sir John (Goodrich)   237–9
      Sir John (Ledbury)   525
      Margaret   338
      Peter, his servant Jankin   224
      Richard, his servant John   19
      Roger, his wife Joan   499–500
      Thomas (Bredwardine)   104
      Thomas (Ross-on-Wye)   336
      Thomas (Staunton)   354
      Walter   999
      William   976
Snede
      Sir John   780–1

      William, his widow Joan   782
Snowe, William   794
Solers, Roger   485, 489
Somerton, Sir John   848
Somon, Brother   71
Soweter, Geoffrey   1289
Specerer, Joan   834
Spermon
      Alice   1272, 1290
      Margaret   1269
Speyser, Walter   548
Spilspekes, John   149
Spyney, Wilkoc   1040
Stafford, Alice   753
Stake, Joan   1089
Staltagh, Roger, his wife Joan   1160–1
Stalworth, Alice   608–9
Stanford, Thomas   663
Stanway
      Richard   955–6
      William   700
Staunton, William   256
Sterr, Sir Richard   xxxiv, 569, 614–15
Stodeherte, Vincent   762
Stokke, Richard   xxxiv, 483
Stone, Sir John   709
Strange
      Helen   16
      Robin   14
Stratedford, Hywel   796
Strawe, John, and his wife Isabel
            Ondys   998
Streton (Stretton)
      Richard   1268
      Roger   443
Sturr, Sir Thomas   1323
Stury, William   966
Style, Cecily de   496
Stywart, John   381
Swayn (Sweyn)
      Emota   967
      John   1101
Sweynshull, William   282
Swinderby, William   xix, xxxix–xl, xli
Swinfield, Richard, bishop of
            Hereford   xvii–xviii, xxiv–xxv
Swone
      Alice   628
      Gylot   799

Symondes
  Harry   555
  Thomas   5
Syre, Alice   833

Taelour (Teylor)
  Agnes   34
  Alice   697
  Cecily (Foy)   323
  Cecily (Mordiford)   552
  David (Clungunford)   1024
  David (Hyssington)   1278
  Geoffrey   1033
  Gruffudd   1282 n.1, 1284
  Harry   149 n.3
  Hugh, his daughter Agnes   335–6
  Ieuan (Kinnersley)   850
  Ieuan (Knighton), his daughter
      Gwenllian   1019
  Ieuan (Presteigne)   942
  Jankin (Culmington)   1065
  Jankin (Much Dewchurch)   195
  Jankin (Stoke Prior)   717
  John (Bishops Frome)   631
  John (Eaton)   720
  John (Goodrich), his wife Joan   233
  John (Leominster)   705
  John (Weobley)   150
  Lewis (Much Cowarne)   575
  Lewis (Much Dewchurch), his wife
      Jonet   195
  Lewis (Presteigne)   941
  Maredudd   1209
  Margaret   306
  Matthew   1061
  Reynold (Westbury-on-Severn), his
      wife Agnes Badron   442
  Reynold (Winforton)   807
  Richard   1166
  Thomas (Bishops Castle), his
      daughter Maud   1120
  Thomas (Monmouth)   275
  Thomas (Wistanstow), his daughter
      Isot   991
  William, his daughter Maiota   306
Talbot(e)
  Angharad ('the lady of
      Corfham')   1074
  Ela   393

Tanner(e)
  Richard, and his son John   929
  Tybota, her servant Sybil   270
Tasger, Jankin   1059
Tasgor, Ieuan   1070
Tattw, Richard   475
Teer, William   351
Teylor *see* Taelour
Thomas
  Ieuan   213
  Maud   277
Thomas ap Iorwerth   77–8
Thomkyns
  Isabel   190
  James   608–9
  William (Goodrich)   242
  William (Shobdon)   963
Thomkys, William *see* Bragger
Thony, Margery   970
Thorpe, William   xl
Thresser
  Davy   834
  Reynold   1025
Toky, Thomas   454
Toppe, Maiota   1165
Torel, Ralph   2
Torr, Alice   49
Tottebury, William, his wife Joan   458
Towe, Isabel, otherwise Isabel verch
      Maredudd   861
Towne, William   704
Trahaearn ap Ieuan Whith (possibly for
      Chwith – left-handed)   334
Tranter, Margaret   1330
Trefnant, John, bishop of Hereford
      as bishop   xviii–xxi, xxv–xxvi
          and Welsh language   xxxviii
          register of Bishop Trefnant   xii,
              xviii, xix, xxix, xxxv
Tresor, John   268
Trillek, John, bishop of Hereford   xviii,
      350
Trosse, William, and his wife
      Maiota   918
Truran, Margaret   xiv
Tryg(e)
  Agnes   337
  Rose   16
Tudrekes, Alison   517

Turnour
    David   46
    Nicholas   744
    Philipot   922
    Robert   639
    William   51
Twycher(e)
    Harry   14
    Joan   15
Tyburton, Alice, wife of Nicholas
        Kolleknafe (Colle Knafe)   432, 437
Tylar (Tyler)
    Joan   525
    John (Holme Lacy), his wife
        Isabel   167
    John (Stretford)   712
    Maiota   1011–12
    Walter   287
Tymberlak, John   166
Tymmys, Sir Robert   809
Tynker, Sir William   127, 130

Uchdrete (Uchdrute), Isot   926, 945
Underwode, Thomas   298
Uton, Jankin   458

Vachan
    Roger   103
    Wilkoc   828
Vadyr, Davy   259
Valedewe, Richard   711
Vammeth, y (recte *y Famaeth* – the
        wet-nurse or foster-mother), her
        daughter Eve   721
Vardd, Philip (recte *Fardd* – the poet)   45
Vawr, David   1014–15
Velinyd, Ieuan (recte *Felinydd* – the
        miller)   1258
Veynsbury *see* Feynsbury
Veyr, Cecily   172
Vicarys, William   1038
Vychan, David   924
Vyell (Fryoll, Vyel), William, his wife
        Isabel   422, 444
Vysaichere (Vysaicher, Vyseichere)
    Alice, otherwise Inchemerssh, wife of
        Thomas London   756, 769–70,
    772

John   755
    his wife Agnes   754–5

Wade
    Helen   333
    Jankin, and his servant Edith   273
    John, his servant Joan   275
    William   1142–3
        his wife Cecily   1142
Wadyns
    Alice   16
    Jankin   14
    William, his wife Joan   16
Waethe, George   1285
Wales
    Gwrwared of   302
    Isabel of   xxxviii, 1065
    Jankin of   749
    Maud of   10
Walissh (Walishe)
    Agnes (Pembridge)   797
    Agnes (Shobdon)   962
    Jack   968
    Joan   795
    John   573–4
    Margaret   639
    Walter   96
    William   108
Walis(s)hmon
    Meurig   846
    Reynold   1163
Walker
    —— 23
    Hayn, his servant Lucy   618
    Joan   378
    Malkyn the   750
    Margery   758
    Philipot   751
    Wilkoc (Kingsland)   769, 771
    Wilkoc, son of Hayn (Cradley)   618
    William, and his wife Joan   924
Walkot, William   1155
Walle, Hugyn oth'   225
Walter, Agnes   848
Walton, Jankin   727
Warde, Jonet   1224
Wardrop, Walter
    his son Andrew   829

his son John   830
his son Roger   819
Waren, Isabel   xxxiv, 483
Wasbe, John, his wife Agnes   545
Wasmair
   Dyddgu   45
   Lucy   251
Watcok, Maiota   238
Water, Margaret Brugge   979
Watkyn(s)
   Jack   351
   Walter   979
   William (Blaisdon), his wife
      Elizabeth   433
   Sir William   212, 218
Waty, Gruffudd   179
Watys
   John (Burghill)   8
   John (Burrington)   1041
   Maiota   84
Webbe
   Adam   730
   Cadwgan   203
   David   185
   Felise   662
   Gwenllian   1022
   Ieuan   204
   Jack   729
   Jankin (Clun)   1193
   Jankin (Shrawardine)   1321
   John   1321
   Julian   406
   Miles   833
   Nicholas   1018
   William (Clunbury)   1175
   William (Montgomery)   1223
Weheddes, Gwenllian   1193
Wele, Christine   480
Wenlock, prior of   1181
Went
   John (Monmouth)   270
   Master John, notary public   1158,
      1367
   Philip   795
Wer, Robert de   744
Werkemon
   David   82
   Einion   746

West(e)
   William (Dorstone)   83–4
   William (Peterchurch)   69
Westhop, Sir William   1089, 1097
Wethy, William   401
Weyndehull, Philip de   923
Whittick, Margaret, née
    Rutherford   xiv
Whylar, Master Richard   1357
Whytebrede, Sir Thomas   697
Wigmore, abbot of   1048–9, 1163
Wilkok (Wilkokes, Wylkok)
   Alice   220
   Roger   1163
Wille (Willes, Wylles)
   David (Bishops Castle)   1122
   David (Pencoyd)   319–20
    his son Hugh   320
   Maiota   629
William ap Roger   96
Wilson
   Maiota   168
   Richard   845
Winchelsey, Robert, archbishop of
   Canterbury   694 n.2
Wlyth *see* Oulyth
Wodeman, Jack   376
Wodemon, Walter   423
Wodewalle, Roger   1366 n.2
Wodeward
   Roger   1043–4
    his wife Alice   1043
   Walter   1058
Wolfe, Clemence   16
Woolaston, Master Reynold of   xviii,
   xxiv, 593, 612
Wotton, William (Wilkoc)   776–7
Wych, Alice   33
Wyclif, John, followers of   xxxix–xli
Wyggemor, Joan   418
Wykes
   Jankin   970
   Roger   972
Wylde, William   560
Wylkes, Joan   1333
Wylkok *see* Wilkok
Wylkyns, Roger   699
Wyllemote, Margaret   1323

Wyne, Hywel   889
Wynnyng, Robert   454
Wynsbury, Jankin   1267
Wyrall, Alice   783
Wysbage, Nicholas   387
Wyse, Thomas   701, 711
Wyston, Sybil   8

Yale, Sir John   1306
Yarsop, Gylym of   132
Yate, John atte, his wife Helen de Pola
    (Helen atte Yate)   431

Yeton, Brother John   1094
Yngeson, Agnes   971
Yong
    Isabel   666
    John   494 n.5, 501
    Maiota   91
    Thomas   1076
Yoyldehalle, Joan   620
Yyfker
    Joan   51
    Sybil   87

Index of subjects

Notes: Roman numerals refer to pages in the Introduction. The text is indexed by item number; references to notes there are to the translation.

accusers (*accusatores*)   xxxi, xxxii, 52, 122,
   297, 332, 352, 405, 410, 545
adultery *see* sexual immorality
altars *see* churches
annulment *see* marriage
antiphonals *see* liturgical books
arbitrated settlements, Eardisley   xxx,
   1340
archdeacons, visitations   xv, xxxiii

'baggerts crafte' *see* begging
bailiffs *see* occupations
bakers *see* occupations
banns
   maliciously challenged to extort
      money   1028
   see also marriage, clandestine
baptism
   chaplain baptizes his own illegitimate
      child   1177
   not performed or done
      incorrectly   xxxiv, 62, 536, 821,
      869, 1145, 1172
   see also fonts
beating   xxix–xxx, 104, 152, 270, 361,
   416, 527, 533, 619, 708, 740, 830,
   883, 888–9, 892, 928, 938, 966, 990,
   1020, 1110, 1169, 1295
   'in due form'   68–9, 77, 84–5, 126,
      151, 182, 184, 224, 245, 259, 264,
      270, 550, 575, 629, 631, 786,
      798, 831, 859, 861–2, 875, 877,
      879–80, 885–7, 892, 894–5, 1009,
      1018, 1084, 1132, 1276, 1295–6,
      1312
   place specified
      around the church   xxix, xxxix,
         107, 126, 151–2, 168, 245–6,
         332, 518–19, 521, 550, 699,

717, 719, 740, 812, 829–31,
   878, 888, 921, 927, 950,
   955–7, 963, 965–6, 969, 979,
   1011, 1033, 1045, 1083, 1112,
   1124, 1169, 1194, 1199, 1201,
   1253, 1262–3, 1279, 1283;
   carrying a candle   xxix, 252,
      254, 297; *see also* through the
      marketplace and around the
      church (*below*)
   before the procession   131, 523,
      618, 1233, 1248, 1264, 1290; at
      Hereford   107, 812, 962
   through the marketplace   xxix,
      523, 1248; at Hereford   107,
      889; at Ludlow   1083; at
      Monmouth   252, 254; at
      Montgomery   1264, 1290;
      carrying a candle   xxix, 1233
   through the marketplace and
      around the church   10, 12,
      20, 301, 391, 702, 746, 760,
      783–5, 833, 886, 919, 962,
      1115, 1247, 1285
begging, fraudulent religious   xxxv, 693
belief *see* religious belief and practice
bell-towers   xxvi, 56, 170, 342, 348, 538,
   546, 549, 632, 685, 860, 961, 1000,
   1036, 1090
bells
   church bells
      lack of bell-ropes   xxxiii, 140,
         539, 571, 842
      monks withhold key from bell-
         ringers   xxxv, 713
      not rung at proper time   xxxv,
         139, 660, 815, 840, 952, 1154,
         1322
      rung by women   xl, 816

lack of bells for visiting the sick at
　　night *see* visiting the sick
bigamy *see* marriage, couples 'unlawfully
　　joined'
bishop's consistory *see* church tribunals
breviaries　xviii, xxxii, 53, 60–1, 135,
　　171, 188, 208, 227, 359, 398, 506,
　　576, 592–3, 623, 814, 881, 910, 1105
brothels　277, 552
burial
　　clergy refusal to conduct burial　317
　　dispute over rights to burial　179
　　irregularly conducted　822, 1174–5
　　lack of required books to conduct
　　　　burial office　xxxiii, 689
butchers　790
　　see also Flesher *in index of personal names*

candles
　　abbot of Wigmore owes alms for
　　　　Easter candle at Bucknell　1049
　　penances　xviii, xxix, 16, 612, 1186
　　　　beating around church or
　　　　　　marketplace carrying a
　　　　　　candle　xxix, 252, 254, 297,
　　　　　　1233
　　see also light in churches
canon law, and visitation　xv, xvi, xxxi,
　　xxxvi
Canterbury, archbishops of,
　　jurisdiction　xix–xxi, 329, 1178
carpenters *see* occupations
central places, in visitation　xxv
chalices
　　bequest to church not
　　　　fulfilled　1219–20
　　missing or damaged　xxix, xxxiii, 79,
　　　　165, 240, 326, 594, 839, 1159
chantries　35, 38, 115, 129, 780, 1303
chapelries　xxv
chapels
　　altar unconsecrated　947
　　chapels within churches　79–80, 728,
　　　　935, 947
　　dependent chapel of Ludford and
　　　　Syde　xxvi, 1088
　　rector fails to maintain/furnish
　　　　adequately　379, 935

rector lets chapel to farm　1299
rector/vicar fails to provide
　　chaplain　65–6, 213, 838, 1067,
　　1080
　　see also chantries
chaplains
　　chantry priests　35, 38, 115, 129, 780,
　　　　1303
　　in charge of chapels　65–6, 213, 838,
　　　　1067, 1080
children
　　husbands refusing to support　xxxvii,
　　　　420
　　see also pregnancy and childbirth
church attendance, absence on Sundays
　　and feast days　15, 186, 191, 348–9,
　　　　360, 460–1, 464, 491, 748, 786, 802,
　　　　811, 836–7, 920, 984–5, 1082, 1122,
　　　　1192, 1257
　　because attending a different
　　　　church　601
　　because of trading/going to
　　　　market　279–80, 282, 284,
　　　　288–9, 491, 977
　　because of work　14, 265–8, 349,
　　　　501, 543, 803, 854, 1040, 1187,
　　　　1191, 1321
　　during harvest　744
　　on feast of the Assumption　501
　　on feast of St Peter in
　　　　Chains　543
　　see also Eucharist, failure to receive
church revenues
　　farmed　52, 114, 174, 209, 305, 512,
　　　　565, 669, 882, 1138, 1232, 1299,
　　　　1328
　　mortuaries　98–9
　　not stored on church land　241, 882
　　see also sequestration; tithes
church tribunals
　　bishop's consistory　xvi, xxxviii
　　　　cases referred to　xxix, 2, 67, 105,
　　　　　　122, 128, 131, 137, 167, 172,
　　　　　　175, 292, 361, 420, 514, 570,
　　　　　　976, 1000, 1046, 1280, 1307
　　　　references to previous decisions
　　　　　　of　xxxi, 323, 776
　　commissary court　xxiv–xxv, xxvi

cases referred to   xxvi, xxix, 177,
    215, 233, 247, 372, 393, 410,
    412, 428–9, 432, 447, 454, 466,
    474, 560, 857, 897, 1000, 1155,
    1359–60
previous appearances at   151–2,
    323, 386, 666, 747, 955
and probate and administration of
    estates   63, 780
scribe of   xii, xxiv–xxv, xxvii,
    xxix
churches
    altars and other furnishings and
        equipment
        altar in chapel not
            consecrated   947
        desks and bench for books   1205
        use of portable altar   1331
        see also bells; fonts; liturgical books;
            liturgical equipment
    attendance *see* church attendance
    beating around the church *see* beating
    behaviour in
        laymen censured for sitting in
            chancel   xxxvii, 450, 900
        pollution by bloodshed   xxxvii,
            381
        talking/disturbing
            services   xxxvii, 29, 449,
                1013, 1166
        women censured for sitting too far
            forward in nave   xxxvii, 899
    bells and bell-towers *see* bell-towers;
        bells
    checking physical condition of church
        fabric   xxxii, *passim*
        chancel   xv, xxix, xxxii, *passim*
        nave   xv, xxxii, *passim*
        windows *see* windows in churches
    goods stored in   841
    lighting *see* light in churches
    services *see* clergy, negligent in
        celebrating services; Eucharist
    straw strewn on floor   605, 635, 1335
    trading in   659
    woman suspended from
        entering   498
churchwardens *see* wardens

churchyards
    boundaries
        defective fencing   xxxii, 64, 158,
            308–9, 311, 324, 535, 597, 964,
            973, 989, 1000, 1030, 1063–4,
            1091, 1148, 1163, 1261, 1329
        defective gate   625
        unfenced   100, 313–14, 324, 648,
            1144, 1326
        wrongly enclosed   3
    misused by clergy   xxxiii, 36, 136,
        200, 597–9, 614, 636
    keeping livestock in   138, 534,
        597, 692
    obstructions to processions   96, 692
    pollution   xxxii, 134
        by bloodshed   xxxvii, 399
    reconsecration   27
Cistercian order, indulgence regarding
    grazing sheep   1337
clandestine marriage *see* marriage
clergy   xv–xvi, xxxii–xxxv
    absence from parish   xxxiii
        case pending about vicarage   585
        chantry priests absent   35, 38,
            115, 129
        rector died and not
            replaced   xxxiii, 255
        rector does not reside   xxxiii,
            330, 503, 526, 668
        rector or vicar fails to provide
            chaplains to serve   181, 213,
                261, 358, 668, 680, 838, 1067,
                1080
        rector or vicar temporarily
            absent   143, 377, 388, 536,
                1047, 1156, 1173
        vicar away at papal court at
            Rome   261
        vicarage vacant   xxxiii, 230, 1203
    celebrating twice in a day   47, 71,
        455, 524, 827, 1039, 1306
        in two different churches   221,
            236–7, 327, 590, 949, 1078
    chaplains not provided for
        chapels   65–6, 213, 838, 1067,
            1080

excommunication   44, 92, 175, 614,
1171, 1314
faults dealt with by bishop,
possible two-tier system of
correction   xxxiv, 1338–9,
1341–2, 1352–4, 1356–7
frequenting taverns   214, 219, 402,
579, 709, 1136
involved in trade   292, 825, 997
dealing in livestock   xxxv, 693,
696
negligent in celebrating
services   xxxiii–xxxiv
failing to stand in pulpit when
making announcements   385
intimidated from celebrating on
Passion Sunday   583
mass celebrated after
midday   384, 596
matins and vespers without
music   257
not celebrating in an appropriate
manner   xxxiii, 534, 1134
services omitted   115, 201, 235, 377,
487–8, 503, 715, 868, 1047, 1173
through drunkenness   402
see also baptism; confession; last
rites
proofs of ordination and
appointment   xv, 350, 1203,
1355
rector's responsibility for chancel   xv
rectors withholding money and goods
from vicar   604, 610, 612
riotous behaviour in parish at
night   615
sexual immorality   xxxiii, xxxiv,
passim
as usurers   132, 507, 825
violence against   xxxvii, 212, 583,
1222
Welsh-speaking   xxxviii, 222
see also chaplains; deacons; last rites;
ordination; religious houses;
sacraments; visiting the sick
Clerk of the Marches   156
clerks of the church *see* parish clerks/
clerks of the church
commissary court *see* church tribunals

commissary general   xxv, xxvi
common fame *see fama* (fame)
communion bread *see* Eucharist
comperta (notes of process and
judgements)   xii, xiii, xliii
concubines *see* clergy, sexual immorality
confession
annual obligation   447
clergy abuses
absolution withheld unless
payment made   xxxiv, 844
failure to provide opportunity for
dying man   818
revealing content of   xxxiv, 219
consistory *see* bishop's consistory *under*
church tribunals
constables *see* occupations
cooks *see* occupations
cruelty *see* domestic violence and cruelty
custodes see wardens

deacons
clergy failure to provide   xxxiii, 137,
189, 232, 570–1, 626, 951, 988,
1182, 1322
faults   515, 1154, 1159
deaneries, visitation organised by   xxiv–
xxv, xxvi, xxx
defamation   xxxvii
by men rather than women   xxxvii,
451, 701, 771, 804, 1010, 1142–3
of adulterous couples   xxix, 133,
392, 422, 458, 500, 581, 617, 749,
771, 782, 804, 998, 1055, 1142,
1155, 1160, 1302
of clergy   95, 454, 617, 782, 1160,
1161
of neighbours   xxxvii, 28, 133, 451,
473, 701, 735, 743, 771, 772, 849,
1054–5
of women incontinent with
monks   444, 1161
dilapidations *see* churches, checking
physical condition of church fabric
diocesan registrar   xii, xxvi, xxvii, 495
disease
leprosy   xxxix, 937
plague   xxxiii, 689
divorce *see* marriage

doctors 890
domestic violence and
    cruelty xxxvi–xxxvii
    cruel or violent husbands given
        chance to amend xxx, 42, 913
Dominican order (Order of
    Preachers) 373, 1352

Easter Sunday, Eucharist *see* Eucharist,
    failure to receive
epithets, Welsh xliii
    ap y coch hir (son of the tall
        redhead) 1270
    ap y penllwyd (son of the grey-haired
        one) 873
    bongam cynydd, y (the bandy-legged
        huntsman) 1198
    ceisiad, y (the serjeant of the peace or
        bailiff) xliii, 1214
    chwith (left-handed) 334, 892, 1215
    crych (wrinkled one) 1007
    cryg (defective of speech/
        stammering) 266, 1034
    cwta (short) xliii, 1202
    dail, y (of the leaves) 1250
    famaeth, y (the wet-nurse or foster-
        mother) xliii, 721
    fardd (poet) 45
    feddyg (doctor) 890
    felinydd (miller) 1258
    gorniog (frowning) 1270
    llwgr y coed (coward of the
        woods) 874
    meueddus (rich) 1139
    moel (bald or barren man) xliii, 1034
    wehydd (weaver) 1263
    wlân (wool) 316
escheator of Herefordshire (John
    Maunce) xxvi, 114
ethnicity *see* Welsh language and people
Eucharist
    communion bread, obligation to
        provide
        abbot of Wigmore for Bucknell
            church 1049
        lay people refusing to provide in
            their turn 13, 258, 448, 1101
        rectors refusing to provide corn
            annually for 396, 577, 625

vicar refusing to provide for
    chaplains 114, 144
failure to receive xl, 489
    on Easter Sunday 173, 419, 447,
        460–1, 711, 776, 811, 824, 832,
        982, 1167
    see also church attendance
given to excommunicates on Easter
    Sunday 212
importance of physical presence
    of Christ in consecrated
    bread xxxiv, 380
pyx 'empty of the body of
    Christ' xxxiv, 380
withheld 832, 845
    unless payment made xxxv, 690,
        844
    until tithes paid 141, 823–4
excommunication xvi, xx, xxx, *passim*
    clergy excommunicated 44, 92, 175,
        614, 1171, 1314
    signification of excommunication,
        indicated by marginal
        procedural notes xxx, 51, 74,
        119, 413, 460, 462, 743, 783,
        877–9, 940, 1041, 1132, 1223,
        1257, 1310
    threatened for not visiting mother
        church 307
    vicar accused of saying 'Lie there,
        you excommunicate!' while
        conducting burial xl, 822
    for violence against chaplain 614
    for withholding 8 pence for a
        light 776
    Wycliffite view xl, xli
extra, significance of xxxviii–xxxix
extreme unction *see* last rites
eyres xvii, xviii

fama (fame) xxviii, 153, 167, 216, 497,
    555, 616, 981, 1035
farming of church revenues *see* church
    revenues, farmed
fasting, as penance 172, 335, 391, 1115,
    1290
feast days *see* church attendance,
    absence on Sundays and feast days;
    Eucharist, failure to receive

fencing *see* churchyards
fonts
    unlocked　xxxiii, 4, 37, 39, 97, 176,
        312, 463, 649, 675, 1051, 1145
    see also holy water
foresters *see* occupations
fornication *see* sexual immorality

gender issues　xxxvii
    see also women
ghosts and spirits　xxxix, 187, 300
    see also magic and sorcery
glass *see* windows
glebe *see* church revenues; rectory estates
graduals *see* liturgical books

harvest　744
HCA 1779 (text of 1397 visitation)
    custodial history　xii
    description of document　xi–xii
    editorial method　xliii
    history of scholarly work　xii–xiv
    possible missing section　xxv n.52
    procedure and composition of
        record　xxvii–xxx
    reasons for preservation　xix–xx, xxi
    watermark　xi
Herefordshire and Shropshire eyres
    (1292)　xvii, xviii
heresy　xxxix–xli
    female ministry　xl, 658
    heresy trials　xix
    see also lollards and Wycliffites
holy bread *see* Eucharist, communion
    bread
holy oils, incorrectly maintained　234,
    650
holy water
    'from the bridge'　688
    refused　451, 489
    see also fonts
hospitals, Ledbury, St Katherine's
    Hospital　510–13, 1353
hours, liturgy of the *see* breviaries;
    matins; vespers
huntsmen *see* occupations

illness *see* disease; visiting the sick
images *see* Mary, Blessed Virgin; saints

impotence　xxxvi, 67
incest　5, 10, 33, 184, 251, 426, 472, 474,
    482, 761–8, 862–3, 887, 893, 902,
    924, 944, 946, 1245, 1254, 1273, 1304
intestacy　58, 63, 122, 372, 496, 1026
Ireland, expeditionary force to　xviii,
    xxxviii, 957, 992, 1038, 1201, 1250,
    1282

last rites, clergy abuses　xxxiv, 262, 380,
    818–20, 1171
lay faults in visitation　xxxvi–xxxvii
    sexual immorality *see* sexual
        immorality, laity
leprosy　xxxix, 937
light in churches
    abbot of Wigmore owes alms for
        Easter candle at Bucknell　1049
    bishop owes 18d yearly for upkeep of
        light at Ledbury　509
    clergy failure to provide lights
        before high altar　145, 404, 479,
            647, 652, 855, 931, 953
        before images of saints　395, 469,
            612, 661
        for processions　465, 653, 1029
        in chapels　935
        to burn day and night　404, 652,
            835, 953
    lack of light impeding conduct
        of services, through clergy
        negligence　xxxiii, 144, 192,
        293, 340
    laity failure to provide or pay for
        upkeep of lights　548
        before high altar　146–9, 341, 367
        before image of Blessed
            Virgin　493, 661, 672, 747,
            776, 1288
        before image of crucifixion　166,
            319, 374, 494
    money bequeathed or given for lights
        withheld　367, 540, 1287
    see also candles
lights for visiting the sick at night *see*
    visiting the sick
liturgical books, missing or
    deficient　xxix, xxxii–xxxiii, xxxv,
    137, 249, 689, 788, 844, 954, 1184

antiphonals   xxxii, 592, 691, 1206
breviaries   xviii, xxxii, 53, 60–1, 135,
      171, 188, 208, 227, 359, 398, 506,
      576, 592–3, 623, 814, 881, 910,
      1105
   graduals   61, 691
   psalters   xxxii, 249, 587, 602, 634,
      954, 1206
liturgical equipment, missing or
   deficient   xxxii, xxxiii, 26, 80, 137,
      197–8, 1137
   bequeathed to church
      withheld by heirs or
         executors   960, 1185, 1218
      withheld by rector   1099–100
   see also chalices; liturgical books;
      pyxes; vestments
livestock, clergy keeping and dealing
   in   xxxv, 138, 534, 597, 692, 693,
      696
lollards and Wycliffites   xxxv, xxxix–xli
   see also heresy

magic and sorcery   xl, 621, 658
   see also ghosts and spirits
marginal procedural notes   xxx
   signification of
      excommunication   xxx, 51, 74,
         119, 413, 460, 462, 743, 783, 877–9,
         940, 1041, 1132, 1223, 1257, 1310
markets
   attending on Sundays and feast
      days   279–80, 282, 284, 288–9,
         491
   beating through the marketplace *see*
      beating
marriage
   annulment   xxix, xxxvi n.82, 251
   banns maliciously challenged to
      extort money   1028
   clandestine marriage   91, 252–4,
      285, 287, 306, 826, 1014, 1071,
      1304
   couples 'unlawfully joined'   67, 91,
      306, 353, 976, 1043, 1076, 1305,
      1358
   bigamy   xxix, 978
   divorce   xxxvi, 9, 67, 638, 859, 1016,
      1162, 1245, 1359

letters testimonial   921, 1024
   outside the diocese   1211
penances deferred in hope of couple
      marrying   xxx, 223, 705, 706,
         785, 888, 903, 943, 1033, 1199,
         1255, 1259
   prevented by man's serious
      illness   1120
   see also incest
Mary, Blessed Virgin
   chaplain of   694
   money owed to service of   2, 654–7,
      1289
   provision of lights before images
      of   395, 493, 661, 672, 747, 776,
         1288
matins   53, 60, 188, 235, 257, 487–8,
   954, 1079
men
   defamation by   xxxvii, 451, 701, 771,
      804, 1010, 1142–3
   interpersonal violence between men
      see violence
   patriarchal authority
      threatened by illicit sexual
         relationships   xxxvii
   see also women
millers *see* occupations
mobility, evidence for   xxxviii
monasteries, monks *see* religious houses
morality
   lay faults   xxxvi, xxxvii
   see also propriety; sexual immorality
mortuaries, owed to vicar   98–9

neighbours, defaming *see* defamation

occupations   xliii
   bailiff   xliii, 499, 1214, 1312
   baker   845
   butcher   790
      see also Flesher *in index of personal
         names*
   carpenter   8, 50
   constable   1109
   cook   1074
   doctor   890
   forester   1212
   huntsman   1198

miller   1258
piper   184
poet   45
sawyer   334 n.1, 339
serjeant of the peace   xliii, 1214
tailor   724, 896
tiler   9
weaver   1263
wet-nurse/foster-mother   xliii, 721
see also occupational surnames in index of
   personal names
omnia bene, significance of   xxxi, xxxii
Order of Preachers *see* Dominican order
ordination
   late ordination   xxxiv, 483
   proofs of ordination and
      appointment   xv, 350, 1203,
      1355

parish clerks/clerks of the church
   failure to fulfil duties   197, 199, 660,
      952
   immorality   752, 1126, 1319
   lack of   101, 688, 815, 951, 1164,
      1316, 1322
   unable to read because of lack of
      light   192
   unable to ring bells because monks
      have the keys   xxxv, 713
parish representatives, peasant elite
   as   xxxi, xxxvi
parishioners   xxvii, xxxi–xxxii
   named at Newland   xxxi, 351
peculiars   xv
penances   xxix–xxx
   avoided by moving away   xxxix,
      1263
   beating *see* beating
   deferred because of
      pregnancy   xxix, 568, 618, 786,
      1045, 1083
   deferred in hope of couple
      marrying   xxx, 223, 705, 706,
      785, 888, 903, 943, 1033, 1199,
      1255, 1259
   deferred on condition of good
      behaviour   895
   fasting   172, 335, 391, 1115, 1290

providing candle for the
   church   xviii, xxix, 16, 612, 1186
perjury   151, 153, 156, 514, 593, 747, 838
pipers *see* occupations
plague   xxxiii, 689
poets   45
pollution of churches and
   churchyards   xxxii, xxxvii, 134,
      381, 399
poor
   Master of St Katherine's Hospital,
      Ledbury, obligation to give
      doles   511, 513
   rector's obligation to distribute
      supplies to   481
preaching, not mentioned in
   presentments   xxxiv
pregnancy and childbirth
   penances deferred because of
      pregnancy   xxix, 568, 618, 786,
      1045, 1083
   readmission of women to church
      after childbirth   xxxii, 386, 1176
   wet-nurses/foster-mothers   xliii, 721
presentments submitted in
   advance   xxvii–xxx
processions
   beating before the procession *see*
      beating
   lack of suitable equipment for   54–5
      processional candles   465, 653,
         1029
   obstructions in churchyard   96, 692
proctors   xxviii, xxxii, 135, 181, 403, 411,
      625, 690, 1139, 1158, 1357–8, 1363,
      1367
   see also wardens
procurations   xv, xvi, xvii, xxvi
propriety, offences against   xxxvi, xxxix
psalters *see* liturgical books
punishments *see* excommunication;
      penances
purgation   xxx
   with a single hand   1096
   with three hands   422, 426
   with five hands   361, 392, 423, 480,
      743, 773, 828, 918, 1162, 1239,
      1280

with six hands   xxx, 131, 150, 390,
   410, 424, 497, 516, 525, 581–2,
   740, 809, 981, 1042, 1046, 1089,
   1097, 1103, 1117, 1307
with twelve hands   95
pyxes
   'empty of the body of Christ'   xxxiv,
      380
   money bequeathed for   587

recidivism   xxix
rectors *see* clergy
rectory estates   xv, xxxii
   barns and other buildings   366, 466,
      470, 1327, 1336
   rectory houses   118, 163, 180, 492,
      504, 526, 566, 586, 671, 678, 1135
   vicarage houses   262, 610–11
register of Bishop Trefnant   xii, xviii,
   xix, xxix, xxxv
religious belief and practice
   complaints by laity about correct
      conduct of services and other
      duties   xxxiii–xxxiv
      see also baptism; clergy, negligent in
         celebrating services; last rites
   unusual beliefs and practices
      reported   xxxix
      see also ghosts and spirits; heresy;
         lollards and Wycliffites
religious houses   xv, xvii, xviii
   Cwmhir Abbey, monk incontinent
      with Llanfair Waterdine
      woman   1208
   Flanesford Priory, prior incontinent
      with Goodrich woman   233
   Flaxley Abbey, monks incontinent
      with Westbury-on-Severn and
      Rudford women   427, 430–44
   Hereford, St Guthlac's Priory
      dispute over parish of Stoke
         Lacy   1356
      prior incontinent with Tarrington
         woman   545
   Leintwardine, canon regular of,
      incontinence with Bromfield
      woman   1094
   Leominster Priory, disputes with
      laity over shared use of priory

church   xxix, xxxv, 688–97,
   713–14
Llanthony Priory
   in possession of breviary
      belonging to Llanwarne   171
   prior incontinent with Lydbury
      North woman   1161
   as rector of Brinsop   1
Monmouth Priory   xviii
   dispute with Llanrothal
      parishioners   210
   disputes with Monmouth
      parishioners   262, 291
   Wenlock Priory, disputes over
      Clunbury and Llanfair
      Waterdine parishes   1181, 1203–7
Wigmore Abbey
   withholds payments and evades
      obligations   101, 1048–9,
      1149, 1163, 1334
   other mentions   865, 1363
   see also Cistercian order; Dominican
      order
rural deans   xxvi, xxx, xxxix, 785, 882,
   890

sacraments
   importance of physical presence
      of Christ in consecrated
      bread   xxxiv, 380
   see also baptism; confession; Eucharist;
      last rites; marriage; ordination
saints
   images of, provision of lights   395,
      469, 493, 612, 661, 672, 747, 776,
      1288
   see also Mary, Blessed Virgin
sawyers   334 n.1, 339
sequestration of revenues   1, 7, 114–15,
   163, 174, 181, 209–10, 213, 261, 305,
   340, 466, 503, 526, 565–6, 603, 647,
   668, 673, 881–2, 1299, 1327
serjeants of the peace   xliii, 1214
service books *see* liturgical books
sextons   1316
sexual immorality
   clergy   xxxiii, xxxiv, *passim*
   laity   xxxvi, *passim*
      at Peterchurch   xxxvi, 67, 68

defamation of adulterous
  couples   xxix, 133, 392, 422,
  458, 500, 581, 617, 749, 771,
  782, 804, 998, 1055, 1142, 1155,
  1160, 1302
and husbands' mistreatment of
  their wives   xxxvi–xxxvii,
  220, 225, 246, 250, 420–1, 913,
  1221, 1225
and husbands refusing to support
  children   xxxvii, 420
unmarried couples, penances
  deferred in the hope of them
  marrying   xxx, 223, 705,
  706, 785, 888, 903, 943, 1033,
  1199, 1255, 1259
  see also brothels; domestic violence;
  incest; marriage
sickness *see* disease; visiting the sick
social control, visitation as organ
  of   xxxi
sorcery *see* magic and sorcery
spirits *see* ghosts and spirits
Sunday church attendance *see* church
  attendance, absence on Sundays
  and feast days; Eucharist, failure to
  receive

tailors *see* occupations
taverns
  clergy frequenting   214, 219, 402,
  579, 709, 1136
  held in rectory   256
taxation, royal, collection for
  subsidy   588
tilers *see* occupations
tithes   xxxiii
  Cistercian order, indulgence
  regarding grazing sheep   1337
  dispute about tithes in Stoke
  Lacy   1356
  not stored on church land   162, 679
  withheld   103, 141, 286, 448, 460,
  584, 790, 823–4, 908, 1048,
  1129–30, 1147
  see also church revenues
trade
  clergy involved in trade   292, 825, 997

dealing in livestock   xxxv, 693,
  696
excuse for church absence on
  Sundays and feast days   977
  attending markets   279–80, 282,
  284, 288–9, 491
making profit on goods by delaying
  sale   1034
trading in churches   659
triennial visitation, evidence for   xviii

usury   480, 1131, 1179–80, 1189, 1235–43
  clergy as usurers   132, 507, 825

vespers   53, 60, 139, 201, 257, 487–8,
  954
vestments, missing or deficient   xxxiii,
  55, 345, 397, 787, 932, 935, 1106,
  1140, 1145, 1153, 1183, 1207, 1306
  dirtied in processions by cow dung in
  churchyard   692
vicarage houses   633
  see also rectory estates
vicars *see* clergy
vills   xxv, xxvi–xxvii
violence
  attacks on clerics   xxxvii, 212, 583,
  1222
  interpersonal violence between
  men   xxxvii, 218
  clerics   983
  involving pollution of churches
  and churchyards   xxxvii,
  381, 399
  see also domestic violence and cruelty
visitation
  in late medieval church   xv–xvii
  in late medieval Hereford   xvii–xxi
  route of 1397 visitation   xxiv–xxvii
  map of route   xxii–xxiii
  text of 1397 visitation *see* HCA 1779
visitation articles   xvi, xxvii, xxxii
visitation centres   xxviii, xxx, xxxi
visiting the sick
  deficiencies in   62, 815
  lack of bell and/or light for visiting
  the sick at night   xxxiii, xxxv,
  688, 1051, 1145, 1306

wardens
  proctors (*procuratores*) of the
    church   xxvii, 213, 261, 613
  wardens (*custodes*) of the goods of the
    church   xxvii, 367, 574
weavers *see* occupations
Welsh language and people
  disharmony between Welsh and
    English speakers   xxxviii
    chaplain unsuitable because
      he does not speak
      Welsh   xxxviii, 222
  Welsh names
    economic migrants indicated by
      locative surnames   xxxviii
    editorial method   xliii
    see also epithets
wet-nurses/foster-mothers   xliii, 721
wills
  accusation of litigating will in a
    secular court   522
  forged   372
  legacies to church not paid/handed
    over   228, 367, 572–3, 587, 960–
    1, 975, 1099–100, 1185, 1219–20
  problems over execution   xxix, 190,
    780, 792, 1218, 1230–1
  see also intestacy
windows in churches, broken or defective
  chancel   48, 70, 93, 112, 207, 226,
    231, 315, 357, 365, 379, 394, 403,

459, 544, 607, 627, 670, 867, 901,
  1146, 1205, 1315
  unspecified   116, 199, 490
women
  censured more harshly than men
    for defamation and unruly
      behaviour   xxxvii
    for sexual immorality   xxxvi
    for sitting too far forward in
      nave   xxxvii, 899
    for talking in church   xxxvii, 29
  church bells rung by women   xl, 816
  defamation of women incontinent
    with monks   444, 1161
  female ministry   xl, 658
  wife-beating seen as acceptable
    behaviour unless
    excessive   xxxvii, 225
  wife mistreating husband seen as
    inversion of proper hierarchy of
    power   xxxvii, 375, 563, 1037
  woman suspended from entering
    church   498
  see also pregnancy and childbirth
words and phrases discussed
  extra   xxxviii–xxxix
  fama   xxviii
  omnia bene   xxxi, xxxii
working, on Sundays and feast days *see*
  church attendance
Wycliffites *see* lollards and Wycliffites